THE KEY

STUDENT STUDY GUIDE

ics 30

THE KEY student study guide is designed to help students achieve success in school. The content in each study guide is 100% curriculum aligned and serves as an excellent source of material for review and practice. To create this book, teachers, curriculum specialists, and assessment experts have worked closely to develop the instructional pieces that explain each of the key concepts for the course. The practice questions and sample tests have detailed solutions that show problem-solving methods, highlight concepts that are likely to be tested, and point out potential sources of errors. ***THE KEY*** is a complete guide to be used by students throughout the school year for reviewing and understanding course content, and to prepare for assessments.

Rao,Gautam,1961 –
THE KEY – Physics 30 Alberta

1. Science – Juvenile Literature. I. Title

Castle Rock Research Corporation
2340 Manulife Place
10180 – 101 Street
Edmonton, AB T5J 3S4

14 15 16 FP 13 12 11

Publisher
Gautam Rao

Contributors
Lloyd Barker
Barry Edgar
Dave Gargus
Powell Jones
Rob Schultz
Steve Sprysak

Reviewers
Chris Cookson
Alison Donner

CASTLE ROCK
RESEARCH CORP

Dedicated to the memory of Dr. V. S. Rao

THE KEY–Physics 30

THE KEY consists of the following sections:

KEY Tips for Being Successful at School gives examples of study and review strategies. It includes information about learning styles, study schedules, and note taking for test preparation.

Class Focus includes a unit on each area of the curriculum. Units are divided into sections, each focusing on one of the specific expectations, or main ideas, that students must learn about in that unit. Examples, definitions, and visuals help to explain each main idea. Practice questions on the main ideas are also included. At the end of each unit is a test on the important ideas covered. The practice questions and unit tests help students identify areas they know and those they need to study more. They can also be used as preparation for tests and quizzes. Most questions are of average difficulty, though some are easy and some are hard—the harder questions are called *Challenger Questions*. Each unit is prefaced by a ***Table of Correlations***, which correlates questions in the unit to the specific curriculum expectations. Answers and solutions are found at the end of each unit.

KEY Strategies for Success on Tests helps students get ready for tests. It shows students different types of questions they might see, word clues to look for when reading them, and hints for answering them.

Practice Tests includes one to three tests based on the entire course. They are very similar to the format and level of difficulty that students may encounter on final tests. In some regions, these tests may be reprinted versions of official tests, or reflect the same difficulty levels and formats as official versions. This gives students the chance to practice using real-world examples. Answers and complete solutions are provided at the end of the section.

For the complete curriculum document (including specific expectations along with examples and sample problems), visit http://education.alberta.ca/teachers/program/science/programs.aspx.

THE KEY *Study Guides* are available for many courses. Check www.castlerockresearch.com for a complete listing of books available for your area.

For information about any of our resources or services, please call Castle Rock Research at 780.448.9619 or visit our website at http://www.castlerockresearch.com.

At Castle Rock Research, we strive to produce an error-free resource. If you should find an error, please contact us so that future editions can be corrected.

CONTENTS

KEY Factors Contributing to School Success

KEY TIPS FOR BEING SUCCESSFUL AT SCHOOL

KEY FACTORS CONTRIBUTING TO SCHOOL SUCCESS

In addition to learning the content of your courses, there are some other things that you can do to help you do your best at school. Some of these strategies are listed below.

- **Keep a positive attitude:** Always reflect on what you can already do and what you already know.
- **Be prepared to learn**: Have ready the necessary pencils, pens, notebooks, and other required materials for participating in class.
- **Complete all of your assignments:** Do your best to finish all of your assignments. Even if you know the material well, practice will reinforce your knowledge. If an assignment or question is difficult for you, work through it as far as you can so that your teacher can see exactly where you are having difficulty.
- **Set small goals for yourself when you are learning new material:** For example, when learning the parts of speech, do not try to learn everything in one night. Work on only one part or section each study session. When you have memorized one particular part of speech and understand it, then move on to another one, continue this process until you have memorized and learned all the parts of speech.
- **Review your classroom work regularly at home:** Review to be sure that you understand the material that you learned in class.
- **Ask your teacher for help**: Your teacher will help you if you do not understand something or if you are having a difficult time completing your assignments.
- **Get plenty of rest and exercise:** Concentrating in class is hard work. It is important to be well-rested and have time to relax and socialize with your friends. This helps you to keep your positive attitude about your school work.
- **Eat healthy meals:** A balanced diet keeps you healthy and gives you the energy that you need for studying at school and at home.

How To Find Your Learning Style

Every student learns differently. The manner in which you learn best is called your learning style. By knowing your learning style, you can increase your success at school. Most students use a combination of learning styles. Do you know what type of learner you are? Read the following descriptions. Which of these common learning styles do you use most often?

- **Linguistic Learner**: You may learn best by saying, hearing, and seeing words. You are probably really good at memorizing things such as dates, places, names, and facts. You may need **to write and then say out loud** the steps in a process, a formula, or the actions that lead up to a significant event.

- **Spatial Learner**: You may learn best by looking at and working with pictures. You are probably really good at puzzles, imagining things, and reading maps and charts. You may need to use strategies like **mind mapping and webbing** to organize your information and study notes.

- **Kinaesthetic Learner**: You may learn best by touching, moving, and figuring things out using manipulative. You are probably really good at physical activities and learning through movement. You may need to **draw your finger over a diagram** to remember it, **"tap out" the steps** needed to solve a problem, or **"feel" yourself writing or typing** a formula.

Scheduling Study Time

You should review your class notes regularly to ensure that you have a clear understanding of all the new material you learned. Reviewing your lessons on a regular basis helps you to learn and remember ideas and concepts. It also reduces the quantity of material that you need to study prior to a test. Establishing a study schedule will help you to make the best use of your time.

Regardless of the type of study schedule you use, you may want to consider the following suggestions to maximize your study time and effort:

- Organize your work so that you begin with the most challenging material first.
- Divide the subject's content into small, manageable chunks.
- Alternate regularly between your different subjects and types of study activities in order to maintain your interest and motivation.
- Make a daily list with headings like "Must Do," "Should Do," and "Could Do."
- Begin each study session by quickly reviewing what you studied the day before.
- Maintain your usual routine of eating, sleeping, and exercising to help you concentrate better for extended periods of time.

CREATING STUDY NOTES

MIND-MAPPING OR WEBBING

Use the key words, ideas, or concepts from your reading or class notes to create a *mind map* or *web* (a diagram or visual representation of the given information). A mind map or web is sometimes referred to as a knowledge map.

- Write the key word, concept, theory, or formula in the centre of your page.
- Write down related facts, ideas, events, and information and then link them to the central concept with lines.
- Use coloured markers, underlining, or other symbols to emphasize things such as relationships, time lines, and important information.
- The following examples of a Frayer Model illustrate how this technique can be used to study scientific vocabulary.

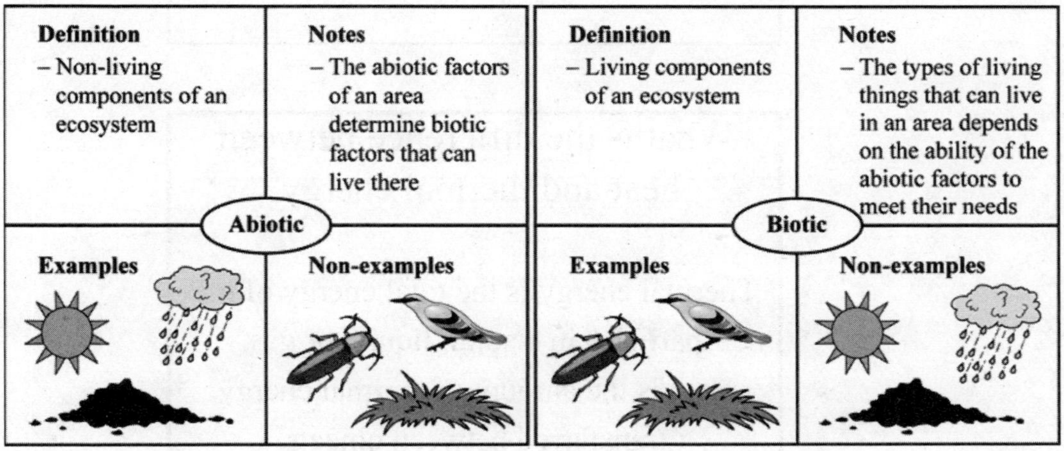

INDEX CARDS

To use index cards while studying, follow these steps:

- Write a key word or question on one side of an index card.
- On the reverse side, write the definition of the word, answer to the question, or any other important information that you want to remember.

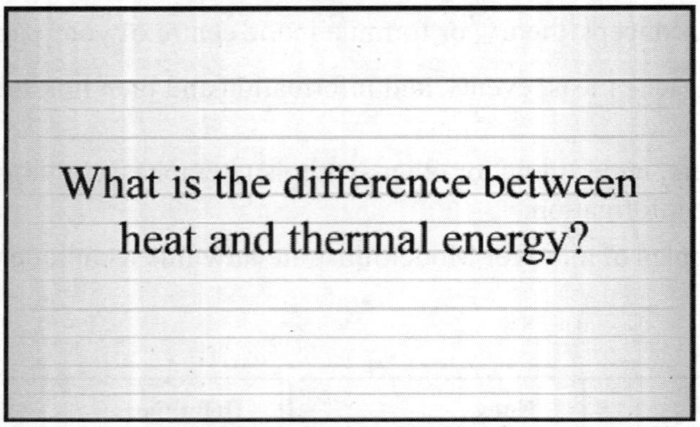

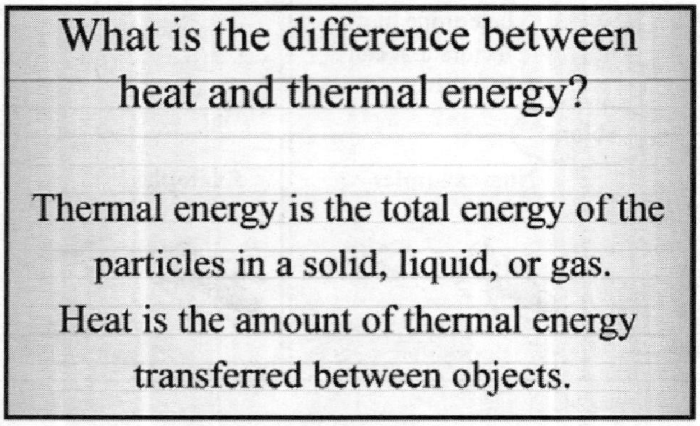

SYMBOLS AND STICKY NOTES—IDENTIFYING IMPORTANT INFORMATION

- Use symbols to mark your class notes. For example, an exclamation mark (!) might be used to point out something that must be learned well because it is a very important idea. A question mark (?) may highlight something that you are not certain about, and a diamond (◊) or asterisk (*) could highlight interesting information that you want to remember.
- Use sticky notes when you are not allowed to put marks in books.
- Use sticky notes to mark a page in a book that contains an important diagram, formula, explanation, etc.
- Use sticky notes to mark important facts in research books.

Memorization Techniques

- **Association** relates new learning to something you already know. For example, to remember the spelling difference between *dessert* and *desert*, recall that the word *sand* has only one *s*. So, because there is sand in a desert, the word *desert* only has on *s*.
- **Mnemonic** devices are sentences that you create to remember a list or group of items. For example, the first letter of each word in the phrase "**E**very **G**ood **B**oy **D**eserves **F**udge" helps you to remember the names of the lines on the treble clef staff (E, G, B, D, and F) in music.
- **Acronyms** are words that are formed from the first letters or parts of the words in a group. For example, **RADAR** is actually an acronym for **Ra**dio **D**etecting **A**nd **R**anging, and **MASH** is an acronym for **M**obile **A**rmy **S**urgical **H**ospital. **HOMES** helps you to remember the names of the five Great Lakes (**H**uron, **O**ntario, **M**ichigan, **E**rie, and **S**uperior).
- **Visualizing** requires you to use your mind's eye to "see" a chart, list, map, diagram, or sentence as it is in your textbook or notes, on the chalk board or computer screen, or in a display.
- **Initialisms** are abbreviations that are formed from the first letters or parts of the words in a group. Unlike acronyms, initialisms cannot be pronounced as a word themselves. For example, **BEDMAS** is an initialism for the order of operations in math (**B**rackets, **E**xponents, **D**ivide, **M**ultiply, **A**dd, **S**ubtract).

Key Strategies for Reviewing

Reviewing textbook material, class notes, and handouts should be an ongoing activity. Spending time reviewing becomes more critical when you are preparing for tests. You may find some of the following review strategies useful when studying during your scheduled study time.

- Before reading a selection, preview it by noting the headings, charts, graphs, and chapter questions.
- Before reviewing a unit, note the headings, charts, graphs and chapter questions.
- Highlight key concepts, vocabulary, definitions and formulas.
- Skim the paragraph and note the key words, phrases, and information.
- Carefully read over each step in a procedure.
- Draw a picture or diagram to help make the concept clearer.

KEY Strategies for Success: A Checklist

Review, review, review: review is a huge part of doing well at school and preparing for tests. Here is a checklist for you to keep track of how many suggested strategies for success you are using. Read each question and then put a check mark (✓) in the correct column. Look at the questions where you have checked the "No" column. Think about how you might try using some of these strategies to help you do your best at school.

***KEY* Strategies for Success**	**Yes**	**No**
Do you attend school regularly?		
Do you know your personal learning style—how you learn best?		
Do you spend 15 to 30 minutes a day reviewing your notes?		
Do you study in a quiet place at home?		
Do you clearly mark the most important ideas in your study notes?		
Do you use sticky notes to mark texts and research books?		
Do you practise answering multiple-choice and written-response questions?		
Do you ask your teacher for help when you need it?		
Are you maintaining a healthy diet and sleep routine?		
Are you participating in regular physical activity?		

Momentum and Impulse

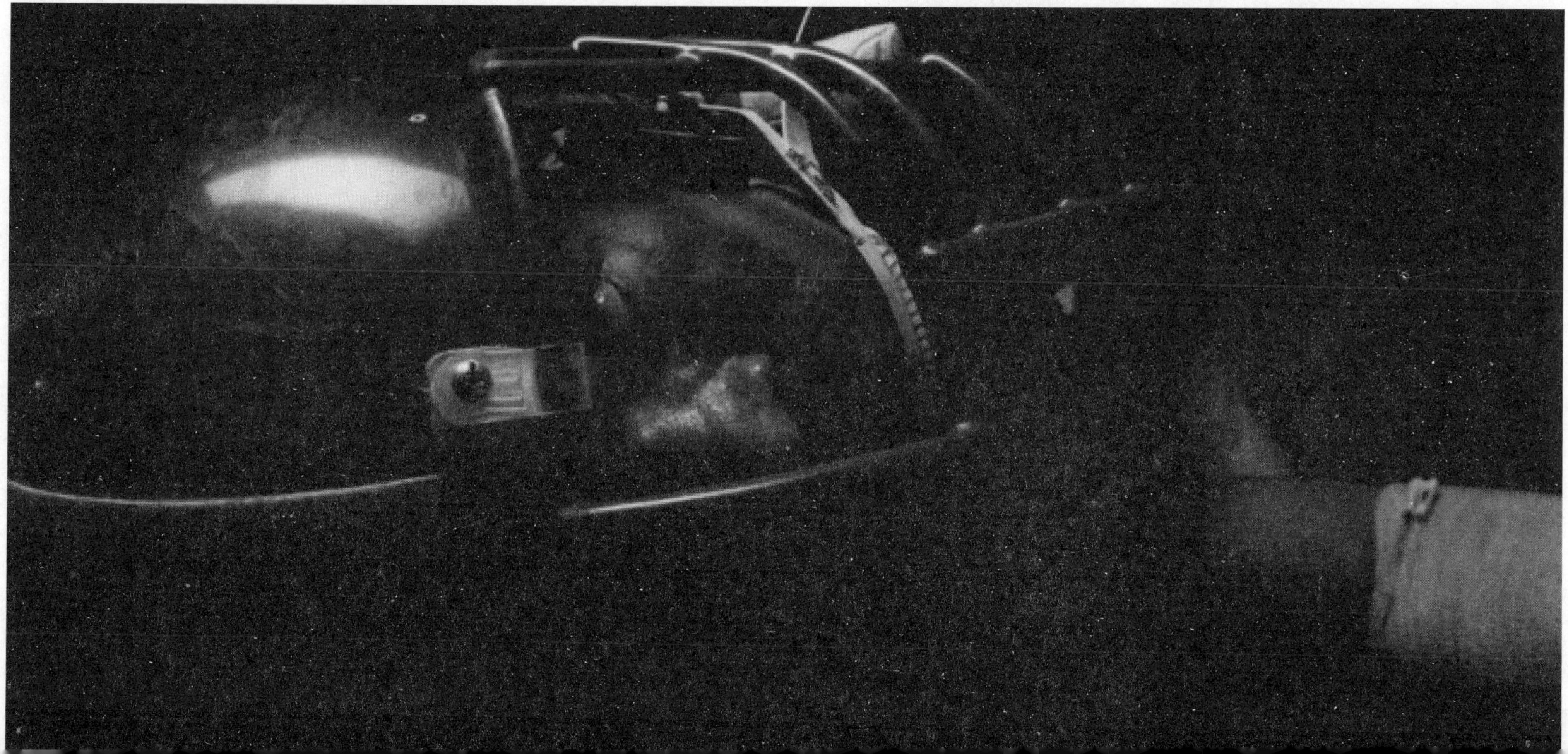

Momentum and Impulse

Table of Correlations

	Outcome	Practice Questions	Unit Test Questions	Practice Test 1	Practice Test 2
A1	explain how momentum is conserved when objects interact in an isolated system.				
30-A1.1k	*define momentum as a vector quantity equal to the product of the mass and the velocity of an object*	1, 2	1	1	1
30-A1.2k	*explain, quantitatively, the concepts of impulse and change in momentum, using Newton's laws of motion*	3, 4, 5, 6, 7	2, 3, 4	2, 3, 4	2, 3, 4
30-A1.3k	*explain, qualitatively, that momentum is conserved in an isolated system*	8, 9	5, 6	5, 6	5, 6
30-A1.4k	*explain, quantitatively, that momentum is conserved in one- and two-dimensional interactions in an isolated system*	10, 11, 12, 13, 14, 15, 16, 17	7, 8, 9	7, 8	7, 8, 9, 10
30-A1.5k	*define, compare and contrast elastic and inelastic collisions, using quantitative examples, in terms of conservation of kinetic energy*	18, 19, 20	10	9	11

30-A1.1k define momentum as a vector quantity equal to the product of the mass and the velocity of an object

Conservation of Momentum in an Isolated System

Vector quantities are described in terms of both magnitude and direction. Momentum is a vector quantity that is the product of an object's mass and velocity. The direction of an object's momentum is the same direction as the object's velocity. Momentum can be calculated using the formula $\vec{p} = m\vec{v}$, where $\vec{p}$ is the object's momentum (measured in $\text{kg} \cdot \text{m/s}$ or $\text{N} \cdot \text{s}$), m is the object's mass, and $\vec{v}$ is the object's velocity.

Example

What is the momentum of a 1 500 kg mass travelling at 20 m/s to the west?

$\vec{p} = m\vec{v}$

$\vec{p} = (1\,500\ \text{kg})(20\ \text{m/s})$

$\vec{p} = 3.0 \times 10^4\ \text{kg} \cdot \text{m/s}$

The momentum of a 1 500 kg mass travelling at 20 m/s to the west is $3.0 \times 10^4\ \text{kg} \cdot \text{m/s}$ to the west.

Example

The momentum of a 95.0 kg football player is $786\ \text{kg} \cdot \text{m/s}$ east. Calculate his velocity.

$\vec{p} = m\vec{v}$

$\vec{v} = \dfrac{\vec{p}}{m}$

$= \dfrac{786\ \text{kg} \cdot \text{m/s}}{95.0\ \text{kg}}$

$= 8.27\ \text{m/s}$

The velocity of the football player is 8.27 m/s east.

---

1. An electron moving with a velocity of 2.63×10^6 m/s north collides with the phosphor screen of a cathode-ray tube. The electron's momentum before the collision is

A. 2.89×10^{-29} kg·m/s north

B. 2.40×10^{-24} kg·m/s north

C. 3.46×10^{-37} kg·m/s south

D. 3.89×10^{-37} kg·m/s east

Numerical Response

2. A car is moving at a speed of 14.0 m/s and has a momentum with a magnitude of 3.92×10^4 kg·m/s. The mass of the car, expressed in scientific notation, is $a.bc \times 10^d$ kg. What is the value of *abcd*? ________(Record your answer as a four-digit number.)

30-A1.2k explain, quantitatively, the concepts of impulse and change in momentum, using Newton's laws of motion

Momentum and Impulse

Newton's second law of motion states that an object's acceleration is directly proportional to the net force acting on it. However, when Newton first published this law in 1686, he described the acceleration as the rate of change to the object's quantity of motion—this is now called momentum.

The relationship between the current statement of Newton's second law and momentum can be demonstrated as follows:

net force = rate of change of momentum

$\vec{F}_{\text{net}} = m\vec{a} = \dfrac{m\Delta\vec{v}}{\Delta t}$, so $\vec{F}_{\text{net}}\Delta t = m\Delta\vec{v}$.

For simplicity, this is often written as $\vec{F}\Delta t = m\Delta\vec{v}$.

The change in momentum is equal to the product of the net force acting on the object and the time over which it acts. The product of force and time is called **impulse**. Similar to momentum, impulse is a vector quantity.

Impulse $= \Delta\vec{p} = m\Delta\vec{v} = F_{\text{net}}\Delta t$

To show that impulse is equal to the change of momentum, compare their units:

Units for Impulse	Units for the Change in Momentum
N·s	$\frac{\text{kg·m}}{\text{s}}$
$\text{N·s} = \left(\frac{\text{kg·m}}{\text{s}^2}\right) \times \text{s} =$	$\frac{\text{kg·m}}{\text{s}}$

Therefore, the units for impulse and the change in momentum are equivalent.

Example

A net force of 25.0 N east acts on an 11.5 kg mass for 5.75 s. If the object's initial velocity is 5.45 m/s west, calculate the impulse (the change in momentum) and the new velocity at the end of 5.75 s.

$$\text{Impulse} = \vec{F}_{\text{net}}\Delta t = (25.0\ \text{N east})(5.75\ \text{s})$$
$$= 144\ \text{N·s east}$$

$$\Delta\vec{p} = \text{Impulse} = 143.8\ \text{kg·m/s east}$$

$$\Delta\vec{p} = m\Delta\vec{v}$$
$$\frac{\Delta\vec{p}}{m} = \vec{v}_{\text{f}} - \vec{v}_{\text{i}}$$
$$\vec{v}_{\text{f}} = \vec{v}_{\text{i}} + \frac{\Delta\vec{p}}{m}$$
$$= (-5.45\ \text{m/s}) + \frac{(143.8\ \text{kg·m/s})}{11.5\ \text{kg}}$$
$$= +7.05$$

Note that east is conventionally understood to be the positive direction, making west the negative direction.

Example

A net force of 12.0 N to the north acts on an object for 2.00×10^{-3} s. What is the impulse on the object? __________ N·s north

Solution

$$\text{Impulse} = \vec{F}_{\text{net}}\Delta t$$
$$= (12.0\ \text{N})(2.00 \times 10^{-3}\text{s})$$
$$= 2.40 \times 10^{-2}\ \text{N·s north}$$

Example

A net force of 14.0 N south acts on a 6.00 kg object for 1.00×10^{-1} s. What is the change in velocity of this object? __________ m/s south

Solution

$$\vec{F}_{\text{net}}\Delta t = m\Delta\vec{v}$$
$$\Delta\vec{v} = \frac{\vec{F}_{\text{net}}\Delta t}{m}$$
$$= \frac{(14.0\ \text{N})(1.00 \times 10^{-1}\ \text{s})}{6.00\ \text{kg}}$$
$$= 0.233\ \text{m/s south}$$

---

3. Which of the following quantities is a scalar quantity?

A. Force **B.** Power
C. Impulse **D.** Momentum

4. The SI units for impulse may be written as

A. $\text{kg·m}^2/\text{s}^2$
B. kg·m / s
C. $\text{kg·m}^2/\text{s}$
D. kg·m/s^2

5. A 12.7 kg mass travelling at 4.85 m/s south collides with and sticks to a wall. The change in the momentum of the mass is

A. 4.85 kg·m/s south
B. 6.16 kg·m/s south
C. 48.5 kg·m/s north
D. 61.6 kg·m/s north

6. The club face of a golf club exerts an average force of 595 N on a golf ball while in contact with the ball. If the ball and club face are in contact for 0.0037 s, what is the impulse given to the golf ball by the club?

A. 1.6 kg · m / s in the direction of the golf club's movement

B. 2.2 N · s in the opposite direction of the golf club's movement

C. 2.2 kg · m / s in the direction of the golf club's movement

D. 1.6×10^5 N · s in the opposite direction of the golf club's movement

Use the following information to answer the next question.

The distribution of energy released while gasoline is burned in a car is illustrated below.

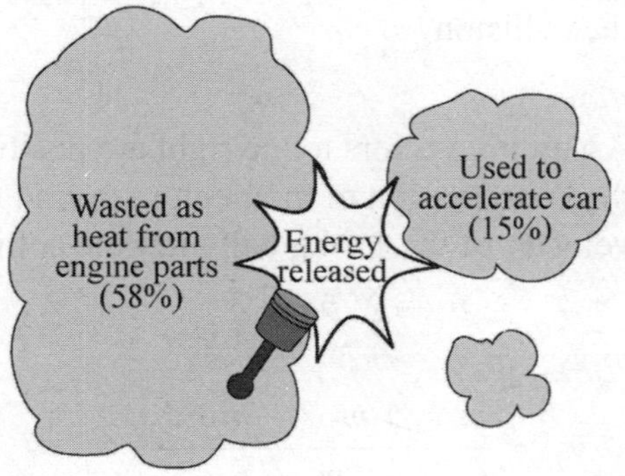

Gasoline releases 30.2 MJ/L during burning. A particular car has a mass of 1.60×10^3 kg. In a test drive, the car accelerated from 3.00 m/s to 15.0 m/s over a distance of 115 m.

Numerical Response

7. The average net force on the car during the test drive, expressed in scientific notation, is $a.bc \times 10^d$ N. The values of *a*, *b*, *c*, and *d* are __________, __________, __________, and __________.
(Record your four-digit answer.)

30-A1.3k explain, qualitatively, that momentum is conserved in an isolated system

Conservation of Momentum

An isolated system is defined as a system that is not influenced by its surroundings. An isolated system is considered an ideal system because the conservation laws (mass, energy, momentum) can be perfectly demonstrated. While a perfectly isolated system cannot be created, physicists attempt to approximate isolated mechanical systems by reducing friction. Thus, in the study of mechanics, an isolated system is often defined as a system in which no net force acts from outside the system.

In an isolated system, momentum is perfectly conserved. In reality, a system is never isolated, and there may appear to be a loss of momentum in the system, even after measurement errors are considered. Two colliding objects transfer some momentum to the air, some to the surface on which they move, and some to the atoms of which they are composed. These losses can be minimized, but they can never be eliminated. For example, two colliding cars on a rough road are not an isolated system because friction acts on them from outside. A ball hitting and compressing a spring can be considered to be isolated as long as friction is very small and the heat and sound produced are also small.

Nevertheless, well-designed experiments have confirmed that momentum is conserved in all interactions. That is, in an isolated system, the total momentum of the system before an interaction will be the same as the total momentum of the system after this interaction.

8. A 1.0 kg mass is held against a 2.0 kg mass on air table. A compressed spring is held between the two masses. When released, the masses recoil from each other on the air table. Which of the following statements about this occurrence is **true**?

A. The momentum of both masses is equal, and momentum is conserved in the recoil.

B. The momentum of the system before the recoil is less than the momentum of the system after the recoil.

C. The magnitude of momentum of the 2.0 kg mass is twice the magnitude of momentum of the 1.0 kg mass.

D. The momentum of the 2.0 kg mass is equal in magnitude but opposite in direction of the momentum of the 1.0 kg mass.

9. Which of the following situations does **not** provide an example of the conservation of momentum in an isolated system?

A. A cannon is attached to the deck of an old naval ship with rope to keep the cannon from rolling backward.

B. An object's gravitational potential energy is increased when it is raised up into the air quickly.

C. A professional pool player makes a difficult shot in the last game of the tournament finals.

D. The space shuttle lifts off from the launch tower in Cape Canaveral, Florida.

30-A1.4k explain, quantitatively, that momentum is conserved in one- and two-dimensional interactions in an isolated system

Conservation of Linear Momentum

The net momentum in a system is conserved as a vector quantity during any interaction between two or more objects.

$$\sum \vec{p}_{\text{before}} = \sum \vec{p}_{\text{after}}$$

$$\sum \vec{p}_{\text{i}} = \sum \vec{p}_{\text{f}}$$

$$\vec{p}_1 + \vec{p}_2 + \ \dots\ + \vec{p}_{\text{n}} = \vec{p}'_1 + \vec{p}'_2 + \ \dots\ + \vec{p}'_{\text{n}}$$

Example

A 1.0 kg ball moving with a velocity of 2.0 m/s to the right collides head-on with a stationary 2.0 kg ball. After the collision, the 2.0 kg ball moves off to the right with a velocity of 1.2 m/s.

What is the velocity of the 1.0 kg ball after the collision?

Solution

Assuming vectors to the right are positive, use the conservation of momentum to find the velocity of the 1.0 kg ball after the collision.

$$\sum \vec{p}_{\text{i}} = \sum \vec{p}_{\text{f}}$$

$$m_1\vec{v}_1 + m_2\vec{v}_2 = m_1\vec{v}_1{}' + m_2\vec{v}_2{}'$$

$$\therefore \vec{v}_1{}' = \frac{m_1\vec{v}_1 + m_2\vec{v}_2 - m_2\vec{v}_2{}'}{m_1}$$

$$= \frac{m_1\vec{v}_1 - m_2\vec{v}_2{}'}{m_1}$$

$$= \frac{(1.0\ \text{kg})(2.0\ \text{m/s}) - (2.0\ \text{kg})(1.2\ \text{m/s})}{1.0\ \text{kg}}$$

$$= -0.40\ \text{m/s}$$

Since moving to the right is positive, the negative velocity means that the 1.0 kg ball moves to the left after the collision. The velocity of the 1.0 kg ball after the collision is 0.40 m/s to the left.

Example

A 90 kg person running at 6.0 m/s east collides with, and sticks to, a 70 kg person walking west at 1.0 m/s. What is the velocity of the pair after the collision?

Solution

$$\sum \vec{p}_i = \sum \vec{p}_f$$

$$m_1\vec{v}_1 + m_2\vec{v}_2 = (m_1 + m_2)\vec{v}'$$

$$\therefore \vec{v}' = \frac{m_1\vec{v}_1 + m_2\vec{v}_2}{m_1 + m_2}$$

$$= \frac{(90\text{ kg})(6.0\text{ m/s}) + (70\text{ kg})(-1.0\text{ m/s})}{90\text{ kg} + 70\text{ kg}}$$

$$= +2.9\text{ m/s}$$

$$= 2.9\text{ m/s east}$$

When a collision occurs in two dimensions, you must be careful to use the vector nature of momentum correctly. Vectors are added by placing them tip-to-tail and using geometry and trigonometry to find solutions.

Example

A 1 500 kg car moving north at 10.0 m/s collides with and sticks to a 2 600 kg truck moving east at 12.0 m/s.

What is the velocity of the pair after the collision?

Solution

Step 1

Use the conservation of momentum to determine the relationship between the initial momentum of the two vehicles and the final momentum of the combined mass.

$$\sum \vec{p}_i = \sum \vec{p}_f$$

$$\vec{p}_{car} + \vec{p}_{truck} = \vec{p}_{total}$$

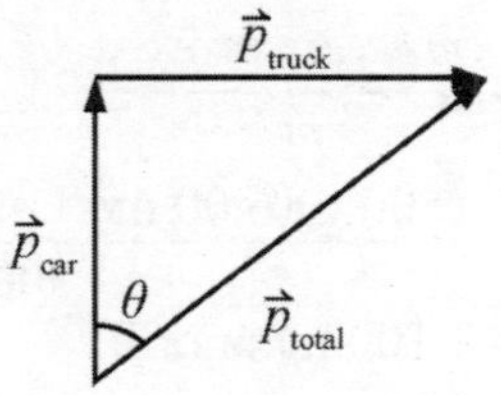

Step 2

Calculate the total momentum of the combined mass using the relation $\vec{p} = m\vec{v}$, the Pythagorean theorem, and trigonometry.

$$\vec{p}_{truck} = m\vec{v}_{truck}$$

$$= 2\ 600\text{ kg}(12.0\text{ m/s east})$$

$$= 31\ 200\text{ kg·m/s east}$$

$$\vec{p}_{car} = m\vec{v}_{car}$$

$$= 1\ 500\text{ kg}(10.0\text{ m/s north})$$

$$= 15\ 000\text{ kg·m/s north}$$

$$p_{total} = \left(\sqrt{15\ 000^2 + 31\ 200^2}\right)\text{ kg·m/s}$$

$$= 34\ 618.5\text{ kg·m/s}$$

$$\theta = \tan^{-1}\left(\frac{31\ 200}{15\ 000}\right)$$

$$= 64.3°$$

Step 3

Use this value for the final momentum to determine the final velocity of the combined mass.

The magnitude of the velocity of the combined vehicles is as follows:

$$v = \frac{p_{total}}{m_{combined}}$$

$$= \frac{34\ 618.5\text{ kg·m/s}}{4\ 100\text{ kg}}$$

$$= 8.44\text{ m/s}$$

Therefore, the final velocity of the two cars stuck together is 8.44 m/s with a heading of 64.3° east of north.

Example

A 500 g puck moving at 6.00 m/s north hits a stationary 200 g puck. After the collision, the smaller puck has a velocity of 8.00 m/s 25.0° east of north.

What is the velocity of the larger puck after the collision?

Solution

Define your known and unknown variables. In this case, use *u* to represent the initial velocities and *v* to represent the final velocities.

$m_1 = 500\text{ g}$
$m_2 = 200\text{ g}$
$\vec{u}_1 = 6.00\text{ m/s north}$
$\vec{u}_2 = 0$
$\vec{v}_1 = ?$
$\vec{v}_2 = 8.00\text{ m/s }25.0°\text{ east of north}$

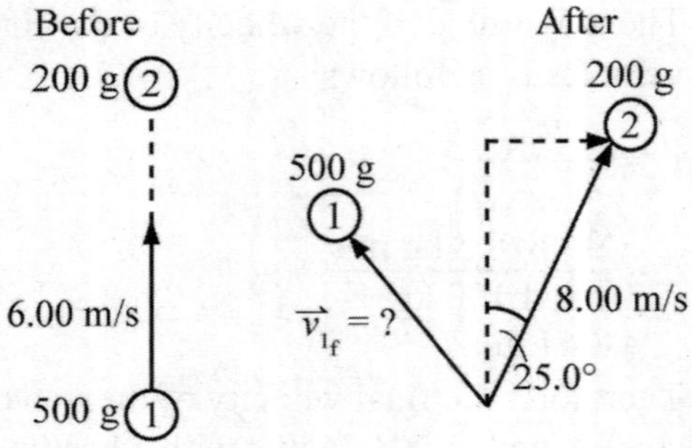

Method 1—Divide the movements into perpendicular components

Define the motion in the horizontal (east-west) direction.

$\vec{u}_{1x} = 0$
$\vec{u}_{2x} = 0$
$\vec{v}_{1x} = ?$

$$\begin{aligned}\vec{v}_{2x} &= (8.00\text{ m/s})\sin 25.0° \\ &= 3.38\text{ m/s east}\end{aligned}$$

Use the conservation of momentum to determine the horizontal component of the larger puck's final velocity.

$$\begin{aligned}\sum \vec{p}_{ix} &= \sum \vec{p}_{fx} \\ m_1\vec{u}_{1x} + m_2\vec{u}_{2x} &= m_1\vec{v}_{1x} + m_2\vec{v}_{2x} \\ m_1(0) + m_2(0) &= m_1\vec{v}_{1x} + m_2\vec{v}_{2x} \\ m_1\vec{v}_{1x} &= -m_2\vec{v}_{2x} \\ \therefore \vec{v}_{1x} &= -\frac{m_2\vec{v}_{2x}}{m_1} \\ &= -\frac{(200\text{ g})(3.38\text{ m/s east})}{500\text{ g}} \\ &= -1.352\text{ m/s east} \\ &= 1.352\text{ m/s west}\end{aligned}$$

Define the motion in the vertical (north-south) direction.

$\vec{u}_{1y} = 6.00\text{ m/s north}$
$\vec{u}_{2y} = 0$
$\vec{v}_{1y} = ?$

$$\begin{aligned}\vec{v}_{2y} &= (8.00\text{ m/s})\cos 25.0° \\ &= 7.250\text{ m/s north}\end{aligned}$$

Use the conservation of momentum to determine the vertical component of the larger puck's final velocity.

$$\begin{aligned}\sum \vec{p}_{iy} &= \sum \vec{p}_{fy} \\ m_1\vec{u}_{1y} + m_2\vec{u}_{2y} &= m_1\vec{v}_{1y} + m_2\vec{v}_{2y} \\ m_1\vec{u}_{1y} + m_2(0) &= m_1\vec{v}_{1y} + m_2\vec{v}_{2y} \\ m_1\vec{u}_{1y} &= m_1\vec{v}_{1y} + m_2\vec{v}_{2y} \\ m_1\vec{u}_{1y} - m_2\vec{v}_{2y} &= m_1\vec{v}_{1y} \\ \therefore \vec{v}_{1y} &= \frac{m_1\vec{u}_{1y} - m_2\vec{v}_{2y}}{m_1} \\ &= \frac{(500\text{ g})(6.00\text{ m/s}) - (200\text{ g})(7.250\text{ m/s})}{500\text{ g}} \\ &= 3.100\text{ m/s north}\end{aligned}$$

Use the Pythagorean theorem to determine the magnitude of the larger puck's velocity, and use the tangent function to determine its direction.

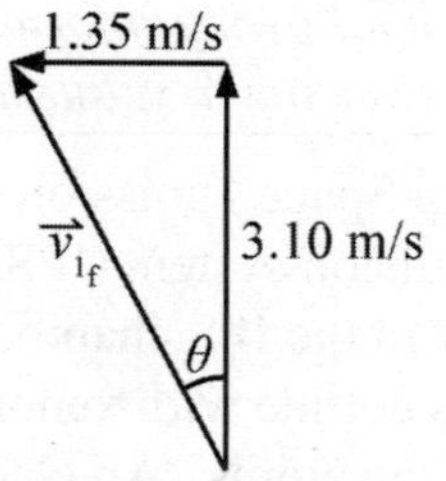

$v_{1f} = \sqrt{(v_{1x})^2 + (v_{1y})^2}$

$v_{1f} = \sqrt{(3.100\text{ m/s})^2 + (1.352\text{ m/s})^2}$

$= 3.38\text{ m/s}$

$\theta = \tan^{-1}\left(\dfrac{1.352}{3.100}\right)$

$= 23.6°$

$\therefore \vec{v}_{1f} = 3.38\text{ m/s N }23.6°\text{ W}$

Therefore, the velocity of the larger puck after the collision is 3.38 m/s23.6° west of north.

Method 2—Use the cosine and sine laws

Use the conservation of momentum, and include the directions with the velocities.

$\sum \vec{p}_{\text{i}} = \sum \vec{p}_{\text{f}}$

$\vec{p}_{1\text{i}} + \vec{p}_{2\text{i}} = \vec{p}_{1\text{f}} + \vec{p}_{2\text{f}}$

$\Rightarrow \vec{p}_{1\text{i}} = \vec{p}_{1\text{f}} + \vec{p}_{2\text{f}}$

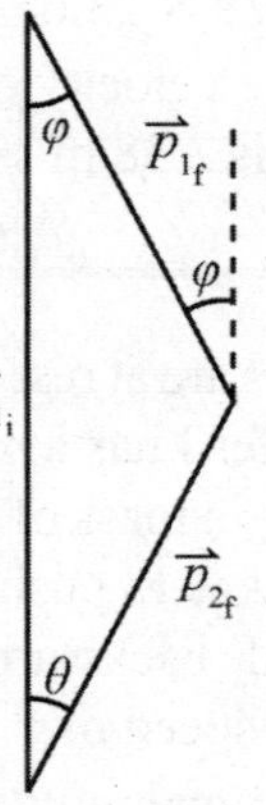

Now determine the known momenta.

$\vec{p}_{1\text{i}} = m_1\vec{u}_1$

$= (500\text{ g})(6.00\text{ m/s N})$

$= 3\,000\text{ g·m/s N}$

$\vec{p}_{2\text{f}} = m_2\vec{v}_2$

$= (200\text{ g})(8.00\text{ m/s N }25.0°\text{ E})$

$= 1\,600\text{ g·m/s N }25.0°\text{ E}$

Use the cosine law to find the magnitude of the velocity of the larger puck after the collision.

$p_{1\text{f}}^2 = p_{1\text{i}}^2 + p_{2\text{f}}^2 - 2p_{1\text{i}}p_{2\text{f}}\cos\theta$

$= (3\,000\text{ g·m/s})^2 + (1\,600\text{ g·m/s})^2 - [2(3\,000\text{ g·m/s})(1\,600\text{ g·m/s}) \times \cos 25.0°]$

$= 2.859 \times 10^6\text{ g}^2\text{·m}^2/\text{s}^2$

$\therefore p_{1\text{f}} = \sqrt{2.859 \times 10^6\text{ g}^2\text{·m}^2/\text{s}^2}$

$= 1.691 \times 10^3\text{ g·m/s}$

Use the sine law to calculate the direction of the larger puck's velocity after the collision.

$\dfrac{p_{1\text{f}}}{\sin\theta} = \dfrac{p_{2\text{f}}}{\sin\varphi}$

$\therefore \sin\varphi = \dfrac{p_{2\text{f}}\sin\theta}{p_{1\text{f}}}$

$= \dfrac{(1\,600\text{ g·m/s})\sin 25.0°}{1.691 \times 10^3\text{ g·m/s}}$

$= 0.4000$

$\therefore \varphi = \sin^{-1}(0.4000)$

$= 23.6°$

$\therefore \vec{p}_{1\text{f}} = 1.69 \times 10^3\text{ g·m/s }23.6°\text{ west of north}$

Calculate the final velocity of the larger puck using the equation for momentum.

$$\vec{v}_{1f} = \frac{\vec{p}_{1f}}{m_1}$$
$$= \frac{1.691 \times 10^3 \text{ g·m/s N } 23.6° \text{ W}}{500 \text{ g}}$$
$$= 3.38 \text{ m/s N } 23.6° \text{ W}$$

Therefore, the velocity of the larger puck after the collision is 3.38 m/s 23.6° west of north.

---

10. Two skaters are at rest on a smooth, frozen pond. Skater I has a mass of 50 kg, and skater II has a mass of 70 kg. Facing each other, the skaters push off of each other. As they glide backward and apart, skater II moves at a speed of 4.0 m/s and has

A. a lower magnitude of momentum than skater I

B. a larger magnitude of momentum than skater I

C. less kinetic energy than skater I

D. more kinetic energy than skater I

Use the following information to answer the next question.

A lump of clay with a mass of 50.0 g is moving south at a speed of 20.0 cm/s. It collides head on with a second lump of clay with a mass of 70.0 g that is moving north at a speed of 40.0 cm/s.

11. The two lumps of clay stick together after the collision, and no external horizontal forces act on the system. The velocity of the combined lump after the collision is

A. 60.0 cm/s south

B. 31.7 cm/s south

C. 20.0 cm/s north

D. 15.0 cm/s north

Use the following information to answer the next question.

The Deep Space 1 mission (DS1) uses an ion propulsion system (IPS) on the DS1 capsule. In the IPS chamber, high-speed electrons collide with xenon atoms, ionizing the atoms. An electric field produced by electrified grids then accelerates the ions and ejects them from the IPS chamber and out into space, propelling the DS1 capsule forward.

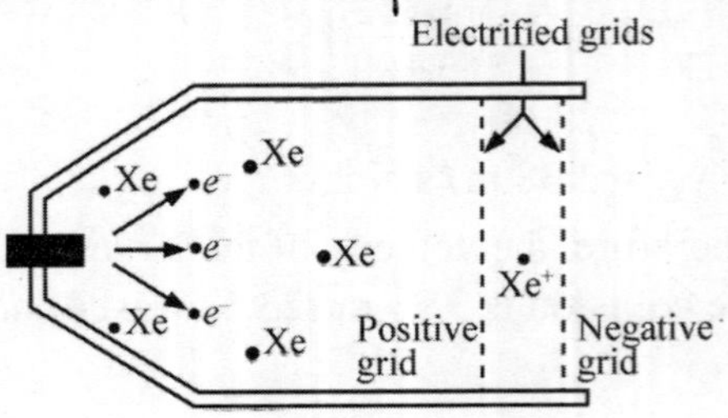

IPS chamber

IPS Operating Specifications for DS1

Propellant ions	Xe^+
Total mass of propellant	81.5 kg
Mass of empty DS1 capsule	489.5 kg

Energy required to ionize a xenon atom = 12.1 eV

Mass of a single xenon atom = 2.18×10^{-25} kg

Average exit speed of the xenon ions = 43.0 km/s

12. If all of the xenon propellant were expelled in a single short burst, the change in the speed of the DS1 capsule after all the fuel is expelled would be

A. 6.14 m/s

B. 7.16 m/s

C. 6.14×10^3 m/s

D. 7.16×10^3 m/s

13. A 1.20 kg grenade at rest on a smooth, frictionless surface suddenly explodes into three pieces. Immediately after the explosion, a 0.50 kg piece travels horizontally to the north at 3.0 m/s, and a 0.30 kg fragment travels horizontally to the southwest at 4.0 m/s. Assuming the third piece is also travelling along the horizontal plane, the velocity of this piece is

A. 3.5 m/s at 52° S of E

B. 3.5 m/s at 38° S of E

C. 2.7 m/s at 52° S of E

D. 2.7 m/s at 38° S of E

CHALLENGER QUESTION

Use the following information to answer the next question.

A 575-g glass ornament sitting on a table experienced a resonant frequency of 440 Hz.
The frequency caused the ornament to break into three pieces which then travelled horizontally across the frictionless tabletop.

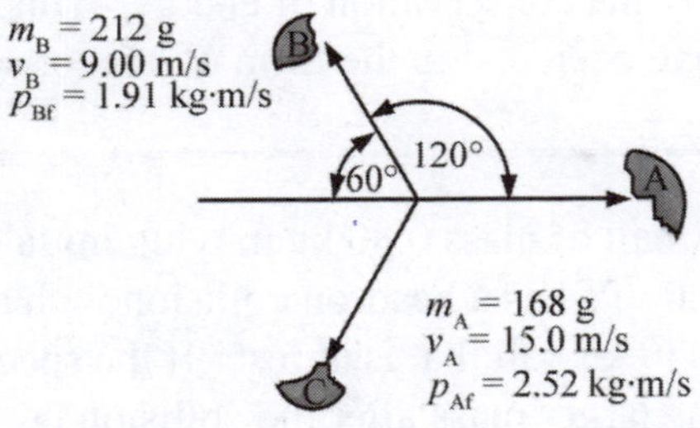

Fragment A had a mass of 168 g, and fragment B had a mass of 212 g.

14. The magnitude of the momentum of fragment C immediately after the ornament broke into pieces was

A. 5.19 kg·m/s

B. 3.85 kg·m/s

C. 2.28 kg·m/s

D. 0.610 kg·m/s

Numerical Response

15. A 1 575 kg car, initially travelling at 10.0 m/s, collides with a stationary 2 250 kg car. The bumpers of the two cars become locked together during the collision. The speed of the combined cars immediately after impact is ________ m/s. (Record your answer to three digits.)

Use the following information to answer the next question.

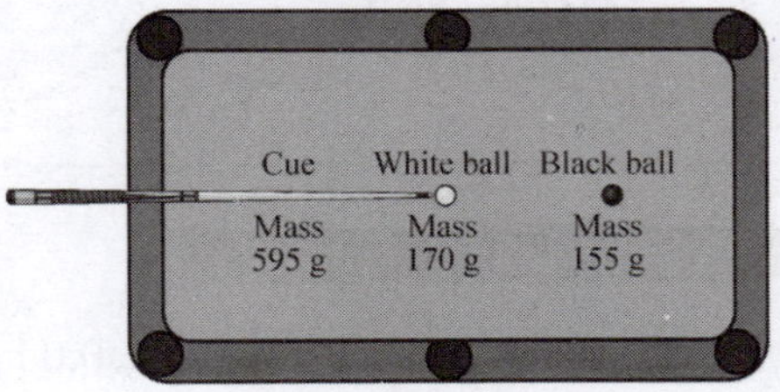

A pool table

Numerical Response

16. On the given pool table, the white ball bounces off of the black ball and moves in the direction opposite to its original direction. If the speed of the white ball immediately after the collision is 3.13 m/s, then the speed of the black ball immediately after the collision is ________ m/s. (Record your three-digit answer.)

Use the following information to answer the next question.

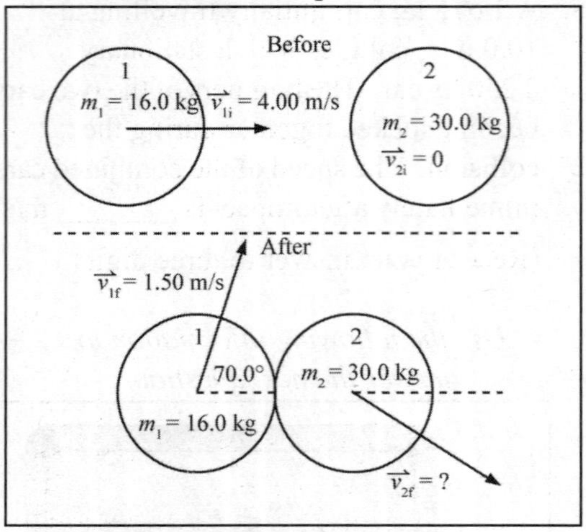

Numerical Response

17. A 16.0 kg disk hits a stationary 30.0 kg disk, as shown in the given diagram. The new speed of the heavier disk is __________ m/s.

30-A1.5k define, compare and contrast elastic and inelastic collisions, using quantitative examples, in terms of conservation of kinetic energy

Elastic and Inelastic Collisions

An elastic collision occurs when both kinetic energy and momentum are conserved. An inelastic collision occurs when the momentum is conserved but some of the kinetic energy is lost as other forms of energy, such as heat, light, or sound.

Example

A 1.0 kg ball travelling with a velocity of 2.0 m/s to the right collides head-on with a stationary 2.0 kg ball. After the collision, the 2.0 kg ball travels to the right with a velocity of 1.2 m/s, while the 1.0 kg ball travels in the opposite direction at 0.40 m/s.

Is this an elastic collision? In other words, does $E_k = E_k{'}$?

$$\begin{aligned} E_k &= \frac{1}{2}m_1 v_1^2 + \frac{1}{2}m_2 v_2^2 \\ &= \frac{1}{2}(1.0\text{ kg})(2.0\text{ m/s})^2 + 0 \\ &= 2.0\text{ J} \end{aligned}$$

$$\begin{aligned} E_k{'} &= \frac{1}{2}m_1(v_1{'})^2 + \frac{1}{2}m_2(v_2{'})^2 \\ &= \frac{1}{2}(2.0\text{ kg})(1.2\text{ m/s})^2 + \frac{1}{2}(1.0\text{ kg})(0.40\text{ m/s})^2 \\ &= 1.5\text{ J} \end{aligned}$$

Note that energy is a scalar quantity, so the directions of the moving objects are not considered in this solution.

Since $E_k \neq E_k{'}$, this collision is not elastic. In fact, since there is some kinetic energy that was present before and is now missing after the collision, energy must have been converted to another form in order to satisfy the conservation of energy. This energy may have been lost in the form of heat or sound.

---

18. A ball of mass 0.80 kg moving initially at 8.0 m/s has a head-on collision with a 0.40 kg ball that is at rest. If the speed of the larger mass after the collision is 2.7 m/s and the speed of the smaller mass is 8.2 m/s, the collision is

A. elastic and momentum is conserved

B. elastic but momentum is not conserved

C. inelastic and 36% of the kinetic energy is lost

D. inelastic and 64% of the kinetic energy is lost

Use the following information to answer the next question.

A projectile with a mass of 28.5 g is fired with a speed of 210 m/s toward a block of wood resting on a frictionless, level surface. The block of wood has a mass of 1.75 kg and moves with a velocity of 3.37 m/s after the bullet embeds in it. The total kinetic energy of the system before impact is ___*i*___; after impact, the total kinetic energy is ___*ii*___.

19. This statement is completed by the information in table

A.

i	*ii*
628 J	4.43 J

B.

i	*ii*
2.99 J	10.1 J

C.

i	*ii*
628 J	10.1 J

D.

i	*ii*
2.99 J	4.43 J

Use the following information to answer the next question.

A 1 600 kg car travelling north at 60.0 km/h collides with a 2 400 kg truck travelling east at 70.0 km/h. After the collision, the velocity of the car is 35.0 km/h10.0° N of E.

Written Response

20. Find the velocity of the truck after the collision.

____

____

____

____

____

____

____

Answers and Solutions
Momentum and Impulse

1. B	5. D	9. B	13. D	17. 2.01
2. 2803	6. C	10. C	14. C	18. C
3. B	7. 1503	11. D	15. 4.12	19. C
4. B	8. D	12. D	16. 3.59	20. WR

1. B

$$\begin{aligned}\vec{p} &= m\vec{v}\\ &= (9.11 \times 10^{-31}\text{ kg})(2.63 \times 10^{6}\text{ m/s north})\\ &= 2.40 \times 10^{-24}\text{ kg·m/s north}\end{aligned}$$

2. 2803

$$\begin{aligned}p &= mv\\ \therefore m &= \frac{p}{v}\\ &= \frac{3.92 \times 10^{4}\text{ kg·m/s}}{14.0\text{ m/s}}\\ &= 2\,800\text{ kg}\\ &= 2.80 \times 10^{3}\text{ kg}\end{aligned}$$

3. B

A scalar quantity only has magnitude (or value), not direction. Therefore, only power is a scalar quantity because the quantities of force, impulse, and momentum each have direction.

4. B

$$\begin{aligned}\text{Impulse} &= \vec{F}_{\text{net}}\Delta t\\ &= \text{N·s}\\ &= (\text{kg·m/s}^2)(\text{s})\\ &= \text{kg·m/s}\end{aligned}$$

5. D

$$\begin{aligned}\Delta\vec{p} &= \vec{p}_{\text{f}} - \vec{p}_{\text{i}}\\ &= 0 - (12.7\text{ kg} \times 4.85\text{ m/s south})\\ &= -61.6\text{ kg·m/s south, or } 61.6\text{ kg·m/s north}\end{aligned}$$

Since momentum is a vector quantity, a direction must be included.

6. C

$$\begin{aligned}\text{Impulse} &= \vec{F}t\\ &= (595\text{ N})(0.0037\text{ s})\\ &= 2.2\text{ N}\cdot\text{s}\\ &= 2.2\text{ kg}\cdot\text{m/s in the direction of the golf club's movement}\end{aligned}$$

7. 1503

$$\begin{aligned}\vec{d} &= \left[\frac{\vec{v}_{\text{f}} + \vec{v}_{\text{i}}}{2}\right]t\\ 115\text{ m} &= \left[\frac{15.0\text{ m/s} + 3.00\text{ m/s}}{2}\right]t\\ t &= 12.78\text{ s}\end{aligned}$$

$$\begin{aligned}\vec{F}\Delta t &= m\Delta\vec{v}\\ \vec{F} &= \frac{m\Delta\vec{v}}{\Delta t}\\ &= \frac{(1.60 \times 10^{3}\text{ kg})(12.0\text{ m/s})}{12.78\text{ s}}\\ &= 1.50 \times 10^{3}\text{ N}\end{aligned}$$

8. D

Momentum is conserved during all interactions. The total momentum before the interaction was zero. After the interaction, the two masses must move in directions opposite of each other.
The momentum for each mass is equal in magnitude and opposite in direction because the spring imparts the energy stored within it according to Newton's third law (for every action there is an equal and opposite reaction).

9. B

The situation in which an object is raised into the air quickly does not have a direct connection to the conservation of momentum.

10. C

It is first necessary to determine the velocity of skater I.

$$\sum \vec{p}_i = \sum \vec{p}_f$$
$$0 = \vec{p}_I + \vec{p}_{II}$$
$$\therefore \vec{p}_I = -\vec{p}_{II}$$
$$\Rightarrow |\vec{p}_I| = |\vec{p}_{II}|$$
$$\therefore p_I = p_{II}$$

$$\begin{aligned} p_{II} &= m_{II}v_{II} \\ &= (70\ \text{kg})(4.0\ \text{m/s}) \\ &= 280\ \text{kg·m/s} \\ &= p_I \end{aligned}$$

So both skater I and skater II have the same magnitude of momentum after they push off of one another.

In order to calculate the kinetic energies of both skaters, the magnitude of their velocities are required. We already have skater II's speed so we now need the speed of skater I.

$$p_I = p_{II}$$
$$m_I v_I = m_{II} v_{II}$$
$$\begin{aligned} \therefore v_I &= \frac{m_{II}v_{II}}{m_I} \\ &= \frac{(70\ \text{kg})(4.0\ \text{m/s})}{50\ \text{kg}} \\ &= 5.6\ \text{m/s} \end{aligned}$$

$$\begin{aligned} E_{k_I} &= \frac{1}{2}m_I v_I^2 \\ &= \frac{1}{2}(50\ \text{kg})(5.6\ \text{m/s})^2 \\ &= 784\ \text{J} \end{aligned}$$

$$\begin{aligned} E_{k_{II}} &= \frac{1}{2}m_{II} v_{II}^2 \\ &= \frac{1}{2}(70\ \text{kg})(4.0\ \text{m/s})^2 \\ &= 560\ \text{J} \end{aligned}$$

$$\therefore E_{k_{II}} < E_{k_I}$$

11. D

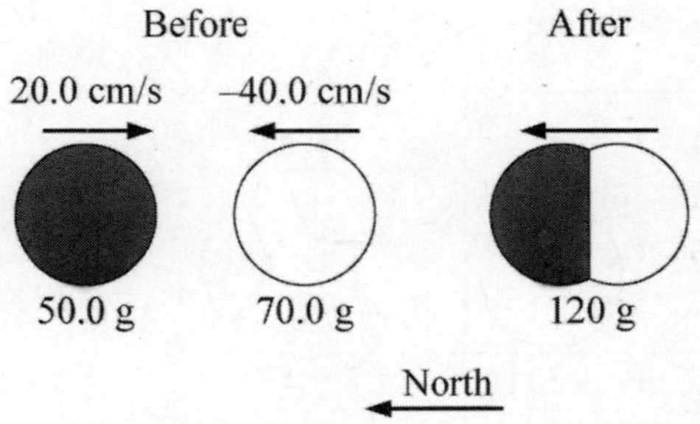

Momentum is always conserved, so (with south being considered the positive direction):

$$\sum \vec{p}_i = \sum \vec{p}_f$$
$$m_1\vec{v}_1 + m_2\vec{v}_2 = (m_1 + m_2)\vec{v}'$$
$$\begin{aligned} \therefore \vec{v}' &= \frac{m_1\vec{v}_1 + m_2\vec{v}_2}{m_1 + m_2} \\ &= \frac{(50.0\ \text{g})(20.0\ \text{cm/s}) + (70.0\ \text{g})(-40.0\ \text{cm/s})}{50.0\ \text{g} + 70.0\ \text{g}} \\ &= \frac{-1\,800\ \text{g·cm/s}}{120\ \text{g}} \\ &= -15.0\ \text{cm/s} \\ &= 15.0\ \text{cm/s north} \end{aligned}$$

Therefore, the velocity of the combined lumps of clay after the collision is 15.0 cm/s north.

12. D

Assume that the initial velocity of both the propellant and the capsule are zero.

The momentum change of the propellant is equal and opposite to the momentum change of the capsule. (Momentum is conserved.)

$$\begin{aligned} \Delta\vec{p}_p &= m_p(\vec{v}_f - \vec{v}_i) \\ &= (81.5\ \text{kg})(43\,000\ \text{m/s} - 0) \\ &= 3.505 \times 10^6\ \text{kg·m/s} \end{aligned}$$

In this case we have chosen the direction of motion of the propellant to be positive. Now it is possible to calculate the velocity of the capsule.

$$\Delta\vec{p}_p = -\Delta\vec{p}_c = -m_c\Delta\vec{v}_c$$
$$\begin{aligned} \therefore \Delta\vec{v}_c &= -\frac{\vec{p}_p}{m_c} \\ &= -\frac{3.505 \times 10^6\ \text{kg·m/s}}{489.5\ \text{kg}} \\ &= -7.16 \times 10^3\ \text{m/s} \end{aligned}$$

So the speed of the DS1 capsule will be 7.16×10^3 m/s.

13. D

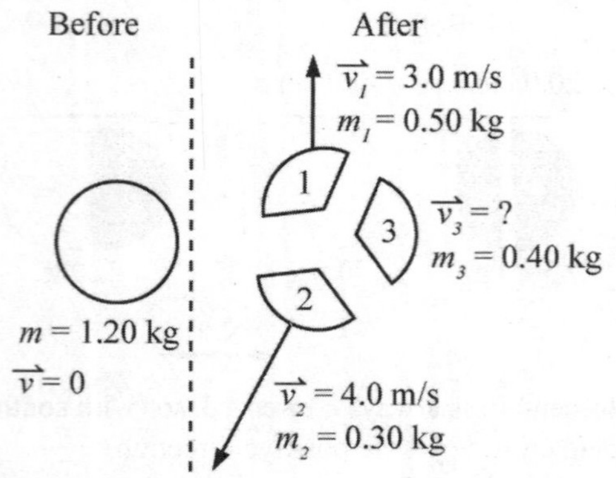

Since the conservation of momentum states that $\sum \vec{p}_\text{i} = \sum \vec{p}_\text{f}$, it is best to start by calculating all relevant known quantities. In this case, since we know that the initial momentum of the system is zero, we need to calculate the final momentum of the two pieces of the grenade for which the velocity and mass are known. Once we have these we can use the cosine law to determine the magnitude of the momentum of the third piece of the grenade since the sum of the three vectors must be zero, and we can use the sine law to determine the direction of this momentum.

$$\begin{aligned}\vec{p}_1 &= m_1\vec{v}_1\\ &= (0.50\text{ kg})(3.0\text{ m/s N})\\ &= 1.5\text{ kg·m/s N}\end{aligned}$$

$$\begin{aligned}\vec{p}_2 &= m_2\vec{v}_2\\ &= (0.30\text{ kg})(4.0\text{ m/s SW})\\ &= 1.2\text{ kg·m/s SW}\end{aligned}$$

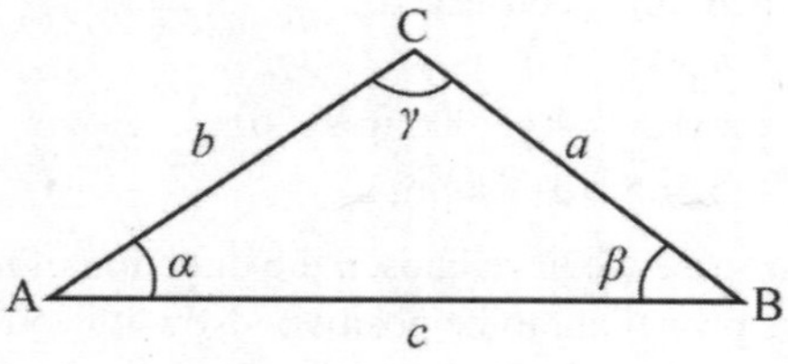

Given the above labels for the angles and lengths of sides for any triangle, the cosine and sine laws are as follows.

Cosine law:

$c^2 = a^2 + b^2 - 2ab\cos\gamma$

Sine law:

$$\frac{a}{\sin\alpha} = \frac{b}{\sin\beta} = \frac{c}{\sin\gamma}$$

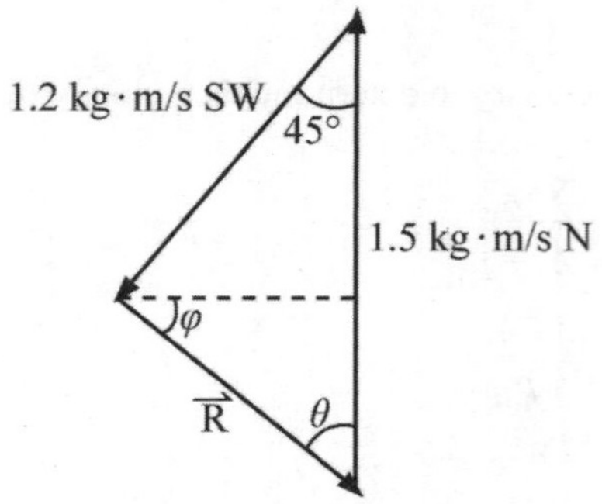

First use the cosine law to determine the magnitude of the resultant vector.

$$\begin{aligned}R^2 &= p_1^2 + p_2^2 - 2p_1p_2\cos 45°\\ &= (1.2\text{ kg·m/s})^2\\ &\quad +(1.5\text{ kg·m/s})^2\\ &\quad -2(1.2\text{ kg·m/s})(1.5\text{ kg·m/s})\cos 45°\\ &= 3.69\text{ kg}^2\text{·m}^2/\text{s}^2\\ &\quad -\left(3.60\text{ kg}^2\text{·m}^2/\text{s}^2\right)\left(\frac{1}{\sqrt{2}}\right)\end{aligned}$$

$$\begin{aligned}R^2 &= 1.144\text{ kg}^2\text{·m}^2/\text{s}^2\\ \therefore R &= \sqrt{1.144\text{ kg}^2\text{·m}^2/\text{s}^2}\\ &= 1.07\text{ kg·m/s}\end{aligned}$$

Use the sine law to determine the angle of the resultant vector.

$$\frac{1.2\text{ kg·m/s}}{\sin\theta} = \frac{1.07\text{ kg·m/s}}{\sin 45°}$$

$\therefore \sin\theta = 0.793 \Rightarrow \theta = 52°$

Now the angle of the third piece of the grenade's momentum can be determined.

$\varphi = 90° - 52° = 38°$

So the final momentum of the third piece of the grenade $(\vec{p}_3)$ is 1.07 kg·m/s 38° S of E. Finally the velocity of the third piece of the grenade can be calculated.

$$\begin{aligned}\vec{p}_3 &= m_3\vec{v}_3\\ \therefore \vec{v}_3 &= \frac{\vec{p}_3}{m_3}\\ &= \frac{1.07\text{ kg·m/s 38° S of E}}{0.40\text{ kg}}\\ &= 2.7\text{ m/s 38° S of E}\end{aligned}$$

14. C

Using the component method:

$$\sum \vec{p}_i = \sum \vec{p}_f$$

The total momentum before is zero, so the total momentum of the three pieces is also zero.

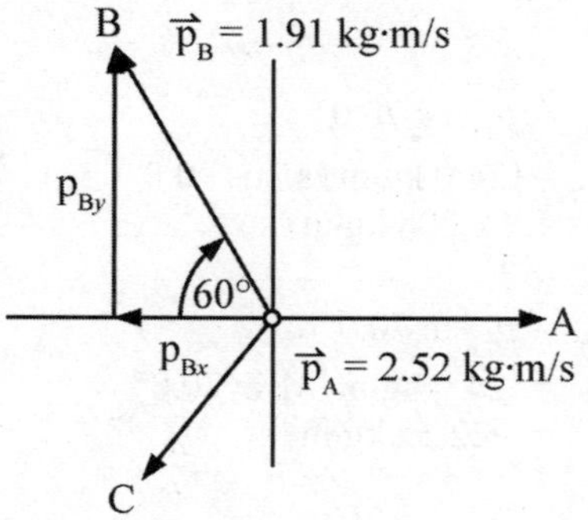

$$0 = \vec{p}_A + \vec{p}_B + \vec{p}_C$$

$$\vec{p}_{Bx} = (1.91 \text{ kg·m/s})\cos 60.0° = 0.955 \text{ kg·m/s to the left}$$

$$\vec{p}_{By} = (1.91 \text{ kg·m/s})\sin 60.0° = 1.654 \text{ kg·m/s up}$$

Horizontally:

$$0 = 2.52 \text{ kg·m/s} - 0.955 \text{ kg·m/s} + \vec{p}_{Cx}$$

$$\vec{p}_{Cx} = -1.565 \text{ kg·m/s to the right}$$

Vertically:

$$0 = 0 + 1.654 \text{ kg·m/s} + \vec{p}_{Cy}$$

$$\vec{p}_{Cy} = -1.654 \text{ kg·m/s up}$$

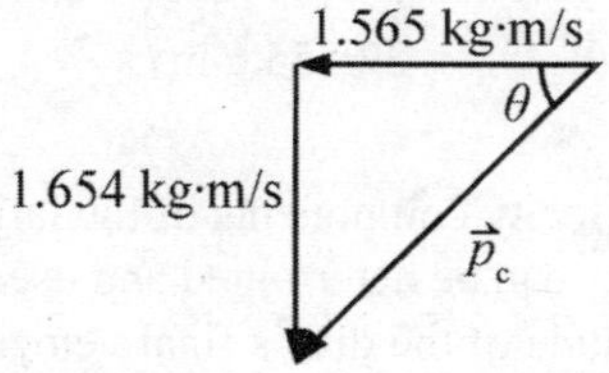

$$|\vec{p}_C| = \sqrt{(1.565 \text{ kg·m/s})^2 + (1.654 \text{ kg·m/s})^2} = 2.28 \text{ kg·m/s}$$

Therefore, the magnitude of the momentum for fragment C is 2.28 kg · m / s.

15. 4.12

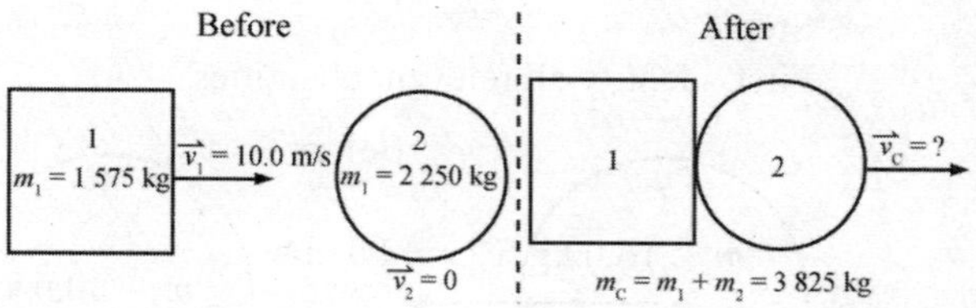

$$\sum \vec{p}_i = \sum \vec{p}_f$$

$$\vec{p}_1 + \vec{p}_2 = \vec{p}_c$$

$$m_1\vec{v}_1 + m_2\vec{v}_2 = m_c\vec{v}_c$$

$$\therefore \vec{v}_c = \frac{m_1\vec{v}_1}{m_c} = \frac{(1\,575 \text{ kg})(10.0 \text{ m/s})}{3\,825 \text{ kg}} = 4.12 \text{ m/s}$$

16. 3.59

$$\sum \vec{p}_i = \sum \vec{p}_f$$

$$m_1\vec{v}_1 + m_2\vec{v}_2 = m_1\vec{v}_1{}' + m_2\vec{v}_2{}'$$

$$170 \text{ g}(3.13 \text{ m/s}) + 0 = 170 \text{ g}(-0.147 \text{ m/s}) + (155 \text{ g})\vec{v}_2{}'$$

$$\vec{v}_2{}' = 3.59 \text{ m/s}$$

17. 2.01

Step 1
First, identify all relevant quantities.

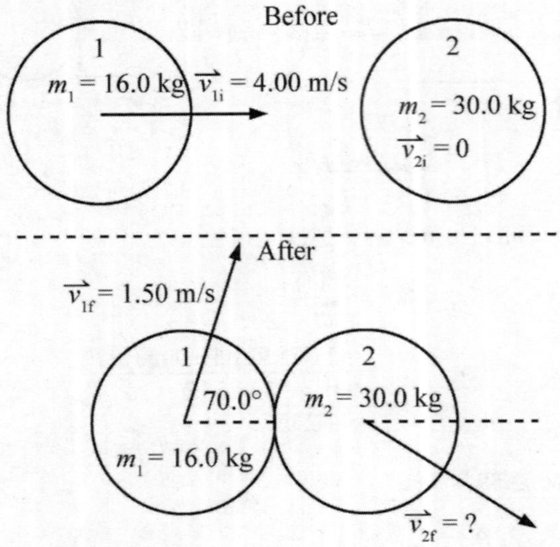

$m_1 = 16.0$ kg
$m_2 = 30.0$ kg
$\vec{u}_1 = 4.00$ m/s at 0°
$\vec{u}_2 = 0$
$\vec{v}_1 = 1.50$ m/s at 70.0°
$\vec{v}_2 = ?$

The initial and final velocities are represented by $\vec{u}$ and $\vec{v}$, respectively.

Step 2
The momenta of this collision problem are also relevant.

$$\begin{aligned}\vec{p}_{1i} &= m_1\vec{u}_1\\ &= (16.0\text{ kg})(4.00\text{ m/s at }0°)\\ &= 64.0\text{ kg·m/s at }0°\end{aligned}$$

$\vec{p}_{2i} = 0$

$$\begin{aligned}\vec{p}_{1f} &= m_1\vec{v}_1\\ &= (16.0\text{ kg})(1.50\text{ m/s at }70.0°)\\ &= 24.0\text{ kg·m/s at }70.0°\end{aligned}$$

$$\begin{aligned}\vec{p}_{2f} &= m_2\vec{v}_2\\ &= ?\end{aligned}$$

Step 3
Next, break the momenta into their vertical and horizontal components (take 0° and 90° to be the positive directions).

$\vec{p}_{1ix} = \vec{p}_{1i} = +64.0$ kg·m/s
$\vec{p}_{2ix} = 0$
$\vec{p}_{1iy} = 0$
$\vec{p}_{2iy} = 0$

$$\begin{aligned}\vec{p}_{1fx} &= p_{1f}\cos 70.0°\\ &= (24.0\text{ kg·m/s})\cos 70.0°\\ &= +8.208\text{ kg·m/s}\end{aligned}$$

$\vec{p}_{2fx} = ?$

$$\begin{aligned}\vec{p}_{1fy} &= p_{1f}\sin 70.0°\\ &= (24.0\text{ kg·m/s})\sin 70.0°\\ &= +22.55\text{ kg·m/s}\end{aligned}$$

$\vec{p}_{2fy} = ?$

Step 4
Use the conservation of momentum along each axis to determine the components of the larger disk's final momentum.

In the horizontal (x) direction,

$$\begin{aligned}\sum \vec{p}_{ix} &= \sum \vec{p}_{fx}\\ \vec{p}_{1ix} + \vec{p}_{2ix} &= \vec{p}_{1fx} + \vec{p}_{2fx}\\ (+64.0\text{ kg·m/s}) + 0 &= (+8.208\text{ kg·m/s}) + \vec{p}_{2fx}\\ \therefore \vec{p}_{2fx} &= +55.79\text{ kg·m/s}\end{aligned}$$

In the vertical (y) direction,

$$\begin{aligned}\sum \vec{p}_{iy} &= \sum \vec{p}_{fy}\\ \vec{p}_{1iy} + \vec{p}_{2iy} &= \vec{p}_{1fy} + \vec{p}_{2fy}\\ 0 + 0 &= (+22.55\text{ kg·m/s}) + \vec{p}_{2fy}\\ \therefore \vec{p}_{2fy} &= -22.55\text{ kg·m/s}\end{aligned}$$

Step 5
The velocity components of the larger disk's final velocity can be determined and used to calculate the magnitude of the disk's final velocity.

$$\begin{aligned}\vec{v}_{2fx} &= \frac{\vec{p}_{2fx}}{m_2}\\ &= \frac{+55.79\text{ kg·m/s}}{30.0\text{ kg}}\\ &= +1.860\text{ m/s}\end{aligned}$$

$$\begin{aligned}\vec{v}_{2fy} &= \frac{\vec{p}_{2fy}}{m_2}\\ &= \frac{-22.55\text{ kg·m/s}}{30.0\text{ kg}}\\ &= -0.7517\text{ m/s}\end{aligned}$$

Use the Pythagorean theorem to determine the final speed of the larger disk.

$$\begin{aligned}\therefore v_{2f} &= \sqrt{(1.860\text{ m/s})^2 + (0.7517\text{ m/s})^2}\\ &= 2.01\text{ m/s}\end{aligned}$$

18. C

Step 1
Examine the kinetic energies involved before the collision.

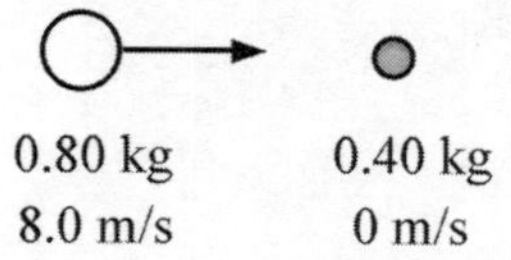

$$E_k = \frac{1}{2}mv_1^2 + \frac{1}{2}mv_2^2$$
$$= \frac{1}{2}(0.80\text{ kg})(8.0\text{ m/s})^2 + 0$$
$$= 25.6\text{ J}$$

Step 2
Examine the kinetic energies involved after the collision.

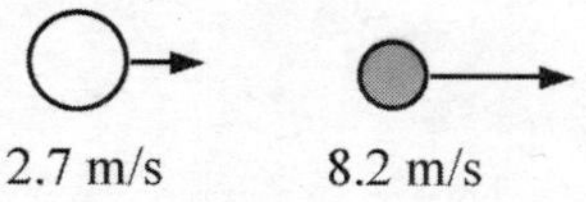

$$E_k' = \frac{1}{2}m(v_1')^2 + \frac{1}{2}m(v_2')^2$$
$$= \frac{1}{2}(0.80\text{ kg})(2.7\text{ m/s})^2 + \frac{1}{2}(0.40\text{ kg})(8.2\text{ m/s})^2$$
$$= 16.4\text{ J}$$

Step 3
Compare the kinetic energy before the collision with the kinetic energy after the collision. It is evident that during the collision, 9.2 J of kinetic energy was lost. This collision was therefore inelastic.

The percentage of kinetic energy lost is calculated as follows:

$$\%_{\text{lost}} = \frac{E_{\text{k lost}}}{E_{\text{k initial}}}$$
$$= \frac{9.2\text{ J}}{25.6\text{ J}} \times 100\%$$
$$= 36\%$$

19. C

Calculate the total kinetic energies before and after the collision.

Before the collision only the projectile is moving so:

$$E_k = \frac{1}{2}m_p v_p^2$$
$$= \frac{1}{2}(0.0285\text{ kg})(210\text{ m/s})^2$$
$$= 628\text{ J}$$

After the collision the combined mass of the projectile and the block moves so:

$$E_k = \frac{1}{2}(m_p + m_b)v'^2$$
$$= \frac{1}{2}(1.7785\text{ kg})(3.37\text{ m/s})^2$$
$$= 10.1\text{ J}$$

20. WR

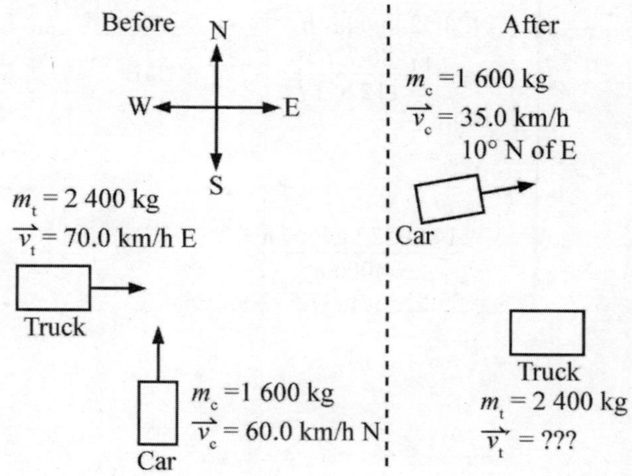

Calculate the initial and final momenta of the car and the initial momentum of the truck.

$$\vec{p}_c = (1\,600\text{ kg})(60.0\text{ km/h})$$
$$= 96\,000\text{ kg}\cdot\text{km/h N}$$
$$\vec{p}'_c = 56\,000\text{ kg}\cdot\text{km/h } 10.0°\text{ N of E}$$
$$\vec{p}_t = (2\,400\text{ kg})(70.0\text{ km/h})$$
$$= 168\,000\text{ kg}\cdot\text{km/h E}$$

Use the principle of conservation of momentum to calculate the final momentum of the truck in the horizontal and vertical planes.

$$\sum \vec{p}_i = \sum \vec{p}_f$$

Horizontally:

$$\vec{p}_c + \vec{p}_t = \vec{p}_c' + \vec{p}_t'$$
$$0 + 168\,000\text{ kg·km/h}$$
$$= 56\,000\text{ kg·km/h}(\cos 10.0°) + \vec{p}_t'$$
$$\vec{p}_t' = 112\,851\text{ kg·km/h east}$$

Vertically:

$$96\,000\text{ kg·km/h} + 0$$
$$= 56\,000\text{ kg·km/h}(\sin 10.0°) + \vec{p}_t'$$
$$\vec{p}_t' = 86\,726\text{ kg·km/h north}$$

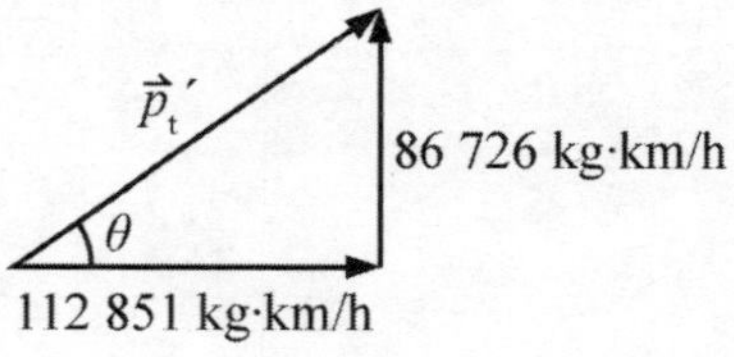

$$\vec{p}_t{}' = \sqrt{(112\ 851\ \text{kg}\cdot\text{km/h})^2 + (86\ 726\ \text{kg}\cdot\text{km/h})^2}$$
$$= 142\ 052\ \text{kg}\cdot\text{km/h}$$
$$\theta = \tan^{-1}\left(\frac{86\ 726}{112\ 851}\right) = 37.5^\circ \text{ N of E}$$
$$\vec{p}_t{}' = m\vec{v}_t{}'$$
$$\vec{v}_t{}' = \frac{\vec{p}_t{}'}{m}$$
$$= \frac{142\ 052\ \text{kg}\cdot\text{km/h}}{2\ 400\ \text{kg}}$$
$$= 59.5\ \text{km/h}\ 37.5^\circ \text{ N of E}$$

UNIT TEST — MOMENTUM AND IMPULSE

1. Which of the following units does **not** represent the momentum of an object?
   A. N·s **B.** g·cm / h
   C. kg·m / s **D.** kg·m / s^2

2. Rock climbers use slightly elastic ropes to prevent injuring themselves in case they fall while climbing. The importance of the elasticity of the climbing rope can be understood in terms of impulse because the rope's elasticity results in a
   A. decreased force on the climber during an increased time interval
   B. increased force on the climber during an increased time interval
   C. decreased force on the climber during a decreased time interval
   D. increased force on the climber during a decreased time interval

3. A 75.0 kg hockey player skating at +10 m / s bodychecks a second, stationary hockey player. After the collision, the two skaters move together at +4.50 m / s. In the collision, the impulse experienced by the second hockey player was
   A. $+3.38 \times 10^2$ kg·m / s
   B. $+4.13 \times 10^2$ kg·m / s
   C. $+7.50 \times 10^2$ kg·m / s
   D. $+1.09 \times 10^3$ kg·m / s

Use the following information to answer the next question.

Foundation piles for tall buildings are hammered into the ground using a pile driver. The pile driver in the given diagram lifts a 900 kg hammer a distance of 3.50 m above the top of the pile and then allows it to drop.

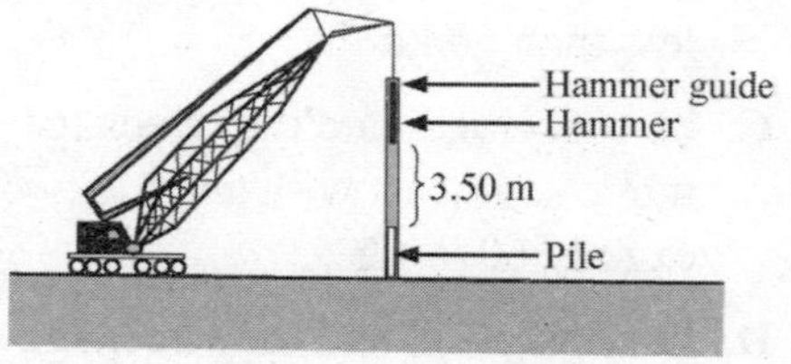

Numerical Response

4. The impulse is delivered by the pile driver in 2.10×10^{-3} s. Expressed in scientific notation, the magnitude of the force the hammer exerts on the pile is $a.bc \times 10^{d}$ N. What is the value of *abcd*?__________

5. Which of the following statements about momentum is **false**?
   A. The momentum of a system remains constant when no external net force acts on the system.
   B. Conservation of momentum can be used to explain rocket propulsion.
   C. Momentum can be transferred from one object to another.
   D. Momentum is not conserved in isolated systems.

6. Two identical cars collide in the middle of an intersection. Car A has a velocity of 60 km/h east, and car B has a velocity of 60 km/h south. If the two cars become entangled during the collision, momentum will

 A. not be conserved, and the wreckage will move southeast with a velocity of exactly 60 km/h

 B. not be conserved, and the wreckage will move southeast with a velocity less than 60 km/h

 C. be conserved, and the wreckage will move southeast with a velocity of exactly 60 km/h

 D. be conserved, and the wreckage will move southeast with a velocity less than 60 km/h

CHALLENGER QUESTION

Use the following information to answer the next question.

Sheet of Curling Ice

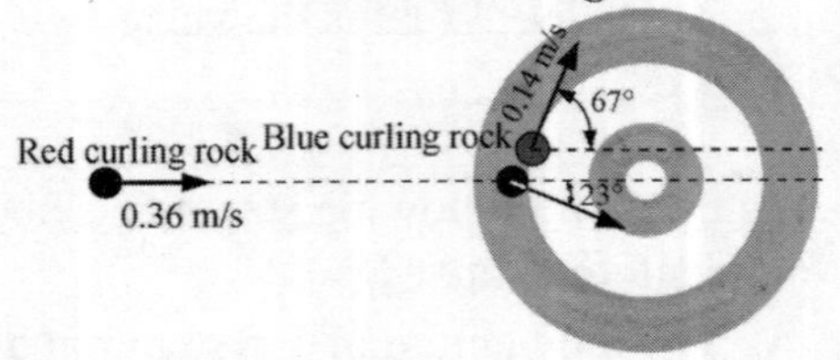

A red curling rock travelling straight down a sheet of ice at 0.36 m/s contacts a stationary blue curling rock. After contact, the blue rock moves at 0.14 m/s at an angle of 67 ° and the red rock moves at an angle of 23 °, as illustrated. The mass of a curling rock is 18.8 kg.

7. The speed of the red rock, after contact, is

 A. 0.15 m/s **B.** 0.22 m/s

 C. 0.33 m/s **D.** 0.39 m/s

Use the following information to answer the next question.

A company that manufactures solid-fuel rocket engines for model rockets runs a test on one of its engines to measure its maximum thrust. The engine is fastened to a force-measuring device and a computer. The forces are read 25 times per second. The given table shows the results of the test.

Model Rocket Engine Test

Time (s)	Force (N)
0	0
0.04	2.8
0.08	5.0
0.12	7.5
0.16	10.9
0.20	13.1

At t = 0.20 s, maximum thrust is achieved.

Written Response

8. The tested engine is used to launch a 17 g model rocket from its position at rest on the ground. Using graphical analysis, determine the speed of the rocket at the time of maximum thrust of the engine. As part of your response, provide a graph of force as a function of time, determine the area under the graph, and relate the area algebraically to a physics equation. State all physics principles and formulas used.

Use the following information to answer the next question.

In a physics lab, students push puck 1, which has a mass of 250 g, toward puck 2, which is stationary and has a mass of 550 g. Puck 1 is pushed with a velocity of 0.35 m/s. The pucks collide as shown in the given diagram.

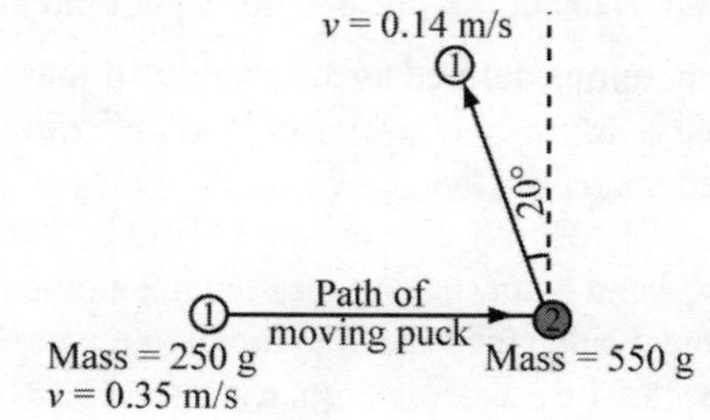

Written Response

9. Determine the velocity of puck 2 after it is hit.

10. Which of the following statements about an elastic collision is **true**?

A. Both the kinetic energy and mometum are conserved.

B. Neither the kinetic energy nor the momentum is conserved.

C. The kinetic energy is not conserved, but the momentum is conserved.

D. The kinetic energy is conserved, but the momentum is not conserved.

Answers and Solutions — Unit Test

1. D	4. 3556	7. C	10. A
2. A	5. D	8. WR	
3. B	6. D	9. WR	

1. D

The measurement of kg·m / s^2 is equivalent to a newton. This unit represents force, not momentum.

Momentum is defined as the product of mass and velocity. Mass can be measured in either grams or kilograms, while the velocity can be measured in terms of m/s, km/h, or even cm/h. Thus both the units kg·m / s and g·cm / h can represent the momentum of an object since they are equivalent to a mass multiplied by a velocity. As well, the unit N·s is a newton-second, which is equivalent to a kg·m / s, so it can also represent the momentum of an object.

2. A

Consider the equation for impulse:
$\Delta\vec{p} = m\Delta\vec{v} = \vec{F}\Delta t$

If the time to change the velocity of an object increases, the force on the object is reduced.
The elasticity of the climbing rope is intended to increase the time it takes to change the velocity of the climber so that the force experienced by the climber is decreased.

3. B

The change in momentum of the first player is equal in magnitude but opposite in direction to the change in momentum of the second player.

$$\begin{aligned}\Delta\vec{p} &= m\Delta\vec{v} = m(\vec{v}_f - \vec{v}_i) \text{ (for player 1)}\\ &= (75.0 \text{ kg})(4.50 \text{ m/s} - 10.0 \text{ m/s})\\ &= -4.13 \times 10^2 \text{ kg·m/s}\end{aligned}$$

Therefore, the second player's change in momentum was

$+4.13 \times 10^2$ kg·m / s

4. 3556

$$\begin{aligned} v_f^2 &= v_i^2 + 2gd\\ \therefore v_f &= \sqrt{0 + 2gd}\\ &= \sqrt{2(9.81 \text{ m/s}^2)(3.50 \text{ m})}\\ &= 8.29 \text{ m/s}\end{aligned}$$

So the final velocity of the hammer will be 8.29 m/s down.

Now it is possible to calculate the momentum change for the hammer. The maximum momentum achieved just before the hammer strikes the pile is

$\vec{p} = m\vec{v} = (900 \text{ kg})(8.29 \text{ m/s})$
$\vec{p} = 7.46 \times 10^3$ kg · m / s down

The impulse exerted on the pile is equal to the momentum of the hammer immediately before it makes contact with the pile, as the hammer will come to a complete stop after its collision with the pile. Therefore, the force can be found using the following equation:

$$\begin{aligned}\Delta\vec{p} &= m\Delta\vec{v} = \vec{F}\Delta t\\ \Rightarrow \vec{F} &= \frac{\Delta\vec{p}}{\Delta t}\\ &= \frac{7.46 \times 10^3 \text{ N·s}}{2.1 \times 10^{-3} \text{ s}}\\ &= 3.55 \times 10^6 \text{ N down}\end{aligned}$$

So the magnitude of the force the hammer exerts on the pile is 3.55×10^6 N.

5. D

The conservation of momentum is best demonstrated in isolated systems. In any isolated system, momentum is always conserved in a collision.
In non-isolated systems, some momentum may be lost to objects that are not included in the system. This would mean that within the non-isolated system, momentum would appear not to be conserved.

6. D

The momentum of the two identical cars that comprise the isolated system will be conserved after the collision. This means that $\sum\vec{p}_i = \sum\vec{p}_f$.

Step 1
First, examine the momentum before the collision.

$$\begin{aligned}\sum\vec{p}_i &= \vec{p}_A + \vec{p}_B\\ &= m\vec{v}_A + m\vec{v}_B\\ &= m(60 \text{ km/h E}) + m(60 \text{ km/h S})\\ &= m(60 \text{ km/h E} + 60 \text{ km/h S})\end{aligned}$$

Step 2
To add these two perpendicular velocities, use the Pythagorean theorem.

$$v = \sqrt{(60\text{ km/h})^2 + (60\text{ km/h})^2}$$
$$= \sqrt{7\,200\text{ km}^2/\text{h}^2}$$
$$= 84.85\text{ km/h}$$
$$\therefore \sum \vec{p}_\text{i} = m(84.85\text{ km/h SE})$$

Step 3
The momentum after the collision must also be equal to the given value for $\sum \vec{p}_\text{i}$.

$$\sum \vec{p}_\text{f} = \sum \vec{p}_\text{i}$$
$$(m_\text{A} + m_\text{B})\vec{v}_\text{A+B} = m(84.85\text{ km/h SE})$$
$$2m\vec{v}_\text{A+B} = m(84.85\text{ km/h SE})$$
$$\therefore \vec{v}_\text{A+B} = 42.4\text{ m/s SE}$$

Momentum will be conserved, as is the case in all isolated collisions, and the wreckage will move with a speed of less than 60 km/h.

7. C

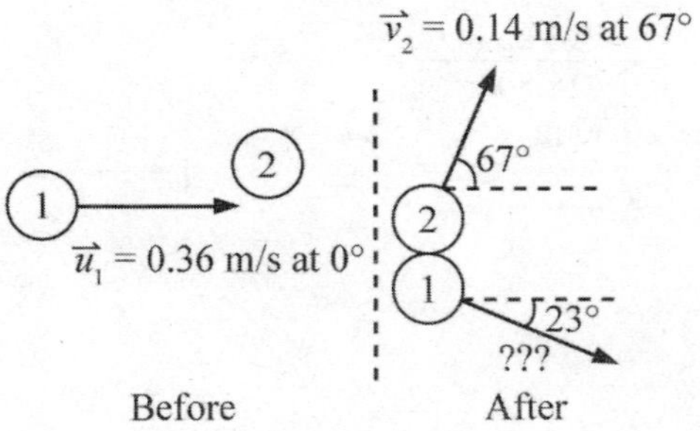

Identify all of the relevant information in the question.

$m = 18.8$ kg
$\vec{u}_1 = 0.36$ m/s at 0°
$\vec{u}_2 = 0$
$\vec{v}_1 = v_1$ at −23°
$\vec{v}_2 = 0.14$ m/s at 67°

You can use any of three different methods to find the speed of the red rock after the collision.

Method 1—Perpendicular components
Calculate the vertical and horizontal components of the given velocities.

$$\vec{u}_{1x} = \vec{u}_1 = +0.36\text{ m/s}$$
$$\vec{u}_{1y} = 0$$
$$\vec{v}_{1x} = v_1\cos(-23°)$$
$$\vec{v}_{1y} = v_1\sin(-23°)$$
$$\vec{v}_{2x} = v_2\cos 67°$$
$$= (0.14\text{ m/s})\cos 67°$$
$$= +0.0547\text{ m/s}$$
$$\vec{v}_{2y} = v_2\sin 67°$$
$$= (0.14\text{ m/s})\sin 67°$$
$$= +0.129\text{ m/s}$$

Apply the conservation of momentum to the horizontal motion to find the speed of the red rock after the collision:

$$\sum \vec{p}_{\text{i}x} = \sum \vec{p}_{\text{f}x}$$
$$m\vec{u}_1 + 0 = m\vec{v}_{1x} + m\vec{v}_{2x}$$
$$\frac{m\vec{u}_1}{m} = \frac{m\vec{v}_{1x}}{m} + \frac{m\vec{v}_{2x}}{m}$$
$$\vec{u}_1 = \vec{v}_{1x} + \vec{v}_{2x}$$
$$\therefore \vec{v}_{1x} = \vec{u}_1 - \vec{v}_{2x}$$
$$v_1\cos(-23°) = 0.36\text{ m/s} - 0.0547\text{ m/s}$$
$$v_1\cos(-23°) = (0.305\text{ m/s})$$
$$v_1 = \frac{0.305\text{ m/s}}{\cos(-23°)}$$
$$= 0.33\text{ m/s}$$

You could also apply the conservation of momentum to the vertical motion to find the speed of the red rock after the collision:

$$\sum \vec{p}_{\text{i}y} = \sum \vec{p}_{\text{f}y}$$
$$0 = m\vec{v}_{1y} + m\vec{v}_{2y}$$
$$\therefore m\vec{v}_{1y} = -m\vec{v}_{2y}$$
$$\frac{m\vec{v}_{1y}}{m} = \frac{-m\vec{v}_{2y}}{m}$$
$$\vec{v}_{1y} = -\vec{v}_{2y}$$
$$v_1\sin(-23°) = -(0.129\text{ m/s})$$
$$\therefore v_1 = \frac{-0.129\text{ m/s}}{\sin(-23°)}$$
$$= 0.33\text{ m/s}$$

Method 2—Cosine law

Draw a vector diagram showing the total momenta before and after the collision.

$\sum \vec{p}_i = \sum \vec{p}_f$

$\Rightarrow \vec{p}_1 = \vec{p}_1' + \vec{p}_2'$

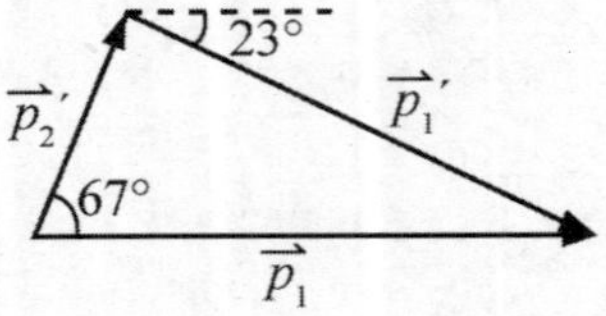

Calculate the momentum for the red rock before the collision.

$$\begin{aligned}\vec{p}_1 &= m\vec{u}_1 \\ &= (18.8\ \text{kg})(0.36\ \text{m/s at } 0°) \\ &= 6.768\ \text{kg·m/s at } 0°\end{aligned}$$

Calculate the momentum for the blue rock after the collision.

$$\begin{aligned}\vec{p}_2' &= m\vec{v}_2 \\ &= (18.8\ \text{kg})(0.14\ \text{m/s at } -67°) \\ &= 2.632\ \text{kg·m/s at } -67°\end{aligned}$$

Use the cosine law states to find the momentum for the red rock after the collision.

$c^2 = a^2 + b^2 - 2ab\cos\gamma$

In this case, the variables are defined as follows:

$c = p_1'$
$a = p_2'$
$b = p_1$
$\gamma = 67°$

Substitute these variables into the cosine law.

$$\begin{aligned}(p_1')^2 &= (p_2')^2 + (p_1)^2 - 2(p_2')(p_1)\cos 67° \\ &= (2.632\ \text{kg·m/s})^2 + (6.768\ \text{kg·m/s})^2 \\ &\quad - 2(2.632\ \text{kg·m/s})(6.768\ \text{kg·m/s})\cos 67° \\ &= 38.81\ \text{kg}^2\text{·m}^2/\text{s}^2 \\ \therefore p_1' &= \sqrt{38.81\ \text{kg}^2\text{·m}^2/\text{s}^2} \\ &= 6.230\ \text{kg·m/s}\end{aligned}$$

Calculate the speed of the red rock using the formula for momentum.

$$\begin{aligned}p_1' &= mv_1 \\ v_1 &= \frac{p_1'}{m} \\ &= \frac{6.230\ \text{kg·m/s}}{18.8\ \text{kg}} \\ &= 0.33\ \text{m/s}\end{aligned}$$

Method 3—Pythagorean theorem

The angle between $\vec{p}_2'$ and $\vec{p}_1'$ in the vector diagram of the momenta is exactly 90 °. Since the vector diagram is a right triangle, use the Pythagorean theorem to solve for the momentum of the red rock.

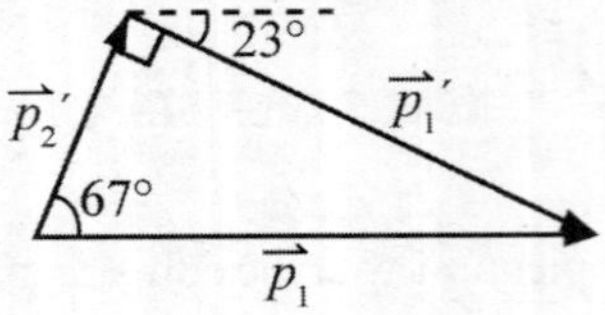

$$\begin{aligned}c^2 &= a^2 + b^2 \\ (p_1)^2 &= (p_1')^2 + (p_2')^2 \\ p_1' &= \sqrt{(p_1)^2 - (P_2')^2} \\ &= \sqrt{(6.768\ \text{kg·m/s})^2 - (2.632\ \text{kg·m/s})^2} \\ &= 6.235\ \text{kg·m/s}\end{aligned}$$

Use the formula for momentum to determine the speed of the red rock.

$$\begin{aligned}p_1' &= mv_1 \\ v_1 &= \frac{p_1'}{m} \\ &= \frac{6.235\ \text{kg·m/s}}{18.8\ \text{kg}} \\ &= 0.33\ \text{m/s}\end{aligned}$$

8. WR

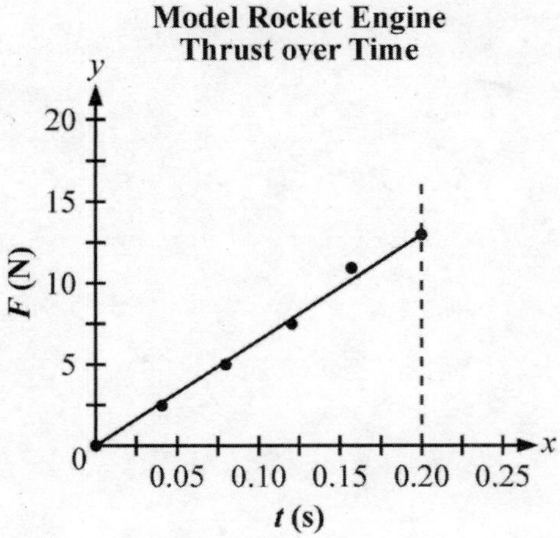

$$\text{Area} = \frac{1}{2}ab$$
$$= \frac{1}{2}(13.1\text{ N})(0.20\text{s})$$
$$= 1.31\text{ N}\cdot\text{s}$$

$$\text{Area} = \text{impulse} = \Delta p = m\Delta v$$
$$\Delta v = v_f - v_i$$
$$= v_f - 0$$
$$\Delta v = v_f$$
$$\therefore v_f = \frac{\text{Area}}{m} = \frac{1.31\text{ N}\cdot\text{s}}{0.017\text{ kg}}$$
$$v_f = 77\text{ m/s}$$

The speed of the rocket at the time of maximum thrust of the engine is 77 m/s.

9. WR

$$\sum \vec{p}_i = \sum \vec{p}_f$$
$$m_1\vec{v}_1 + m_2\vec{v}_2 = m_1\vec{v}_1{}' + m_2\vec{v}_2{}'$$

Determine the horizontal velocity of puck 2 after the collision.

$$(250\text{ g})(0.35\text{ m/s}) + 0$$
$$= (250\text{ g})(-0.14\text{ m/s})(\sin 20°) + (550\text{ g})(\vec{v}_{2x}{}')$$
$$\vec{v}_{2x}{}' = 0.1809\text{ m/s}$$

Determine the vertical velocity of puck 2 after the collision.

$$0 + 0 = (250\text{ g})(0.14\text{ m/s})(\cos 20°) + (550\text{ g})(\vec{v}_{2y}{}')$$
$$\vec{v}_{2y}{}' = -0.059\ 80\text{ m/s}$$

Using the results of these two calculations, draw a vector addition diagram to determine the angle travelled by puck 2.

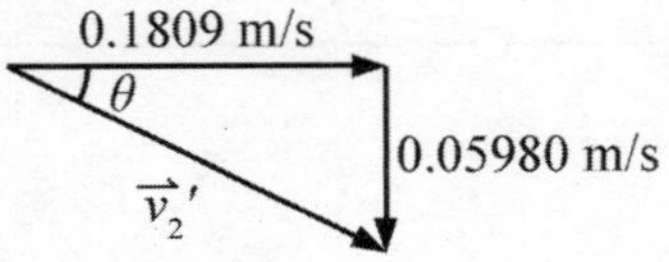

Find the velocity of puck 2.

$$v_2{}' = \sqrt{(0.1809\text{ m/s})^2 + (0.059\ 80\text{ m/s})^2}$$
$$\cong 0.19\text{ m/s}$$
$$\theta = \tan^{-1}\left(\frac{0.0598}{0.1809}\right) \cong 18°$$

The velocity of puck 2 after it is hit is 0.19 m/s, 18° down from the original direction of puck 1.

10. A

In an elastic collision, both the kinetic energy and the momentum are conserved.

NOTES

Forces and Fields

FORCES AND FIELDS

Table of Correlations

Outcome		Practice Questions	Unit Test Questions	Practice Test 1	Practice Test 2
B1	explain the behaviour of electric charges, using the laws that govern electrical interactions				
30-B1.1k	*explain electrical interactions in terms of the law of conservation of charge*	1			
30-B1.2k	*explain electrical interactions in terms of the repulsion and attraction of charges*	2			
30-B1.3k	*compare the methods of transferring charge (conduction and induction)*	3, 4	1	10, 11	12
30-B1.4k	*explain, qualitatively, the distribution of charge on the surfaces of conductors and insulators*	5, 6, 7	2		13, 14
30-B1.5k	*explain, qualitatively, the principles pertinent to Coulomb's torsion balance experiment*	8	3	12	
30-B1.6k	*apply Coulomb's law, quantitatively, to analyze the interaction of two point charges*	9, 10	4, 5, 6	13, 14	
30-B1.7k	*determine, quantitatively, the magnitude and direction of the electric force on a point charge due to two or more other point charges in a plane*	11, 12, 13, 14a, 14b	7	15	15
30-B1.8k	*compare, qualitatively and quantitatively, the inverse square relationship as it is expressed by Coulomb's law and by Newton's universal law of gravitation*	15	8		16, 17
B2	describe electrical phenomena, using the electric field theory				
30-B2.1k	*define vector fields*	16			
30-B2.2k	*compare forces and fields*	17			
30-B2.3k	*compare, qualitatively, gravitational potential energy and electric potential energy*			16, 17	18
30-B2.4k	*define electric potential difference as a change in electric potential energy per unit of charge*	23, 24	9		19
30-B2.5k	*calculate the electric potential difference between two points in a uniform electric field*	25, 26a, 26b, 27	10	18	20, 21
30-B2.6k	*explain, quantitatively, electric fields in terms of intensity (strength) and direction, relative to the source of the field and to the effect on an electric charge*	18, 19, 20, 21, 22	11	19	22
30-B2.7k	*define electric current as the amount of charge passing a reference point per unit of time*	34	12	20	23
30-B2.8k	*describe, quantitatively, the motion of an electric charge in a uniform electric field*	28, 29, 30	13	21	
30-B2.9k	*explain, quantitatively, electrical interactions using the law of conservation of energy*	31a, 31b	14	22	24
30-B2.10k	*explain Millikan's oil-drop experiment and its significance relative to charge quantization*	32, 33	15	23	25
B3	explain how the properties of electric and magnetic fields are applied in numerous devices.				
30-B3.1k	*describe magnetic interactions in terms of forces and fields*				
30-B3.2k	*compare gravitational, electric and magnetic fields (caused by permanent magnets and moving charges) in terms of their sources and directions*	35	16	24, 25	26

30-B3.3k	*describe how the discoveries of Oersted and Faraday form the foundation of the theory relating electricity to magnetism*	36, 37	22	26	
30-B3.4k	*describe, qualitatively, a moving charge as the source of a magnetic field and predict the orientation of the magnetic field from the direction of motion*	41	17		27, 28
30-B3.5k	*explain, qualitatively and quantitatively, how a uniform magnetic field affects a moving electric charge, using the relationships among charge, motion, field direction and strength, when motion and field directions are mutually perpendicular*	42, 43, 44, 45	18	27, 28	29, 30
30-B3.6k	*explain, quantitatively, how uniform magnetic and electric fields affect a moving electric charge, using the relationships among charge, motion, field direction and strength, when motion and field directions are mutually perpendicular*	46, 47, 48, 49, 50	19	29, 30	31
30-B3.7k	*describe and explain, qualitatively, the interaction between a magnetic field and a moving charge and between a magnetic field and a current-carrying conductor*	38	20		
30-B3.8k	*explain, quantitatively, the effect of an external magnetic field on a current-carrying conductor*	39	21		32, 33
30-B3.9k	*describe, qualitatively, the effects of moving a conductor in an external magnetic field, in terms of moving charges in a magnetic field.*	40		31	

30-B1.1k explain electrical interactions in terms of the law of conservation of charge

Law of Conservation of Charge

It has been known for centuries that there are two types of electric charge: positive and negative. Investigations into the nature of matter in the past two centuries have revealed that matter is mostly composed of charged particles. Through these investigations, scientists identified the following particles and their charges:

- Protons are positively charged.
- Electrons are negatively charged.
- Neutrons are neutral (have no net charge).

Experiments have also shown that charge is conserved in any interaction with matter. This **law of conservation of charge** means the net charge must remain constant within an isolated system (matter cannot enter or leave the system). For example, consider a system consisting of a metal sphere with +2.00 C of electrostatic charge and a metal sphere with –1.00 C of electrostatic charge. When these two spheres are brought into contact, the charges rearrange between them such that the net charge on each sphere is +0.50 C.

Before the spheres came in contact with each other, the net charge on the system was +1.00 C.
$(+2.00\text{ C}) + (-1.00\text{ C}) = +1.00\text{ C}$

Once the spheres came into contact, the charges rearranged according to the rules of electrostatic attraction and repulsion. The net charge on each sphere became +0.50 C. The net charge of the system, however, remained +1.00 C.
$(+0.50\text{ C}) + (+0.50\text{ C}) = +1.00\text{ C}$

Chemical Reactions

By definition, an atom is neutral, meaning that it has an equal number of protons and electrons. When an atom or molecule has a net charge, it is called an ion. Chemical reactions involving ions demonstrate the law of conservation of charge.

$$Ca^{2+} + 2Cl^- + 2Ag^+ + 2NO_3^-$$
$$\rightarrow Ca^{2+} + 2NO_3^- + 2AgCl$$

Before the reaction, the net charge on the ions was 0.
$(+2) + 2(-1) + 2(-1) + 2(+1) = 0.$

After the reaction, the net charge changed as follows:
net charge $= (+2) + 2(-1) = 0$

Therefore, charge was conserved in the reaction.

Electric Circuits

In an electric circuit, the current going into a junction is equal to the current leaving the junction. This is called the **junction rule**. This is considered to be a corollary of the law of conservation of charge.

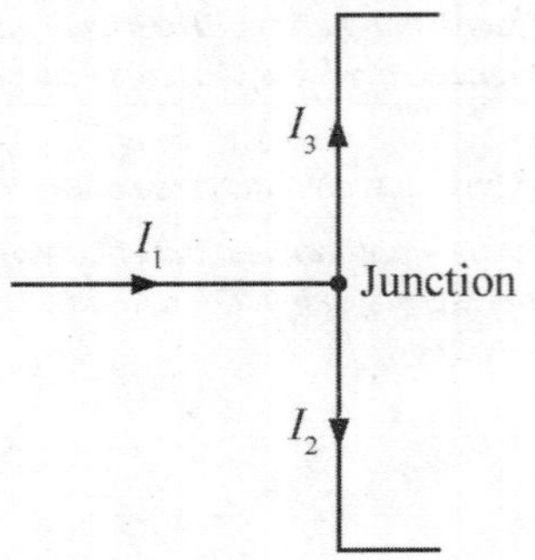

In this junction, a wire splits into two possible paths that the electric current can take. The total current before the junction must split such that $I_1 = I_2 + I_3$.

The current represents the amount of charge flowing past a point in the circuit. Thus, I_1 indicates how much charge enters into the junction. This quantity of charge is equal to the amount of charge leaving the junction. The net charge in the circuit is conserved.

1. Two neutral objects are rubbed together and become charged. Which of the following statements about this occurrence is **true**?
   A. Both objects are positively charged.
   B. Both objects are negatively charged.
   C. One object is positively charged, and the other object is negatively charged.
   D. One object remains neutral, while the other object is either positively or negatively charged.

30-B1.2k explain electrical interactions in terms of the repulsion and attraction of charges

BEHAVIOUR OF CHARGES IN MATTER

Like charges (e.g., positive and positive) exert repulsion forces on each other.
Unlike charges (e.g., negative and positive) exert attraction forces on each other.

- Like charges repel each other.
- Opposite charges attract each other.
- Electrons move easily through conductors and with difficulty through insulators (or not at all).

Use the following information to answer the next question.

> Two charged spheres are seen to repel each other. A third sphere attracts both of these other spheres. The third sphere has ___*i*___ the first two spheres, which have ___*ii*___.

2. This statement is completed by the information in table

A.

i	*ii*
the same charge as	the same charge

B.

i	*ii*
the opposite charge of	opposite charges

C.

i	*ii*
the same charge as	opposite charges

D.

i	*ii*
the opposite charge of	the same charge

30-B1.3k compare the methods of transferring charge (conduction and induction)

METHODS FOR TRANSFERRING CHARGE

Sometimes when different materials are rubbed together, the electrons from one material may move to the other. One material is then positively charged; the other is negatively charged. For example, when ebonite, a black plastic, is rubbed on fur, the ebonite becomes negatively charged and the fur becomes positively charged. This is often referred to as **charging by friction**.

When a piece of charged metal touches a neutral one, charge transfers to the neutral one until both objects have the same charge. This is called **charging by conduction**.

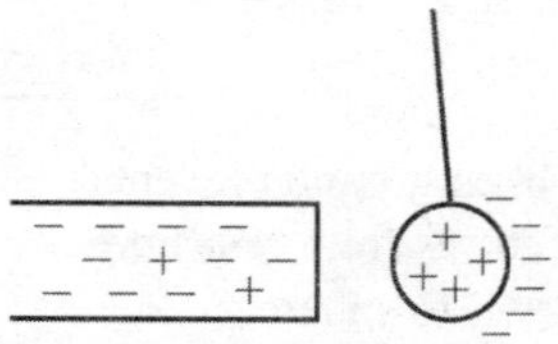

Negative rod repels electrons in sphere to opposite side. Charges are separated within the sphere.

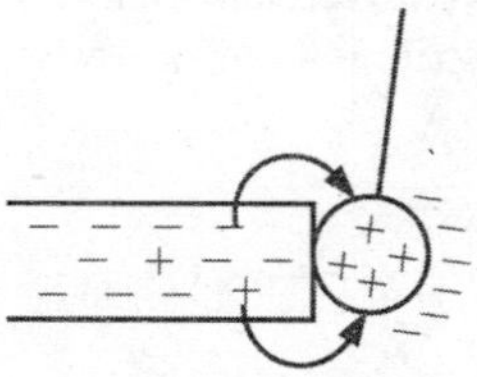

Rod attracts near side of sphere. Upon contact, electrons move to sphere.

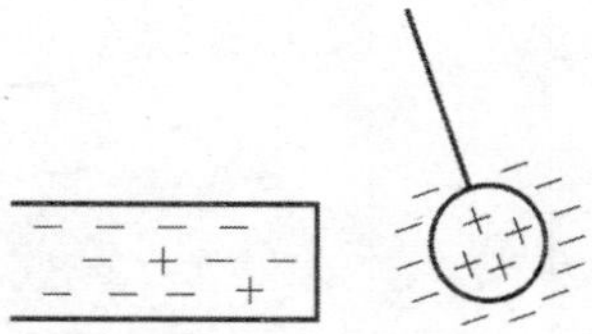

Rod and sphere are both negative and now repel each other.

A piece of neutral metal is grounded to Earth. If a charged object is placed near it and the ground is removed while the charged object is still near, the neutral object becomes charged opposite to the charged object. This is called **charging by induction**.

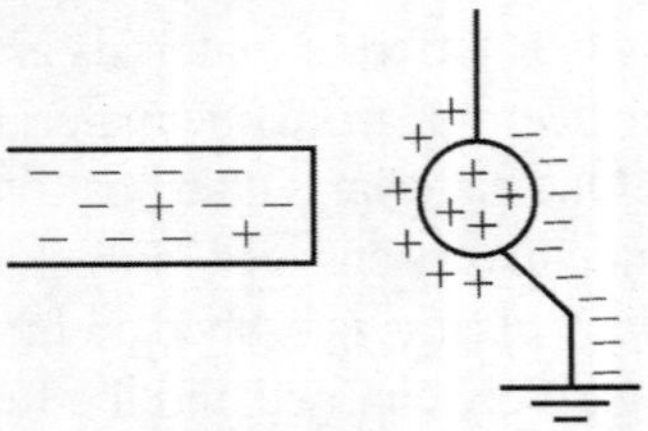

Rod repels electrons from sphere to ground.

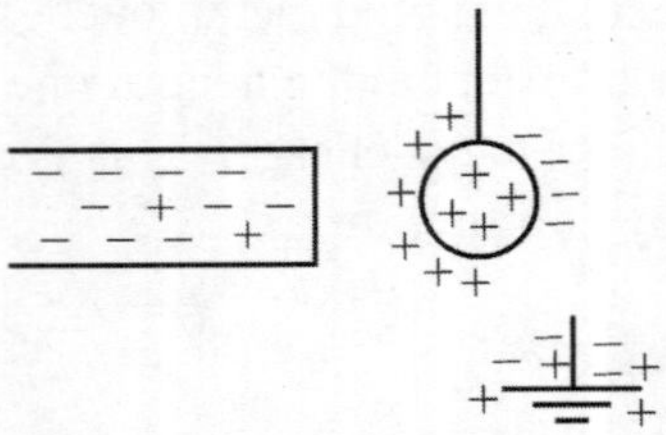

Broken ground prevents electrons from returning to sphere.

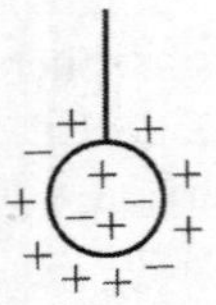

Rod is removed and charge is redistributed uniformly.

Use the following information to answer the next question.

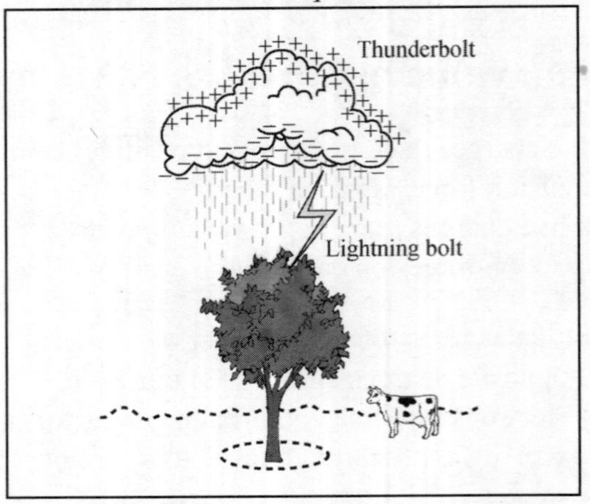

3. The bottom of a thundercloud usually becomes negatively charged. Before lightning strikes, the charge of the ground directly beneath the thundercloud will become

A. positive by induction

B. negative by induction

C. positive by conduction

D. negative by conduction

4. Arianna ran a comb through her hair and found that afterward, the comb attracted small pieces of paper known to be neutral. She correctly inferred that the comb

A. created charges when it rubbed against her hair

B. became charged by conduction, and the charges in the paper were separated by induction

C. became positively charged, and the paper nearest to the comb became negatively charged

D. became negatively charged, and the paper nearest to the comb became positively charged

30-B1.4k explain, qualitatively, the distribution of charge on the surfaces of conductors and insulators

Distribution of Charge on Conductors and Insulators

Any charge placed on an insulator will stay where it is since electrons cannot flow through the insulator. Charges placed on a conductor can move, and they will distribute themselves as far from each other as they can, since they repel one another. As a result, the excess charge is found on the outside surface of a conductor. The pointier the surface is, the more charge that collects there.

An *electroscope* is a device that detects excess charges. Electroscopes have moving leaves that open when they are charged.

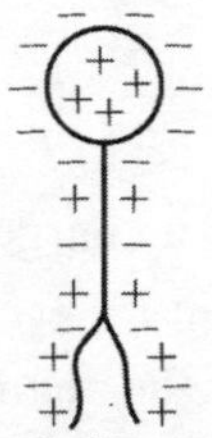

Neutral electroscope
leaves closed

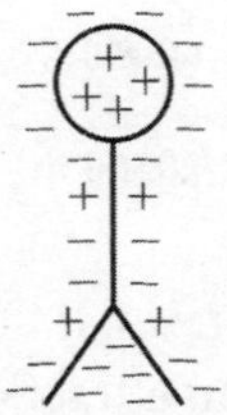

Charged electroscope
leaves open
(they repel each other)

Use the following information to answer the next question.

> During an experiment, Pablo touched the ball of an electroscope to ground the device. He then brought a negatively charged ebonite rod near the ball of the electroscope. Pablo observed that the metal foil leaves repelled. While the ebonite rod was still near the electroscope, Pablo touched the electroscope with his finger. He then removed his finger from the ball, and then he removed the ebonite rod. After removing the ebonite rod, Pablo observed that the foil leaves again repelled.

5. What was the charge on the foil leaves the first and second time they repelled, respectively?

A. negative, negative

B. negative, positive

C. positive, negative

D. positive, positive

6. Which of the following statements is **false**?

A. Electric forces of attraction occur only between particles that have opposite electrical charges.

B. Charges are created when two surfaces are rubbed together.

C. A negative ion consists of more electrons than protons.

D. Charged objects can attract some neutral objects.

7. Three identical spherical conductors, spheres A, B, and C, were each suspended from a thread. The spheres had charges of −200 μC, 400 μC, and −500 μC, respectively. Spheres B and C were brought into contact momentarily and then separated. The total charge of the system and the charge on each of the spheres after spheres B and C were brought into contact and separated were

A. 300μC, 200 μC, 400 μC, −500 μC

B. −300 μC, −200 μC, 400 μC, −500 μC

C. −300 μC, −200 μC, −50 μC, −50 μC

D. 300 μC, 200 μC, −50 μC, −50 μC

30-B1.5k explain, qualitatively, the principles pertinent to Coulomb's torsion balance experiment

30-B1.6k apply Coulomb's law, quantitatively, to analyze the interaction of two point charges

COULOMB'S LAW

Charles-Augustin de Coulomb applied a charge, q_1, to one end of a torsion balance. He then placed a second charge, q_2, near q_1. The repulsion or attraction between the charges caused the balance to twist.

By measuring the angle of twist, Coulomb determined the force of repulsion or attraction between the charges. He also found a relation between the force, the distance between the two charges, and the magnitudes of both charges.

Through his torsion balance experiments, Coulomb determined that the magnitude of the electrical force could be found using the following equation:

$$F_e = \frac{kq_1q_2}{r^2}$$

where

F_e = force on a charged object (N)

k = Coulomb's constant $(8.99 \times 10^9\ \text{N} \cdot \text{m}^2/\text{C}^2)$

r = distance between the centres of two charged objects (m)

q_1 and q_2 = magnitude of charges on the two objects (C)

This equation only gives the magnitude of the electrical force. The direction of the force is always along a straight line between the centres of the two charges. A positive value of electric force indicates a repulsive force. A negative value indicates an attractive force.

Example

Two spheres, one with a charge of $+1.60 \times 10^{-8}$ C and one with a charge of -2.50×10^{-8} C, are placed 5.00 cm apart. What is the magnitude of the electric force between them?

$$F_e = \frac{kq_1q_2}{r^2}$$

$$= \frac{\left(8.99 \times 10^9 \frac{\text{N·m}^2}{\text{C}^2}\right)(1.60 \times 10^{-8}\ \text{C})(-2.50 \times 10^{-8}\ \text{C})}{(0.0500\ \text{m})^2}$$

$$= -1.44 \times 10^{-3}\ \text{N}$$

The minus sign indicates that the charges are opposites, so there is an attraction between the two spheres.

Example

A neutral metallic sphere is brought into contact with an identical sphere that has a charge of −2.5 μC. The two spheres are then placed 32 cm apart. What is the electric force between them?

Touching the spheres allows the excess charge to spread out as far as possible, giving each sphere half the total charge, or −1.25 μC each.

$$F_e = \frac{kq_1q_2}{r^2}$$

$$= \frac{\left(8.99 \times 10^9\ \text{N}\cdot\frac{\text{m}^2}{\text{C}^2}\right)\left(-1.25 \times 10^{-6}\ \text{C}\right)^2}{(0.32\ \text{m})^2}$$

$$= +0.14\ \text{N}$$

The positive sign indicates that the charges are the same, so the two spheres repel each other.

8. The strength of the electrical force of attraction between two charged objects is F_e. If the distance between the centres of the two objects is doubled, and one of the charges is touched to a neutral sphere of the same size, the new electrical force of attraction will be

A. $\frac{1}{2}F_e$ **B.** $\frac{1}{8}F_e$

C. $\frac{1}{4}F_e$ **D.** F_e

9. Conducting sphere X has an initial charge of $+2.0 \times 10^{-8}$ C and an identical conducting sphere Y has an initial charge of -3.0×10^{-8} C. The two spheres are touched together and then separated. After they are separated, the charge on sphere X is

A. -5.0×10^{-9} C

B. -1.0×10^{-8} C

C. -2.5×10^{-8} C

D. -5.0×10^{-8} C

10. Which of the following graphs **best** illustrates Coulomb's law?

A.

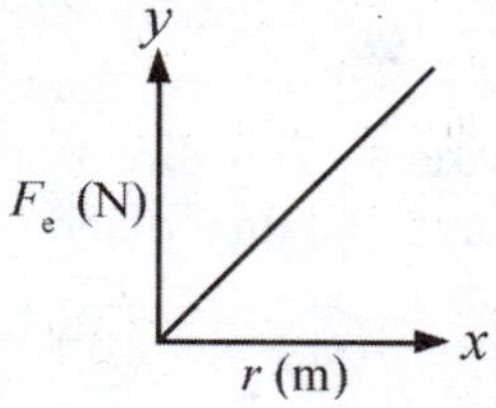

B.

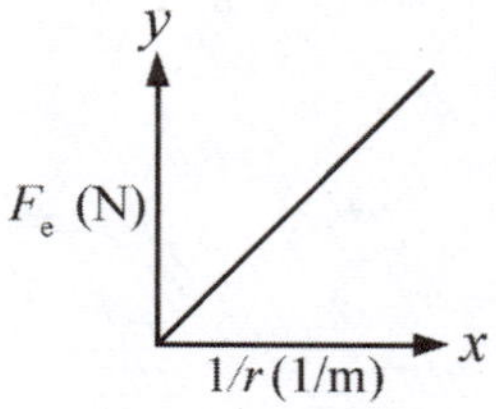

C.

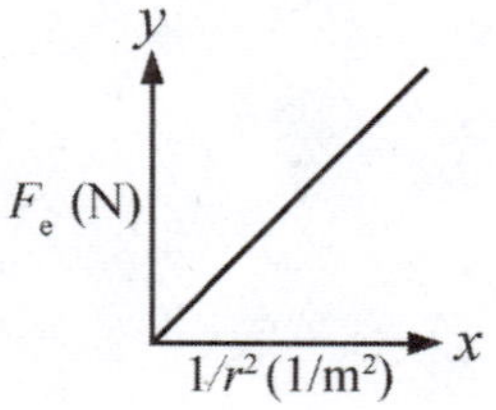

D.

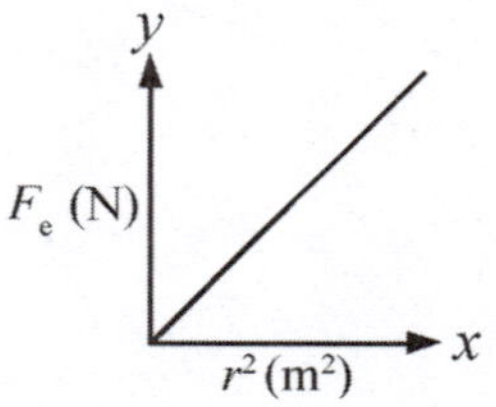

30-B1.7k determine, quantitatively, the magnitude and direction of the electric force on a point charge due to two or more other point charges in a plane

Electric Forces Due to More Than Two Charges

Coulomb's law addresses the force between two charges, so the force is either repulsive or attractive, depending on the polarity of the charges. The force will always act in the direction of the line connecting the two charges. Coulomb's law is used to calculate the magnitude of the electric force.

Force is a vector quantity, so the direction is important. The direction is determined by analyzing the natures of the charges interacting (e.g., whether they are positive or negative) and the relative positions of the charges. This direction is essential if several point charges lie on a plane.

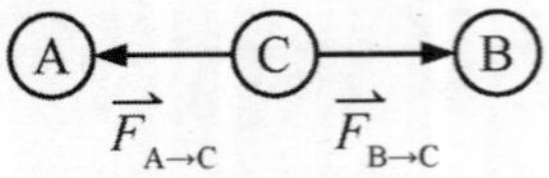

Example

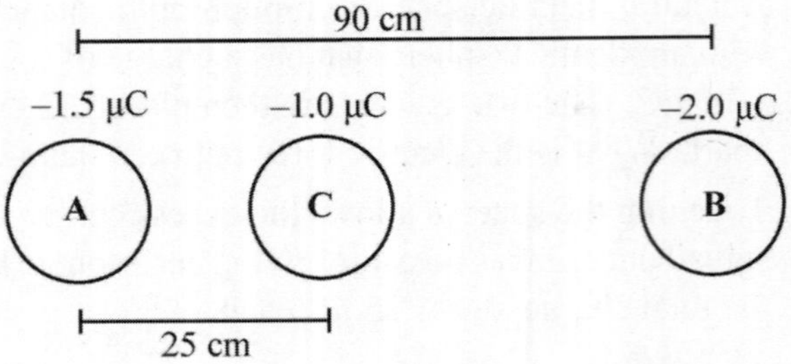

Two point charges, $q_A = -1.5\ \mu C$ and $q_B = -2.0\ \mu C$, are 90.0 cm apart. Another charge, $q_C = -1.0\ \mu C$, is placed between charges A and B, 25.0 cm from point charge A. What is the net electric force acting on point charge C?

Solution

$$F_{\text{A on C}} = \frac{kq_Aq_C}{r^2}$$

$$= \frac{\left(8.99 \times 10^9 \frac{\text{N·m}^2}{\text{C}^2}\right)(-1.5 \times 10^{-6}\ \text{C})(-1.0 \times 10^{-6}\ \text{C})}{(0.25\ \text{m})^2}$$

$= 0.216$ N

$\therefore \vec{F}_{\text{A on C}} = 0.216$ N to the right

$$F_{\text{B on C}} = \frac{kq_Bq_C}{r^2}$$

$$= \frac{\left(8.99 \times 10^9 \frac{\text{N·m}^2}{\text{C}^2}\right)(-2.0 \times 10^{-6}\ \text{C})(-1.0 \times 10^{-6}\ \text{C})}{(0.65\ \text{m})^2}$$

$= 0.0426$ N $\therefore \vec{F}_{\text{B on C}} = 0.0426$ N to the leftto the left

Let forces acting toward the right be positive values.

$\vec{F}_{\text{net}} = \vec{F}_{\text{A on C}} + \vec{F}_{\text{B on C}}$

$\vec{F}_{\text{net}} = 0.216\ \text{N} - 0.0426\ \text{N}$

$\vec{F}_{\text{net}} = 0.173\ \text{N} \approx 0.17\ \text{N}$

The net force acting on charge C is 0.17 N acting to the right.

Use the following information to answer the next question.

The force exerted on sphere X by sphere Y has a magnitude of 6.0 N. A third sphere, Z, with a charge –3.0*Q* is introduced, as shown in the diagram.

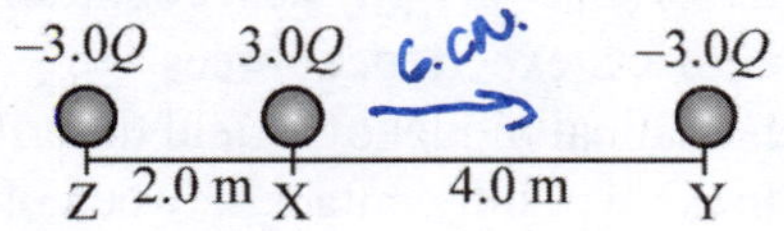

11. The magnitude of the net force on sphere X, due to spheres Y and Z, is

A. 9.0 N **B.** 12 N
C. 18 N **D.** 24 N

Use the following information to answer the next question.

Three charges are placed on a plane.

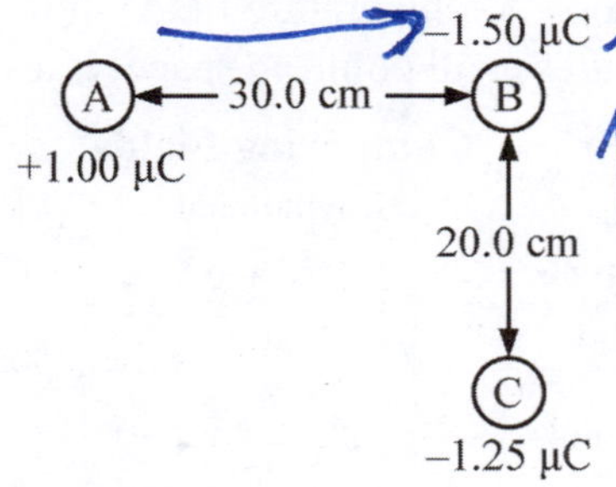

12. Find the magnitude of the net force on sphere B.

A. 0.447 N **B.** 0.894 N
C. 0.0955 N **D.** 0.191 N

Numerical Response

13. Three point charges, charges A (+4.50 μC), B(–3.00 μC), and C (+2.00 μC), were placed along one straight line. If the distance between charges A and C is 12.0 cm and the distance between charges B to C is twice the distance between charges B to A, the magnitude of the net electrical force acting on charge B is $a.bc \times 10^d$ N. The value of *abcd* is ________. (Record your answer as a four digit number.)

Use the following information to answer the next multipart question.

14. Sphere *A* had a negative charge 3.50 times larger than the magnitude of the charge on sphere B, which was identical in size and mass. Initially the spheres were 30.0 cm apart, at which point they experienced an attraction force of 8.00×10^{-5} N. The two spheres were then touched together momentarily. They were then separated and placed 20.0 cm apart.

Written Response

a) What was the value of the charge on each sphere before they touched each other?

____
____
____
____
____

b) What was the force acting on the spheres after they were separated?

____
____
____
____
____
____

30-B1.8k compare, qualitatively and quantitatively, the inverse square relationship as it is expressed by Coulomb's law and by Newton's universal law of gravitation

Comparing Coulomb's Law and Newton's Law

The gravitational force that acts between masses and the electrical force that acts between charges are similar. The equations for Coulomb's law and Newton's universal law, which describe these two types of forces, have essentially the same form.

Coulomb's law	$F_e = \dfrac{kq_1q_2}{r^2}$
Newton's universal law	$F_g = \dfrac{Gm_1m_2}{r^2}$

While the causes of both forces are different, there is a relationship between the magnitudes of the forces and the distances separating the objects producing those forces. In both cases, the force diminishes as the distance between the objects increases. In other words, the magnitudes of both forces are inversely proportional to the square of the distances between the objects, as shown by $F \propto \dfrac{1}{r^2}$.

While the relationships between the forces are similar, the magnitudes of the two forces are significantly different. Compare the magnitudes of the two constants k and G as a ratio. The ratio of $\dfrac{k}{G}$ shows approximately how much larger electrical forces are compared to gravitational forces.

$$\frac{k}{G} = \frac{8.99 \times 10^9}{6.67 \times 10^{-11}} = 1.35 \times 10^{20}$$

This is an enormous value, and it illustrates exactly how much larger the electrical forces are. You can observe this difference when you use a charged comb to pick up bits of paper. The electrical force holding the paper to the comb is much stronger than the gravitational force pulling the paper toward the ground.

Numerical Response

15. An electron and a proton are separated by 5.3×10^{-11} m in a hydrogen atom. Expressed in scientific notation, the electrical force of attraction is $a.b \times 10^{cd}$ times as large as the gravitational attraction between the particles. The value of *abcd* is ________?

30-B2.1k define vector fields

30-B2.2k compare forces and fields

Electric-Field Theory

A **field** in this study is a physical condition on space in which objects experience forces.
The mathematical model of a field describes how forces can act without contact between objects. For example, the mass of an object experiences the effects of a gravitational field around a planet. The field exists even if no object is present to experience the force.

In a similar fashion, the charge of a charged object experiences an electric force when the object is inside an electric field. The field exists even if no charge is present to experience its force.

Since forces are vectors, gravitational and electric fields are **vector fields**. Fields can be defined with scalars, too. A temperature field (showing temperatures at all points in space) is a **scalar field**.

Comparing Fields

	Gravitational	Electrical
Acts on	Mass	Charge
Unit	N/kg	N/C
Formula	$\vec{g} = \dfrac{\vec{F}_g}{m}$	$\vec{E} = \dfrac{\vec{F}_e}{q}$
Direction	Attractive	Same as force on a + test charge
Near a point (spherical mass/ charge)	$g = \dfrac{Gm}{r^2}$	$E = \dfrac{kq}{r^2}$

CHALLENGER QUESTION

16. Which of the following pairs of fields are examples of vector fields?

A. Electric and air pressure

B. Gravitational and electric

C. Temperature and electric

D. Air pressure and gravitational

17. In order to determine the direction of an electric field surrounding a source charge, it is necessary to place a

A. neutral test charge in various locations around the source charge and measure the electrical force exerted on this test charge

B. positive test charge in various locations around the source charge and measure the electrical force exerted on the test charge

C. negative test charge in various locations around the source charge and measure the electrical force on the test charge

D. positive test charge in the field if the source charge is negative, or negative test charge in the field if the source charge is positive, and measure the force of attraction in various locations around the source

30-B2.6k explain, quantitatively, electric fields in terms of intensity (strength) and direction, relative to the source of the field and to the effect on an electric charge

Forces and Fields

Calculating Electric Field Strength

Similar to the force exerted on a mass by the gravitational field, electric fields exert forces on charged objects. Therefore, the electric force on a charge can be calculated using this formula:

$\vec{F}_e = \vec{E}q$,

where $\vec{F}_e$ is the force on the charged object (N), $\vec{E}$ is the strength of the electric field (N/C), and q is the magnitude of the charge on the object in the electric field (C).

This can be rewritten in order to determine the strength of the electric field.

$$\vec{E} = \frac{\vec{F}_e}{q}$$

The direction of the field is the same as the direction of the electric force acting on a positive test charge. The electric field is oriented to repel positively charged objects and to attract negatively charged objects.

If the electric field is the result of a point charge, it will be a non-uniform field. If the electric field is the result of two charged parallel plates, the electric field will be uniform in the region between the plates.

The electric field inside a hollow conductor is zero.

The electric field strength can also be calculated based upon the charge that creates it, using the formula $E = \frac{kq}{r^2}$, where q is the source charge.

In this case, a positive electric field represents a field directed away from the positive charge forming it. A negative electric field represents a field that is directed toward the negative charge forming it.

18. Which of the following graphs illustrates the relationship between the force of an electric field and its distance from a point charge?

A.

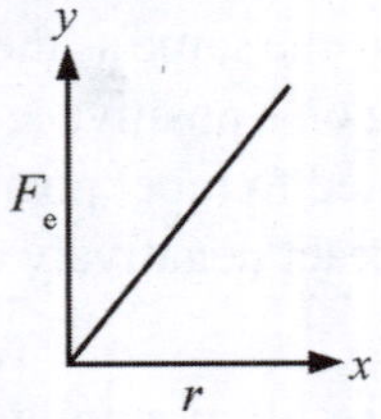

B.

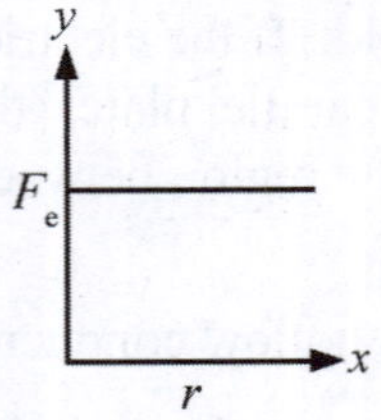

C.

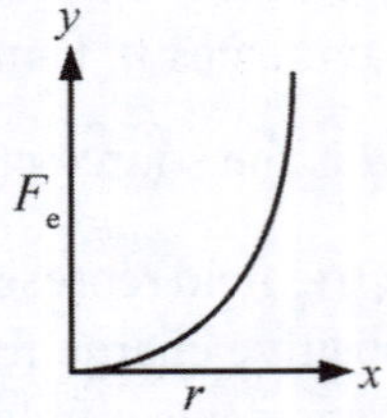

D.

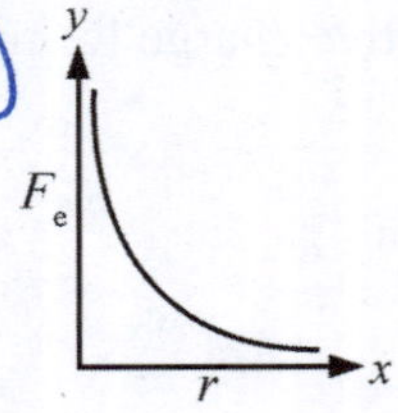

19. A -2.00×10^{-7} C charge is placed into an electric field of 2.50×10^{4} N/C south. The force acting on the charge is

A. 5.00×10^{-3} N south

B. 5.00×10^{-3} N north

C. 200 N south

D. 200 N north

20. A point charge of magnitude 6.9×10^{-5} C produces an electric field of 1.0×10^{3} N/C at point P. The distance from the point charge to point P is

A. 4.3×10^{-2} m

B. 2.1×10^{-1} m

C. 2.5×10^{1} m

D. 6.2×10^{2} m

Use the following information to answer the next question.

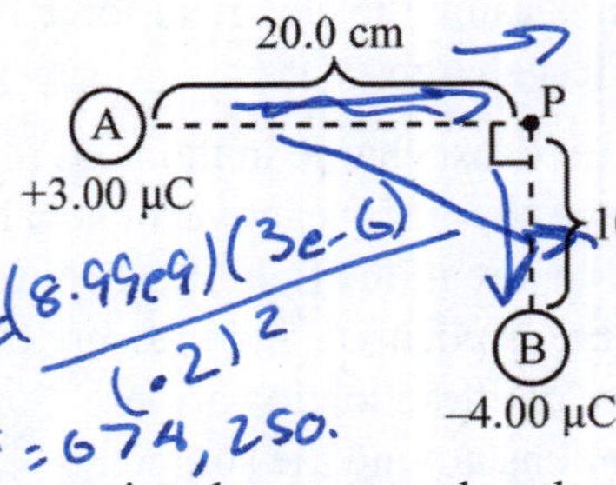

Two point charges are placed near each other on the same plane.

21. The magnitude of the electric field strength at point P in the given diagram is

A. 6.74×10^{5} N/C

B. 3.66×10^{6} N/C

C. 2.60×10^{6} N/C

D. 2.92×10^{6} N/C

Numerical Response

22. A test charge experiences a 0.200 N attractive force when placed 15 cm from an unknown charge. Expressed in scientific notation, the force experienced 45 cm from the unknown charge is $a.b \times 10^{-c}$ N. What is the value of *abc*?__________

30-B2.3k compare, qualitatively, gravitational potential energy and electric potential energy

30-B2.4k define electric potential difference as a change in electric potential energy per unit of charge

Comparing Gravitational and Electrical Potential Energies

Since the form of the equations for forces due to electric charges and forces due to gravitation are remarkably similar, it is often useful to compare them when first thinking about potential energies. There is often a very similar conformation in situations of gravitational and electrical potential energy.

For example, assuming Earth's gravitational field is uniform over small distances and a mass of 2.0 kg is raised a distance of 3.0 m, the work done on the mass can be calculated. From the work completed, the increase in the gravitational potential energy of the mass can be determined (work-energy theorem).

When the mass was lifted, the work was done against the gravitational field. If the mass is dropped, the gravitational field does work on the mass, and the gravitational potential energy converts into kinetic energy.

Precisely the same transformations occur when a charge moves within a uniform electric field set up between two parallel charged plates. When a positive charge moves from the negatively charged plate to the positively charged plate, work is done against the electric field. The electric potential energy gained by the charge is equal to the work done to move the charge.

Again, if the charge is released, the electric field does work on the charge. The electric potential converts into kinetic energy.

Electric Potential Difference

Work is done when a charge moves against an electric field, so the electric potential energy of the charge increases. If a larger charge also moves in the same field, more work is done, so more electric potential energy is stored in the system.

Electric potential difference (V), also called voltage, is the change in potential energy per unit charge between two points in an electric field. It is equal to the work done in moving a unit charge from one position to another within the electric field.

$$\Delta V = \frac{\Delta E}{q}$$

The units for the electric potential difference are $\frac{\text{J}}{\text{C}} = \text{volt} = \text{V}$.

Numerical Response

23. Expressed in scientific notation, the energy gained by a proton that moves through a potential difference of 1.0 V is $a.b \times 10^{-cd}$. The value of *abcd* is ________.

24. The energy gained by a proton that moves through a potential difference of 1.0 V is

A. 1.0 J

B. 1.0 eV

C. 6.3×10^{-18} J

D. 1.6×10^{-19} eV

30-B2.5k calculate the electric potential difference between two points in a uniform electric field

Calculating Electric Potential Difference

A uniform electric field exists between two charged plates, as long as they are close together and the strength of the field is ignored near the edges.

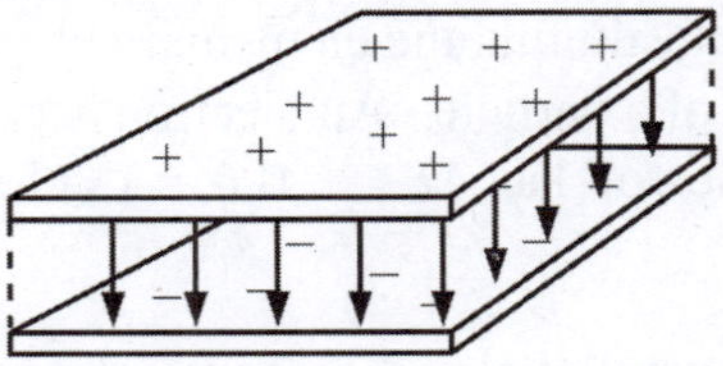

The work done against an electric field when a unit charge is moved from the negative to the positive plate is as follows:

$W = \Delta E_p = -Eqd$

This relationship can be used to find an algebraic expression for the electric potential difference between two points in a uniform electric field.

$\Delta V = -Ed$

The change in the potential difference is positive when the test charge moves against the electric field and negative when the charge moves in the same direction as the electric field. Potential always decreases in the direction of the electric field. You can also determine the change in the potential energy using the potential.

$\Delta E_p = q\Delta V$

For a positive particle, an increase in the potential results in an increase in potential energy since the value of q is positive. For a negative particle, an increase in potential results in a decrease in potential energy since the value of q is negative.

In many applications involving parallel charged plates, the relationship between the potential difference and electric field can be expressed as follows:

$$E = \frac{V}{d}$$

Using this equation, the change in the potential, the charge, and the magnitude of the electric field are always given as positive values. The direction of motion of the particle and electric field must then be decided upon based on the configuration of the system.

These different relationships give many ways to express the units of an electric field. These different forms help with the physical understanding of electric fields.

$$\frac{\text{V}}{\text{m}} = \frac{\text{J}}{\text{C} \cdot \text{m}} = \frac{\text{N} \cdot \text{m}}{\text{C} \cdot \text{m}} = \frac{\text{N}}{\text{C}}$$

Electron Volts

A smaller energy unit is the electron volt (eV). It is found by substituting the elementary charge (e) for the charge of a particle. An electron accelerated through one volt has $\Delta E_p = \Delta Vq = 1\text{V}(1\text{e}) = 1\text{ eV}$ of energy.

25. Two parallel plates 2.00 cm apart are connected to a 1.50 V battery.
The strength of the electric field between the plates is

A. 75.0 V/m

B. 3.00 V/m

C. 0.750 V/m

D. 0.0300 V/m

Use the following information to answer the next multipart question.

26. In an experiment, a charged particle moves in the space between two charged plates. The potential difference between the plates is 6.00 V.

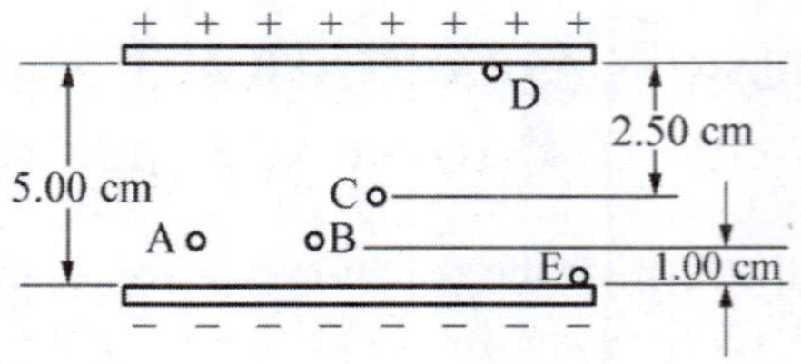

a) The potential difference between points A and C is

A. 6.00 V **B.** 3.00 V

C. 1.80 V **D.** 1.50 V

b) The work done moving a 3.00×10^{-9} C charge from point A to point B is

A. 0

B. 3.00×10^{-9} J

C. 1.50×10^{-8} J

D. 7.50×10^{-7} J

27. The electric potential difference from a negatively charged plate to a positively charged plate when the two plates are 0.250 m apart is 3.50×10^3 V. If a single electron increases its electric potential energy by moving a distance of 0.100 m, the electron had to move toward the

A. positive plate through a potential difference of 1.40×10^3 V

B. positive plate through a potential difference of 3.50×10^3 V

C. negative plate through a potential difference of 1.40×10^3 V

D. negative plate through a potential difference of 3.50×10^3 V

30-B2.8k describe, quantitatively, the motion of an electric charge in a uniform electric field

DYNAMICS OF CHARGES IN ELECTRIC FIELDS

The electric field between two parallel plates is a uniform field. Therefore, the field between two parallel plates will exert a constant force on charges within it. This means that Newton's laws of motion can be used to describe the forces acting on the charges.

The electric force on a subatomic particle is huge compared to the gravitational force on the same particle. An electron can accelerate freely in a vacuum without colliding with air, liquid, or solid particles.

Example

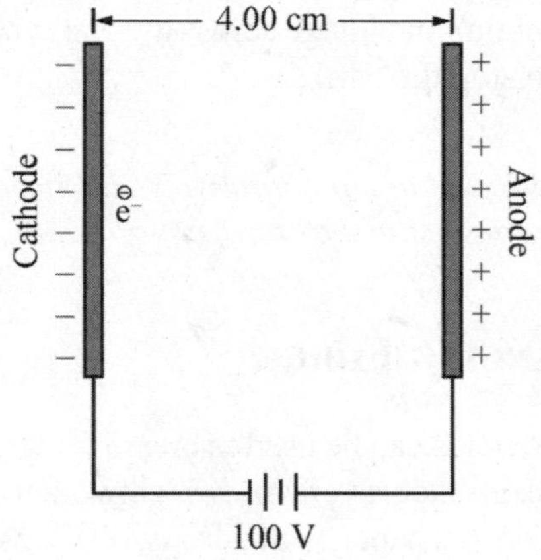

The given electric field is used to accelerate an electron.

What will be the speed of the electron when it reaches the positive plate?

Solution

Step 1
Use conservation of energy to solve for the change in kinetic energy of the electron.

$$\Delta E_k + \Delta U_E = 0$$
$$\Delta E_k = -\Delta U_E$$

Step 2
Substitute the known variables for the potential and kinetic energy into the equation, and solve for the final speed.
The electron started from rest, so its initial speed (v_i) was zero. The electric field lines begin at the positive plate and terminate at the negative plate, so the electron moves in the opposite direction of the electric field. Since the electric potential decreases in the direction of the electric field, the electric potential at the electron's final position must be greater than the electric potential at its initial position.
Therefore, the potential difference is positive.

$$\Delta E_k = -\Delta U_E$$
$$\left(\frac{1}{2}mv_f^2 - \frac{1}{2}mv_i^2\right) = -q\Delta V$$
$$\frac{1}{2}mv_f^2 = -q\Delta V$$
$$\Rightarrow v_f = \sqrt{\frac{-2q\Delta V}{m}}$$
$$= \sqrt{\frac{-2(-1.6 \times 10^{-19}\ \text{C})(100\ \text{V})}{9.11 \times 10^{-31}\ \text{kg}}}$$
$$= 5.93 \times 10^6\ \text{m/s}$$

This calculation can also be done using equations from dynamics and kinematics, but the solution will be significantly longer.
The solution requires more equations and the use of vectors to properly work out the negative signs. Electric potential is the most efficient way to solve most problems involving charges.

Step 1
Identify the forces involved in the given scenario. The net force on the electron is the electric force (assuming that gravity is negligible).
$F_{net} = ma$

The electric force is related to the electric field by $F_e = qE$.

In this case, the only the force due to the electric field contributes to the net force.

$$\vec{F}_{net} = \vec{F}_e$$
$$\therefore ma = -qE$$

The negative sign indicates that the force is in the opposite direction of the electric field.

Step 2
Calculate the magnitude of the electric field.

$$E = \frac{|\Delta V|}{d}$$
$$= \frac{100 \text{ V}}{0.0400 \text{ m}}$$
$$= 2\,500 \text{ V/m or N/C}$$

Step 3
Calculate the acceleration of the electron.

$$a = -\frac{qE}{m}$$
$$= -\frac{(2\,500 \text{ N/C})(-1.60 \times 10^{-19} \text{ C})}{9.11 \times 10^{-31} \text{ kg}}$$
$$= 4.39 \times 10^{14} \text{ m/s}^2$$

Step 4
Use the kinematic equation for non-uniform motion to calculate the speed of the electron as it reaches the positive plate. Substitute in the magnitudes of each known variable.

$$v_f^2 = v_i^2 + 2ad$$
$$v_f^2 = 0 + 2(4.39 \times 10^{14} \text{ m/s}^2)(0.0400 \text{ m})$$
$$\therefore v_f = 5.93 \times 10^6 \text{ m/s}$$

Therefore, the speed of the electron when it reaches the surface of the anode will be 5.93×10^6 m/s.

---

28. An electron accelerates from rest across the gap between two parallel charged plates, reaching a final velocity of $\vec{v}$. If the potential difference across the plates triples, the final speed of an electron accelerating from rest across the gap would be

A. $\frac{1}{3}v$ **B.** $\frac{1}{\sqrt{3}}v$

C. $\sqrt{3}v$ **D.** $9v$

CHALLENGER QUESTION

Numerical Response

29. An electron is held against the negative plate of an apparatus consisting of two parallel charged plates 2.50 cm apart. If a 3.50 kV source is connected across the plates, the electron's acceleration is $a.bc \times 10^{de}$ m/s^2 as it travels the distance between the charged plates. The value of *abcde* is ________. (State your answer as a five digit number.)

Numerical Response

30. An alpha particle moving at 5.34×10^4 m/s enters the region between two parallel plates. If the particle enters through a hole in the cathode, the minimum voltage across the plates needed to stop the particle is ________ V.

30-B2.9k explain, quantitatively, electrical interactions using the law of conservation of energy

Balancing Forces

Electric fields can be used to create forces about the same magnitude as gravity. Lightweight objects like pith balls, paper, water drops, oil drops, and dust allow these forces to balance.

Example

A 7.6×10^{-6} kg pith ball is suspended from a string and brought near a charged Van de Graaff generator, as shown. The strength of the electric field a the pith ball's location is 10 400 N/C.

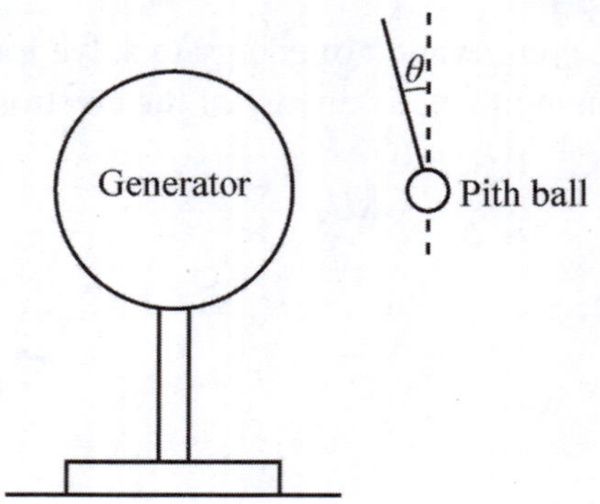

Find the magnitudes of the electric force and the charge on the pith ball if the pith ball makes an angle of 15° with respect to the vertical.

Solution

If the pith ball is suspended, the net force on it must be zero. There are three forces, as shown in this free-body diagram.

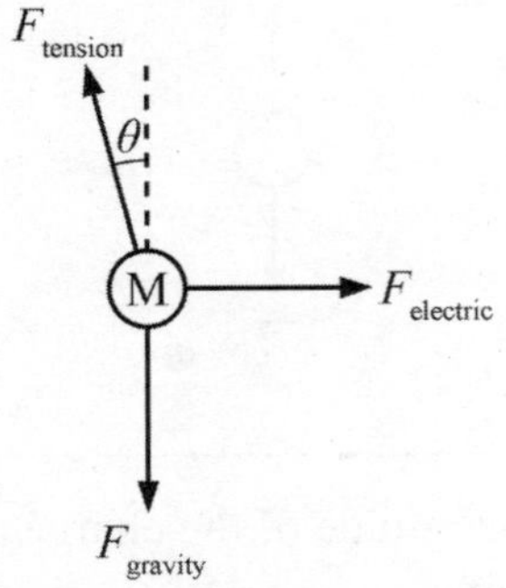

The force of tension balances the other two forces. Resolve the force of tension into components.

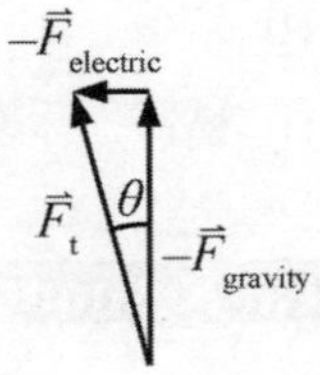

$$\frac{F_e}{F_g} = \tan\theta$$

$$F_e = F_g \tan\theta$$
$$= (mg)\tan\theta$$
$$F_e = (7.6 \times 10^{-6}\ \text{kg})(9.81\ \text{m/s}^2)\tan 15°$$
$$F_e = 2.00 \times 10^{-5}\ \text{N}$$
$$q = \frac{F_e}{|\vec{E}|}$$
$$= \frac{2.00 \times 10^{-5}\ \text{N}}{10\ 400\ \text{N/C}}$$
$$= 1.92 \times 10^{-9}\ \text{C}$$

So, the electrostatic force acting on the pith ball has a magnitude of 2.00×10^{-5} N and the charge on the pith ball has a magnitude of 1.92×10^{-9} C.

CHALLENGER QUESTION

Use the following information to answer the next multipart question.

31. A 3.0×10^{-4} kg pith ball hangs from a 1.0 m long thread between two vertical, parallel plates that are 0.10 m apart, as shown in the given diagram. When the potential difference across the plates is 420 V, the pith ball deflects 1.0 cm to the side and comes to rest.

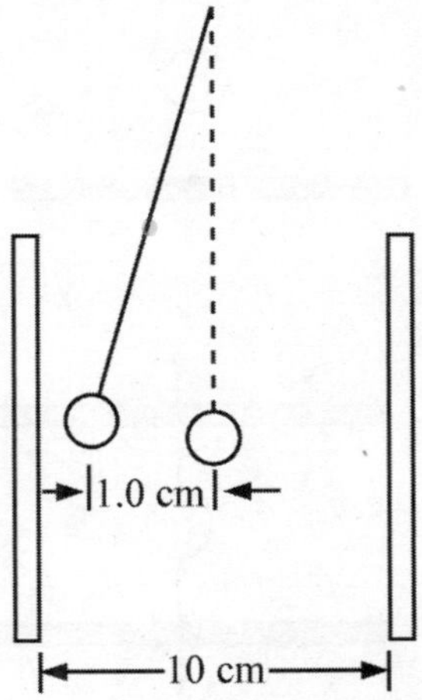

a) What is the magnitude of the electric force that deflects the pith ball?

A. 2.9×10^{-5} N

B. 3.0×10^{-4} N

C. 6.4×10^{-4} N

D. 7.7×10^{-5} N

b) What is the electric field intensity between the plates?

A. 4.2×10^3 N/C

B. 4.2×10^2 V/m

C. 42 V/m

D. 4.2 N/C

30-B2.10k explain Millikan's oil-drop experiment and its significance relative to charge quantization

MILLIKAN'S OIL-DROP EXPERIMENT

Robert Millikan used an electric field to suspend charged oil droplets in order to determine the charge on the droplets. He found that the charge on every oil droplet was a multiple of 1.60×10^{-19} C.

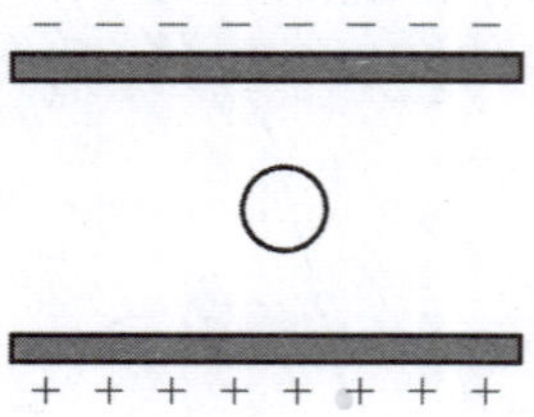

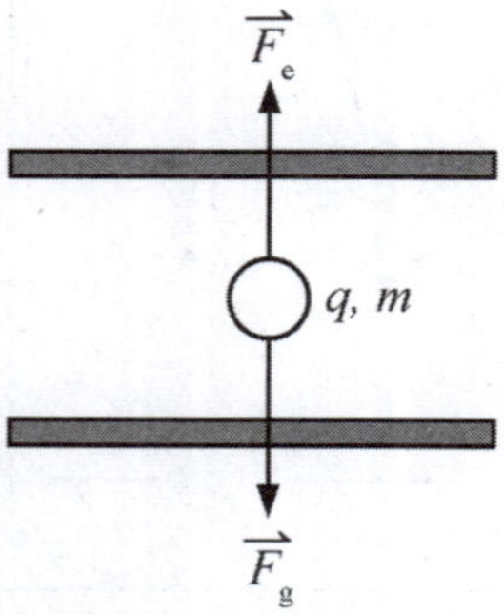

Millikan inferred that the value 1.60×10^{-19} C is the charge for a single electron. By determining that an electron had this specific charge, Millikan defined charge as a quantized value. In other words, the charge on any object must be a whole-number multiple of this elementary charge.

Use the following information to answer the next question.

An oil drop is suspended between the two parallel plates as shown. The magnitude of the electric field is 2 200 N/C and the mass of the oil drop is 2.87×10^{-16} kg.

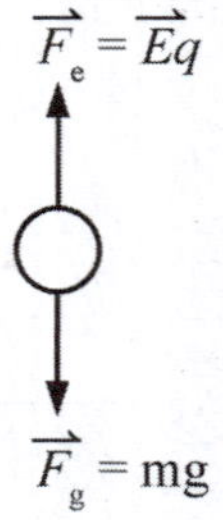

32. The magnitude of the charge on the oil drop is

A. 6.31×10^{-13} C

B. 6.19×10^{-12} C

C. 1.30×10^{-18} C

D. 1.28×10^{-18} C

D.

Numerical Response

33. Earth has an electric field that is oriented opposite to the direction of its gravitational field. An oil drop with a mass of 2.00×10^{-15} kg and a charge of 1.96×10^{-16} C remains suspended as a result of this electric field. Expressed in scientific notation, the electric field has a value of $a.bc \times 10^{d}$ N/C. What are the values of a, b, and c?

Variable	Value
a =	1
b =	0
c =	0
d =	1

m = 2.00e-15kg.

q = 1.96e-16.

30-B2.7k define electric current as the amount of charge passing a reference point per unit of time

Electric Current

Electrical current, I, is defined as the rate at which electric charges flow past any given point in a conductor. Therefore, the current is a measure of the change in charge per unit of time.

$$I = \frac{\Delta q}{\Delta t}$$

This formula is often simplified to appear as

$$I = \frac{q}{t}.$$

One ampere (A) is equal to the flow of one coulomb (C) past a given point in one second (s).
1 A = 1 C/s

By convention, current flows from positive to negative.

Example

If 75.0 C of charge flow from a car battery in 1.2 minutes, calculate the current flow in amperes.

$$I = \frac{q}{t} = \frac{75.0\ \text{C}}{1.2\ \text{min} \times 60\frac{\text{s}}{\text{min}}} = 1.0\ \text{A}$$

---

34. A car engine was started by engaging the starter motor for 0.25 min. If the average current passing through the starter motor during this time was 92 A, the total charge flowing through the starter motor was

A. 6.1 C

B. 23 C

C. 3.7×10^2 C

D. 1.4×10^3 C

30-B3.1k describe magnetic interactions in terms of forces and fields

30-B3.2k compare gravitational, electric and magnetic fields (caused by permanent magnets and moving charges) in terms of their sources and directions

Magnetic Field Theory

Certain metals are attracted to magnets. They have particular arrangements of electrons that can be affected by the forces from a magnetic field.

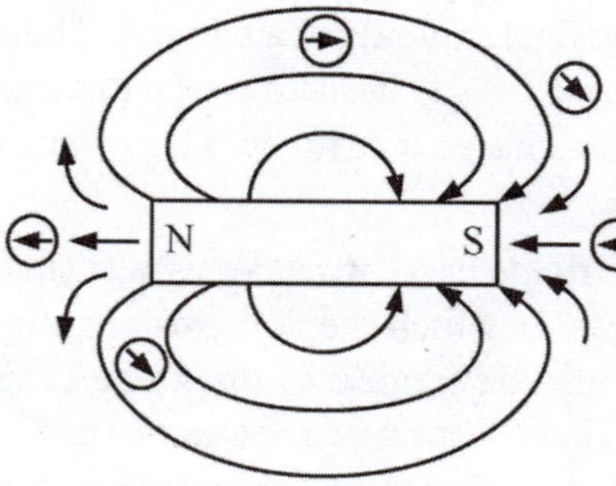

In order to determine the direction of a magnetic field, place a small compass (a test magnet) in the field. The north-seeking pole of the compass will then point in the direction of the magnetic field. This is because the compass' north-seeking pole is technically a south-seeking pole, since Earth's north magnetic pole is actually a south magnetic pole. This means that the north pole of the compass will point in the direction that the magnetic field travels in order to reach the south magnetic pole.

Magnetic fields are also vector fields. Two vector fields can be added together. For example, a magnetic field of 2.0 T east and a magnetic field of 3.0 T west interact to create a magnetic field with a net magnitude of 1.0 T to the west.

This explains how an electromagnet is created. The magnetic fields around each coil of the electromagnet adds together to create a single large magnetic field.

Comparing Gravitational, Electrical, and Magnetic Fields

Gravitational fields are caused by the presence of matter. A large amount of matter is required to create a significant gravitational field. The direction of a gravitational field is defined as the direction that a test mass will move if placed within the gravitation field, usually toward the centre of gravity of the more massive body generating the field.

Similarly, **electric fields** exist around charges. A uniform electric field can be created by a potential difference across two parallel metal plates attached to the opposite terminals of a battery. The direction of an electric field is defined as the direction that a positive test charge will move when placed within the electric field.

Magnetic fields exist around magnets (masses, usually iron, in which the domains are aligned). They can also be created by moving electric charges. The direction of a magnetic field is defined as the direction that the north pole (south-seeking pole) of a magnet will point when placed within the magnetic field. This is the direction that a compass needle's north pole (south-seeking pole) will point since it is built to point toward Earth's magnetic south (geographic north) pole.

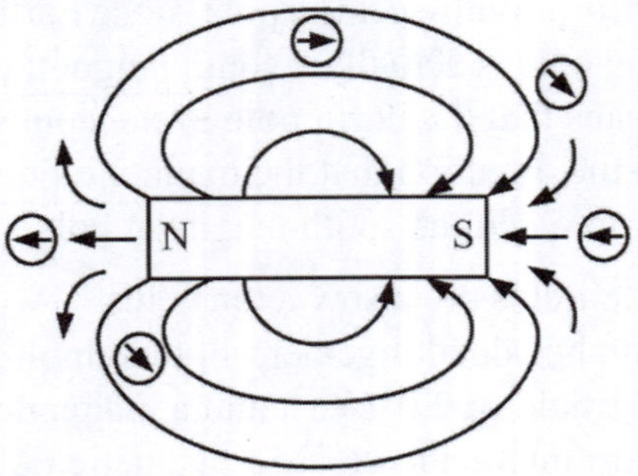

Use the following information to answer the next question.

A compass measures the direction of the magnetic field at point *P*.

35. Which of the following diagrams indicates the direction of the compass needle at point *P*?

A. ↗ **B.** ↙

C. ↖ **D.** ↘

30-B3.3k describe how the discoveries of Oersted and Faraday form the foundation of the theory relating electricity to magnetism

Oersted and Ampère's Contributions

Hans Christian Oersted discovered that a moving charge, such as the current in a wire, produces a magnetic field perpendicular to the direction of its motion. Andrè Ampère found the direction of this magnetic field and described its direction using a hand rule.

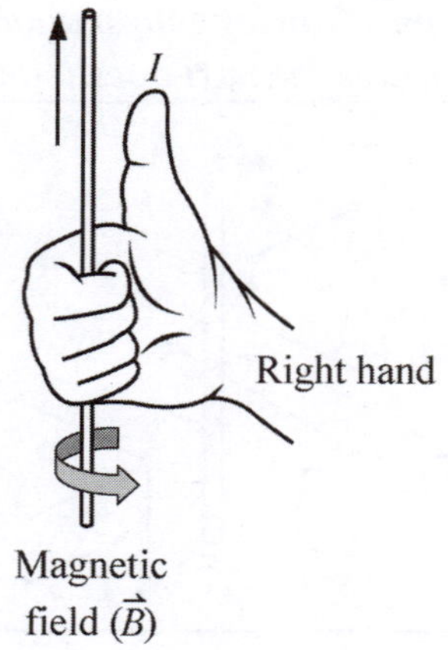

Using the right hand for conventional current, the thumb on the points in the direction of the current. The fingers then curl around wire in the direction of the magnetic field. Use the left hand for electron flow.

The magnetic field around a current-carrying wire has direction but no poles. Wrapping a wire into a spiral (called a solenoid) also wraps the magnetic field around the spiral. The resulting magnetic field is very similar to that of a bar magnet. Its poles can be found with a second hand rule.

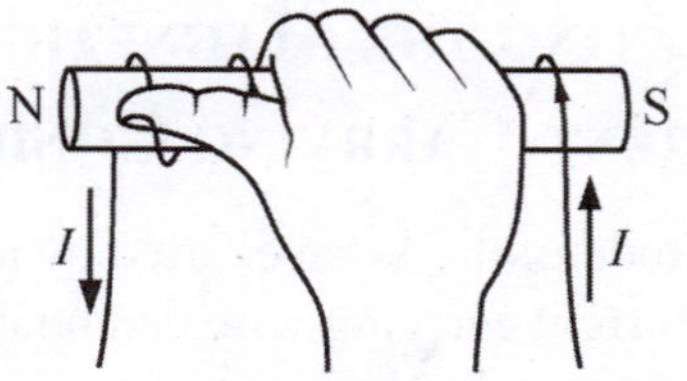

Grasp the solenoid with the right hand with the fingers following the conventional current around the spiral. The thumb then points to the north pole of the electromagnet. Use the left hand for electron flow.

Michael Faraday discovered that the motion of a magnetic field relative to a conductor (change in flux) creates a current in the conductor.

Use the following information to answer the next question.

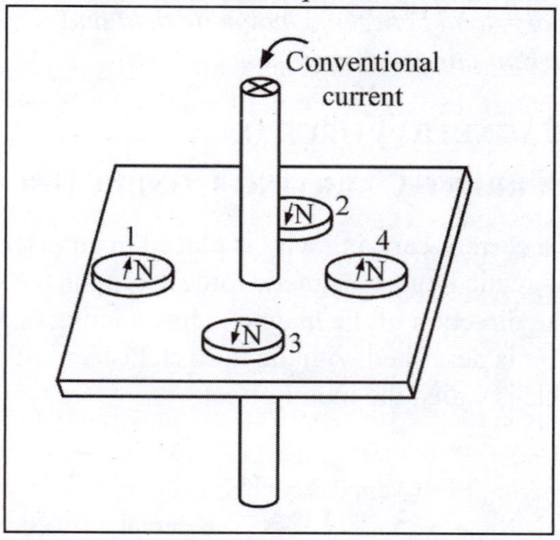

36. The direction of conventional current flow through a wire is shown in the diagram. The compass showing the correct orientation is labeled with the number

A. 1 **B.** 2
C. 3 **D.** 4

Use the following information to answer the next question.

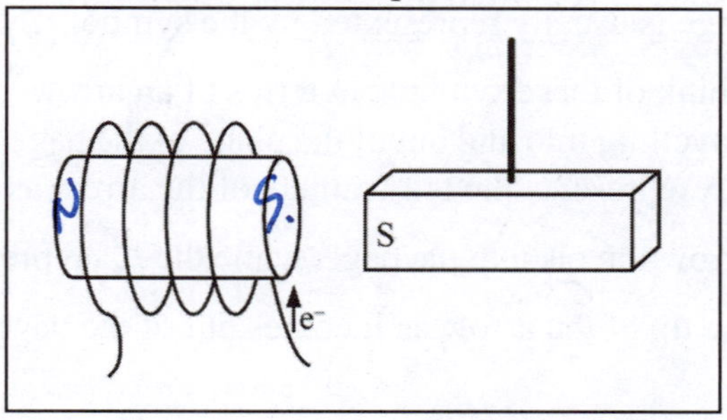

37. Electrons flow through a solenoid that is then brought near a suspended bar magnet. The end of the bar magnet marked as the south pole will be

A. forced upward

B. forced downward

C. attracted by the solenoid

D. repelled away from the solenoid

30-B3.7k describe and explain, qualitatively, the interaction between a magnetic field and a moving charge and between a magnetic field and a current-carrying conductor

Magnetic Force on a Current-Carrying Conductor

If a current-carrying wire is placed in an external magnetic field, a magnetic force acts upon the wire. The direction of the magnetic force acting on the wire is described with the third right-hand rule. This is called the motor effect.

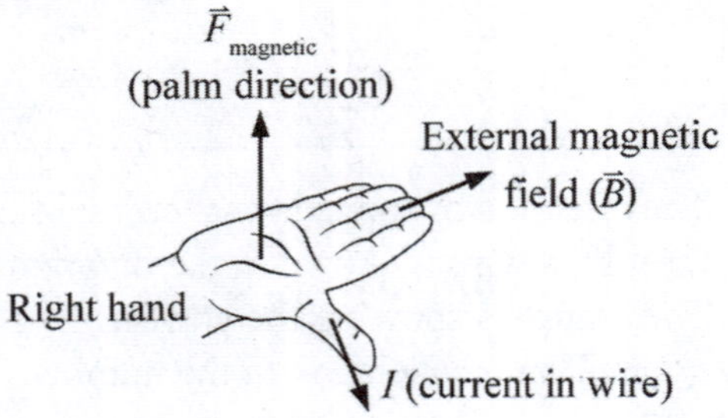

Use the left hand to determine the direction of the magnetic force acting on moving electrons.

A field directed into the page is usually represented by the symbol $\otimes$, and a field directed out of the page is usually represented by the symbol $\odot$.

Think of these symbols in terms of an arrow travelling into and out of the plane of the page. The $\otimes$ represents the tail feathers of the arrow as the arrow travels into the page, while the $\odot$ represents the tip of the arrow as it comes out of the page.

Use the following information to answer the next question.

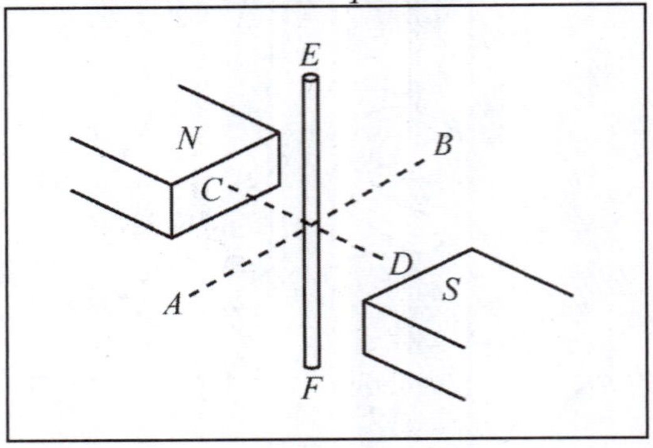

38. If a current runs through the wire from point E to point F in the wire, in what direction will the magnetic force act on the wire?

A. Point A **B.** Point B

C. Point C **D.** Point D

30-B3.8k explain, quantitatively, the effect of an external magnetic field on a current-carrying conductor

Calculating the Magnetic Force of Current-Carrying Conductors

The magnitude of the force exerted by a magnetic field on a current carrying wire can be determined by using the formula $F_m = B_{\perp}Il$

where F_m is the magnitude of the force,

I is the current in the wire,

l is the length of wire exposed to the field,

and $B_{\perp}$ is the magnitude of the magnetic field perpendicular to the wire.

Use the following information to answer the next question.

A conductor 1.5 cm long is placed between the poles of a magnet, as shown. The conductor carries a conventional current of 6.5 A in the direction shown.

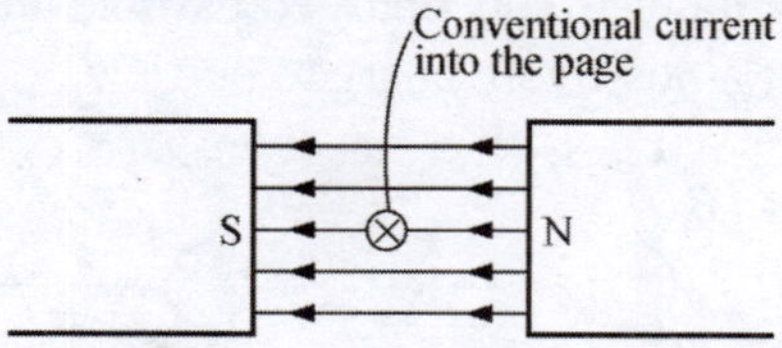

39. If the magnetic field between the poles is uniform and has a value of 1.5×10^{-2} T, the magnetic force acting on the conductor is

A. 0.15 N up

B. 1.5 mN up

C. 0.15 N down

D. 1.5 mN down

30-B3.9k describe, qualitatively, the effects of moving a conductor in an external magnetic field, in terms of moving charges in a magnetic field.

FARADAY'S CONTRIBUTION

Michael Faraday discovered that the motion of a magnetic field relative to a conductor induces a voltage across the conductor. This voltage can produce an electric current. This is the generator effect. The third hand rule can be used to find the direction of the generated current. The thumb points in the direction of the velocity of the wire relative to the magnet. The palm points in the direction of the magnetic force on the electrons in the conductor, which generates the current in the wire.

Example

A wire is pushed through a magnetic field from point A to point B as shown. Which end of the wire will become negatively charged?

Use the left hand for electron flow.

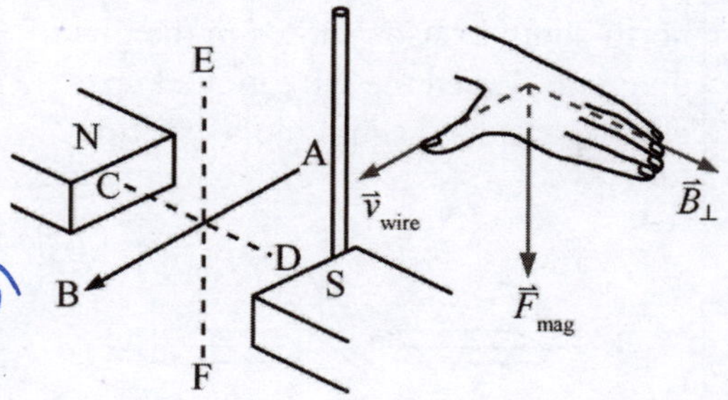

The electrons are pushed down the wire toward point F. The wire will become negatively charged at point F, and it will become positively charged at point E.

Use the following information to answer the next question.

Two bar magnets are aligned along an east-west axis, and a piece of wire is placed between the magnets along the north-south axis, as shown in the given diagram. When the wire moved up, electrons moved south in this section of wire.

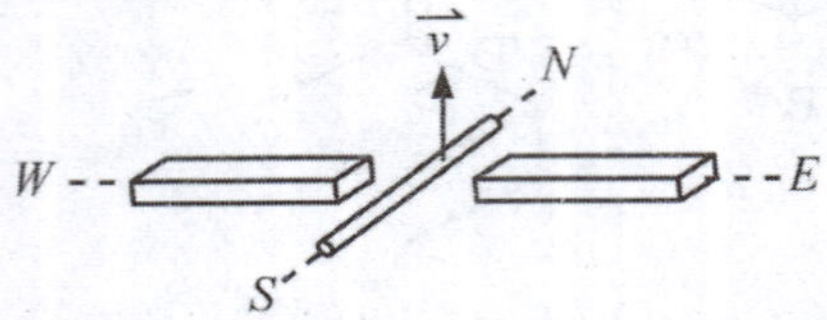

40. What will the polarity of the bar magnets and the direction of the conventional current be if the wire moves east?

A. The north pole will be on the left, the south pole will be on the right, and the conventional current will be zero.

B. The north pole will be on the right, the south pole will be on the left, and the conventional current will be zero.

C. The north pole will be on the left, the south pole will be on the right, and the conventional current will be north.

D. The north pole will be on the right, the south pole will be on the left, and the conventional current will be south.

30-B3.4k describe, qualitatively, a moving charge as the source of a magnetic field and predict the orientation of the magnetic field from the direction of motion

Magnetic Fields Produced by Moving Charges

The magnetic field created by a single moving charge can be visualized as ripples moving out from the charge in the space directly behind the moving charge. The field dissipates as the charge moves forward.

The direction of a magnetic field around a current-carrying conductor can be determined using the first hand rule. The thumb should point in the direction of the velocity of the moving charge in the conductor and the fingers curl around the conductor in the direction of the magnetic field. Use the left hand for a negatively charged particle and the right hand for a positively charged particle.

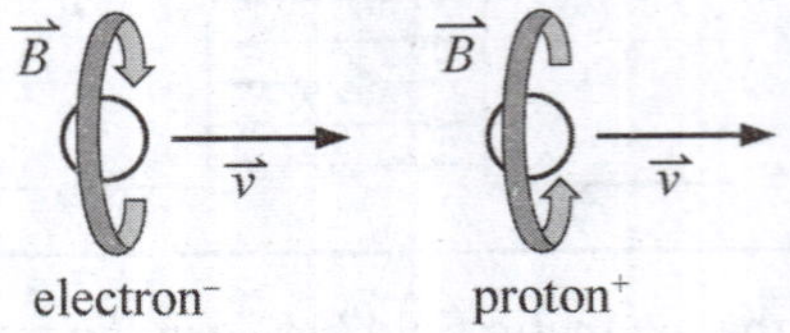

1. Point the thumb in the direction of the current within the conductor.
2. Curl the fingers of your hand around the conductor.
3. The curled fingers indicates the direction of the field.

The magnetic field can be represented by drawing a cross-section view of the wire. Consider what an arrow would look like from its ends going into and out of the page.

Consider the current in the following image to be electron flow.

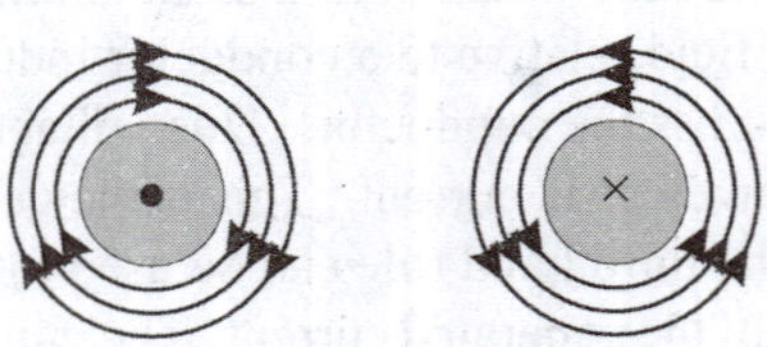

A dot in the centre of the wire indicates current flow out of the plane of the page, toward the reader. An "X" in the centre of the wire indicates current flow into the plane of the page, away from the reader. So using the left hand for electron flow, point the thumb in the direction of the current and the direction of the magnetic field is in the same direction as the fingers curl.

41. An electron travels into the plane of the page. Which of the following diagrams correctly shows the magnetic field around the electron?

A.
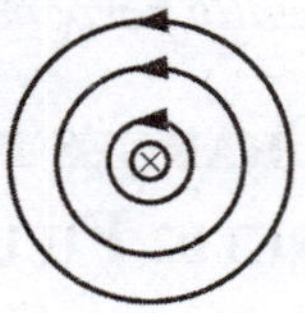

B.

C.
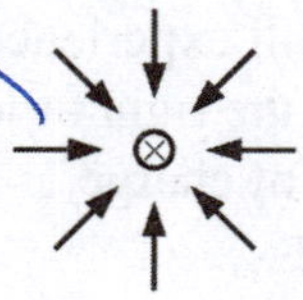

D.
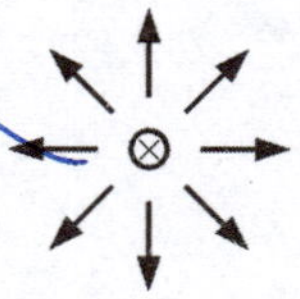

30-B3.5k explain, qualitatively and quantitatively, how a uniform magnetic field affects a moving electric charge, using the relationships among charge, motion, field direction and strength, when motion and field directions are mutually perpendicular

Magnetic Force on Moving Charges

The force a magnetic field exerts on a moving charge can be determined using this formula:
$F_m = qvB_\perp$,
where F_m is the magnitude of the force, q is the magnitude of the charge on the object, v is the magnitude of the object's velocity, and $B_\perp$ is the magnitude of the magnetic field perpendicular to the particle's motion.

If the motion of the particle and direction of the magnetic field are not perpendicular, then the magnetic force is calculated using this formula:
$F_m = qvB\sin\theta$
where θ is the angle between $\vec{v}$ and $\vec{B}$.

The direction of the magnetic force is always perpendicular to the direction of the motion.

To determine the direction of the force, ignore the signs associated with the quantities. Instead, use the left-hand and right-hand rules.

Use your left hand with negative charges and your right hand with positive charges.

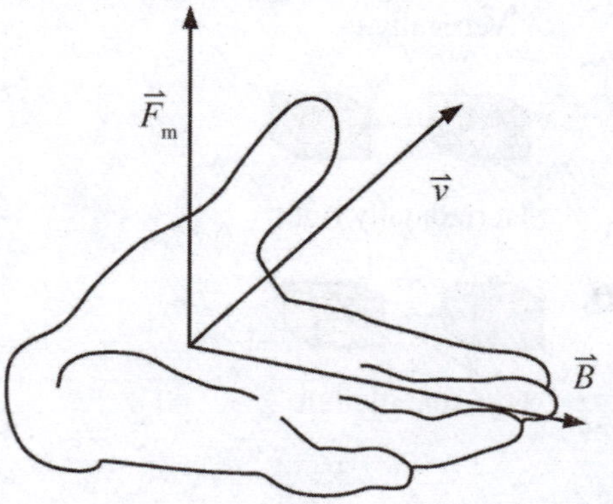

To use the hand rules, follow these steps:

1. Flatten your hand, and extend your thumb perpendicular to the fingers.
2. Point your thumb in the direction of the moving charge (the velocity).
3. Point your fingers in the direction of the magnetic field.

The palm of your hand then points in the direction of the force.

42. If a cathode ray (electron beam) tube is placed in a magnetic field, the cathode ray passes undeflected only when the direction of the ray is

A. parallel to the magnetic field

B. perpendicular to the magnetic field

C. at a 30° angle to the magnetic field

D. at a 45° angle to the magnetic field

43. The path followed by a moving proton in an external magnetic field is shown in

A.

Vertically down

B.
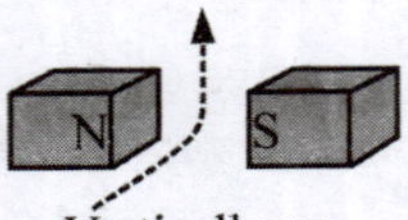

Vertically up

C.

Horizontally right

D.

Horizontally left

Use the following information to answer the next question.

Magnetic lines of force are directed into the plane of the page, and a proton is moving into this field, as shown in the given diagram.

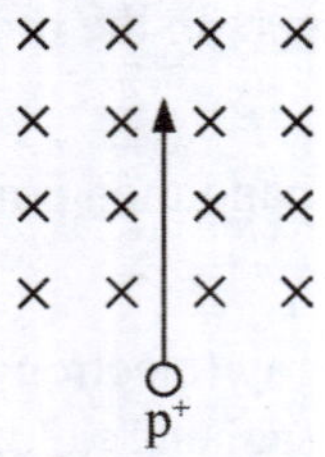

44. The magnetic force acting on the proton will deflect it

A. to the left

B. to the right

C. out of the plane of the page

D. into the plane of the page

Numerical Response

45. An electron moving at 4.0×10^6 m/s perpendicularly to a 0.050 T magnetic field experiences a magnetic force of $a.b \times 10^{-cd}$ N. What is the value of *abcd*? __________

30-B3.6k explain, quantitatively, how uniform magnetic and electric fields affect a moving electric charge, using the relationships among charge, motion, field direction and strength, when motion and field directions are mutually perpendicular

Moving Electric Charges in Electric and Magnetic Fields

Electric charges can be affected by both electric and magnetic fields. An electric charge moving in an electric field experiences a force that is directed along the electric field direction dependent upon the magnitude and type of charge. An electric charge moving in a magnetic field, that is perpendicular to the motion of the particle, will experience a force that is directed according to the right or left hand rules depending on the type of charge.

Circular Paths of Charged Particles in Magnetic Fields

The magnetic force on a moving charged particle is perpendicular to the velocity of the particle.
The force remains perpendicular to the velocity as the velocity changes direction. Consider the case of an electron moving to the right into a region with a constant magnetic field directed into the page. According to the left-hand rule for negative charges, the thumb will point in the direction of the electron's initial velocity and the fingers will point into the page in the direction of the magnetic field. Therefore, the electron will first experience a force directed down. As this force causes the electron to change direction, the force experienced by it due to the constant magnetic field also changes direction. This result continues as the electron is forced into a circular path. Since the magnetic force acts toward the centre of this circle anywhere along the path, this fits the definition of a centripetal force.

Electron in a Constant Magnetic Field

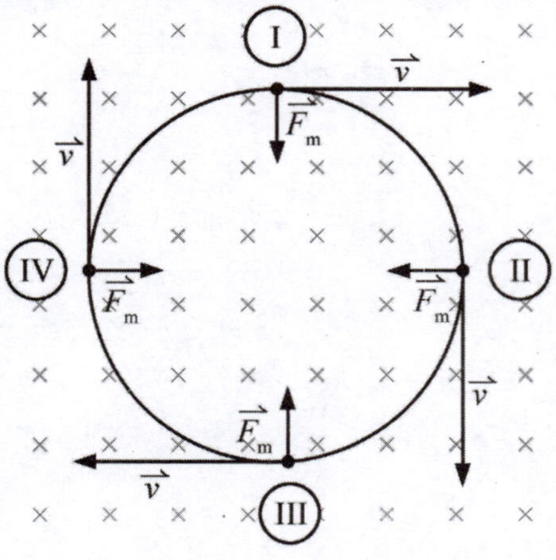

Moving Charges in Magnetic and Electric Fields

A charge moving through a uniform electric field will experience an electric force that is directly proportional to the magnitude of the charge and the electric field strength. For a positive charge, the direction of the force is the same as the direction of the electric field; for a negative charge, the direction of the force is opposite to the direction of the electric field.

$F_e = qE = \frac{qV}{d}$

A charge moving perpendicularly through a uniform magnetic field will experience a magnetic force that is directly proportional to the magnitude of the charge, the charge's velocity, and the magnetic field strength.

$F_m = qvB_\perp$

Use the following information to answer the next question.

A proton, with 894 eV of energy, travels perpendicular to a magnetic field and moves in a circular path with a radius of 3.60×10^{-4} m.

46. The speed of the proton is

A. 4.14×10^5 m/s

B. 1.77×10^7 m/s

C. 1.71×10^{11} m/s

D. 3.14×10^{14} m/s

47. A potential difference of 3.25 kV accelerates an alpha particle from rest eastward. The alpha particle then enters into a uniform magnetic field with a field strength of 2.90×10^{-1} T north.
The magnetic force acting on the alpha particle is

A. 1.64×10^{-19} N up

B. 2.60×10^{-15} N down

C. 2.90×10^{-8} N down

D. 5.19×10^{-14} N up

Use the following information to answer the next question.

Charged particles moving toward Earth become trapped within a field near Earth where they cause the *aurora borealis* (northern lights) and *aurora australis* (southern lights).

48. The field in which the particles are trapped is

A. a gravitational field

B. an induction field

C. a magnetic field

D. an electric field

Use the following information to answer the next question.

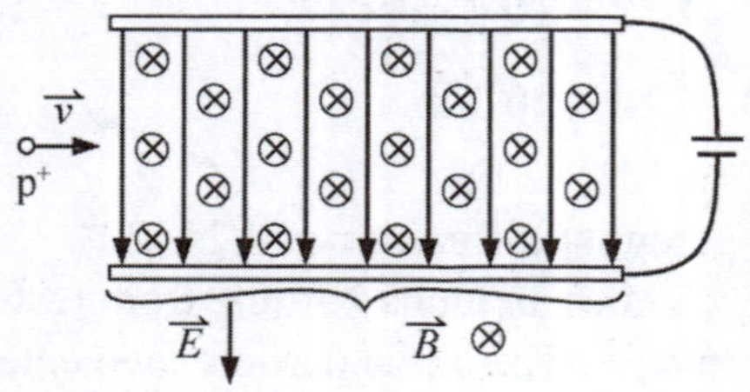

A proton moving at 2.9×10^5 m/s enters a region in which perpendicular electric and magnetic fields exist, as shown in the given diagram. The magnitude of the electric field is 5.0×10^4 N/C.

Numerical Response

49. If the proton passes undeflected through this region, then the magnitude of the magnetic field is ________ T. (Assume that gravity is negligible.)

Numerical Response

50. An alpha particle accelerates westward as it travels between two charged parallel plates with a potential difference of 10.5 kV between them. The plates are fixed 4.55 cm apart. The alpha particle then enters into a uniform magnetic field of 6.22×10^{-2} T directed north. Expressed in scientific notation, the radius of curvature of the alpha particle's path is $a.bc \times 10^{-d}$ J. What is the value of *abcd*?________

Answers and Solutions
Forces and Fields

1. C	12. A	22. 222	b) A	42. A
2. D	13. 6741	23. 1619	32. D	43. A
3. A	14. a) WR	24. B	33. 1002	44. A
4. B	b) WR	25. A	34. D	45. 3214
5. B	15. 2339	26. a) C	35. C	46. A
6. B	16. B	b) A	36. A	47. D
7. C	17. B	27. C	37. D	48. C
8. B	18. D	28. C	38. A	49. 0.17
9. A	19. B	29. 24616	39. B	50. 3361
10. C	20. C	30. 29.6	40. A	
11. C	21. B	31. a) A	41. A	

1. C

When two objects are rubbed together, one takes electrons from the other. An excess of electrons means a negative charge, while a shortage of electrons means a positive charge. Therefore, the object that gains electrons becomes negatively charged, while the object that lost electrons will become positively charged.

2. D

The third sphere attracts the others, so it has the opposite charge of the first two spheres. If the third sphere attracts both other spheres, these other spheres must have the same charge.

3. A

Earth, for purposes of electrostatics, is considered to be a conductor. Since the bottom of a thundercloud is negative, it repels electrons away from the region of Earth directly beneath it, leaving that region with a positive charge. Since no charge is actually transferred from the cloud to Earth during this process, this redistribution of charge is due to induction.

4. B

Charges can neither be created nor destroyed; instead, they are transferred and rearranged. After Arianna ran the comb through her hair, the comb became charged by conduction. The charges in the small pieces of paper were then separated by induction.

As the charge on the comb was brought close to the bits of paper, the charges in the paper (equal number positive and negative) were forced to separate. The charges that were the same as those on the comb were forced farther away, while the opposite charges were attracted toward the comb. The paper was attracted to the comb because the force of attraction to the nearer opposite charges in the paper was stronger than the force of repulsion from the farther similar charges.

5. B

The leaves repelled the first time because of the negative rod, which caused electrons to flow from the ball toward the leaves by induction. Therefore, the leaves were negatively charged when they repelled.

The leaves repelled the second time after the electrons flowed to ground through the finger. Thus the electroscope became deficient in electrons. Therefore, the leaves were then positively charged when they repelled.

6. B

According to the law of conservation of charge, charges can neither be created nor destroyed. Therefore, the statement that charges are created by rubbing two surfaces together is false.

7. C

A	B	C
−200 μC	400 μC	−500 μC

$$\frac{B+C}{2} = \frac{400\ \mu C + (-500\ \mu C)}{2}$$
$$= -50\ \mu C = B = C$$
$$A = -200\ \mu C$$
$$q_{total} = -200\ \mu C + 400\ \mu C + (-500\ \mu C)$$
$$q_{total} = -300\ \mu C$$

Therefore, the total charge of the system and the charge on each sphere, respectively, was –300 μC, –200 μC, –50 μC, –50 μC.

8. B

Recall that $F_e \propto \frac{q_1 q_2}{r^2}$.

When one charged object touches the neutral sphere of the same size, the charge on the object becomes $\frac{1}{2}$ as large. Therefore, one of the charges decreases by $\frac{1}{2}$.

Apply the factor changes to q_2 and r:

$$\frac{1 \times \frac{1}{2}}{(2)^2} = \frac{\frac{1}{2}}{4} = \frac{1}{8}$$

$\therefore F_e$ becomes $\frac{1}{8}$ as large.

9. A

Since the two spheres are identical, they will divide the total charge evenly between them.

$$\begin{aligned} q_{total} &= q_X + q_Y \\ &= (+2.0 \times 10^{-8}\ C) + (-3.0 \times 10^{-8}\ C) \\ &= -1.0 \times 10^{-8}\ C \end{aligned}$$

$$q_{X\ final} = \frac{-1.0 \times 10^{-8}\ C}{2} = -5.0 \times 10^{-9}\ C$$

10. C

Coulomb's law states that the electric force of one point charge on another is directly related to the inverse square of the distance between two charges. Graph C best illustrates this law.

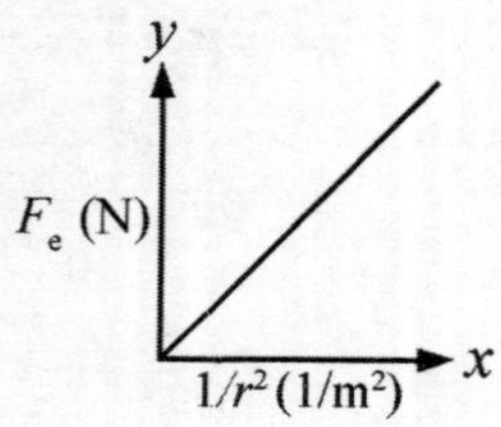

11. C

The force on sphere X due to sphere Y is attractive because the charges on spheres X and Y are opposite. Therefore, this force is 6.0 N to the right.

The electrostatic force between two charges is given by the formula $F_e = \frac{kq_1q_2}{r^2}$. Use this formula to determine the force exerted by the same magnitude charge at half the distance.

$$\begin{aligned} F_{XZ} &= \frac{F_{XY}}{\left(\frac{1}{2}\right)^2} \\ &= 4F_{XY} \\ &= 4(6.0\ N) \\ &= 24\ N \end{aligned}$$

Since the force on sphere X due to sphere Z is also attractive, because of the opposite nature of the charges, it will be directed in the opposite direction of the force on sphere X due to sphere Y.

$$\vec{F}_{XY} = 6.0\ N \text{ to the right} = +6.0\ N$$
$$\vec{F}_{XZ} = 24\ N \text{ to the left} = -24\ N$$
$$\begin{aligned} \vec{F}_{net} &= \vec{F}_{XY} + \vec{F}_{XZ} \\ &= +6.0\ N + (-24\ N) \\ &= -18\ N = 18\ N \text{ to the left} \end{aligned}$$

The net force on sphere X due to spheres Y and Z is 18 N.

12. A

Use the formula for the electric force between two points charges to find the net force on sphere B.

$$F_{A\ on\ B} = \frac{kq_Aq_B}{r^2}$$
$$= \frac{\left(8.99 \times 10^9 \frac{N\cdot m^2}{C^2}\right)(1.00 \times 10^{-6}\ C)(-1.50 \times 10^{-6}\ C)}{(0.300\ m)^2}$$
$$= -0.150\ N$$

Therefore, $F_{A\ on\ B} = 0.150$ N to the left.

$$F_{C\ on\ B} = \frac{kq_Bq_C}{r^2}$$
$$= \frac{\left(8.99 \times 10^9 \frac{N\cdot m^2}{C^2}\right)(-1.50 \times 10^{-6}\ C)(-1.25 \times 10^{-6}\ C)}{(0.200\ m)^2}$$
$$= 0.421\ N$$

Therefore, $F_{\text{C on B}} = 0.421$ N up.

Use the Pythagorean theorem to find the magnitude of the net force on sphere B.

$$F_{\text{net}} = \sqrt{(0.150\text{ N})^2 + (0.421\text{ N})^2}$$
$$= 0.447\text{ N}$$

13. 6741

Draw a free-body diagram of the scenario.

$3x = 12.0$ cm
$x = 4.00$ cm

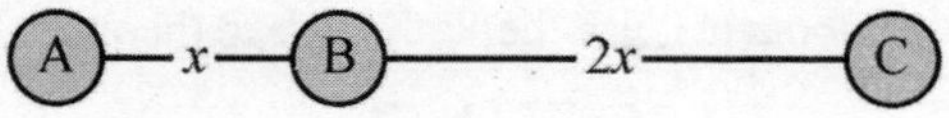

$$F_{\text{A on B}} = \frac{kq_{\text{A}}q_{\text{B}}}{r^2}$$
$$= \frac{8.99 \times 10^9 \frac{\text{N·m}^2}{\text{C}^2}(4.50 \times 10^{-6}\text{ C})(-3.00 \times 10^{-6}\text{ C})}{(4.00 \times 10^{-2}\text{ m})^2}$$
$$= -7.585 \times 10^1\text{ N}$$

Therefore, charge A attracts charge B toward itself along the line between them. In this case, the force on charge B pulls it toward the left.

$$F_{\text{C on B}} = \frac{kq_{\text{B}}q_{\text{C}}}{r^2}$$
$$= \frac{8.99 \times 10^9 \frac{\text{N·m}^2}{\text{C}^2}(3.00 \times 10^{-6}\text{ C})(2.00 \times 10^{-6}\text{ C})}{(8.00 \times 10^{-2}\text{ m})^2}$$
$$= -8.428\text{ N}$$

Therefore, charge C attracts charge B toward itself along the line between them. In this case, the force on charge B pulls it toward the right.

$$F_{\text{net}} = -7.585 \times 10^1\text{ N} + 8.428\text{ N}$$
$$= -6.74 \times 10^1\text{ N}$$

This is equivalent to 6.74×10^1 N acting to the left.

14. a) WR

Since sphere *A* had a negative charge and the initial force was an attraction force, the charge of sphere *B* must have been positive. The force $F_{\text{A and B}}$ is also negatve because it is an attraction force.

$$F_{\text{A and B}} = \frac{kq_Aq_B}{r^2}$$
$$-8.00 \times 10^{-5}\text{ N} = \frac{k(-3.50q_{\text{B}})(q_{\text{B}})}{(0.30\text{ m})^2}$$
$$q_{\text{B}}^2 = \frac{(-8.00 \times 10^{-5}\text{ N})(0.30\text{ m})^2}{\left(8.99 \times 10^9 \frac{\text{N·m}^2}{\text{C}^2}\right)(-3.50)}$$
$$q_{\text{B}} = 1.51 \times 10^{-9}\text{ C}$$
$$q_{\text{A}} = -3.50(1.58 \times 10^{-8}\text{ C})$$
$$= -5.29 \times 10^{-8}\text{ C}$$

Therefore, sphere *A* initially had a charge of -5.29×10^{-8} C and sphere *B* initially had a charge of 1.51×10^{-8} C.

b) WR

Determine the charge on each sphere after they touch using the conservation law.

$$q = \frac{q_A + q_B}{2}$$
$$= \frac{(-5.29 \times 10^{-8}\text{ C}) + (1.51 \times 10^{-8}\text{ C})}{2}$$
$$q = -1.89 \times 10^{-8}\text{ C}$$
$$F_{\text{e}} = \frac{kq_1q_2}{r^2}$$
$$= \frac{8.99 \times 10^9 \frac{\text{N·m}^2}{\text{C}^2}(-1.86 \times 10^{-8}\text{ C})(-1.86 \times 10^{-9}\text{ C})}{(0.200\text{ m})^2}$$
$$= 8.03 \times 10^{-5}\text{ N}$$

The two spheres would have a repulsive force of 8.03×10^{-5} N acting on them.

15. 2339

$$\frac{F_{\text{e}}}{F_{\text{g}}} = \frac{\frac{kq_1q_2}{r^2}}{\frac{Gm_1m_2}{r^2}} = \frac{kq_1q_2}{Gm_1m_2}$$
$$= \frac{\left(8.99 \times 10^9 \frac{\text{N·m}^2}{\text{C}^2}\right) \times (1.60 \times 10^{-19}\text{ C})^2}{\left(6.67 \times 10^{-11} \frac{\text{N·m}^2}{\text{kg}^2}\right) \times (1.67 \times 10^{-27}\text{ kg})(9.11 \times 10^{-31}\text{ kg})}$$
$$= 2.3 \times 10^{39}$$

The value of *abcd* is 2339.

16. B

Vector fields have both a magnitude and a direction. Scalar fields only have a magnitude. Both electric and gravitational fields have direction. Temperature and air pressure do not.

17. B

An electric field has been defined in terms of the electrical force acting on a positive test charge placed in various locations within the field.

18. D

The electric field near a point charge falls off following an inverse square law. This is illustrated in graph D.

19. B

The negative sign changes direction.

A test charge is being used in a field.

$$E = \frac{F_e}{q} \Rightarrow F_e = Eq$$

$$= \left(2.5 \times 10^4 \frac{\text{N}}{\text{C}}\right)\left(-2 \times 10^{-7}\ \text{C}\right)$$

$$= -5.00 \times 10^{-3}\ \text{N south}$$

$$= 5.00 \times 10^{-3}\ \text{N north}$$

The negative sign means opposite the field direction—in this case, to the north.

20. C

$$E = \frac{kq}{r^2} \Rightarrow r = \sqrt{\frac{kq}{E}}$$

$$r = \sqrt{\frac{(8.99 \times 10^9\ \text{N}\cdot\text{m}^2/\text{C})(6.9 \times 10^{-5}\ \text{C})}{1.0 \times 10^3\ \text{N/C}}}$$

$$r = 2.5 \times 10^1\ \text{m}$$

21. B

Find the electric field created by charge A at point P.

$$(E)_A = \frac{kq}{r^2}$$

$$= \frac{(8.99 \times 10^9\ \text{N/C})(3.00 \times 10^{-6}\ \text{C})}{(0.200\ \text{m})^2}$$

$$= 6.74 \times 10^5\ \text{N/C}$$

E_A is positive, so the field is directed outward. Therefore, the electric field created by charge A at point P is 6.74×10^{-5} N/C to the right.

Find the electric field created by charge B at point P.

$$E_B = \frac{kq}{r^2}$$

$$= \frac{(8.99 \times 10^9\ \text{N/C})(-4.00 \times 10^{-6}\ \text{C})}{(0.100\ \text{m})^2}$$

$$= -3.60 \times 10^6\ \text{N/C}$$

E_B is negative, so the electric field is directed inward. Therefore, the electric field created by charge B at point P is 3.6×10^6 N/C down.

In order to add these perpendicular electric field components, use the Pythagorean theorem.

$$E_{net} = \sqrt{(6.74 \times 10^5\ \text{N/C})^2 + (3.60 \times 10^6\ \text{N/C})^2}$$

$$E_{net} = 3.66 \times 10^6\ \text{N/C}$$

22. 222

Compare the forces at both distances.

$$\frac{F_{45\ \text{cm}}}{F_{15\ \text{cm}}} = \frac{\vec{E}_{45\ \text{cm}}q}{\vec{E}_{15\ \text{cm}}q}$$

$$= \frac{\dfrac{kq}{(0.45\ \text{m})^2}}{\dfrac{kq}{(0.15\ \text{m})^2}}$$

$$= \frac{(0.15\ \text{m})^2}{(0.45\ \text{m})^2}$$

$$= \frac{1}{9}$$

$$F_{45\ \text{cm}} = \frac{1}{9}(F_{15\ \text{cm}}) = \frac{1}{9}(0.200\ \text{N})$$

$$= 0.022\ \text{N}$$

$$= 2.2 \times 10^{-2}\ \text{N}$$

23. 1619

Let the charge of the proton be q, the energy gained be ΔE_p, and the potential difference be ΔV.

$$\Delta E_p = q\Delta V$$

$$= (1.60 \times 10^{-19}\ \text{C})(1.0\ \text{V})$$

$$= 1.6 \times 10^{-19}\ \text{J}$$

24. B

$$\Delta E = Vq$$

$$= (1.0\ \text{V})(+1e)$$

$$= 1.0\ \text{eV}$$

25. A

$$E = \frac{V}{d} = \frac{1.50\ \text{V}}{0.0200\ \text{m}} = 75.0\ \text{V/m}$$

26. a) C

The vertical displacement from A to C is 1.50 cm. The electric potential increases as the charge moves against the electric field.

$$\frac{1.50\text{ cm}}{5.00\text{ cm}} = \frac{n}{6.00\text{ V}}$$
$$n = 1.80\text{ V}$$

b) A

Moving horizontally does not change the potential energy. Since points A and B are the same distance from the plates, there is no difference in potential. This means the difference in potential at point A is the same as the potential at point B and there is no change in moving a charged particle in this way. Therefore, $\Delta V = 0$. Since there is no change in potential, there is no work done in moving the particle against the electric field.

27. C

In order for the electric potential to increase, the electron must move toward the negative plate.

The work done on a charge to move it through the uniform electric field is proportional to the distance the charge moves.

$$\frac{3.50 \times 10^3\text{ V}}{0.250\text{ m}} = \frac{x}{0.100\text{ m}}$$
$$\therefore x = 1.40 \times 10^3\text{ V}$$

The actual potential difference is negative because the particle has a negative charge. Negative particles gain potential energy when they move through a decrease in potential in an electric field.

$$\Delta V = \frac{\Delta E_p}{q}$$

where $q = 1$ electron

$$\Delta V = -\frac{\Delta E_p}{e}$$
$$\therefore \Delta V \propto -\Delta E_p$$

28. C

Use the conservation of energy to equate the potential and kinetic energies.

$$\Sigma E_{\text{i}} = \Sigma E_{\text{f}}$$
$$E_{p_{\text{i}}} = E_{k_{\text{f}}}$$

The electric potential energy of the particle in its initial state is equal to the kinetic energy of the particle in its final state.

$$V_{\text{i}} q_e = \frac{1}{2} m_e v_{\text{f}}^2$$
$$\therefore v_{\text{f}}^2 \propto V_{\text{i}}$$
$$v_{\text{f}} \propto \sqrt{V}_{\text{i}}$$
$$v_{\text{f}} \propto \sqrt{3}$$

If the potential difference is tripled, the speed will increase by a factor of 3.

29. 24616

Method 1 - Conservation of energy

$$E_{\text{p}} = E_{\text{k}}$$
$$qV = \frac{1}{2} m v^2$$
$$\therefore v = \sqrt{\frac{2qV}{m}}$$
$$= \sqrt{\frac{2\left(1.60 \times 10^{-19}\text{ C}\right)\left(3.50 \times 10^3\text{ V}\right)}{9.11 \times 10^{-31}\text{ kg}}}$$
$$= 3.506 \times 10^7\text{ m/s}$$
$$v_{\text{f}}^2 = v_{\text{i}}^2 + 2ad$$
$$\therefore a = \frac{v_{\text{f}}^2 - v_{\text{i}}^2}{2d}$$
$$= \frac{\left(3.506 \times 10^7\text{ m/s}\right)^2 - 0}{2 \times \left(2.50 \times 10^{-2}\text{ m}\right)}$$
$$= 2.458 \times 10^{16}\text{ m/s}^2$$
$$\approx 2.46 \times 10^{16}\text{ m/s}^2$$

Method 2 - Force analysis

$$F_{\text{e}} = F_{\text{net}}$$
$$q\frac{V}{d} = ma$$
$$a = \frac{qV}{md}$$
$$= \frac{\left(1.60 \times 10^{-19}\text{ C}\right)\left(3.50 \times 10^3\text{ V}\right)}{\left(9.11 \times 10^{-31}\text{ kg}\right)\left(2.50 \times 10^{-2}\text{ m}\right)}$$
$$= 2.459 \times 10^{16}\text{ m/s}^2$$
$$\approx 2.46 \times 10^{16}\text{ m/s}^2$$

30. 29.6

$$V = \frac{\Delta E_k}{q}$$
$$\Delta E_k = \frac{1}{2}m\Delta v^2$$
$$Vq = \frac{1}{2}m\Delta v^2$$
$$V(3.20 \times 10^{-19}\text{ C})$$
$$= \frac{1}{2}(6.65 \times 10^{-27}\text{ kg})$$
$$= (5.34 \times 10^4\text{ m/s} - 0)^2$$
$$V = 29.6\text{ V}$$

31. a) A

The free-body diagram for this scenario involves a total of three forces. Since the pith ball is in static equilibrium, all three forces must cancel out. Since the force of tension in the string is the only force not acting solely in either the horizontal or vertical plane, the electrical force must be equal in magnitude and opposite in direction to the horizontal component of the force of tension.

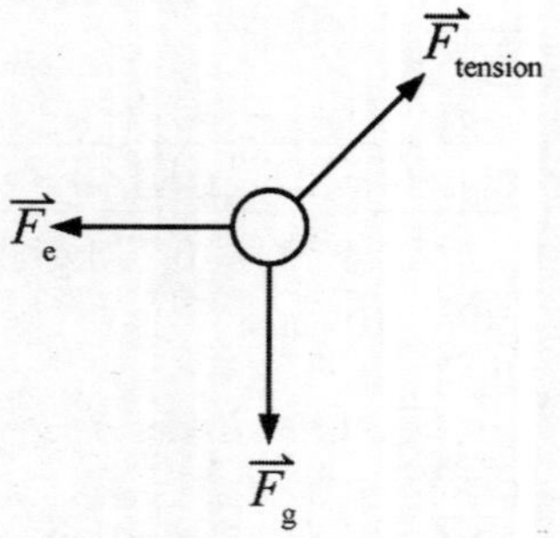

$$\tan\theta \cong \frac{x_{deflection}}{x_{length}} = \frac{0.010\text{ m}}{1.0\text{ m}}$$
$$\tan\theta = \frac{F_e}{mg} \Rightarrow F_e = mg(\tan\theta)$$
$$F_e = (3.0 \times 10^{-4}\text{ kg})(9.81\text{ N/kg})\frac{0.010\text{ m}}{1.0\text{ m}}$$
$$= 2.9 \times 10^{-5}\text{ N}$$

b) A

$$E = \frac{V}{d} = \frac{420\text{ V}}{0.10\text{ m}} = 4.2 \times 10^3\text{V/m or}$$
$$4.2 \times 10^3\text{ N/C}$$

32. D

When an oil drop is suspended between two horizontal parallel plates, the upward electric force balances out the downward force of gravity.

$$F_e = F_g$$
$$= Eq$$
$$= mg$$
$$q = \frac{mg}{E}$$
$$= \frac{2.87 \times 10^{-16}\text{ kg}(9.81\text{ m/s}^2)}{2\,200\text{ N/C}}$$
$$= 1.28 \times 10^{-18}\text{ C}$$

33. 1002

$$F_g = F_e$$
$$mg = qE$$
$$E = \frac{mg}{q}$$
$$= \frac{(2.00 \times 10^{-15}\text{ kg})(9.81\text{ m/s})}{1.96 \times 10^{-16}\text{ C}}$$
$$= 1.00 \times 10^2\text{ N/C}$$

34. D

$$I = \frac{q}{t}$$
$$\Rightarrow q = It$$
$$= (92\text{ A})(0.25\text{ min})(60\text{ s/min})$$
$$= 1.4 \times 10^3\text{ C}$$

35. C

The compass needle will follow the magnetic field lines, which exit the magnet at the north pole and enter the magnet at the south pole. Therefore, the compass needle will point toward the south pole at point *P*.

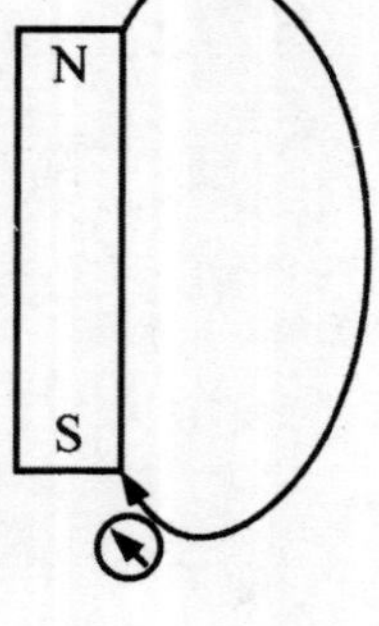

36. A

Since the current flow is conventional current (positive), use the right-hand rule to determine the direction of the magnetic field around the wire. The right-hand rule shows that the magnetic field is directed clockwise around the wire by pointing the thumb of the right hand in the direction of the conventional current and curling the fingers in the direction of the induced magnetic field.

37. D

Since the scenario is concerning electron flow, use the left-hand rule. From this, with the fingers curling in the direction of the electron current, the thumb shows that the magnetic field inside the solenoid is directed to the left. Therefore, the left-hand side of the solenoid will act as a north pole while the right-hand side will act as a south magnetic pole. Therefore, the magnet will be repelled.

38. A

Use the right-hand rule for current flow. Your thumb should point toward *F* in the direction of the current. Your fingers should point toward *D* in the direction of the magnetic field. Your palm will then face the direction of the magnetic force, which is directed toward point *A*.

39. B

Determine the magnitude of the magnetic force acting on the conductor.

$$F_m = B_{\perp}Il$$
$$= (1.5 \times 10^{-2}\ \text{T})(6.5\ \text{A})(1.5 \times 10^{-2}\ \text{m})$$
$$= 1.5 \times 10^{-3}\ \text{N} = 1.5\ \text{mN}$$

Use the right-hand rule for positive charges moving perpendicularly through a magnetic field to determine the direction of the magnetic force.

Your fingers should point to the right, your thumb should point into the page, and your palm should point upward. This shows that the magnetic force acts upward on the charges.

Therefore, the magnetic force acting on the conductor is 1.5 mN up.

40. A

Use the left-hand rule to detemine that the magnetic field is oriented toward the east. When the wire moves east, no current is induced in the wire because the motion is parallel to the magnetic field lines.

41. A

To find the correct magnetic field orientation for the moving electron, use the left-hand rule for electron flow. Your left thumb should point in the direction of the electron's movement into the page. Your fingers will then curl counterclockwise around the electron for the direction of the magnetic field. Therefore, the diagram that correctly shows the orientation of the magnetic field is diagram A.

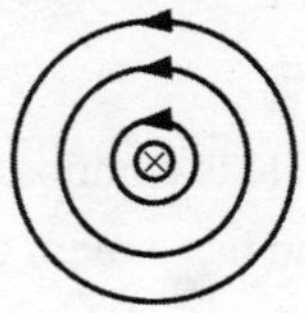

42. A

The force exerted on a moving charged particle within a magnetic field can be calculated using the formula $F_m = qvB\sin\theta$. When $\theta = 0°$, $F_m = 0$; therefore, when the cathode ray is parallel to the direction of the magnetic field, no magnetic force acts on the ray and no deflection of the ray occurs.

43. A

Using the third right hand rule (positive particle), the thumb points in the direction of the particle movement, the fingers point in direction of the magnetic field, and the palm points in the direction of the force on the particle.

Since the proton moves into the page and the magnetic field points to the right, the palm faces downward. This means that the proton will experience a force due to the magnetic field, directed vertically down.

44. A

Use the right-hand rule for protons (positively charged). The thumb will follow the proton's motion, the fingers will follow the magnetic field, and the palm will point in the direction of the force. The magnetic force acting on the proton will deflect it to the left.

45. 3214

$$F_m = qvB_{\perp}$$
$$= (1.6 \times 10^{-19}\ \text{C})(4.0 \times 10^{6}\ \text{m/s})(0.050\ \text{T})$$
$$= 3.2 \times 10^{-14}\ \text{N}$$

46. A

$$E_k = \frac{1}{2}mv^2$$

$$\Rightarrow v = \sqrt{\frac{2E_k}{m}}$$

$$= \sqrt{\frac{2(894\text{ eV})(1.60 \times 10^{-19}\text{ J/eV})}{1.67 \times 10^{-27}\text{ kg}}}$$

$$= 4.14 \times 10^5\text{ m/s}$$

47. D

An alpha particle is composed of two neutrons and two protons and has a mass of 6.64×10^{-27} kg and a charge of 3.20×10^{-19} C.

$$qV = \frac{1}{2}mv^2$$

$$\therefore v = \sqrt{\frac{2qV}{m}}$$

$$= \sqrt{\frac{2(3.20 \times 10^{-19}\text{ C})(3.25 \times 10^3\text{ V})}{6.64 \times 10^{-27}\text{ kg}}}$$

$$= 5.597 \times 10^5\text{ m/s}$$

$$F_m = qvB_\perp$$

$$= (3.20 \times 10^{-19}\text{ C})(5.597 \times 10^5\text{ m/s})(2.90 \times 10^{-1}\text{ T})$$

$$= 5.19 \times 10^{-14}\text{ N}$$

Use the right-hand rule for positive particles with the thumb pointing to the east and the fingers pointing north. The result is that the magnetic force on the alpha particle will be directed vertically up.

$\vec{F}_m = 5.19 \times 10^{-14}$ N up

48. C

The *aurora borealis* and *aurora australis* are caused by excited particles trapped within Earth's magnetic field, which is why the effects are most intense near Earth's magnetic poles, where the magnetic field lines converge as they exit the South Pole and enter the North Pole.

49. 0.17

$$F_m = F_e$$

$$qvB_\perp = |\vec{E}|q$$

$$\therefore B_\perp = \frac{|\vec{E}|}{v}$$

$$= \frac{5.0 \times 10^4\text{ N/C}}{2.9 \times 10^5\text{ m/s}}$$

$$= 0.172\text{ T} \cong 0.17\text{ T}$$

50. 3361

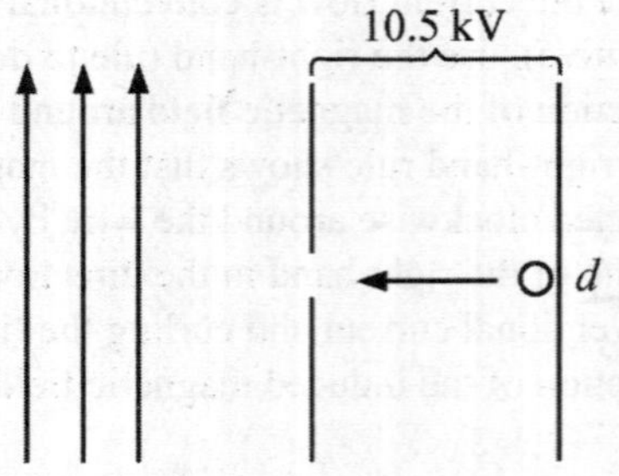

$\vec{B} = 6.22 \times 10^{-2}$T

The proton is accelerated as the electrical potential energy is converted into kinetic energy.

$$\sum E_i = \sum E_f$$

$$qV_i = \frac{1}{2}mv_f^2$$

$$v_f = \sqrt{\frac{2qV_i}{m}}$$

$$= \sqrt{\frac{2(3.20 \times 10^{-19}\text{ C})\left(10.5 \times 10^3 \frac{\text{J}}{\text{C}}\right)}{6.65 \times 10^{-27}\text{ kg}}}$$

$$= 1.005 \times 10^6\ \frac{\text{m}}{\text{s}}$$

As the rapidly moving proton enters the perpendicular magnetic field, it is forced into a circular path, with the magnetic force acting as the centripetal force. The magnetic force balances the centripetal force for a given radius at the calculated speed.

$$F_m = ma_c$$

$$B_\perp qv = \frac{mv^2}{r}$$

$$r = \frac{mv^2}{B_\perp qv} = \frac{mv}{B_\perp q}$$

$$= \frac{(6.65 \times 10^{-27}\text{ kg})(1.005 \times 10^6\text{ m/s})}{(6.22 \times 10^{-2}\text{ T})(3.20 \times 10^{-19}\text{ C})}$$

$$= 3.36 \times 10^{-1}\text{ m}$$

UNIT TEST — FORCES AND FIELDS

1. A piece of neutrally charged fur was rubbed against a neutral ebonite rod. The rod was then brought near a positively charged pith ball suspended from a silk thread. The pith ball was attracted to the ebonite rod. From this information, which of the following statements is **true**?
   A. The ebonite rod became positively charged by friction.
   B. Both the ebonite rod and the fur are negatively charged.
   C. The ebonite rod became negatively charged by induction.
   D. The fur would repel the pith ball if it were brought close to the pith ball.

Use the following information to answer the next question.

Cable TV sends it's signal on a coaxial cable that has a central copper wire. The central wire is surrounded by a layer of plastic that is then surrounded by a conducting cylinder of fine wire mesh. The outer layer of the cable is a durable plastic.

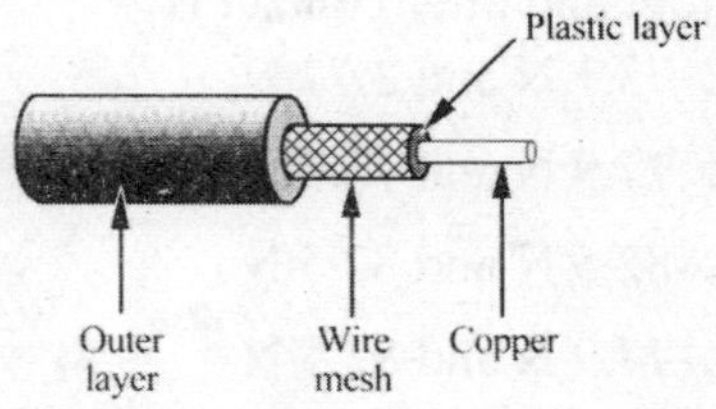

2. The wire mesh layer is necessary because the
   A. cable needs a rigid reinforcing layer
   B. electric force inside a conductor is not zero
   C. electrical signals need to be shielded from strong magnetic and electric fields
   D. electrical signals will travel better if they have two different transmitting wires

3. Coulomb was able to measure the electrical force acting between two charged spheres experimentally by precisely measuring
   A. the centre-to-centre distance separating the two spheres
   B. the amount of twist in the wire suspending his torsion balance
   C. the distance of separation between the charged spheres and the mass of each sphere
   D. the distance of separation between the charged spheres and the charges on each sphere

Use the following information to answer the next question.

Two identical metal spheres, one with a negative charge of 2.60×10^{-6} C and the other with a negative charge of 4.20×10^{-6} C, had a distance of 3.55 cm between their centres. The two spheres are then brought into momentary contact and then separated to the same distance as before.

4. The magnitude of the electrostatic force before and after contact is
   A. 73.1 N and 2.77 N
   B. 77.9 N and 77.9 N
   C. 82.5 N and 82.5 N
   D. 77.9 N and 82.5 N

Use the following information to answer the next question.

An experiment is carried out to test Coulomb's law. A small sphere, with a mass of 2.80 g, is hung from a thread near a charged van de Graaf generator, as shown. The sphere is touched to the generator and comes to rest.

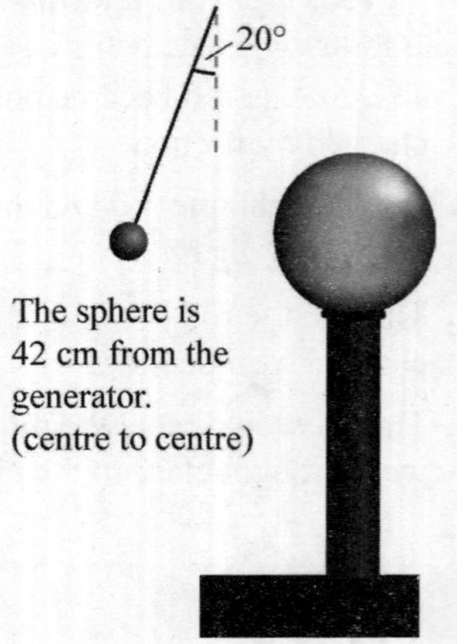

Written Response

5. If the small sphere has a charge of $+3.0 \times 10^{-8}$ C, what is the initial electric force acting on the sphere and the charge on the Van de Graaf generator?

   Analyse this situation by showing the forces acting on the sphere and use these forces to find the electric force acting on the sphere. (Be sure to use proper vector notation in your solution.)

Use the following information to answer the next question.

An experiment is carried out to test Coulomb's law. The force of repulsion between two charged spheres is measured at various distances between the spheres. Here are the results.

r(m)	$F\left(\times 10^{-4}\ \text{N}\right)$	$\frac{1}{r^2}\left(\frac{1}{\text{m}^2}\right)$
0.35	4.5	8.2
0.40	3.2	6.3
0.50	2.3	4.0
0.60	1.5	2.8
0.70	1.0	2.0

The charge on the fixed sphere is $+2.0 \times 10^{-7}$ C.

Written Response

6. Graphically show the force as a function of the reciprocal of the distance squared $\left(\frac{1}{r^2}\right)$. Find the slope of the graph and use the slope to find the charge on the moving sphere.

____

____

____

____

____

____

____

Use the following information to answer the next question.

Two point charges of equal magnitude, $+Q$ and $-Q$, are each placed at an equal distance, x, from point P, as shown below.

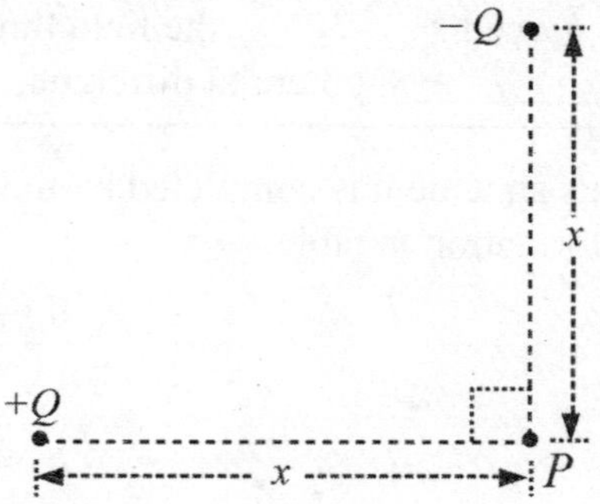

7. The direction of the resultant electric field at point P is

A. 

B. 

C. 

D. 

8. A 1.50×10^{-7} C charge experiences a 4.50×10^{-1} N force to the right. The electric field is

A. 3.00×10^{6} N/C right

B. 3.00×10^{6} N/C left

C. 3.33×10^{-7} N/C right

D. 3.33×10^{-7} N/C left

9. At some distance from a point charge, the electric field strength is 500 N/C. If the charge is tripled, what will be the field strength at twice the original separation?

A. 250 N/C **B.** 375 N/C

C. 750 N/C **D.** 1 000 N/C

Use the following information to answer the next question.

If 2.4×10^{-17} J of work is done on a 6.4×10^{-19} C charge to move it between two parallel charged plates, the charge will be moved ___*i*___ the field through a ___*ii*___ potential difference.

10. This statement is completed by the information in table

A.

i	*ii*
with	38 V

B.

i	*ii*
with	0.027 V

C.

i	*ii*
against	38 V

D.

i	*ii*
against	0.027 V

11. A pith ball with a mass of 3.0×10^{-4} kg is hanging from a light thread near a large charged sphere. The thread makes an angle of 40° with the vertical, showing a repulsive force. Which of the following force diagrams shows the forces acting on the pith ball?

A.

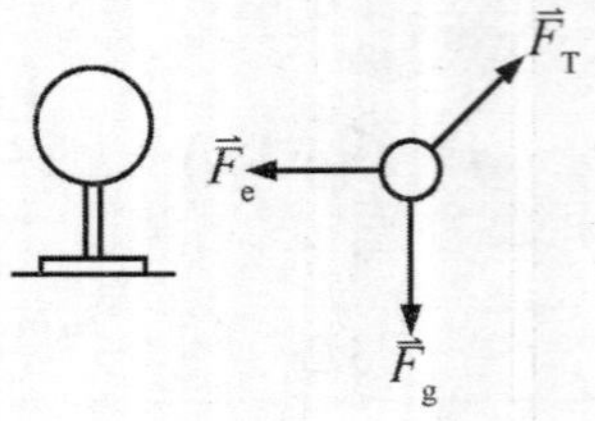

B.

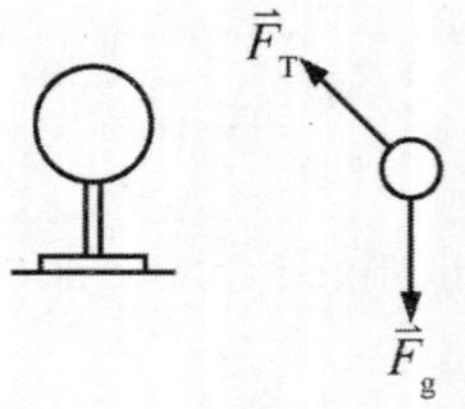

C.

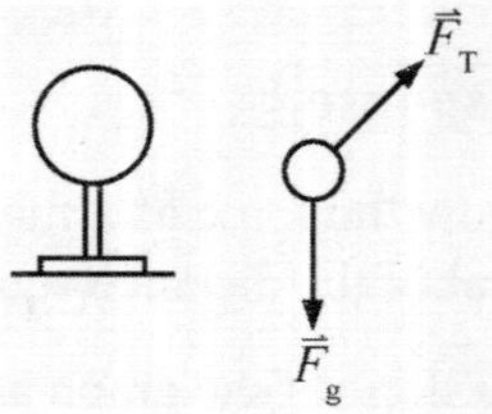

D.

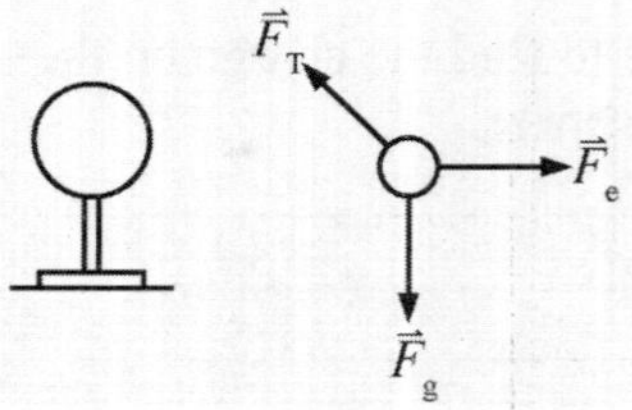

12. What is the electric current through a conductor 5.0 cm long when 12 C of charge pass the midpoint of this length of conductor in 3.0 s?

A. 4.0 A **B.** 2.4 A
C. 8.0 A **D.** 2.7 A

Use the following information to answer the next question.

An electron is held against a negative plate while a proton is held against a positive plate in a setup of two parallel charged plates. The two plates are 2.50 cm apart and charged by a potential difference of 4.50 kV.

Numerical Response

13. If the two elementary particles are released simultaneously, the proton will impact the negative plate with a momentum that is $a.bc \times 10^d$ times larger than the electron's momentum just before it collides with the positive plate. The value of *abcd* is __________.

14. During a lightning strike, 30 C of charge may move through a potential difference of 1.0×10^8 V in 2.0×10^{-2} seconds. The total energy released by this lightning bolt is

A. 3.0×10^9 J

B. 6.0×10^7 J

C. 3.3×10^6 J

D. 1.5×10^3 J

15. A 7.45×10^{-15} kg oil droplet is placed in an electric field of 2.10×10^5 N/C acting downward. If the oil drop has an excess charge of eight electrons, what is the acceleration experienced by the oil drop in the electric field?

A. 2.15×10^{17} m/s^2 down

B. 26.3 m/s^2 up

C. 9.81 m/s^2 down

D. 0 m/s^2

16. An electron travelling east passes perpendicularly through a magnetic field directed south. The directions of the magnetic and the gravitational forces acting on the electron respectively will be

A. up and down

B. down and down

C. due west and up

D. due north and down

17. A negative ion travels south through perpendicular electric and magnetic fields. The electric field is generated by two horizontal, parallel charged plates, and its direction is down. Assuming that the gravitational field is negligible, the direction of the magnetic field in order for no deflection to occur must be

A. north **B.** south

C. west **D.** east

Numerical Response

18. A 10 cm length of wire with a 4.0 A current running through it is suspended against gravity by a 0.95 T magnetic field. The wire has 6.0 cm of its length inside and perpendicular to the field. Expressed in scientific notation, the mass of the wire is $a.b \times 10^{-c}$ kg. What is the value of *abc*? __________

Use the following information to answer the next question.

In preparation for an experiment in which the charge-to-mass ratio of an electron will be measured, the electrons must be brought to a speed of 8.50×10^6 m/s. Then the beam will pass through a magnetic field of 1.50×10^{-4} T.

Written Response

19. Determine the required accelerating voltage and the expected radius of the circular motion of the electrons.

____

____

____

____

____

____

____

20. Two 0.50 m long wires are parallel to one another. The electrical current travelling through one wire is equal and opposite in direction to the current travelling through the other. The two wires will experience

A. a repulsion force because the magnetic fields between the wires are in the same direction

B. an attraction force because the magnetic fields between the two wires are in the same direction

C. a repulsion force because the magnetic fields between the two wires is weaker than the magnetic fields outside the two wires

D. an attraction force because the magnetic fields between the two wires is weaker than the magnetic fields outside the two wires

Use the following information to answer the next question.

Electrons are accelerated by a 450 V potential difference and sent through a magnetic field, as shown in the given diagram.

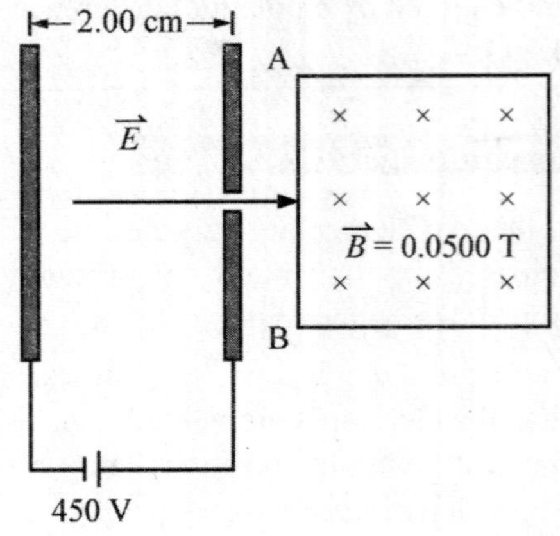

Written Response

21. Find the radius of circular motion of the electrons in the magnetic field.
Which location, A or B, is closest to the final position of the electrons? State all physics principles and formulas used.

____

____

____

____

____

____

____

Use the following information to answer the next question.

A compass is held above a wire in which a conventional current is flowing, as shown in the given diagram.

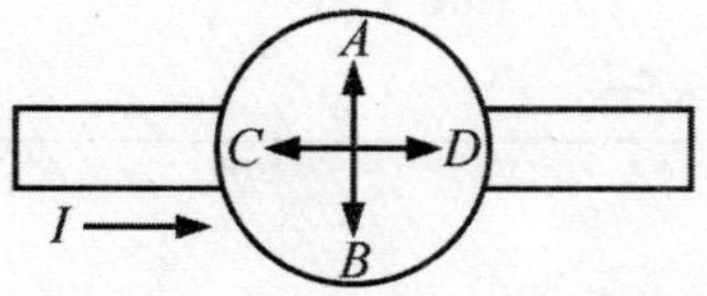

22. In which direction will the north pole of the compass point?

A. Direction A **B.** Direction B

C. Direction C **D.** Direction D

ANSWERS AND SOLUTIONS — UNIT TEST

1. D	6. WR	11. D	16. A	21. WR
2. C	7. C	12. A	17. D	22. B
3. B	8. A	13. 4281	18. 232	
4. D	9. B	14. A	19. WR	
5. WR	10. C	15. B	20. A	

1. D

The positive pithball is attracted to the ebonite rod, therefore the rod gained a negative charge from the fur. This would leave the fur with a net positive charge which would repel the pith ball.

2. C

External magnetic and electric fields will not enter a region enclosed by a metal conductor, so fine wire mesh is used to shield the central copper wire—and the signals it carries—from such external fields.

3. B

Coulomb understood that the the amount of twist in the wire that suspended the torsion balance was directly propotional to the force causing the wire to twist.

4. D

Determine the force between the spheres before contact.

$$F_e = \frac{kq_1q_2}{r^2}$$

$$= \frac{\left(8.99 \times 10^9 \frac{\text{N·m}^2}{\text{C}^2}\right)(-2.60 \times 10^{-6}\text{ C})(-4.20 \times 10^{-6}\text{ C})}{(3.55 \times 10^{-2}\text{m})^2}$$

$$= 77.9\text{ N}$$

The force before contact is positive, so it is repulsive.

Determine the force between the spheres after contact.

$$F_e = \frac{kq_1q_2}{r^2}$$

$$= \frac{\left(8.99 \times 10^9 \frac{\text{N·m}^2}{\text{C}^2}\right)\left(\frac{-2.60 \times 10^{-6}\text{ C} + (-4.20 \times 10^{-6}\text{ C})}{2}\right)^2}{(3.55 \times 10^{-2}\text{m})^2}$$

$$= 82.5\text{ N}$$

The force after contact is positive, so it is repulsive.

5. WR

Draw a free-body diagram to determine the forces on the small sphere.

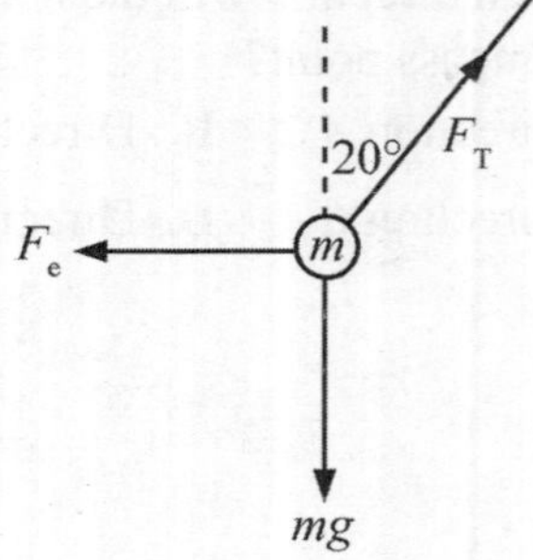

Use trignometry relations for right angle triangles to find the electric force.

$$\frac{F_e}{mg} = \tan 20°$$

$$F_e = mg\tan 20°$$
$$= (0.002\ 80\text{ kg})(9.81\text{ m/s}^2)\tan 20°$$
$$= 1.00 \times 10^{-2}\text{ N}$$

$$F_e = \frac{kq_1q_2}{r^2}$$

$$\Rightarrow q_2 = \frac{F_e r^2}{kq_1}$$

$$= \frac{(1.00 \times 10^{-2}\text{ N})(0.42\text{ m})^2}{(8.99 \times 10^9\text{ N·m}^2/\text{C}^2)(3.0 \times 10^{-8}\text{ C})}$$

$$= 6.54 \times 10^{-6}\text{ C}$$

$$\approx 6.5 \times 10^{-6}\text{ C}$$

6. WR

The graph of the data values should be as follows:

Coulomb's Law - Force is Function of $1/r^2$

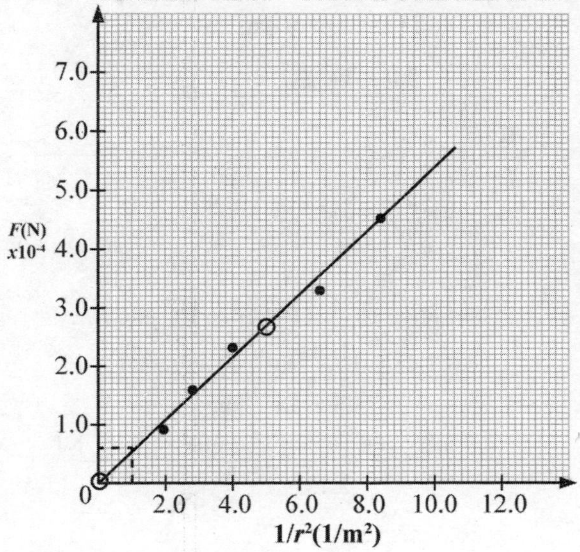

Calculate the slope using its formula.

$$\text{Slope} = \frac{\text{rise}}{\text{run}}$$

$$= \frac{(2.75 \times 10^{-4} - 0)\text{ N}}{(5 - 0)\frac{1}{\text{m}^2}}$$

$$= 5.5 \times 10^{-5}\text{ N·m}^2$$

Rewrite the formula for the electric force to identify the slope. The variables in the graph are F_e and $\left(\frac{1}{r^2}\right)$.

$$F_e = \frac{kq_1q_2}{r^2}$$

$$F_e = kq_1q_2\left(\frac{1}{r^2}\right)$$

$$y = mx + b$$

Therefore, the slope of the equation is kq_1q_2.

$$kq_1q_2 = \text{Slope}$$

$$\therefore q_1 = \frac{\text{Slope}}{kq_2}$$

$$= \frac{5.5 \times 10^{-5}\text{ N·m}^2}{\left(8.99 \times 10^9 \frac{\text{N·m}^2}{\text{C}^2}\right)(2.0 \times 10^{-7}\text{ C})}$$

$$= 3.1 \times 10^{-8}\text{ C}$$

The charge must be positive because the electric force is repulsive. Therefore, the charge on the moving sphere is $+3.1 \times 10^{-8}$ C.

7. C

The direction of an electric field is defined as the direction of the force acting on a positive test charge. A positive test charge would experience a repulsion force $\vec{F}_1$ due to $+Q$ and an attraction force $\vec{F}_2$ due to $-Q$. The vector sum of $\vec{F}_1$ and $\vec{F}_2$, added tip-to-tail, is answer C from the choices given. This is, by definition, the direction of the electric field.

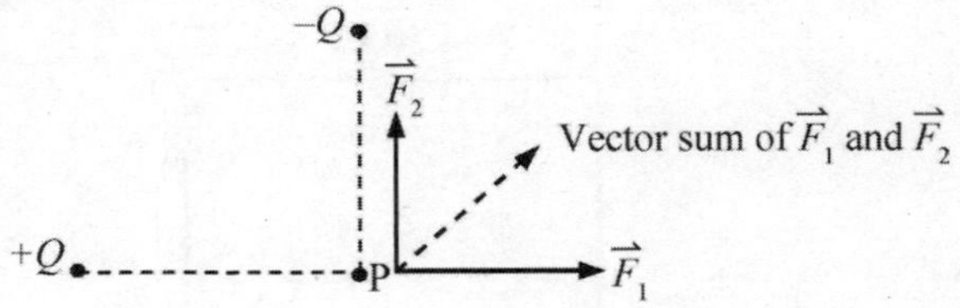

8. A

$$\vec{E} = \frac{\vec{F}_e}{q} = \frac{4.5 \times 10^{-1}\text{ N}}{1.5 \times 10^{-7}\text{ C}} = 3.00 \times 10^6\text{ N/C right}$$

Since q is positive, $\vec{F}_e$ and $\vec{E}$ are in the same direction.

9. B

$$\frac{E_{new}}{E_{old}} = \frac{\frac{kq_n}{r_n^2}}{\frac{kq_o}{r_o^2}} = \frac{\frac{q_n}{r_n^2}}{\frac{q_o}{r_o^2}} = \frac{\frac{3q_o}{(2r_o)^2}}{\frac{q_o}{r_o^2}} = \frac{3}{2^2} = \frac{3}{4}$$

$$E_{new} = \frac{3}{4}E_{old} = \frac{3}{4}(500\text{ N/C}) = 375\text{ N/C}$$

10. C

If 2.4×10^{-17} J of work is done, the potential energy of the charge increases by 2.4×10^{-17} J. Since the charge is positive, it must be moving toward the positive plate, which is opposite the field.

$$\Delta V = \frac{\Delta E_p}{q}$$

$$= \frac{2.4 \times 10^{-17}\text{ J}}{6.4 \times 10^{-19}\text{ C}}$$

$$= 37.5\text{ V}$$

$$\approx 38\text{ V}$$

11. D

There are three forces that add (as vectors) to zero because the pith ball is in static equilibrium. Only diagram D shows this with a repulsive electric force. If the electrical force were attractive as in diagram A, the pith ball would be attracted into the large charged sphere.

12. A

$$I = \frac{q}{t} = \frac{12\ \text{C}}{3.0\ \text{s}} = 4.0\ \text{A}$$

13. 4281

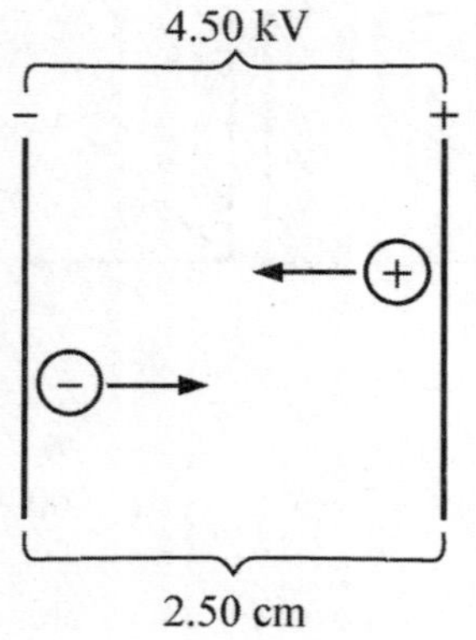

Electron

$$qV = \frac{1}{2}mv^2$$
$$v = \sqrt{\frac{2qV}{m}}$$
$$= \sqrt{\frac{2(1.6 \times 10^{-19}\ \text{C})(4.50 \times 10^3\text{V})}{9.11 \times 10^{-31}\ \text{kg}}}$$
$$= 3.976 \times 10^7 \text{m / s}$$
$$p_e = m_e v$$
$$= (9.11 \times 10^{-31}\ \text{kg})(3.976 \times 10^7\ \text{m / s})$$
$$= 3.62 \times 10^{-23}\ \text{kg·m / s}$$

Proton

$$v = \sqrt{\frac{2qV}{m}}$$
$$= \sqrt{\frac{2(1.60 \times 10^{-19}\ \text{C})(4.50 \times 10^3\ \text{V})}{1.67 \times 10^{-27}\ \text{kg}}}$$
$$= 9.286 \times 10^5\ \text{m/s}$$
$$p_p = m_p v$$
$$= (1.67 \times 10^{-27}\ \text{kg})(9.286 \times 10^5\ \text{m/s})$$
$$= 1.55 \times 10^{-21}\ \text{kg·m/s}$$

$$\frac{p_p}{p_e} = \frac{1.55 \times 10^{-21}}{3.62 \times 10^{-23}}$$
$$= 4.28 \times 10^1$$

14. A

Energy

$$\Delta E_p = \Delta Vq$$
$$= (1.0 \times 10^8\ \text{V})(30\ \text{C})$$
$$= 3.0 \times 10^9\ \text{J}$$

15. B

$$\vec{F}_{\text{net}} = \vec{F}_e + \vec{F}_g$$
$$m\vec{a} = q\vec{E} + m\vec{g}$$
$$\vec{a} = \frac{q\vec{E} + m\vec{g}}{m}$$
$$= \frac{8(1.60 \times 10^{-19}\ \text{C})(2.10 \times 10^5\ \text{N/C}) + (7.45 \times 10^{-15}\ \text{kg})(-9.81\ \text{m/s}^2)}{7.45 \times 10^{-15}\ \text{kg}}$$
$$= \frac{2.688 \times 10^{-13}\ \text{N} + (-7.308 \times 10^{-14}\ \text{N})}{7.45 \times 10^{-15}\ \text{kg}}$$
$$= 26.3\ \text{m/s}^2\ \text{up}$$

16. A

Use the left-hand rule for a negative charge moving in a perpendicular magnetic field. The fingers of your left hand should point south, and your thumb should point east in the direction of motion of the electron. This will result in tour palm facing up, so the magnetic force on the charge will be up. The gravitational forces on the electron will act down.

17. D

Since the electric field is down, the electric force on the negative ion will be directed up. In order for no deflection to occur, the magnetic force must be directed down. Using the left-hand rule for negative particles, the palm will be directed downward and the thumb will be directed south. This results in the fingers pointing east, so the magnetic field must be pointed east in order for no net deflection to occur.

18. 232

$$F_g = F_m$$
$$mg = B_\perp Il$$
$$\therefore m = \frac{B_\perp Il}{g}$$
$$= \frac{(0.95\ \text{T})(4.0\ \text{A})(0.060\ \text{m})}{9.81\ \text{m/s}^2}$$
$$= 0.0232\ \text{kg}$$
$$\cong 2.3 \times 10^{-2}\ \text{kg}$$

19. WR

Use the conservation of energy to find the speed of the electrons.

$$\sum E_i = \sum E_f$$

$$Vq = \frac{1}{2}mv^2$$

$$V = \frac{mv^2}{2q}$$

$$= \frac{(9.11 \times 10^{-31}\ \text{kg})(8.5 \times 10^6\ \text{m/s})^2}{2(1.6 \times 10^{-19}\ \text{C})}$$

$$= 206\ \text{V}$$

To find the radius of the circular path, an unbalanced force causes circular motion.

$$F_m = ma_c$$

$$qvB_\perp = \frac{mv^2}{r}$$

$$\therefore r = \frac{mv}{qB_\perp}$$

$$= \frac{(9.11 \times 10^{-31}\ \text{kg})(8.5 \times 10^6\ \text{m/s})}{1.60 \times 10^{-19}\ \text{C} \times 1.5 \times 10^{-4}\ \text{T}}$$

$$= 0.323\ \text{m or } 32.3\ \text{cm}$$

Therefore, the required accelerating voltage was 206 V, and the expected radius of the electron's circular motion was 32.3 cm.

20. A

Using either the left hand rule for moving negative charges or the right hand rule for moving positive charges we see that setting the thumb in the direction of current flow through the wire results in magnetic fields acting in the same direction from both wires. Like polarities repel and opposite polarities attract. Direction of $\vec{B}$ between the wires is the same, that is they have the same magnetic polarity and as a result a repulsive force will result between them.

21. WR

To find the radius of the circular motion, you must first find the speed of the electrons as they enter the magnetic field. You can find the speed of the electrons as they exit the electric field by using the principles of energy conservation or the principles of unbalances forces and accelerated motion.

Method 1—Conservation of Energy

Choose $E_p = 0$ at the positive plate.

$$\sum E_i = \sum E_f$$

$$Vq = \frac{1}{2}mv_f^2$$

$$v = \sqrt{\frac{2Vq}{m}}$$

$$= \sqrt{\frac{2(450\ \text{V})(1.60 \times 10^{-19}\ \text{C})}{9.11 \times 10^{-31}\ \text{kg}}}$$

$$= 1.257 \times 10^7\ \text{m/s}$$

Method 2—Unbalanced forces and accelerated motion

Assume that gravity is negligible.

$$F_{net} = (F_e)$$

$$ma = (Eq)$$

$$a = \frac{Vq}{dm}$$

$$= \frac{(450\ \text{V})(1.60 \times 10^{-19}\ \text{C})}{(0.0200\ \text{m})(9.11 \times 10^{-31}\ \text{kg})}$$

$$= 3.952 \times 10^{15}\ \text{m/s}^2$$

$$v_f^2 = v_i^2 + 2ad$$

$$v_f^2 = 0 + 2(3.952 \times 10^{15}\ \text{m/s}^2)(0.0200\ \text{m})$$

$$v_f = 1.257 \times 10^7\ \text{m/s}$$

Now, find the radius of the circular motion using the principles of unbalanced forces and circular motion.

$\vec{F}_m$ acts as the centripetal force.

$$F_m = ma_c = \frac{mv^2}{r}$$

$$qvB_\perp = \frac{mv^2}{r}$$

$$r = \frac{mv}{qB_\perp}$$

$$= \frac{(9.11 \times 10^{-31}\ \text{kg})(1.257 \times 10^7\ \text{m/s})}{(1.60 \times 10^{-19}\ \text{C})(0.0500\ \text{T})}$$

$$= 1.43 \times 10^{-3}\ \text{m}$$

$$= 1.43\ \text{mm}$$

Using the left-hand rule for electrons, your thumb will point in the direction of the electrons' velocity, and your fingers will point in the direction of the magnetic field. This will result in your palm pointing in the direction of the magnetic force. Your palm should point toward B, so the final position of the electrons is closest to B.

22. B

To solve this problem, use the right-hand rule for conventional current. Point your thumb in the direction of the current, and curl your fingers around the wire. Your fingers will point in the direction that the north pole of the compass will point. This is the direction that the magnetic field generated by the current will be pointing, in this case that means down towards *B*.

Electromagnetic Radiation

Electromagnetic Radiation

Table of Correlations

	Outcome	Practice Questions	Unit Test Questions	Practice Test 1	Practice Test 2
C1	explain the nature and behaviour of EMR, using the wave model				
30-C1.1k	*describe, qualitatively, how all accelerating charges produce EMR*	1		32	
30-C1.2k	*compare and contrast the constituents of the electromagnetic spectrum on the basis of frequency and wavelength*	2, 3		33	34
30-C1.3k	*explain the propagation of EMR in terms of perpendicular electric and magnetic fields that are varying with time and travelling away from their source at the speed of light*	4	1, 21		35
30-C1.4k	*explain, qualitatively, various methods of measuring the speed of EMR*	5, 6		34	
30-C1.5k	*calculate the speed of EMR, given data from a Michelson-type experiment*	7, 8, 9, 10	2	35	36
30-C1.6k	*describe, quantitatively, the phenomena of reflection and refraction, including total internal reflection*	11, 12, 13, 14	3, 4	36, 37, 38	37, 38
30-C1.7k	*describe, quantitatively, simple optical systems, consisting of only one component, for both lenses and curved mirrors*	15, 16, 17, 18	5	39, 40	39, 40
30-C1.8k	*describe, qualitatively, diffraction, interference and polarization*	19, 20, 21	6	41	
30-C1.9k	*describe, qualitatively, how the results of Young's double-slit experiment support the wave model of light*	22	7, 8		41
30-C1.10k	*solve double-slit and diffraction grating problems using,* $\lambda = \frac{xd}{nl}$, $\lambda = \frac{d \sin \theta}{n}$	23, 24, 25, 26	9, 10	42, 43	42, 43
30-C1.11k	*describe, qualitatively and quantitatively, how refraction supports the wave model of EMR, using* $\sin \frac{\theta_1}{\sin}\theta_2 = \frac{n_2}{n_1} = \frac{v_1}{v_2} = \frac{\lambda_1}{\lambda_2}$	27, 28	11		44
30-C1.12k	*compare and contrast the visible spectra produced by diffraction gratings and triangular prisms*	29	12, 22	44	45
C2	explain the photoelectric effect, using the quantum model				
30-C2.1k	*define the photon as a quantum of EMR and calculate its energy*	30, 31	13, 14		
30-C2.2k	*classify the regions of the electromagnetic spectrum by photon energy*	32, 33		45, 46, 47	46, 47
30-C2.3k	*describe the photoelectric effect in terms of the intensity and wavelength or frequency of the incident light and surface material*	34, 35, 36			48
30-C2.4k	*describe, quantitatively, photoelectric emission, using concepts related to the conservation of energy*	37, 38, 39	15	48	49
30-C2.5k	*describe the photoelectric effect as a phenomenon that supports the notion of the wave-particle duality of EMR*		16, 17		50
30-C2.6k	*explain, qualitatively and quantitatively, the Compton effect as another example of wave-particle duality, applying the laws of mechanics and of conservation of momentum and energy to photons.*	40, 41, 42, 43	18, 19, 20	49	51

30-C1.1k describe, qualitatively, how all accelerating charges produce EMR

Producing Electromagnetic Radiation

Electromagnetic radiation (EMR) is a self-sustaining chain of interactions between electric charges and magnetic fields.

EMR always begins with an accelerating charge. This can be an electron changing its position within an atom and emitting visible light, the entire atom or molecule vibrating or rotating and emitting infrared or microwave radiation, or electrons oscillating within a conductor and emitting radio waves.

EMR can be considered as two waves. One consisting of an electric field, and the other consisting of a magnetic field. Both waves have the same frequency travelling in phase together in perpendicular planes to form one EMR wave.

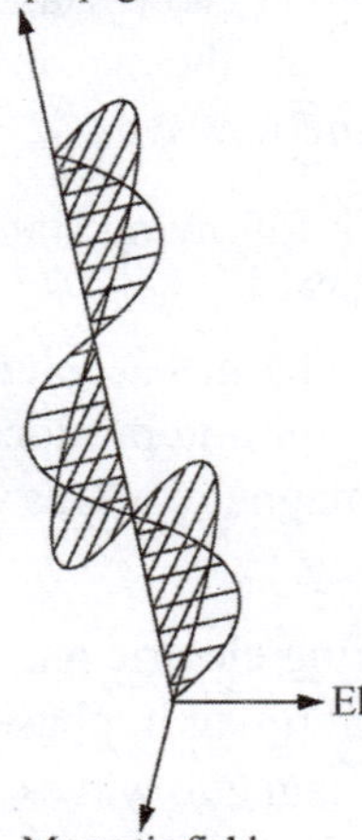

1. Electromagnetic radiation is always produced as a result of the
   - **A.** acceleration of electric charges
   - **B.** movement of electric charges
   - **C.** acceleration of masses
   - **D.** magnetic fields

30-C1.2k compare and contrast the constituents of the electromagnetic spectrum on the basis of frequency and wavelength

The Electromagnetic Spectrum

Different types of electromagnetic radiation differ from one another according to their frequencies, wavelengths, or energies. The frequency of EMR with a given energy never changes.
The corresponding wavelength is inversely related to the frequency.

$$\lambda \propto \frac{1}{f}$$

The proportionality constant is the speed of EMR, c.

$$\lambda = (c)\frac{1}{f}$$

This results in the universal wave equation as it applies to EMR.

$$c = f\lambda$$

The value of c is 3.00×10^8 m/s in vacuum (or air). This speed can be affected by the medium through which the EMR travels.

Placing the different forms of EMR in order of increasing frequencies or energies, or in order of decreasing wavelengths, results in the electromagnetic spectrum.

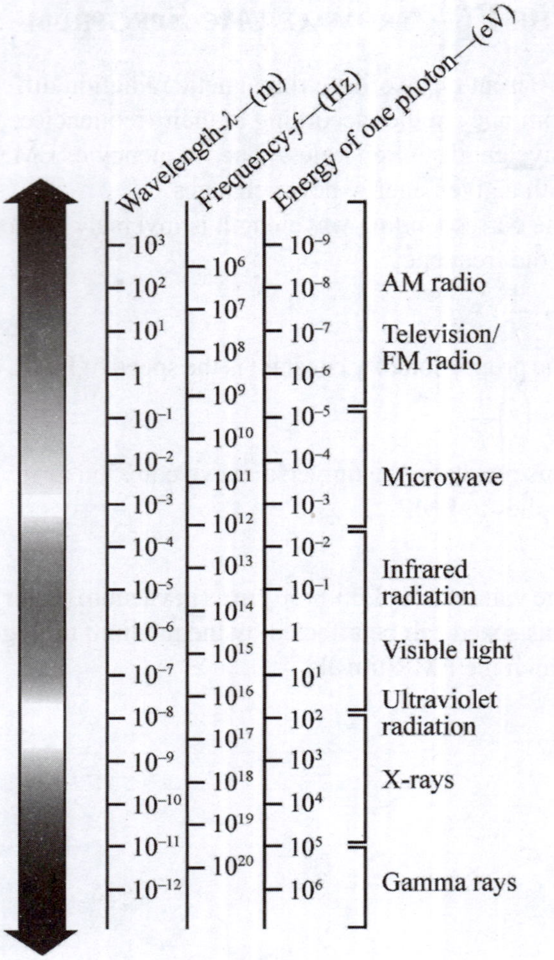

The electromagnetic spectrum

2. A pale blue light with a wavelength of 500 nm illuminates an ice rink. The period of the light is

   A. 1.67×10^{-15} s

   B. 8.33×10^{-13} s

   C. 6.00×10^{5} s

   D. 6.00×10^{14} s

3. Which of the following types of radiation has the longest period?

   A. Radio waves

   B. Infrared light

   C. Ultraviolet light

   D. Gamma radiation

30-C1.3k explain the propagation of EMR in terms of perpendicular electric and magnetic fields that are varying with time and travelling away from their source at the speed of light

WAVE MODEL OF EMR

James Maxwell explained that an accelerating charge produces an electric field that changes with time. This changing electric field produces a changing magnetic field, which in turn produces a changing electric field. These mutually induced electric and magnetic fields move away from the source of the accelerating charge at the speed of light. These changing electric and magnetic fields that travel as waves are the reason that the waves are called electromagnetic waves.

4. Which of the following statements about EMR is **false**?

   A. Electric charges accelerated in periodic motion produce electromagnetic waves with the same frequency.

   B. Oscillating electric and magnetic field that travel in phase comprise electromagnetic waves.

   C. Electromagnetic waves are produced whenever electric charges are accelerated.

   D. Electromagnetic waves always travel with a velocity of 3.00×10^{8} m/s.

30-C1.4k explain, qualitatively, various methods of measuring the speed of EMR

Measuring the Speed of EMR

The speed of EMR is so large that a successful measurement of this speed required either the accurate measurement of very large distances or of very small intervals of time.

Christian Huygens used Ole Roemer's data of the eclipse of Jupiter's moon, Io. He recognized that the delay in the predicted occurrence of Io's eclipse was caused by the increase in Earth's distance from Jupiter over 6 months and its decrease for the other 6 months of the year. Huygens used the diameter of Earth's orbit and a maximum eclipse delay of about 22 minutes to calculate a value for *c*.

This technique was reproduced on a smaller scale by Hippolyte Fizeau. Fizeau's apparatus used a rotating toothed wheel that permitted intermittent views of a beam of light that reflected off a distant mirror (about 8 km away). A small interval of time could be observed in this experiment, which was used to calculate the speed of light.

A.A. Michelson, building on Fizeau's design, used a rotating octagonal mirror to accomplish a similar phenomena. Using a rotation of the octagonal mirror with a known frequency, the time for $\frac{1}{8}$ of a rotation is easily determined. Michelson was able to adjust the frequency so that light travelled from the source to a distant fixed mirror and back (a round trip distance of 70 km) in the time the mirror rotated $\frac{1}{8}$ rotation. His measurement of *c* was very precise.

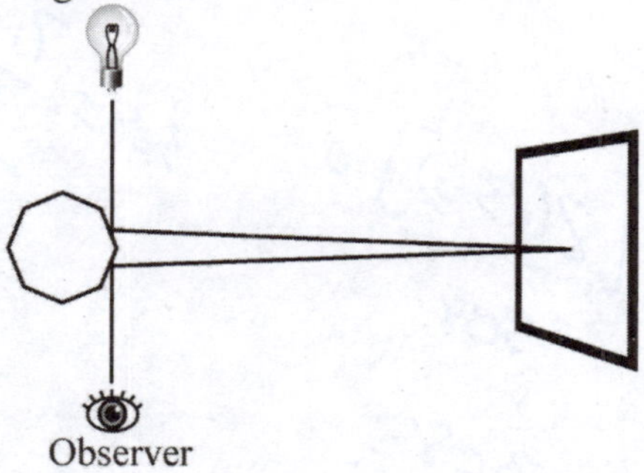

5. The period of one revolution of Io around Jupiter was known to be 42.5 h. Ole Roemer was able to calculate the speed of light by
   - **A.** using this period of 42.5 h and the diameter of Earth's orbit
   - **B.** concluding the actual period of Io changed depending on Earth's position relative to Jupiter's position
   - **C.** multiplying the time difference between longest and shortest periods (22 min) and the diameter of Earth's orbit
   - **D.** noticing the eclipse of Io by Jupiter was delayed when Earth was furthest from Jupiter and occurred sooner than expected when Earth was closest to Jupiter.

Written Response

6. Describe, using a labelled diagram, how A.A. Michelson determined the speed of light.

Had a rotating mirror and he new the frequency it took for the light to come and back

30-C1.5k calculate the speed of EMR, given data from a Michelson-type experiment

Calculating the Speed of Electromagnetic Radiation

The exact speed of electromagnetic radiation (EMR) is very difficult to calculate precisely. The less precise the measurements, the less precise the calculation is.

Example

In a Michelson-type experiment, an octagonal mirror rotates at 64 000 rpm. If the mirror rotates just $\frac{1}{4}$ of a complete rotation in the time a beam of light reflects off a rotating face onto a fixed mirror 35.0 km away and back again, calculate the speed of light.

$$f = (64\ 000\ \text{rpm})\left(\frac{1\ \text{min}}{60\ \text{s}}\right)$$

$$= 1.067 \times 10^3\ \text{Hz}$$

$$T = \frac{1}{f} = 9.375 \times 10^{-4}\ \text{s}$$

$$t = \frac{1}{4}T = 2.344 \times 10^{-4}\ \text{s}$$

$$c = \frac{d}{t} = \frac{2(35.0\ \text{km})(1\ 000\ \text{m/km})}{2.344 \times 10^{-4}\ \text{s}}$$

$$= 2.99 \times 10^8\ \text{m/s}$$

From these measurements, the speed of light is $2.99 \times 10^8\ \text{m/s}$.

---

7. In a Michelson-like experiment to determine the speed of light, a rotating octagonal mirror spins with a frequency of 750 Hz($T = 1.33 \times 10^{-3}$ s). The remote mirror is 24.8 km away. If the ray of light returns to the rotating mirror after it completes $\frac{1}{8}$ of one turn, the resulting calculated value for the speed of light in this experiment is

   A. 1.49×10^8 m/s

   B. 1.99×10^8 m/s

   C. 2.98×10^8 m/s

   D. 5.96×10^8 m/s

8. In an experiment that simulates Michelson's historic experiment, light from a source reflects off an eight-sided rotating mirror toward a fixed mirror and back again to the rotating mirror, before being observed in the telescope. If the distance from the rotating mirror to the fixed mirror is 23.5 km, and the rotating mirror makes just $\frac{1}{8}$ of a complete rotation in the time the light travels to the fixed mirror and back again, the frequency with which the mirror rotates is

   A. 9.97×10^1 Hz

   B. 7.98×10^2 Hz

   C. 1.25×10^3 Hz

   D. 6.38×10^3 Hz

9. In a Michelson-like experiment to determine the speed of light, a rotating hexagonal mirror is used. The distance from the rotating mirror to the fixed mirror is 35.7 km. The rotating mirror moves through an angle of 60.0° in the time it takes for a light pulse to reflect off the rotating mirror, onto the fixed mirror, and back again. The period of rotation of the mirror is

   A. 2.38×10^{-4} s

   B. 7.14×10^{-4} s

   C. 1.43×10^{-3} s

   D. 6.99×10^{-2} s

Numerical Response

10. In a Michelson-type experiment to determine the speed of light, an octagonal mirror rotating with a frequency of 720 Hz is used to reflect light onto a distant, fixed mirror and back again in the time the octagonal mirror makes $\frac{1}{8}$ rotation. If the accepted speed of light is used, the distance between the octagonal mirror and the fixed mirror is $a.bc \times 10^{d}$ m. The value of *abcd* is ________. (Record your answer as a four-digit number.)

30-C1.6k describe, quantitatively, the phenomena of reflection and refraction, including total internal reflection

Reflection

A ray of light will always obey the two laws of reflection:

1. The incident and reflected rays, as well as the normal line, all lie on the same plane.
2. The angle of incidence is equal to the angle of reflection.

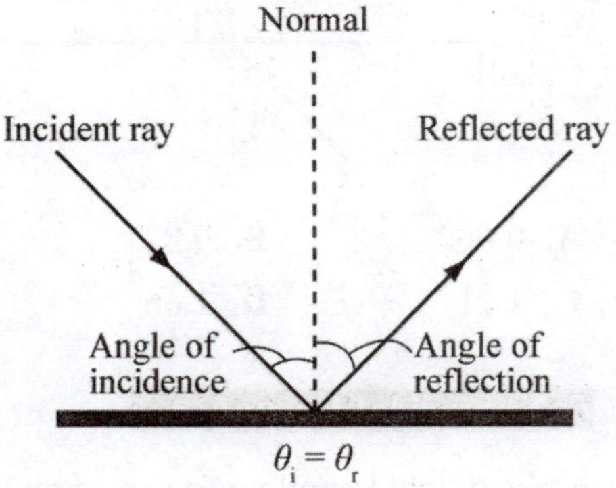

These angles are always measured between the ray and the normal to the surface at the point of incidence. The laws of reflection hold for plane mirrors and curved mirrors.

Snell's Law (The Law of Refraction)

When a ray of light travels from one medium into another, the ray will **refract**, or bend, toward the normal if the second medium is more optically dense. The light will also slow down and its wavelength will decrease. The absolute index of refraction of a substance is the factor by which light is slowed down as it enters into that substance. The absolute index of refraction assumes that the light travels from the air or a vacuum into the medium. The direction of the light, from vacuum into the medium, is important because it is how all refractive indices are defined.

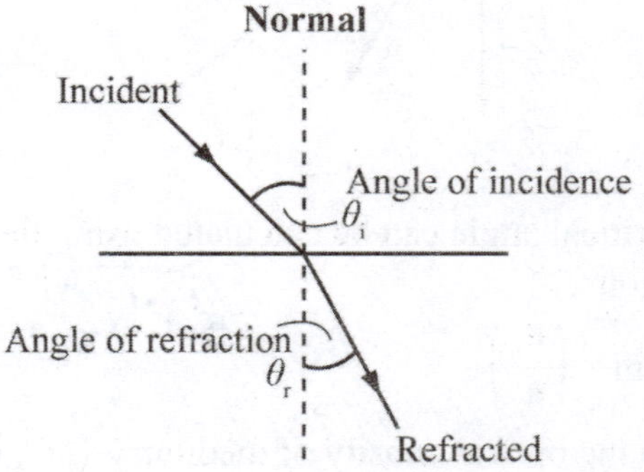

The absolute index of refraction for two substances can be used to calculate the angle of refraction for a ray of light as it passes from one substance into another.

The relative index of refraction of the second medium with respect to the first medium is given by Snell's Law.

$$\frac{\sin\theta_1}{\sin\theta_2} = \frac{v_1}{v_2} = \frac{\lambda_1}{\lambda_2} = \frac{n_2}{n_1}$$

where n_1 and n_2 are the absolute indices of refraction of medium 1 and 2, respectively.

Total Internal Reflection

When light travels from an optically denser medium into a less dense medium at a certain angle, the angle of refraction will be 90°. This incident angle is called the critical angle. Any incident angle greater than the critical angle will cause total internal reflection to occur at the interface between the two media. Again, the direction of the light is important.

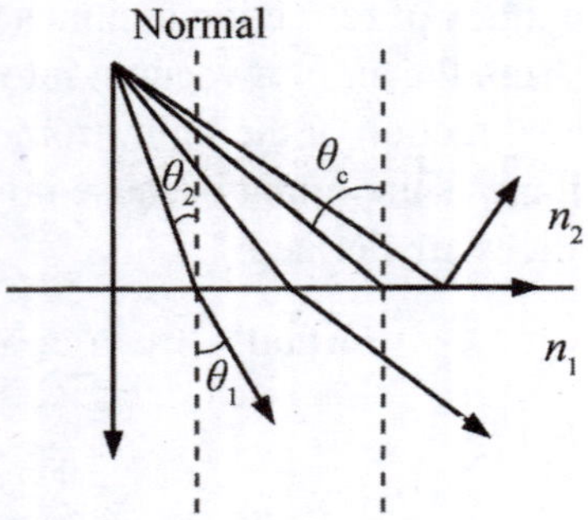

The critical angle can be calculated using the equation

$$\theta_c = \sin^{-1}\left(\frac{n_1}{n_2}\right)$$

where the optical density of medium 2 (i.e., water) must be greater than the optical density of medium 1 (i.e., air).

Use the following information to answer the next question.

Two plane mirrors make an angle of 120° with each other as shown in the diagram.

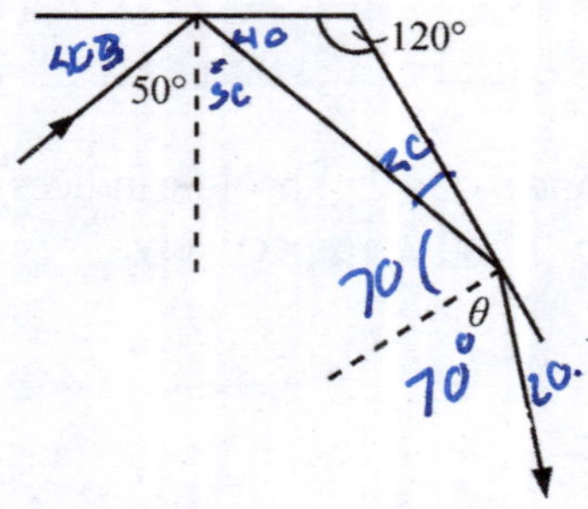

11. If a ray of light strikes the first mirror with an angle of incidence of 50°, the angle of reflection off the second mirror is

A. 20° **B.** 40°

C. 50° **D.** 70°

Use the following information to answer the next question.

A ray of light entered into an aquarium filled with water (n = 1.33) with an angle of incidence of 55.0° and then passed into a glass block (n = 1.55) resting at the bottom of the tank, as shown.

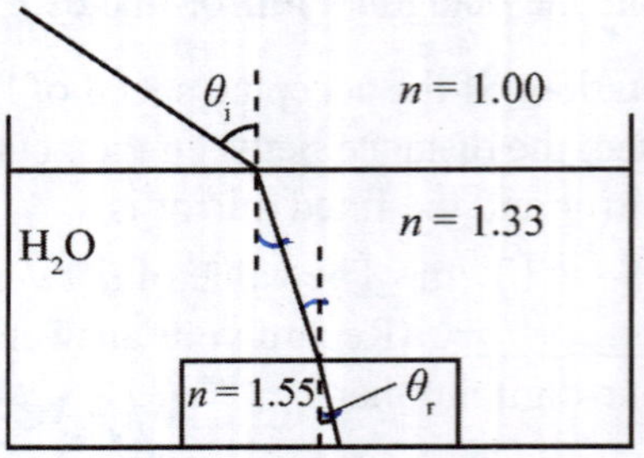

12. The angle of refraction measured in glass was

A. 31.9° **B.** 33.1°

C. 38.0° **D.** 55.0°

13. A light ray passes from a clear plastic block into air at an angle of incidence so that the angle of refraction is 90.0°. If the critical angle for this plastic is 37.0°, it's absolute index of refraction is

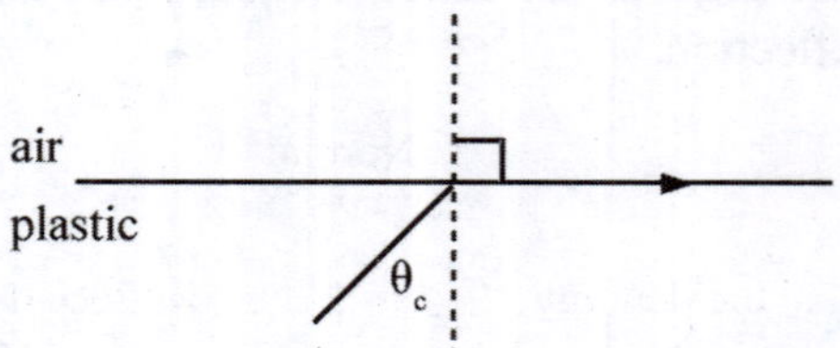

A. 0.602 **B.** 0.827

C. 1.21 **D.** 1.66

Numerical Response

14. A ray of light travelling from a crystal into air strikes the interface between the two materials at an angle of 20.0° and enters the air at an angle of 30.0°. The absolute index of refraction of the crystal is *a.bc*. The value of *a.bc* is ________.

30-C1.7k describe, quantitatively, simple optical systems, consisting of only one component, for both lenses and curved mirrors

Optics

To evaluate an optic system involving curved mirrors or thin lenses, use these formulas:

$$\frac{1}{f}=\frac{1}{d_o}+\frac{1}{d_i}$$

$$M=\frac{h_i}{h_o}=-\frac{d_i}{d_o}$$

where
f = focal length
d = distance of object and image
h = heights of object and image
M = magnification factor

Sign conventions must be observed in order to correctly apply these formulas to both concave (converging) and convex (diverging) mirror systems.

The sign conventions are as follows:

- Distances that are virtual (objects, images, or foci) are given negative numbers.
- Distances that are real (objects, images, or foci) are given positive numbers.

15. An object is located 30.0 cm in front of a converging mirror with a radius of curvature of 10.0 cm. If the object is 4.00 cm high, at what distance from the mirror will the image form, and is the image real or virtual?

A. 0.80 cm, real
B. 0.80 cm, virtual
C. 6.00 cm, real
D. 6.00 cm, virtual

16. A converging mirror has a focal length of 20.0 cm. Where should an object be placed in order for its virtual image to be twice as tall as its real height?

A. 5.00 cm **B.** 10.0 cm
C. 20.0 cm **D.** 30.0 cm

17. An 8.00 cm tall object stands 18.0 cm in front of a converging lens that has a focal length of 10.0 cm. What is the distance of the image to the lens and the nature of the image?

A. 6.43 cm, real, inverted
B. 6.43 cm, virtual, erect
C. 22.5 cm, real, inverted
D. 22.5 cm, virtual, erect

Numerical Response

18. A projector lens projects an image from a 6.35 cm wide LCD screen onto a screen 3.25 m wide. If the focal length of the projector lens is 13.8 cm, the screen must be __________ m from the projector.

30-C1.8k describe, qualitatively, diffraction, interference and polarization

Electromagnetic Radiation

Wave Diffraction, Interference, and Polarization

Diffraction refers to the spreading or bending of waves as the wave fronts move past the edge of a barrier or pass through a small opening. Diffraction varies inversely with the size of the opening, d, and directly with the wavelength. Diffracted waves often subsequently interfere with one another.

Constructive interference occurs where a crest or trough from one source meet a crest or trough from another source, respectively. Points of constructive interference can be connected by a line, called an antinodal line. Destructive interference occurs where a crest from one source meets a trough from another. A line connecting points of destructive interference is called a nodal line.

The relationships of the distance between the nodes or antinodes can be expressed by the following formula:

$$n\lambda = \frac{dx}{l} = d\sin\theta$$

where

n = an integer greater than zero that describes the location of the nth node, or $n + \frac{1}{2}$ for the nth antinode

x = the distance between the nodes or antinodes

d = the distance between the two sources

l = the distance from the sources to the screen

θ = the angle between the central antinode and the position on the interference pattern

The electric and magnetic fields of electromagnetic radiation (EMR) vibrate along an infinite number of planes, which are always perpendicular to each other and to the direction of propagation of the radiation. Thus, EMR travels as a transverse wave. Unlike other types of waves, transverse waves can be polarized.

Polarization is the process of filtering out the different planes of transverse waves. To polarize EMR, the vibration of the electric field is filtered to a single plane. For example, visible light is plane polarized when it reflects off a horizontal non-metallic surface because the electric field of the reflected light oscillates primarily along the horizontal plane.

Light can be polarized when it travels through certain natural crystals, such as tourmaline.

A Polaroid lens is made of plastic that is strained to cause its molecules to align. Light becomes plane polarized as it passes through the plastic.

Diffraction, interference, and polarization provided convincing empirical evidence to support the wave model of EMR.

Huygen's Principle

Huygen's principle states that every point on a wavefront behaves like a point source of circular wavefronts that are in phase and propagate out in front of the wave to produce a new wavefront.

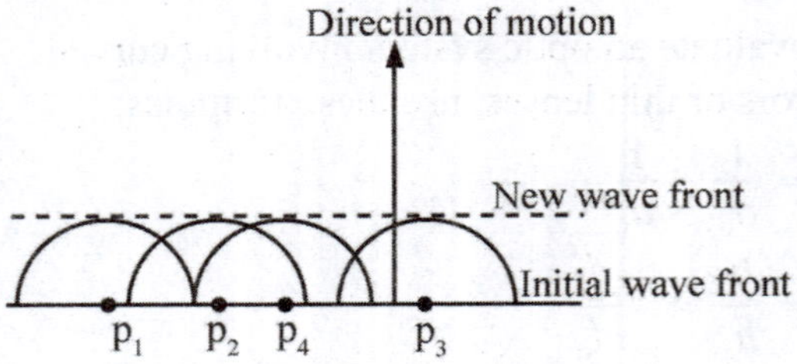

This principle can be used to explain the diffraction of a wave around an obstacle or through a small slit. It can also explain the propagation of a curved wave from a point source.

Use the following information to answer the next question.

i. A water wave wraps around the large wooden supports of a pier.
ii. A sound wave can be heard at one end of your home when the sound system is located at the other end.
iii. Microwaves are kept within the metallic wall of the oven.

19. Which of the given statements illustrates only the diffraction property of waves?

A. i **B.** iii

C. i and ii **D.** ii and iii

20. Light is plane polarized when

A. it is reflected off a flat surface

B. light is absorbed by certain substances

C. the electric field of the EMR is oriented along a single plane

D. the observer's head is tilted horizontally while looking at a part of the sky that is blue in colour

Written Response

21. Using Huygens's principle and appropriate diagrams, illustrate how a
   A. plane wave diffracts around an obstacle
   B. plane wave diffracts through a small opening
   C. curved wave front from a point source propagates over a short distance

30-C1.9k describe, qualitatively, how the results of Young's double-slit experiment support the wave model of light

YOUNG'S DOUBLE-SLIT EXPERIMENT

In 1803, Thomas Young published a paper in which he attempted to prove the wave nature of light once and for all. The experiment he performed was the now famous double-slit experiment.

In the double-slit experiment, light from a coherent source was directed at an opaque screen with a single slit in it. The ray of light emerging from this slit was used to illuminate two closely spaced slits in another screen. These two slits simulated two in-phase sources of light, and the two rays were then projected on a screen.

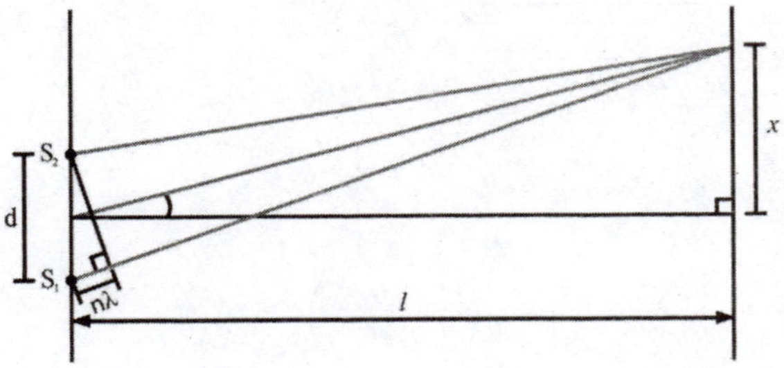

The interference pattern on the screen consisted of a bright central band with equally spaced dark bands (nodes) and bright bands (antinodes) on either side.

Directly in front of the slits, the light coming from each slit travels equal distances to the screen. The light was in phase at the slits and is therefore in phase at the screen. This marks the central antinode.

Off to one side, the wave from one slit has farther to go than from the other. This path difference ($n\lambda$ in the diagram) may cause constructive or destructive interference. If n is a whole number, an antinode results, and if n is "something plus $\frac{1}{2}$," a node results.

Young's experiment provided strong evidence in favour of the wave model of electromagnetic radiation (EMR). It was not until more than 100 years later that Albert Einstein finally disproved the wave nature of light for a more precise wave-particle duality.

Use the following information to answer the next question.

The following diagram illustrates the circular wave fronts generated by two point sources. Each line represents the crest of the wave front, and the midpoint between each line is the trough of the wave front.

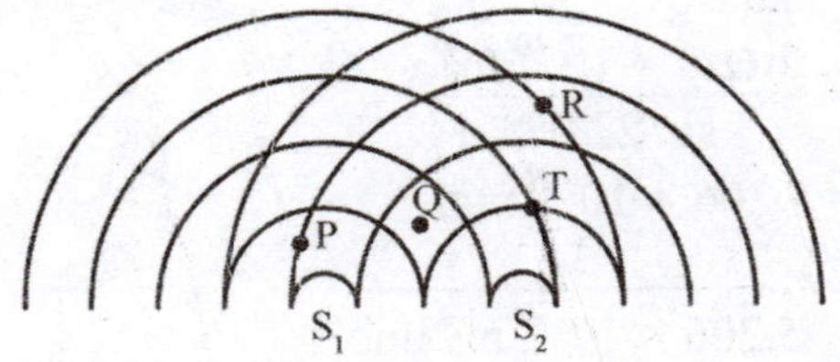

22. Which of the following statements about the diagram is **true**?
   A. Both sources are in phase, and point Q is a nodal point.
   B. Both sources are in phase, and points Q and T are antinodal points.
   C. Both sources are 180° out of phase, and point T is an antinodal point.
   D. Both sources are 90° out of phase, and points P and R are nodal points.

30-C1.10k solve double-slit and diffraction grating problems using, $\lambda = \dfrac{xd}{nl}$, $\lambda = \dfrac{d\sin\theta}{n}$

Diffraction Problems

Use the following formula to calculate problems involving double-slit or multi-slit apparatuses. A multi-slit apparatus is also referred to as a diffraction grating.

$$n\lambda = \frac{dx}{l} = d\sin\theta$$

The formula $n\lambda = \dfrac{dx}{l}$ is used only if angle θ is less than 10°. A diffraction grating has many slits very close together. If it has 500 lines/mm, the slits are separated by $\dfrac{1}{500}$ m or 2.00×10^{-6} m.

Example

When light with a wavelength of 650 nm is shone on a diffraction grating and the third-order maximum occurs at an angle of 22.0°, how many lines per centimetre have been ruled on the diffraction grating?

$$n\lambda = d\sin\theta$$

$$d = \frac{n\lambda}{\sin\theta}$$

$$= \frac{3(650 \times 10^{-9}\text{ m})}{\sin 22.0°}$$

$$= 5.206 \times 10^{-6}\text{ m}$$

$$= \frac{1}{5.206 \times 10^{-6}\text{ m/line}}$$

$$= 1.92 \times 10^{5}\text{ lines/m}$$

$$= 1.92 \times 10^{3}\text{ lines/cm}$$

---

23. A monochromatic yellow light with a wavelength of 610 nm shines through a double-slit apparatus. If the two slits are 0.450 mm apart, what is the angle between the central axis and the third antinode ($n = 3$)?

A. 0.233° **B.** 1.41°
C. 2.37° **D.** 2.86°

CHALLENGER QUESTION

24. Trace amounts of sodium in a flame create a characteristic yellow color in its centre, which creates two closely spaced emission lines with the wavelengths of 589.59 nm and 589.00 nm. A diffraction grating with 105 lines/mm is used to diffract the yellow light emitted from the burning sodium. If the distance from the midpoint of the two emission lines to the central maximum is 3.45 cm, the distance from diffraction grating to the screen must be

A. 1.63×10^{-3} m

B. 5.58×10^{-1} m

C. 1.63 m

D. 5.57 m

Numerical Response

25. A diffraction grating with 8.00×10^{3} lines per centimeter is illuminated with light from a hydrogen lamp. In the first-order spectrum, the angular separation between the 656 nm and 410 nm emission lines is ________ degrees. (Give your answer to three digits.)

Numerical Response

26. Light with a wavelength of 565 nm passes through two narrow slits. Adjacent maxima near the centre of the interference pattern are separated by 1.50°. The distance between the slits is $a.bc \times 10^{-d}$ m. The value of *abcd* is ________.

30-C1.11k describe, qualitatively and quantitatively, how refraction supports the wave model of EMR, using

$$\frac{\sin\theta_1}{\sin\theta_2} = \frac{n_2}{n_1} = \frac{v_1}{v_2} = \frac{\lambda_1}{\lambda_2}$$

Refraction and the Wave Model of Light

The law of refraction, also called Snell's law, can be used to find wavelengths and also speeds of electromagnetic radiation (EMR) in different media.

$$\frac{\sin\theta_1}{\sin\theta_2} = \frac{v_1}{v_2} = \frac{\lambda_1}{\lambda_2} = \frac{n_2}{n_1}$$

Note that the frequency of EMR does not change during refraction.

The wavelength of EMR changes with the medium through which it travels. Also, if the EMR enters the medium at an angle, it will changes direction. These are intrinsic properties that all waves exhibit when crossing a boundary into different media. Refraction of light is further evidence for the wave model of EMR.

Example

Red light with a wavelength of 730 nm passes from the air into glass, which has an index of refraction of 1.50. What is the wavelength of red light as it travels through the glass?

$$\frac{n_g}{n_a} = \frac{\lambda_a}{\lambda_g}$$

$$\lambda_g = \frac{\lambda_a}{n_g}$$

$$= \frac{730\text{ nm}}{1.50}$$

$$= 487\text{ nm}$$

---

27. A ray of red light from a laser has a wavelength of 630 nm and travels from air into diamond ($n = 2.42$). If the angle between the surface of the diamond crystal and the ray is 55.0°, the wavelength and the speed of the red light as it passes through the diamond is

A. 2.60×10^{-7} m, 1.24×10^{8} m/s

B. 5.10×10^{-7} m, 2.10×10^{8} m/s

C. 6.30×10^{-7} m, 1.24×10^{8} m/s

D. 1.52×10^{-6} m, 3.00×10^{8} m/s

Numerical Response

28. The wavelength of a microwave changes from 3.45 cm to 2.44 cm as it travels from air into a low density plastic. The index of refraction for the plastic with respect to the air is ________.

30-C1.12k compare and contrast the visible spectra produced by diffraction gratings and triangular prisms

The Visible Spectrum

The dispersion of white light, by either a prism or a diffraction grating, results in a continuous spectrum of the colours of light that white light is composed of.

However, while long wavelengths of light will diffract more than short wavelengths when they pass through a diffraction grating, the reverse is true for the refraction of light through the prism. When the white light passes through the prism, the long wavelengths will refract less. Therefore, the continuous spectra are indistinguishable except that the order that the colours of light appear in. The spectrum produced by a prism will be in exactly the opposite order of the spectrum produced by a diffraction grating.

29. A ray of white light is split into its composite colours by a diffraction grating, while another ray of white light is split by a glass prism. Which of the following statements is **false**?

A. Both the diffraction grating and the prism will create dispersion spectra from the white light.

B. The longer wavelengths in the white light both refract and diffract less than the shorter wavelengths.

C. Starting at the end closest to the original direction of the white light, the order of the spectral colours is red, orange, yellow, green, blue, indigo, and violet.

D. Starting at the end closest to the central antinode, the order of the spectral colours created by the diffraction grating is violet, indigo, blue, green, yellow, orange, and red.

30-C2.1k define the photon as a quantum of EMR and calculate its energy

30-C2.2k classify the regions of the electromagnetic spectrum by photon energy

Photoelectric Effect and the Photon Model

Prior to Planck's work on blackbody radiation, theories that were used to predict the behaviour of radiation could not be applied to electromagnetic radiation (EMR) beyond the ultraviolet. Planck introduced the idea of a quantum of energy in order to explain these blackbody radiation curves. To obtain an agreement with theory and experimental curves, Planck assumed that the energy of an oscillator could only have discrete values or fixed quantities.

He derived the following formula to explain these blackbody radiation curves:
$E = nhf$,

where E is the energy of the oscillator, n is a whole number, h is Planck's constant $(6.63 \times 10^{-34}\ \text{J}\cdot\text{s}$ or $4.14 \times 10^{-15}\ \text{eV}\cdot\text{s})$, and f is the frequency of the emitted radiation.

It was discovered later that the n in Planck's equation represented the number of packages (fixed quantity) of light being emitted. These packages were given the name photon.

Classifying Electromagnetic Radiation by Photon Energy

The energy of a photon is directly proportional to its frequency.
$E = hf = \dfrac{hc}{\lambda}$

Consequently, a photon of electromagnetic radiation (EMR) corresponding to a radio wave with a wavelength of 1.00 m is much less energetic than an X-ray photon with a wavelength of 1.00×10^{-11} m. In fact, the X-ray photon has an energy that is 1.00×10^{11} times larger than the radio photon.

Example

Characteristics of Three Types of EMR

1. Radio wave $f = 80.0$ MHz
2. Green light $\lambda = 550$ nm
3. X-ray $f = 6.00 \times 10^{18}$ Hz

Determine which of the given photons has the greatest energy (in eV).

Solution

Calculate the energy of each photon type.

1. $E = hf = 4.14 \times 10^{-15}\ \text{eV·s}(80 \times 10^{6}\ \text{Hz})$
   $= 3.31 \times 10^{-7}$ eV
2. $E = \dfrac{hc}{\lambda} = \dfrac{4.14 \times 10^{-15}\ \text{eV·s}(3 \times 10^{8}\ \text{m/s})}{5.5 \times 10^{-7}\ \text{m}}$
   $= 2.26$ eV
3. $E = hf = 4.14 \times 10^{-15}\ \text{eV·s}(6 \times 10^{18}\ \text{Hz})$
   $= 24.8$ keV

The X-ray photon has a much greater energy than the other two photons. The X-ray is the most dangerous of the three types of EMR.

CHALLENGER QUESTION

Use the following information to answer the next question.

Fusion Research

Interest in nuclear fusion is growing because of the amount of energy available from nuclear reactions. A major difficulty in producing a nuclear fusion reaction is that the nuclei must possess a large amount of kinetic energy in order for nuclei to fuse. Under most circumstances, 0.25 MeV per nucleus is sufficient. At such high energies, the nuclear fuel is a plasma. The average kinetic energy of a nucleus within a plasma can be found using

$$E_k = \frac{3}{2}bT$$

where T is the temperature of the plasma (K), and b is a physical constant equal to 1.4×10^{-23} J/K.

One method for obtaining the temperatures necessary for fusion is to use a high-intensity laser to heat a small cluster of nuclei. One such laser emits a 1.0×10^{15} W pulse of ultraviolet radiation that lasts for 1.0×10^{-12} s. The wavelength of this laser is 280 nm.

30. From the given information, what is the energy of a single photon of the ultraviolet laser used to heat the small nuclei cluster?

A. 7.1×10^{-19} J

B. 1.9×10^{-28} J

C. 7.1×10^{-28} J

D. 1.9×10^{-40} J

Use the following information to answer the next question.

In a medical procedure, a patient may be injected with a radioactive isotope. As the isotope decays, the gamma ray emissions are detected, and a computer builds images of the patient's blood flow and organs.

A radioactive isotope commonly used in this procedure is technetium-99. This isotope has a half-life of 6.00 h, and it decays to a stable isotope by gamma ray emission.

31. A photon of gamma radiation emitted by the radioactive decay of technetium-99 has 3.85 MeV of energy. This radiation has a wavelength of

A. 5.17×10^{-16} m

B. 3.23×10^{-13} m

C. 3.10×10^{4} m

D. 9.29×10^{12} m

Use the following information to answer the next question.

The different colours seen in exploding fireworks are produced using different elements.

Element	Predominant Colour
Strontium	Red
Barium	Green
Copper	Blue-Green
Sodium	Yellow-Orange

32. Given the information above, the element that emits the lowest energy photon of visible light is

A. strontium **B.** barium

C. copper **D.** sodium

Numerical Response

33. A beam from a laser has a wavelength of 633 nm and an intensity of 3.0 mW. The number of photons that are emitted by this device per second is $a.b \times 10^{cd}$. The value of *abcd* is ________. (Record your answer as a four-digit number.)

30-C2.3k describe the photoelectric effect in terms of the intensity and wavelength or frequency of the incident light and surface material

30-C2.4k describe, quantitatively, photoelectric emission, using concepts related to the conservation of energy

DESCRIBING THE PHOTOELECTRIC EFFECT

The photoelectric effect occurs when a metal surface, called a photoelectric surface, in a photoelectric cell is exposed to light. When light shines on the surface, a current begins to flow in the circuit connected to the photoelectric cell. This is because electrons are ejected from the surface if the light has a high enough frequency. Electrons ejected during the photoelectric effect are often called photoelectrons.

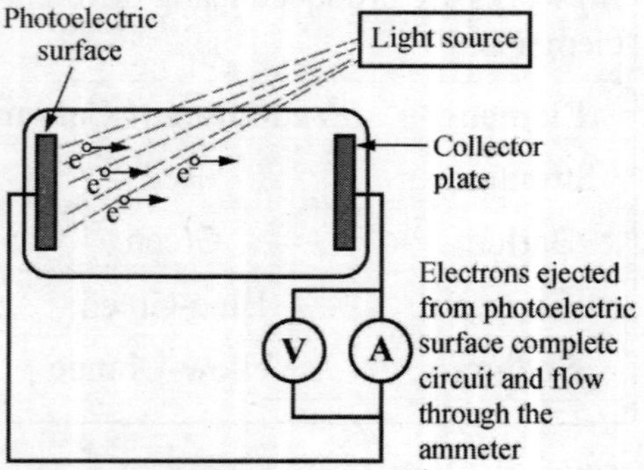

A photoelectric cell

The following important observations have been made during experiments investigating the photoelectric effect.

- The energy of the photoelectrons increased as the frequency of incident light increased.
- The energy of the photoelectrons increased as the wavelength of the incident light decreased.
- Each material tested had a minimum frequency (f_0) that was required before any photoelectrons were emitted. This is called the threshold frequency of a material. For example, sodium metal has a threshold frequency of 5.5×10^{14} Hz (in the visible range), and aluminum metal has threshold frequency of 9.9×10^{14} Hz (in the ultraviolet range).
- An increase in the intensity (brightness) of incident light had no effect if the frequency of the incident light was less than the threshold frequency.
- If the intensity was increased for frequencies of light greater than the threshold frequency, the photoelectric current increased, as measured by the ammeter.
- Photoelectrons were emitted almost instantly when the incident light struck the surface.

The photoelectric effect is very important in the history of physics because a new theory of light had to be proposed to explain these results. It also led to accurate experimental values of Planck's constant, and to the invention of photoelectric cells for generating electrical power.

EINSTEIN'S EXPLANATION OF THE PHOTOELECTRIC EFFECT

Albert Einstein first proposed that light came in bundles, which he called photons. He also proposed that a single photon would transfer all of its energy to a single electron, but that the transfer followed the law of conservation of energy. For the photon to knock an electron out of a material, it must have a sufficient amount of energy. Einstein suggested that the energy of a photon could be determined using Planck's formula:
$E = hf$

The minimum amount of work (energy) required to remove an electron from a photoelectric surface is called the work function, W. The energy carried by a photon of the threshold frequency, f_0, is just large enough to do so:

$W = hf_0$

Any additional energy possessed by the incoming photon converts into the kinetic energy of the emitted photoelectron. Thus, the energy of the incident photon is equal to the sum of the maximum kinetic energy of the emitted photoelectron and the work function of the material:

$hf = E_{\text{k}_{\text{max}}} + W$

To measure the kinetic energy of the photoelectrons, the collector plate is made negative by providing a voltage, or potential difference, to the photoelectric cell. The potential difference that prevents the photoelectrons from reaching the collector plate is the voltage needed to stop the fastest of the photoelectrons. This is called the stopping voltage (V_{stop}).

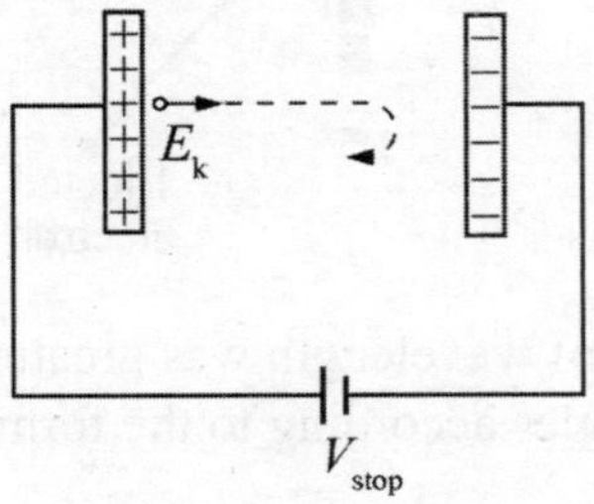

The stopping voltage is determined using the principles of energy conservation.

$$E_{\text{k}} \Rightarrow E_{\text{p}}$$

$$\frac{1}{2}mv^2 = qV_{\text{stop}}$$

34. A photon that approached a photoelectric cell has X units of energy. Each of the surface electrons in the photoelectric surface were held with a binding energy of Y units of energy. The interaction releases an electron with a kinetic energy of Z units of energy. Which of the following mathematical statements shows this interaction?

A. $Z = X + Y$ **B.** $Z = X - Y$

C. $X = Y - Z$ **D.** $X = Y - X$

Use the following information to answer the next question.

Four Observations about Electromagnetic Radiation

I. The number of electrons released by a metal is proportional to the intensity of the electromagnetic radiation (EMR) incident on the surface, given that the EMR is above the threshold frequency.

II. The kinetic energy of ejected electrons is dependent only upon the frequency of the EMR used, not upon its intensity.

III. Below the threshold frequency, no electrons are ejected, no matter the intensity of the EMR.

IV. Every surface has a different threshold frequency.

35. Which of the given observations can be explained using a classical wave model of EMR?

A. I and III **B.** I and IV

C. II and III **D.** II and IV

Numerical Response

36. A copper surface has a work function of 4.45 eV. The longest wavelength EMR that will successfully emit electrons from the surface of this metal is $a.bc \times 10^{-d}$ m. The value of $abcd$ is __________. (Record your answer as a four-digit number.)

Use the following information to answer the next question.

While designing a photocell, which will operate using the photoelectric effect with visible light, Haseeb had to select a photoelectric surface from one of the following four materials. The work function for each material was provided.

Material Name	Work Function (eV)
Barium	2.5
Tantalum	4.2
Tungsten	4.5
Aluminum	4.2

37. Which of the given materials would **most likely** work in a photocell for visible light (λ_{red} = 750 nm, λ_{blue} = 450 nm)?

A. Barium (2.5 eV)

B. Tantalum (4.2 eV)

C. Tungsten (4.5 eV)

D. Aluminum (4.2 eV)

38. If electromagnetic radiation (EMR) with a frequency of 3.45×10^{15} Hz is directed at a metallic surface with a work function of 2.31 eV, the maximum kinetic energy of the emitted photoelectrons is

A. 3.70×10^{-19} J

B. 1.92×10^{-18} J

C. 14.0 eV

D. 18.0 eV

Numerical Response

39. A photoelectric surface with a threshold frequency of 3.86×10^{14} Hz emits photoelectrons when illuminated with visible light. If the maximum speed of the emitted electrons was 3.50×10^{5} m/s, the stopping voltage was $a.bc \times 10^{-d}$ V. The value of *abcd* is __________.

30-C2.6k explain, qualitatively and quantitatively, the Compton effect as another example of wave-particle duality, applying the laws of mechanics and of conservation of momentum and energy to photons.

The Compton Effect

Arthur Compton studied collisions between incident X-ray or gamma ray photons with electrons in a target material. He found the scattered photons had longer wavelengths, which indicated the photons lost energy in the collision. Compton was able to show that this lost energy was transferred to the emitted electrons and that the conservation of energy was evident.

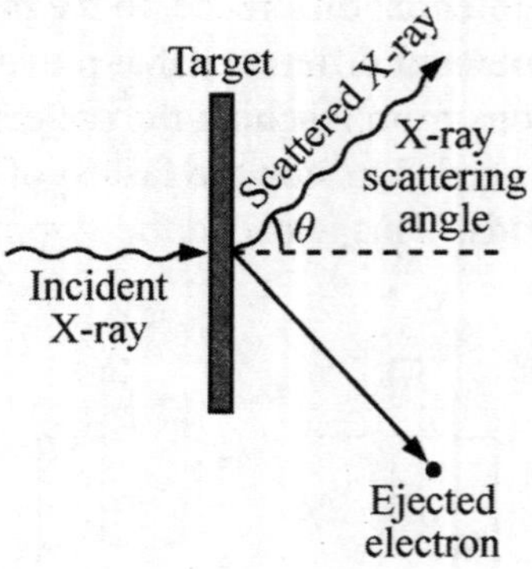

The change of wavelength was greater for larger scattered angles according to the formula

$\Delta\lambda = \frac{h}{mc}(1 - \cos\theta)$, where $\Delta\lambda$ is the change in wavelength, h is Planck's constant in joule seconds (J·s), m is the electron's mass, θ is the X-ray scattering angle, and c is the speed of light.

More significantly, Compton confirmed the conservation of momentum occurred as long as the photon's momentum could be defined. Recall that since photons have no rest mass, their momentum cannot be defined using the formula $\vec{p} = m\vec{v}$.

Compton defined the magnitude of the photon's momentum using this formula:

$$p = \frac{h}{\lambda} = \frac{hf}{c}$$

Compton's theory was further evidence supporting the particle nature of electromagnetic radiation (EMR). Since photons are able to collide with electrons, photons clearly possess momentum, a property of particles.

40. The magnitude of the momentum of an X-ray photon with a frequency of 6.56×10^{19} Hz is

A. 1.01×10^{-43} kg·m/s

B. 1.45×10^{-22} kg·m/s

C. 2.21×10^{-22} kg·m/s

D. 3.03×10^{-43} kg·m/s

Use the following information to answer the next question.

> An X-ray with a wavelength of 4.60×10^{-11} m is incident upon a target. A scattered X-ray with 4.80×10^{-11} m is observed. The scattered angle is ___*i*___ degrees, and the loss of energy is ___*ii*___ J.

41. This statement is completed by the information in table

A.

i	*ii*
79.9°	1.80×10^{-16} J

B.

i	*ii*
34.5°	1.80×10^{-16} J

C.

i	*ii*
79.9°	9.95×10^{-14} J

D.

i	*ii*
34.5°	9.95×10^{-14} J

42. Which of the following statements does **not** describe Compton's conclusions based on his scattering data?

A. The scattered X-ray's momentum and energy both changed as predicted, just like if a small particle had collided elastically with an electron.

B. The vector sum of the momenta of the scattered electron and the scattered X-ray could not be determined.

C. The longer wavelength of the scattered X-ray indicated that the X-ray had lost energy in the collision.

D. The momentum of the scattered X-ray was less than the momentum of the incident X-ray.

Numerical Response

43. In a Compton scattering experiment, an incident X-ray is scattered at an angle of 70.0°. Expressed in scientific notation, the change in wavelength is $a.bc \times 10^{-de}$ m. The value of *abcde* is __________. (Record your answer as a five-digit number.)

30-C2.5k describe the photoelectric effect as a phenomenon that supports the notion of the wave-particle duality of EMR

Wave-Particle Duality of EMR

At the beginning of the twentieth century, physicists believed that EMR travelled as a wave. However, Einstein's explanation of the photoelectric effect proposed a particle model of light.

Most scientists now accept that both models are needed to explain all the properties that light exhibits. This is known as the wave–particle model of light.

Answers and Solutions
Electromagnetic Radiation

1. A	**10. 2604**	**19. A**	**28. 1.41**	**37. A**
2. A	**11. D**	**20. C**	**29. B**	**38. B**
3. A	**12. A**	**21. WR**	**30. A**	**39. 3491**
4. D	**13. D**	**22. B**	**31. B**	**40. B**
5. D	**14. 1.46**	**23. A**	**32. A**	**41. A**
6. WR	**15. C**	**24. B**	**33. 9515**	**42. B**
7. C	**16. B**	**25. 12.5**	**34. B**	**43. 16012**
8. B	**17. C**	**26. 2165**	**35. B**	
9. C	**18. 6.92**	**27. A**	**36. 2797**	

1. A

Accelerating electric charges create changing electric and magnetic fields. This becomes the source of an electromagnetic wave. For example, the accelerating electrons in a radio antenna produce the radio waves that can travel great distances.

2. A

Recall that the period can be found using $T = \frac{1}{f}$

$c = f\lambda$

$\frac{1}{f} = \frac{\lambda}{c}$

$T = \frac{\lambda}{c}$

$T = \frac{500 \times 10^{-9}\ \text{m}}{3 \times 10^{8}\ \text{m/s}}$

$T = 1.67 \times 10^{-15}\ \text{s}$

3. A

Since $T = \frac{1}{f}$, period will get longer as frequency gets lower. On the EMR spectrum, the form of EMR with the lowest frequency is radio waves. Thus they have the longest period.

4. D

EMR travels at 3.00×10^{8} m/s (c) in a vacuum. EMR travels more slowly in more optically dense materials, such as water or glass. Note that the speed of light in air is generally taken to be the same as that in a vacuum although there would be some slowing of light since air is more optically dense than a vacuum.

5. D

Roemer was able to deduce that the differences in observed times of eclipses of Jupiter's moon Io was due to light taking some time to reach us from this distant event. This demonstrates that light has a finite velocity.

6. WR

Michelson was able to determine the speed of light quite precisely by focusing a very intense light source at a rotating octagonal mirror, which reflected the beam at a distant fixed mirror 35.7 km away as shown.

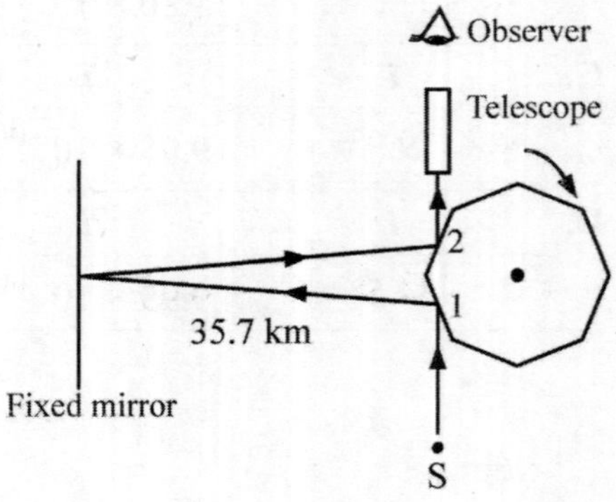

Assume that the octagonal mirror makes $\frac{1}{8}$ of a rotation in the time that light reflects off a face at position 1, travels to the fixed mirror and back to the octagonal mirror, just in time for the light to reflect off the same face that has just moved into position 2. The period of time that passes as the mirror makes $\frac{1}{8}$ of a rotation can be used to determine the speed of light as it travelled the distance from the rotating mirror to the fixed mirror and back.

$$v = \frac{d}{t} = \frac{2(35.7\text{ km})}{\text{time for } \frac{1}{8} \text{ rotation}}$$

If the frequency of the rotation is known, then

$$T = \frac{1}{f}$$

The time required is merely $\frac{1}{8}T$.

$$\therefore c = \frac{2(35.7\text{ km})}{\frac{1}{8}T}$$

7. C

$$c = \frac{d}{t} = \frac{\text{distance to fixed mirror and back}}{\text{time for } \frac{1}{8} \text{ rotation}}$$

$$= \frac{2(24\ 800\text{ m})}{\frac{1}{8}(1.33 \times 10^{-3}\text{ s})}$$

$$= 2.98 \times 10^{8}\text{ m/s}$$

8. B

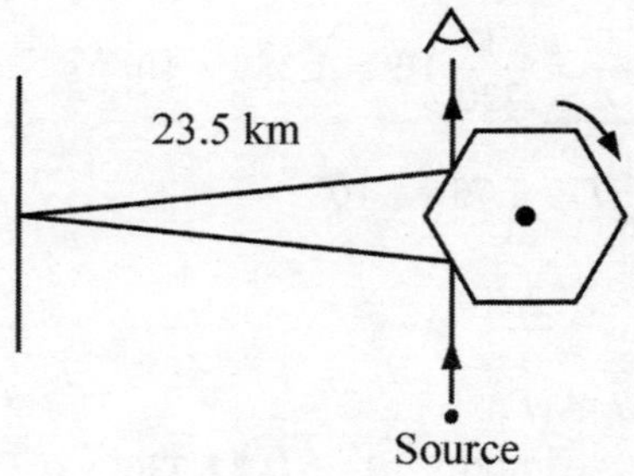

$$c = \frac{d}{t}$$

$$\Rightarrow t = \frac{d}{c} = \frac{2(23.5 \times 10^{3}\text{ m})}{3.00 \times 10^{8}\text{ m/s}}$$

$$= 1.5667 \times 10^{-4}\text{ s}$$

$$\therefore \frac{1}{8}T = 1.5667 \times 10^{-4}\text{ s}$$

$$T = 1.253 \times 10^{-3}\text{ s}$$

$$f = \frac{1}{T}$$

$$= \frac{1}{1.253 \times 10^{-3}\text{ s}}$$

$$= 7.98 \times 10^{2}\text{ Hz}$$

9. C

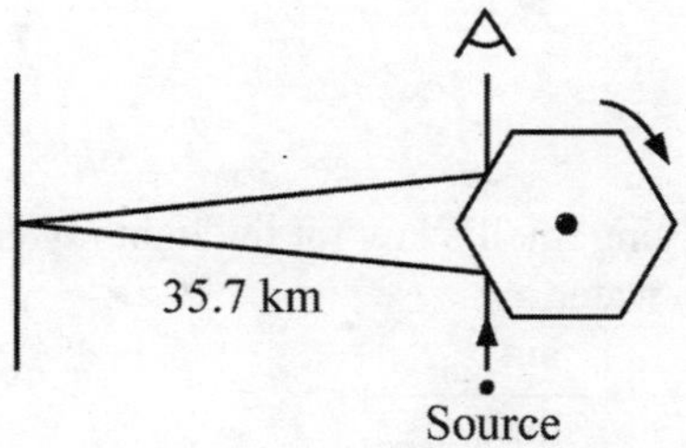

One full rotation of the mirror involves a rotation through an angle of 360°. Therefore, if the mirror rotates through an angle of 60° in the time it takes for a light pulse to travel from the surface of the rotating mirror to a fixed mirror and back to the rotating mirror, the time is

$$\frac{60°}{360°}T = \frac{1}{6}T.$$

$$c = \frac{d}{t}$$

$$\Rightarrow t = \frac{d}{c}$$

$$= \frac{2(35.7 \times 10^{3}\text{ m})}{3.00 \times 10^{8}\text{ m/s}}$$

$$= 2.38 \times 10^{-4}\text{ s}$$

$$T = 6(2.38 \times 10^{-4}\text{ s}) = 1.43 \times 10^{-3}\text{ s}$$

10. 2604

$$T = \frac{1}{f} = \frac{1}{720}\ \text{Hz} = 1.389 \times 10^{-3}\ \text{s}$$

$$t = \frac{1}{8}T = 1.736 \times 10^{-4}\ \text{s}$$

$$\begin{aligned} v &= \frac{2d}{t} \\ \Rightarrow 2d &= vt \\ &= (3.00 \times 10^{8}\ \text{m/s})(1.736 \times 10^{-4}\ \text{s}) \\ &= 5.208 \times 10^{4}\ \text{m} \\ \therefore d &= 2.60 \times 10^{4}\ \text{m} \end{aligned}$$

11. D

Each of the angles between the incident and reflection rays with the mirror surfaces are shown in the given diagram.

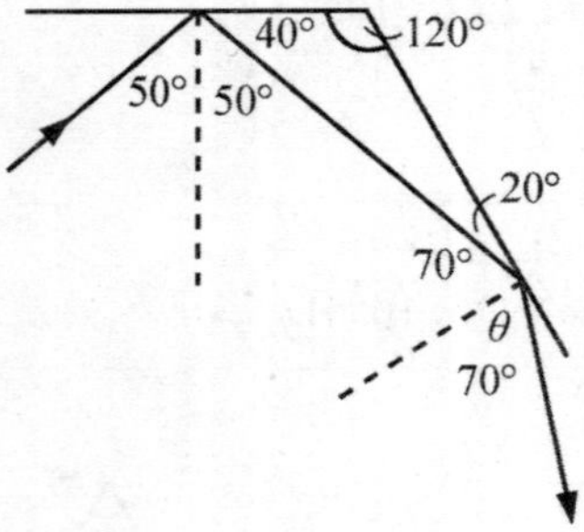

12. A

Applying Snell's law for the light ray entered from air to water

$$\frac{n_{\text{water}}}{n_{\text{air}}} = \frac{\sin\theta_{\text{air}}}{\sin\theta_{\text{water}}} \quad (1)$$

Applying Snell's law for the light ray entered from water to glass

$$\frac{n_{\text{glass}}}{n_{\text{water}}} = \frac{\sin\theta_{\text{water}}}{\sin\theta_{\text{glass}}} \quad (2)$$

Multiplying equation (2) by equation (1)

$$\frac{n_{\text{glass}}}{n_{\text{water}}} \times \frac{n_{\text{water}}}{n_{\text{air}}} = \frac{\sin\theta_{\text{water}}}{\sin\theta_{\text{glass}}} \times \frac{\sin\theta_{\text{air}}}{\sin\theta_{\text{water}}}$$

$$\therefore \frac{n_{\text{glass}}}{n_{\text{air}}} = \frac{\sin\theta_{\text{air}}}{\sin\theta_{\text{glass}}} \Rightarrow \sin\theta_{\text{glass}} = \frac{n_{\text{air}}\sin\theta_{\text{air}}}{n_{\text{glass}}}$$

$$\sin\theta_{\text{glass}} = \frac{(1.00)(\sin 55.0°)}{1.55} = 0.528$$

$$\therefore \theta_{\text{glass}} = 31.9°$$

Notice that it would have been possible to ignore the intermediary medium and just look at the light as having passed from the air into the glass. This is always the case when light passes through regions of different refractive indices.

13. D

$$\begin{aligned} \frac{n_{\text{p}}}{n_{\text{a}}} &= \frac{\sin\theta_{\text{a}}}{\sin\theta_{\text{p}}} \\ \Rightarrow n_{\text{p}} &= \frac{n_{\text{a}}\sin\theta_{\text{a}}}{\sin\theta_{\text{p}}} \\ &= \frac{(1.00)\sin 90.0°}{\sin 37.0°} \\ &= 1.66 \end{aligned}$$

The absolute index of refraction of the plastic is 1.66.

14. 1.46

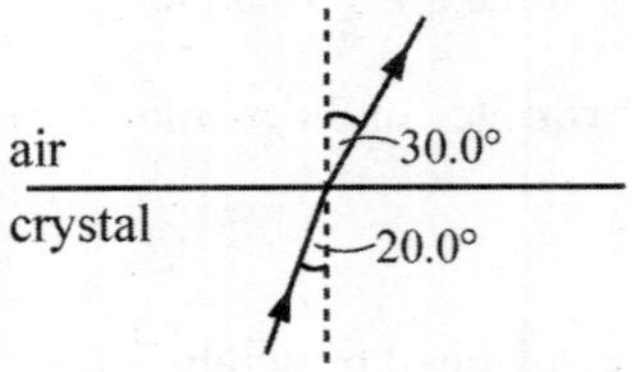

$$\begin{aligned} \frac{n_{\text{cr}}}{n_{\text{a}}} &= \frac{\sin\theta_{\text{a}}}{\sin\theta_{\text{cr}}} \\ \Rightarrow n_{\text{cr}} &= \frac{n_{\text{a}}\sin\theta_{\text{a}}}{\sin\theta_{\text{cr}}} \\ &= \frac{(1.00)\sin 30.0°}{\sin 20.0°} \\ &= 1.46 \end{aligned}$$

15. C

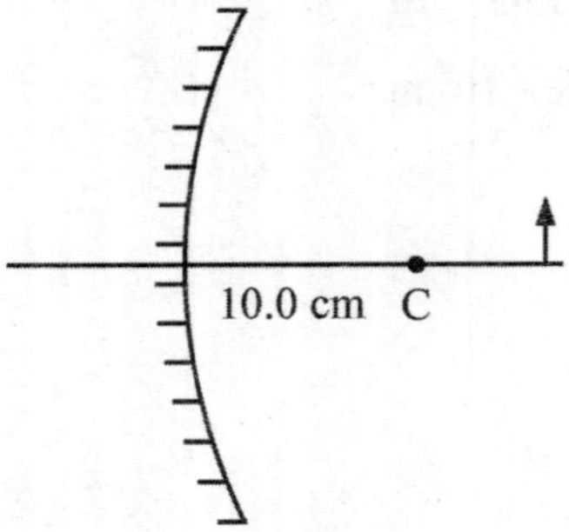

$$\begin{aligned} \frac{1}{f} &= \frac{1}{d_{\text{i}}} + \frac{1}{d_{\text{o}}} \\ \frac{1}{5.00\ \text{cm}} &= \frac{1}{d_{\text{i}}} + \frac{1}{30.0\ \text{cm}} \\ \frac{1}{d_{\text{i}}} &= \frac{1}{5.00\ \text{cm}} - \frac{1}{30.0\ \text{cm}} \\ &= \frac{6.00 - 1.00}{30.0\ \text{cm}} \\ d_{\text{i}} &= \frac{30.0\ \text{cm}}{5.00} = 6.00\ \text{cm} \end{aligned}$$

Since the object is positioned beyond the radius of curvature (which is twice the focal length), the image will be real, inverted, and smaller than the object.

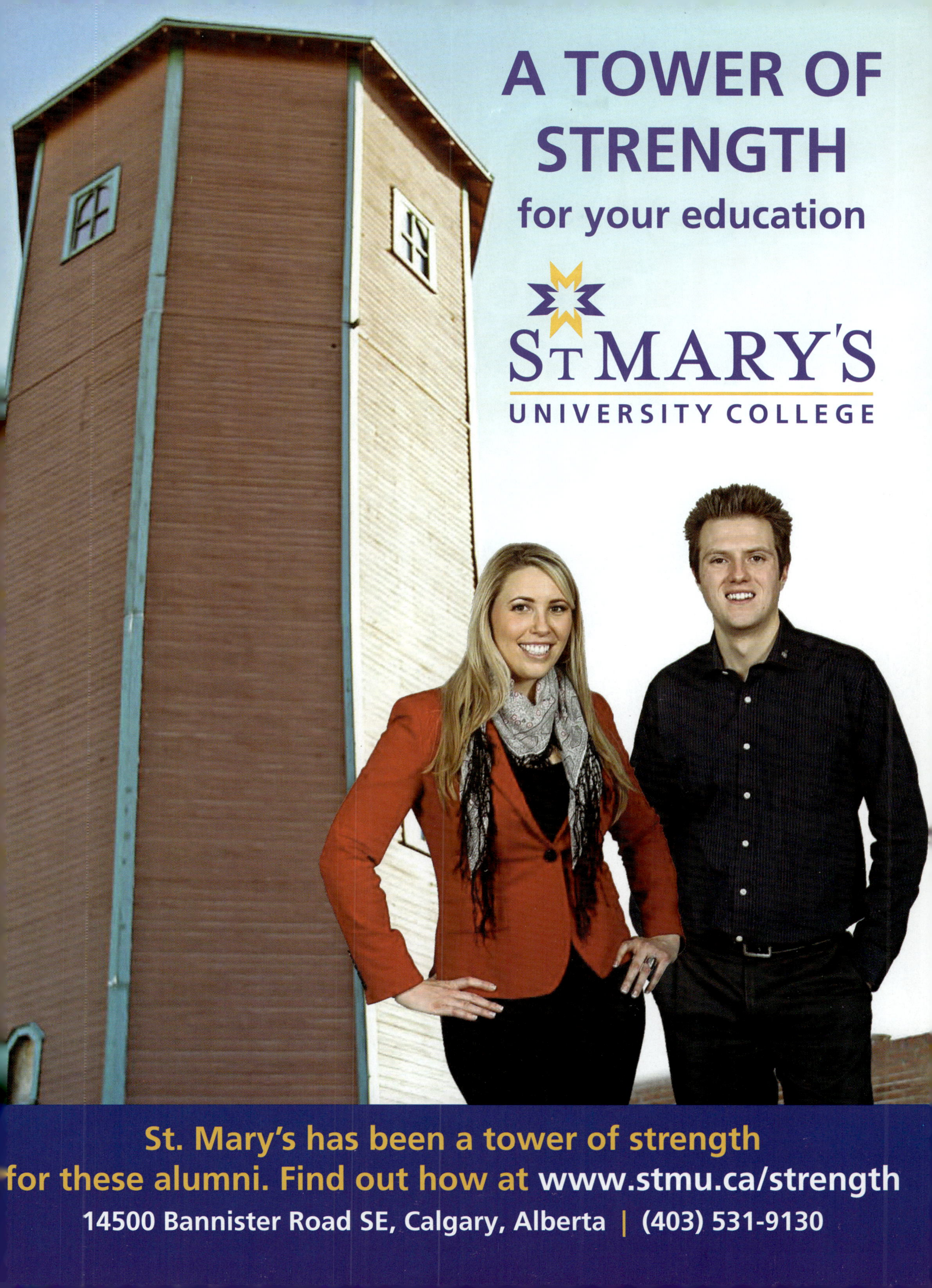
A TOWER OF STRENGTH
for your education
ST MARY'S
UNIVERSITY COLLEGE
St. Mary's has been a tower of strength for these alumni. Find out how at www.stmu.ca/strength
14500 Bannister Road SE, Calgary, Alberta | (403) 531-9130

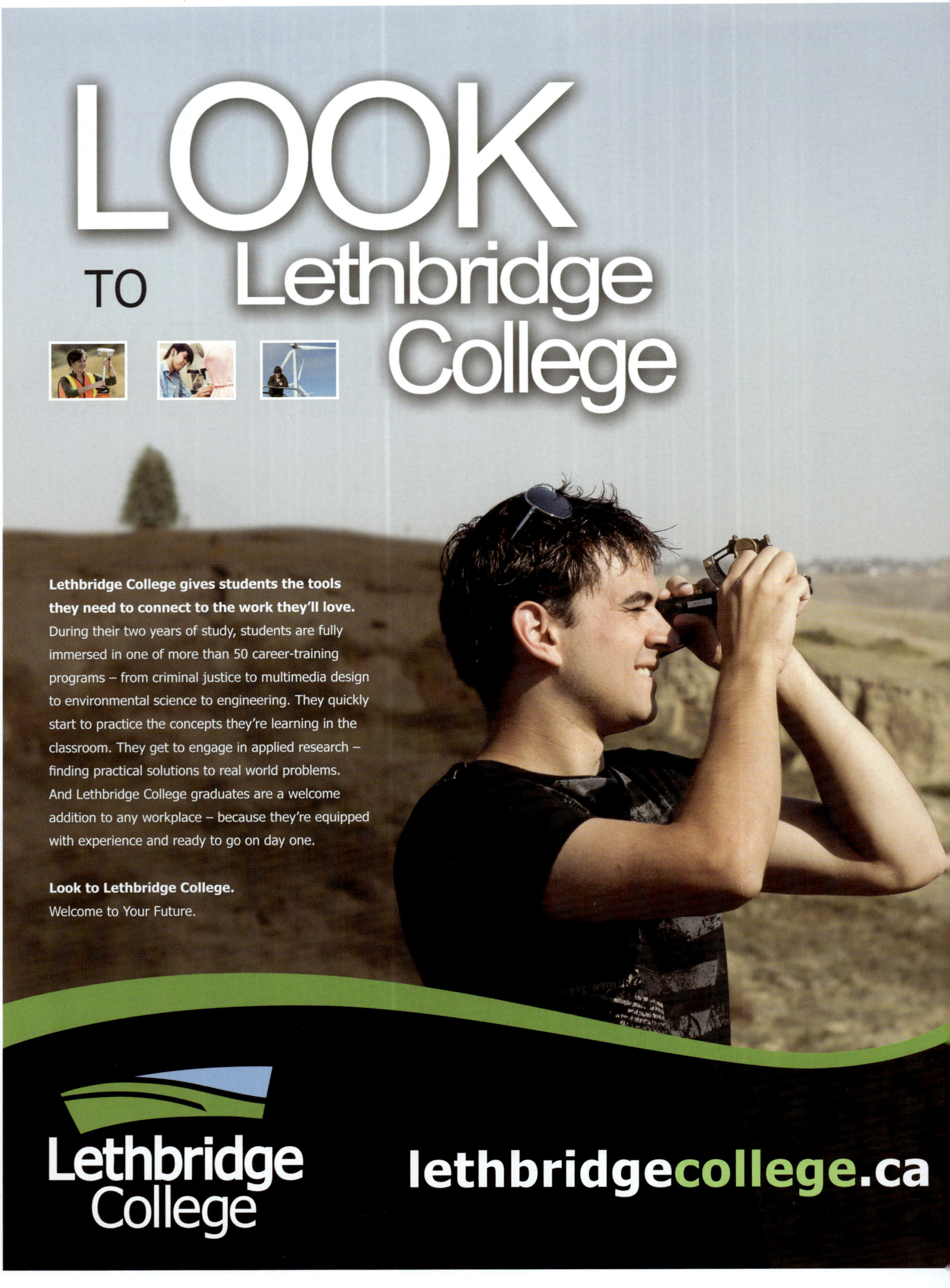
LOOK
TO Lethbridge College
Lethbridge College gives students the tools they need to connect to the work they'll love. During their two years of study, students are fully immersed in one of more than 50 career-training programs – from criminal justice to multimedia design to environmental science to engineering. They quickly start to practice the concepts they're learning in the classroom. They get to engage in applied research – finding practical solutions to real world problems. And Lethbridge College graduates are a welcome addition to any workplace – because they're equipped with experience and ready to go on day one.
Look to Lethbridge College.
Welcome to Your Future.
Lethbridge College
lethbridgecollege.ca

OVERWHELMED?

uncertain
I'm too hot
unloved
unheard
Sighhhh Im sooo bored
I WANNA B LEFT ALONE
i have too much to do
i have nothing to do
my friends never include me
ugh! my mom took my phone away
i'm not a morning person
I wanna get high
does anybody care about how i feel?
my paents r soooo weird
EVERYBODY IS GIVING ME A HEADACHE
OMG I HAVE A ZITT!!
my little brother is annoying
please stop talking to me
BAD HAIR DAY!
UGH I CAN'T TAKE THIS ANYMORE
I HATE WAKING UP EARLY
DON T GET ME STARTED
I'M MISUNDERSTOOD
Y DOES MY SISTER GET TO STAY UP LATE?
booooorring
HOMEWORK GRRRRRRRRRRRRR :(
i hate my nose I'M HUNGRY
my head hurts
SIGH.... IM BORED
its not ez being me
I WANNA BE LEFT ALONE
i feel sad
i have nothing to do
MIDTERMS R KILLING ME
OMG! I'M BORED
im so bored I HATE MY LIFE
now im really bored
i need new friends
GRRRRRRR
my room is NOT a mess!
I DON'T WANNA STUDY
I'M BORED UGH!
is anybody listening?
Y CAN'T I GO TO THE MOVIES?
WHY ME?
im always being picked on
help me
he doesnt even know im alive
I'M NOT OVERREACTING
IT'S NOT MY FAULT
i have crampsss
MY STOMACH HURTS
I'M LONELY
EVERY BODY PICKS ON ME
im too fat
THIS IS THE WORST DAY EVER!!!!!
I M TOO COLD
AND NO, I DON'T WANNA TALK ABOUT IT
ugh boys!!! I need to get blazed and forget about all of this.

We can help you with that.

CleanScene
NETWORK FOR YOUTH

Call Clean Scene at 780-488-0036 or 1-866-481-DRUG
Visit us any time at www.cleanscene.ca

DRUGS DON'T HELP - MENTORS DO.

AU BComm student Teang

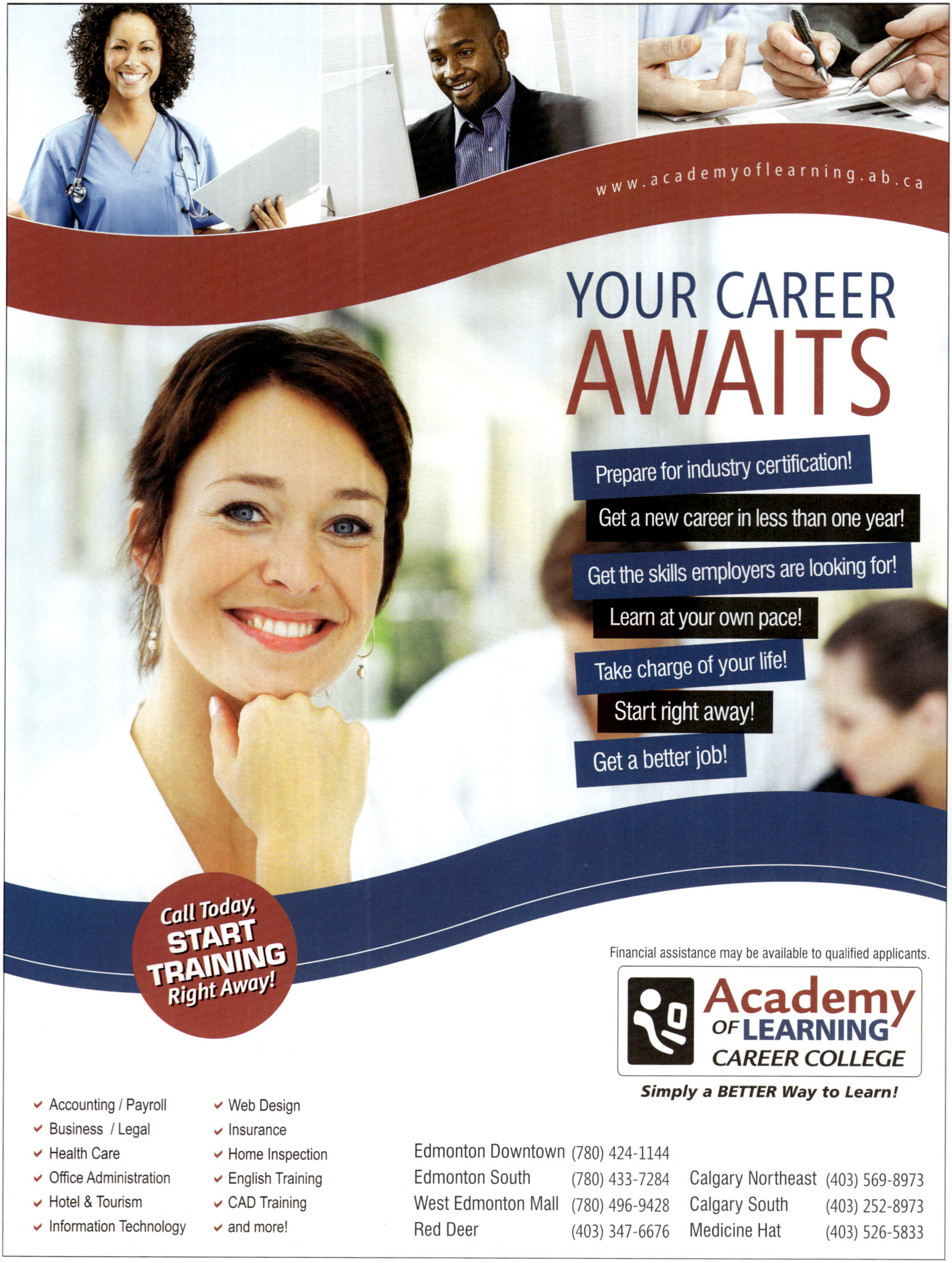
www.academyoflearning.ab.ca
YOUR CAREER
AWAITS
Prepare for industry certification!
Get a new career in less than one year!
Get the skills employers are looking for!
Learn at your own pace!
Take charge of your life!
Start right away!
Get a better job!
Call Today, START TRAINING Right Away!
Financial assistance may be available to qualified applicants.
Academy OF LEARNING CAREER COLLEGE
Simply a BETTER Way to Learn!
Accounting / Payroll
Business / Legal
Health Care
Office Administration
Hotel & Tourism
Information Technology
Web Design
Insurance
Home Inspection
English Training
CAD Training
and more!
Edmonton Downtown (780) 424-1144
Edmonton South (780) 433-7284
West Edmonton Mall (780) 496-9428
Red Deer (403) 347-6676
Calgary Northeast (403) 569-8973
Calgary South (403) 252-8973
Medicine Hat (403) 526-5833

Access a tutor from your mobile device.
Any Time. Any Where.
motuto
Your first session is FREE
Lets review the relationship on the whiteboard...
If you compare a cone and a cylinder of the same base and height in terms of their respective volumes, you will find that the volume of the cylinder is exactly 3 times the volume of the cone!
New whiteboard created by tutor.
Take a look at the board... The base of a cylinder and the base of a cone are both circular...
Do you see?
Yes
This means that, the formula used to calculate the volume of a cone can be derived or taken from the formula used for the volume of a cylinder.
Can you remember the formula for the volume of a cylinder?
Yes
That is great, would you like to write it
Send
EndSession
Done
1/3
V = πr² × h
V = 1/3 (πr² × h)
V = πr² × h / 3
End Session
New whiteboard created by Motuto.
Hi and welcome to Motuto.
Hi
I see you have sent me a copy of your homework assignment. Would you like me to help you review question 1?
Send
Live Mobile Tutoring for Math and Science in grades 6-12.
www.motuto.com
Available on the App Store
Available in Android Market

16. B

To solve this problem both the mirror equation and the magnification formula will be required. First use the magnification formula to find the relationship between the object distance and the image distance, then use the mirror equation to calculate the object distance.

$$M = -\frac{d_i}{d_o} = 2$$

$$\therefore d_i = -2d_o$$

$$\frac{1}{f} = \frac{1}{d_i} + \frac{1}{d_o}$$

$$\frac{1}{20.0 \text{ cm}} = \frac{1}{-2d_o} + \frac{1}{d_o}$$

$$\frac{1}{20.0 \text{ cm}} = \frac{1}{-2d_o} + \frac{-2}{-2d_o}$$

$$\frac{1}{20.0 \text{ cm}} = \frac{-1}{-2d_o}$$

$$2d_o = 20.0 \text{ cm}$$

$$d_o = 10.0 \text{ cm}$$

17. C

$$\frac{1}{f} = \frac{1}{d_i} + \frac{1}{d_o}$$

$$\frac{1}{10.0 \text{ cm}} = \frac{1}{d_i} + \frac{1}{18.0 \text{ cm}}$$

$$\frac{1}{d_i} = \frac{1}{10.0 \text{ cm}} - \frac{1}{18.0 \text{ cm}} = \frac{18.0 - 10.0}{180 \text{ cm}}$$

$$d_i = \frac{180 \text{ cm}}{8.00} = 22.5 \text{ cm}$$

A converging lens with the object located between the focus and the centre of curvature will result in an image that is real and inverted.

18. 6.92

In this case the height of the image is the size of the projection screen, and the height of the object is the height of the LCD screen. First, calculate the relationship between the image and object heights, then use this information to calculate the distance between the LCD screen and the projection screen.

$$M = \frac{h_i}{h_o} = \frac{3.25 \times 10^2 \text{ cm}}{6.35 \text{ cm}} = 5.118 \times 10^1 = -\frac{d_i}{d_o}$$

$$\therefore d_i = \left(-5.118 \times 10^1\right)d_o$$

Use the lens equation to determine the object distance (distance between LCD screen and the lens).

$$\frac{1}{f} = \frac{1}{d_i} + \frac{1}{d_o}$$

$$\frac{1}{13.8 \text{ cm}} = \frac{1}{\left(-5.118 \times 10^1\right)d_o} + \frac{1}{d_o}$$

$$\frac{1}{13.8 \text{ cm}} = \frac{1 - 51.18}{(-51.18)d_o}$$

$$(-51.18)d_o = (13.8 \text{ cm})(-50.18)$$

$$d_o = 1.35 \times 10^1 \text{ cm}$$

$$\therefore d_i = (-51.18)d_o$$
$$= -6.92 \times 10^2 \text{ cm}$$
$$= -6.92 \text{ m}$$

In order to get the required magnification to fit the projected image onto the screen, the LCD screen would need to be located 13.5 cm in front of the lens. This would cause the projected image to appear on the 3.25 m wide screen at a distance of 6.92 m behind the projecting lens.

19. A

Statement iii relates to the absorption of the $\vec{E}$ of EMR by the metallic walls of the oven and some reflection but no significant diffraction. Statement ii may deal with some diffraction as the sound waves move through the house but it also deals with reflection from the walls. Only statement i deals solely with diffraction around the support pier.

20. C

For unpolarized EMR, the electric and magnetic fields exist at all orientations perpendicular to the direction of motion.

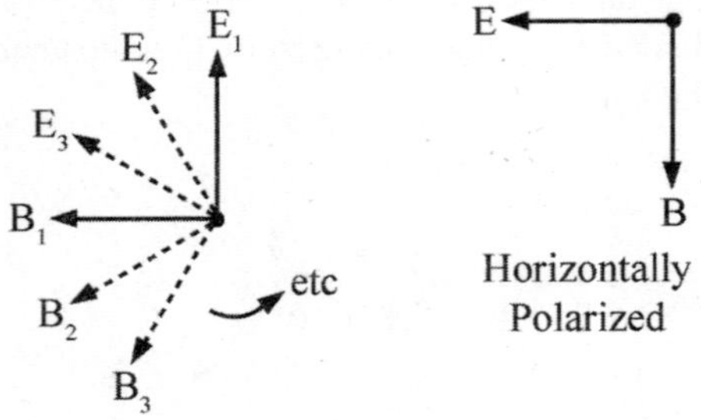

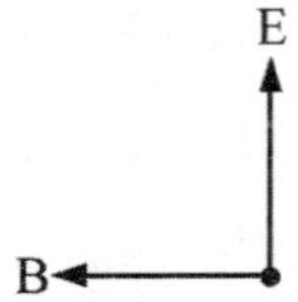

If the electric field oscillates in only one plane, the EMR is polarized along that plane. Light may be polarized when it is reflected off of some flat surfaces, but not all. For example, light reflected from the surface of water is plane polarized but light that is reflected from a household mirror is not. Light absorption does not cause polarization and neither does adjusting the position from which light is viewed.

21. WR

A. Huygens's principle states that every point on a wave front behaves like a point source of circular wave fronts that are in phase and propagate out in front of the wave to produce a new wave front.

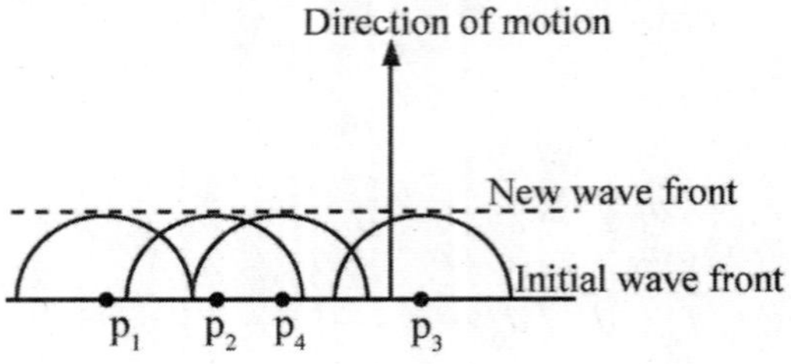

Huygens used this idea to explain diffraction, the bending of a wave front around an obstacle.

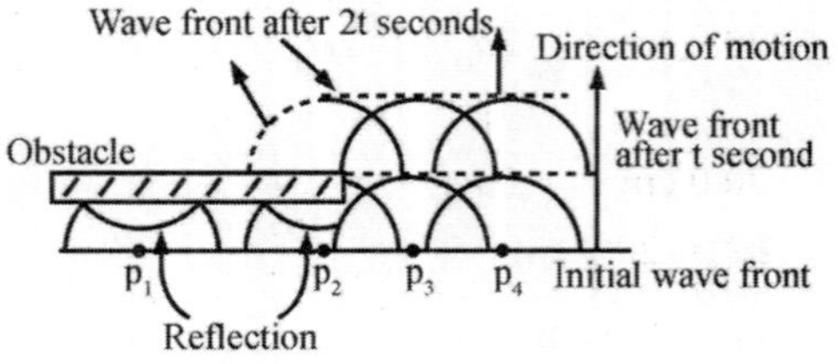

Wave fronts from point sources at times t and $2t$ show that energy in the wave front is transmitted behind the obstacle. This is diffraction.

B. Diffraction by a small slit is similar to the situation when waves are diffracting around objects. Every point on the wave front acts as an individual circular wave front propagating out from the slit.

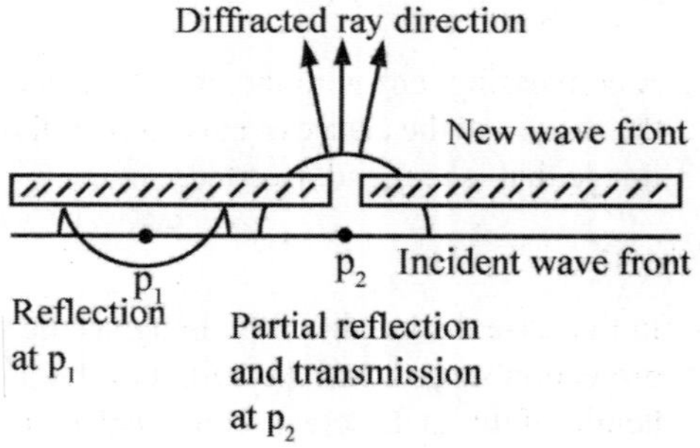

C. Huygens's principles easily explains the propagation of a curved wave front from a point source.

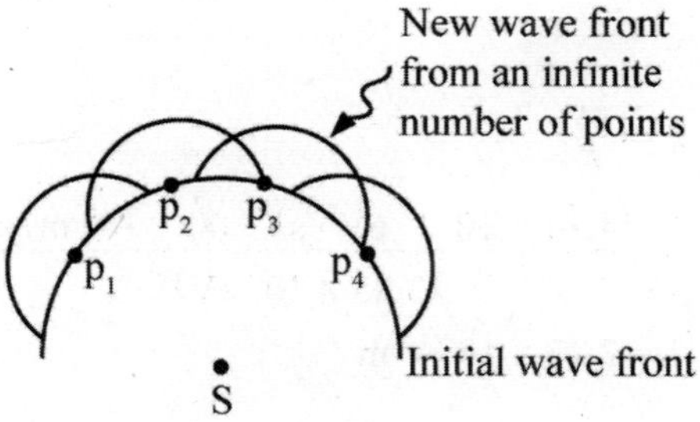

22. B

The sources are in phase because the crests were produced simultaneously. When two lines meet, two crests are intersecting, so point T lies at a point of constructive interference. In contrast, point Q lies at a point where the midpoints between two different pairs of lines meet. This is a point of constructive interference if two troughs. Therefore, both points are anti-nodal points.

23. A

$$n\lambda = d\sin\theta$$
$$\therefore \sin\theta = \frac{n\lambda}{d}$$
$$\Rightarrow \theta = \sin^{-1}\left(\frac{n\lambda}{d}\right)$$
$$= \sin^{-1}\left(\frac{3(610 \times 10^{-9}\ \text{m})}{0.450 \times 10^{-3}\ \text{m}}\right)$$
$$= 0.233°$$

24. B

First, find the average wavelength of the two closely spaced emission lines.

$$\frac{589.59\ \text{nm} + 589.00\ \text{nm}}{2} = 589.3\ \text{nm}$$

Next, use the average wavelength as the wavelength for the light to find the value of l.

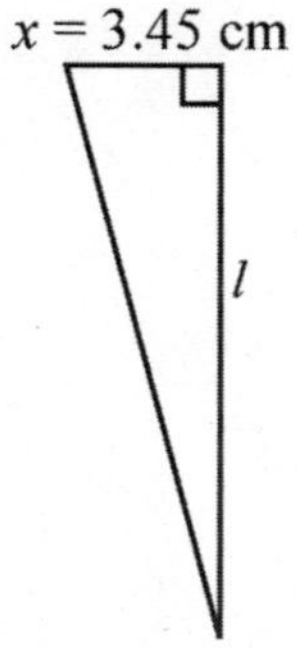

$$d = \frac{1}{105 \times 10^3}\ \text{m}$$
$$d = 9.524 \times 10^{-6}\ \text{m}$$
$$n\lambda = \frac{dx}{l} \Rightarrow l = \frac{dx}{n\lambda}$$
$$l = \frac{(9.524 \times 10^{-6}\ \text{m})(3.45 \times 10^{-2}\ \text{m})}{(1)(589.3 \times 10^{-9}\ \text{m})}$$
$$= 5.58 \times 10^{-1}\ \text{m}$$

25. 12.5

First, find the value of d.

$$d = \frac{1}{8.00 \times 10^5\ \text{lines/m}}$$
$$= 1.25 \times 10^{-6}\ \text{m}$$

Next, find the value of θ for both wavelengths using

$$n\lambda = d\sin\theta$$
$$\Rightarrow \sin\theta = \frac{n\lambda}{d}$$
$$\therefore \theta = \sin^{-1}\left(\frac{n\lambda}{d}\right)$$

for $\lambda = 656$ nm

$$\theta = \sin^{-1}\left(\frac{n\lambda}{d}\right) = \sin^{-1}\left(\frac{1(656 \times 10^{-9}\ \text{m})}{1.25 \times 10^{-6}\ \text{m}}\right)$$
$$= 31.65°$$

for $\lambda = 410$ nm

$$\theta = \sin^{-1}\left(\frac{n\lambda}{d}\right) = \sin^{-1}\left(\frac{1(410 \times 10^{-9}\ \text{m})}{1.25 \times 10^{-6}\ \text{m}}\right)$$
$$= 19.15°$$

angular separation = 31.65° – 19.15° = 12.5°

26. 2165

$$n\lambda = d\sin\theta$$
$$d = \frac{n\lambda}{\sin\theta}$$
$$= \frac{(1)(565 \times 10^{-9}\text{ m})}{\sin 1.50°}$$
$$= 2.16 \times 10^{-5}\text{ m}$$

27. A

$$\frac{n_d}{n_a} = \frac{v_a}{v_d}$$
$$\Rightarrow v_d = \frac{v_a}{2.42} = \frac{3.00 \times 10^8\text{ m/s}}{2.42}$$
$$= 1.24 \times 10^8\text{ m/s}$$
$$\frac{n_d}{n_a} = \frac{\lambda_a}{\lambda_d}$$
$$\Rightarrow \lambda_d = \frac{\lambda_a}{2.42} = \frac{630\text{ nm}}{2.42}$$
$$= 2.60 \times 10^2\text{ nm}$$
$$= 2.60 \times 10^{-7}\text{ m}$$

28. 1.41

According to Snell's Law we have

$$\frac{n_p}{n_a} = \frac{\lambda_a}{\lambda_p}$$
$$\frac{n_p}{1.00} = \frac{3.45\text{ cm}}{2.44\text{ cm}}$$
$$n_p = 1.41$$

29. B

While long wavelengths diffract more than short wavelengths, the reverse is true for refraction. In refraction, long wavelengths refract less than short wavelengths.

30. A

$$E = \frac{hc}{\lambda}$$
$$= \frac{(6.63 \times 10^{-34}\text{ J} \cdot \text{s})(3.00 \times 10^8\text{m/s})}{(2.80 \times 10^{-7}\text{ m})}$$
$$E = 7.1 \times 10^{-19}\text{ J}$$

31. B

Use the energy equation. Insert the values provided in the question, to find the wavelength.

$$E = \frac{hc}{\lambda}$$
$$\lambda = \frac{hc}{E}$$
$$= \frac{(4.14 \times 10^{-15}\text{ eV} \cdot \text{s})(3.00 \times 10^8\text{ m/s})}{(3.85 \times 10^6\text{ eV})}$$
$$\lambda = 3.23 \times 10^{-13}\text{ m}$$

32. A

The visible spectrum of light from the lowest frequency to the highest is red, orange, yellow, green, blue, indigo, and violet. A photon's energy is calculated using $E = hf$. Since strontium emits red light, it has the lowest frequency, so it produces the photon with the lowest energy.

33. 9515

Energy emitted each second is 3.00×10^{-3} J (1 watt = 1 J/s)

$$E = \frac{hc}{\lambda}$$
$$= \frac{(6.63 \times 10^{-34}\text{J} \cdot \text{s})(3.00 \times 10^8\text{ m/s})}{633 \times 10^{-9}\text{ m}}$$
$$= 3.142 \times 10^{-19}\text{ J/photon}$$
$$\#\text{ photons} = \frac{3.00 \times 10^{-3}\text{ J/s}}{3.142 \times 10^{-19}\text{ J/photon}}$$
$$= 9.5 \times 10^{15}\text{ photons/s}$$

34. B

$$E_{k_{max}} = Z$$
$$hf = X$$
$$W = Y$$
$$E_{k_{max}} = hf - W$$
$$\therefore Z = X - Y$$

35. B

The particle model can be used to explain all four observations, but only observations I and IV can be explained using a classical wave model of EMR. Intensity is measured by the amplitude of the wave. It is harder to remove electrons from some metals than from others (IV), and more energy in the wave (amplitude) would remove more electrons (I).

36. 2797

$$E = W = \frac{hc}{\lambda}$$

where W is the work function

$$\lambda = \frac{hc}{W}$$

$$= \frac{(6.63 \times 10^{-34}\ \text{J·s})(3.00 \times 10^{8}\ \text{m/s})}{(4.45\ \text{eV})(1.60 \times 10^{-19}\ \text{J/eV})}$$

$$= 2.79 \times 10^{-7}\ \text{m}$$

37. A

Energy carried by a photon of red light (750 nm)

$$E = \frac{hc}{\lambda}$$

$$= \frac{(6.63 \times 10^{-34}\ \text{J·s})(3.00 \times 10^{8}\ \text{m/s})}{750 \times 10^{-9}\ \text{m}} \times \frac{1\ \text{eV}}{1.60 \times 10^{-19}\ \text{J}}$$

$$= 1.66\ \text{eV}$$

Energy carried by a photon of blue light (450 nm)

$$E = \frac{hc}{\lambda}$$

$$= \frac{(6.63 \times 10^{-34}\ \text{J·s})(3.00 \times 10^{8}\ \text{m/s})}{450 \times 10^{-9}\ \text{m}} \times \frac{1\ \text{eV}}{1.60 \times 10^{-19}\ \text{J}}$$

$$= 2.76\ \text{eV}$$

Since the photon of blue light carries enough energy to overcome the work function of Barium, the correct answer is Barium. Visible light does not carry enough energy to overcome the work function of any of the other three materials.

38. B

Find the maximum kinetic energy expressed in both joules and in electron-volts. To do this, convert the work function (2.31 eV) into joules by multiplying by 1.60×10^{-19} J/eV.

$$E_{\text{k max}} = hf - W$$

$$= (6.63 \times 10^{-34}\ \text{J·s})(3.45 \times 10^{15}\ \text{Hz}) - (2.31\ \text{eV})(1.60 \times 10^{-19}\ \text{J/eV})$$

$$= 1.92 \times 10^{-18}\ \text{J}$$

$$= 12.0\ \text{eV}$$

Therefore, the maximum kinetic energy of the emitted photoelectrons is 1.92×10^{-18} J or 12.0 eV.

39. 3491

$$E_{\text{k}_{\text{max}}} = \frac{1}{2}mv^2 = qV_{\text{stop}}$$

$$\Rightarrow V_{\text{stop}} = \frac{\frac{1}{2}mv^2}{q}$$

$$= \frac{\frac{1}{2}(9.11 \times 10^{-31}\ \text{kg})(3.50 \times 10^{5}\ \text{m/s})^2}{1.60 \times 10^{-19}\ \text{C}}$$

$$= 3.49 \times 10^{-1}\ \text{V}$$

40. B

Use the equation for the momentum of a photon of EMR.

$$p = \frac{h}{\lambda} = \frac{hf}{c}$$

$$= \frac{(6.63 \times 10^{-34}\ \text{J·s})(6.56 \times 10^{19}\ \text{Hz})}{3.00 \times 10^{8}\ \text{m/s}}$$

$$= 1.45 \times 10^{-22}\ \text{kg·m/s}$$

41. A

Find the scattered angle using the following formula:

$$\Delta\lambda = \frac{h}{mc}(1 - \cos\theta)$$

$$\Delta\lambda = \frac{h}{mc} - \frac{h\cos\theta}{mc}$$

$$\frac{h\cos\theta}{mc} = \frac{h}{mc} - \Delta\lambda$$

$$\cos\theta = 1 - \frac{\Delta\lambda mc}{h}$$

$$= 1 - \frac{(0.20 \times 10^{-11}\ \text{m})(9.11 \times 10^{-31}\ \text{kg}) \times (3.00 \times 10^{8}\ \text{m/s})}{6.63 \times 10^{-34}\ \text{J·s}}$$

$$= 1 - 0.8244$$

$$= 0.1756$$

$$\therefore \theta = 79.9^\circ$$

To calculate the change in energy of the X-rays before and after the collision, use the following formula:

$$\Delta E = E_{\text{f}} - E_{\text{i}} = \frac{hc}{\lambda_{\text{f}}} - \frac{hc}{\lambda_{\text{i}}}$$

$$E_i = \frac{(6.63 \times 10^{-34}\ \text{J·s})(3.00 \times 10^8\ \text{m/s})}{4.60 \times 10^{-11}\ \text{m}}$$
$$= 4.32 \times 10^{-15}\ \text{J}$$

$$E_f = \frac{(6.63 \times 10^{-34}\ \text{J·s})(3.00 \times 10^8\ \text{m/s})}{4.80 \times 10^{-11}\ \text{m}}$$
$$= 4.14 \times 10^{-15}\ \text{J}$$

$$\Rightarrow \Delta E = E_f - E_i$$
$$= -1.80 \times 10^{-16}\ \text{J}$$

This is equivalent to a loss in energy of 1.80×10^{-16} J.

42. B

Compton's experiment found that when X-rays interact with matter, both the momentum and energy are conserved. An X-ray photon interacts with an electron in the same manner as a small particle with the same kinetic energy as the photon would interact with the electron.

The vector sum of the momenta of the scattered electron and photon can be determined by conservation of momentum.

43. 16012

Use the following formula to calculate the change in wavelength:

$$\Delta\lambda = \frac{h}{mc}(1 - \cos\theta)$$
$$= \frac{(6.63 \times 10^{-34}\ \text{J·s})(1 - \cos 70.0°)}{(9.11 \times 10^{-31}\ \text{kg})(3.00 \times 10^8\ \text{m/s})}$$
$$= 1.60 \times 10^{-12}\ \text{m}$$

UNIT TEST — ELECTROMAGNETIC RADIATION

1. James Maxwell, in his theory of electromagnetism, hypothesized a cause of electromagnetic waves. Which of the following statements **best** describes this cause?
   A. An electric current in a wire produces a magnetic field that circles the wire.
   B. A current is induced in a conductor that moves across a magnetic field.
   C. An electric field that changes with time generates a magnetic field.
   D. Two parallel current-carrying wires exert a force on each other.

Numerical Response

2. An eight-sided rotating mirror, similar to that used by Michelson, rotated with a frequency of 510 Hz. A fixed mirror was located 35.8 km away from the octagonal mirror. If the rotating mirror makes $\frac{1}{8}$ of a rotation in the time a light pulse travels the entire length of the experimental apparatus, the empirically determined value of c is $a.bc \times 10^{d}$ m/s. The value of *abcd* is _________.

CHALLENGER QUESTION

Use the following information to answer the next question.

A ray of light entered into a rectangular box resting on its side, as shown in the given diagram. Both the top and bottom surfaces are plane mirrors. The light ray grazed the box opening and reflected off the upper surface with an incident angle of 21.8°. The ray then reflected several times off the top and bottom before striking the far end of the box.

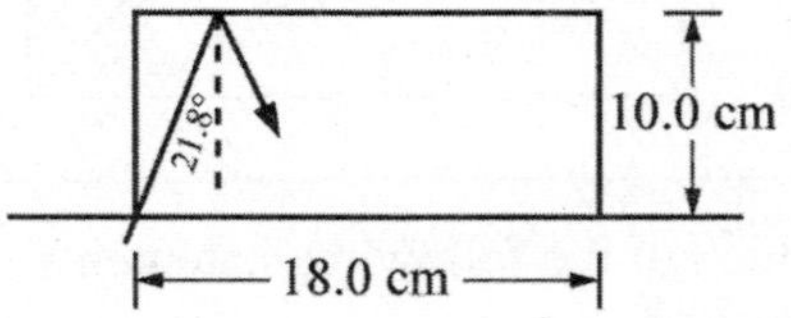

3. At what height did the light ray strike the back of the box?
   A. 2.00 cm **B.** 4.00 cm
   C. 5.00 cm **D.** 8.00 cm

4. A light beam passing through glass is incident upon a layer of water sitting on top of the glass. Given that n_{H_2O} is 1.33 and n_{glass} is 1.55, the critical angle is
   A. 40.2° **B.** 48.8°
   C. 59.1° **D.** 90.0°

5. A diverging mirror with a focal length of 5.00 cm produced an image of an object located 15.0 cm from the mirror. What is the distance from the image to the mirror and the magnification of the image?
   A. 3.80 cm, –0.250
   B. 3.80 cm, 0.250
   C. 7.50 cm, 4.00
   D. 7.50 cm, –4.00

Use the following information to answer the next question.

A room is fitted with windows made of polarized glass, and people are standing on either side of the windows, as shown in the given diagram. The arrows indicate the plane of polarization of the glass.

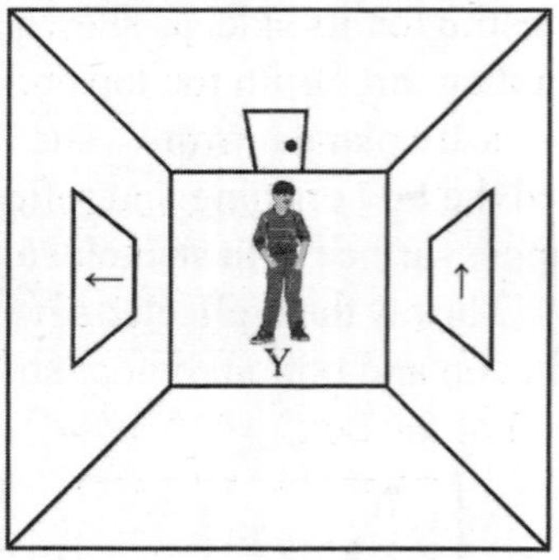

6. Which of the following statements is **true**?
   A. Person X can see both person Y and person Z.
   B. Person Y can see both person X and person Z.
   C. Person Z can see both person X and person Y.
   D. None of the people can see each other.

7. The following diagram shows the circular wavefronts coming from two point sources. Which of the following pairs of rays will have a path difference of 1.5λ?

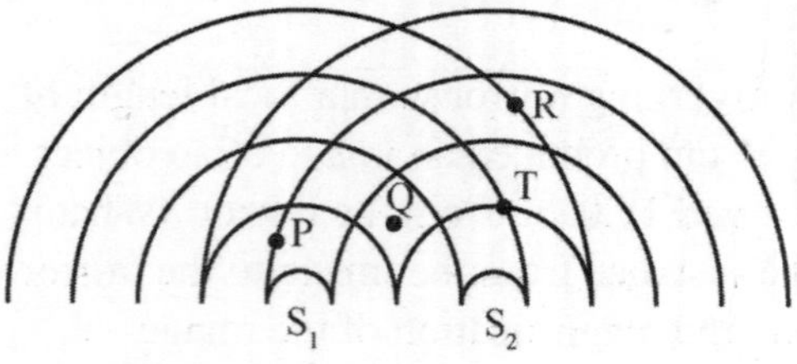

   A. PS_1 and PS_2
   B. RS_1 and RS_2
   C. QS_1 and QS_2
   D. TS_1 and TS_2

Written Response

8. Analyze Thomas Young's double-slit experiment using the following aspects:
   - Explain how Young's experiment favours the wave theory of electromagnetic radiation and not the particle theory.
   - Explain how varying the distance between the slits affects the experiment.

____
____
____
____
____
____
____

9. A diffraction grating is ruled with 425 lines per millimetre. A yellow light with a wavelength of 600 nm illuminates the grating. What is the angle between the first two bright lines on one side of the central maximum?
   A. 14.8° **B.** 15.9°
   C. 29.5° **D.** 30.7°

Numerical Response

10. A screen with two small slits, separated 4.24×10^{-4} m apart, is located 1.00 m from a solid screen. If the distance between the central fringe and the second fringe that appear on the solid screen is 2.35 mm, the wavelength of light creating this interference pattern must be $a.bc \times 10^{-d}$ m. The values of a, b, c, and d are ________, ________, ________, and ________. (Give your answer to four digits.)

Numerical Response

11. Microwave radiation, with a wavelength of 3.45 cm in air, entered into a medium in which the speed of the wave decreased by a factor of 0.755. The wavelength of the microwave in the medium was $a.bc \times 10^{-d}$ m. The value of *abcd* is __________.

12. The formula for double slit diffraction, $n\lambda = \frac{dx}{l}$, shows that red light will be positioned

A. closer to the central antinode than blue light

B. farther from the central antinode than will blue light

C. only at the central antinode

D. at the same distance from the central antinode as blue light

13. At what speed must an electron travel in order to have the same momentum as a photon of blue light (λ = 450 nm)?

A. 8.82×10^{-1} m/s

B. 8.82×10^{1} m/s

C. 1.62×10^{3} m/s

D. 1.62×10^{5} m/s

Use the following information to answer the next question.

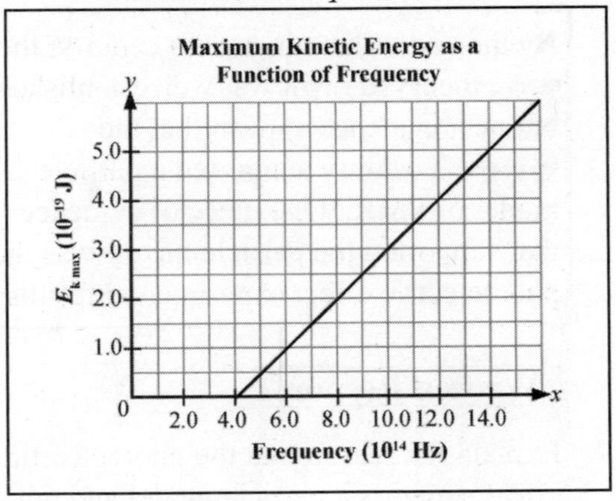

14. Based on the given graph, Planck's constant has a value of

A. 6.6×10^{-34} J·s

B. 5.0×10^{-34} J·s

C. 3.6×10^{-34} J·s

D. 3.0×10^{-34} J·s

Numerical Response

15. The work function of a given metal is 2.5 eV. Expressed in scientific notation, its threshold frequency is $a.b \times 10^{cd}$ Hz. The value of *abcd* is __________.

16. In his explanation of the photoelectric effect, Einstein proposed that

A. the speed of light is constant

B. light energy is contained in distinct "packets"

C. light energy is evenly distributed over the entire wave front

D. metallic surfaces emit electrons when illuminated with short-wavelength light

Use the following information to answer the next question.

By the end of the nineteenth century, the wave theory of EMR was well established, but new evidence appeared in the twentieth century supported a particle model of EMR. One piece of evidence that supported the particle theory was the photoelectric effect experimental results.

Written Response

17. Explain the reason that the photoelecrtic effect supports a particle model and not a wave model of EMR (choose one clear argument.), and explain what effect intensity has on the photoelectric current produced.

____

____

____

____

____

____

____

18. The Compton effect was significant because it demonstrated that photons have

A. mass

B. momentum

C. wave properties

D. a speed of 3.00×10^8 m/s

Written Response

19. Using the concepts of wave refraction, wave interference, and the conservation of energy and momentum, analyze the current understanding of the model of light by addressing the following points:

- Explain an experiment (classroom lab or "famous" experiment) that favours a particle theory of EMR
- Explain an experiment that favours a wave theory of EMR
- Explain what the term *wave-particle duality* means

____

____

____

____

____

____

____

Use the following information to answer the next question.

In a Compton scattering type experiment, X-rays with a wavelength of 7.00×10^{-11} m bombard a metal target, as shown.

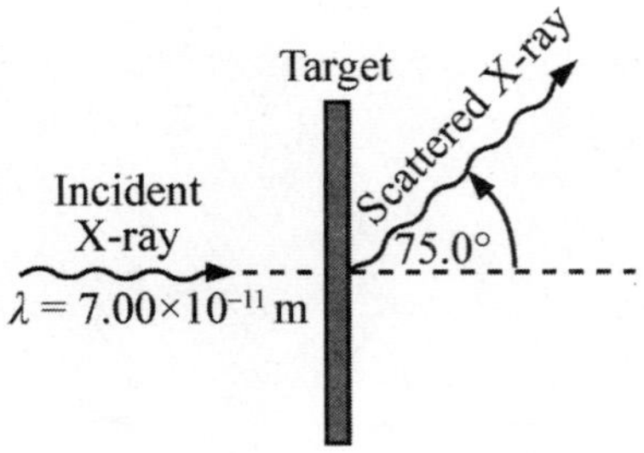

Written Response

20. Determine the momentum of the scattered electron. As part of your response, draw an diagram to represent the electron's momentum after the collision, sketch a vector addition diagram consistent with the method you use, and state all necessary physics principles and formulas.

____

____

____

____

____

____

____

Use the following information to answer the next question.

Three properties of electromagnetic radiation in a vacuum:

1. Wavelength
2. Frequency
3. Speed

Numerical Response

21. Match each of the given properties with the description that applies to it. (Record your answer as a three-digit number.)

Description	Number
Remains the same regardless of location in the electromagnetic spectrum	________
Decreases from gamma rays to radio waves	________
Increases from gamma rays to radio waves	________

Use the following information to answer the next question.

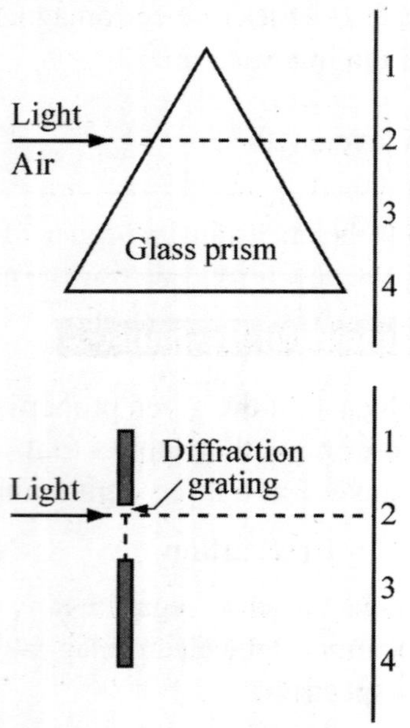

The possible positions for red and violet light in the spectra produced in the given scenarios are marked as the numbers 1 through 4.

The position of red and violet light in the prism spectra are *a* and *b*, respectively. The position of red and violet light in the diffraction grating spectrum are *c* and *d*, respectively.

Numerical Response

22. What are the values of *a*, *b*, *c*, and *d*? (Give your answer as a four-digit number.)

Variable	**Value**
a =	________
b =	________
c =	________
d =	________

Answers and Solutions — Unit Test

1. C	6. B	11. 2602	16. B	21. 321
2. 2928	7. B	12. B	17. WR	22. 3443
3. C	8. WR	13. C	18. B	
4. C	9. B	14. B	19. WR	
5. B	10. 4987	15. 6014	20. WR	

1. C

Maxwell suggested that electric fields that changed with time could produce a time-varying magnetic field, creating an electromagnetic wave that could travel through the vacuum of space.

2. 2928

$$T = \frac{1}{f}$$
$$= \frac{1}{510\text{ Hz}}$$
$$= 1.96 \times 10^{-2}\text{ s}$$
$$t = \frac{1}{8}T$$
$$= \frac{1.96 \times 10^{-2}\text{ s}}{8}$$
$$= 2.45 \times 10^{-4}\text{ s}$$
$$v = \frac{2d}{t}$$
$$= \frac{2(35.8 \times 10^{3}\text{ m})}{2.45 \times 10^{-4}\text{ s}}$$
$$= 2.92 \times 10^{8}\text{ m/s}$$

3. C

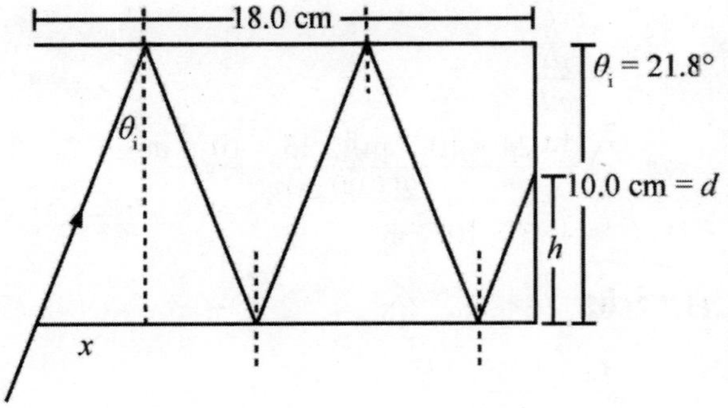

The distance x in the given diagram can be calculated using the following trigonometric relation:

$$\tan 21.8° = \frac{x}{10.0\text{ cm}}$$
$$x = (10.0\text{ cm})(\tan 21.8°) = 4.00\text{ cm}$$

Therefore, before its final reflection off the bottom surface, the light ray travelled a total horizontal distance of $4x$, which is 16.0 cm. This means that the distance between the final reflection and the back wall of the box is 2.00 cm.

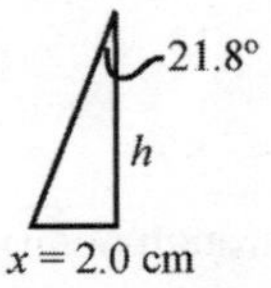

It is now possible to calculate the height at which the light ray struck the back wall of the box.

$$\tan 21.8° = \frac{2.00\text{ cm}}{h}$$
$$h = \frac{2.00\text{ cm}}{\tan 21.8°} = 5.00\text{ cm}$$

4. C

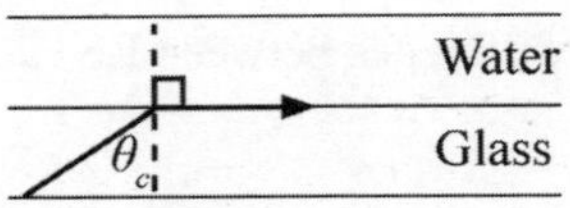

Use Snell's law to solve this critical angle problem.

$$\frac{\sin \theta_1}{\sin \theta_2} = \frac{n_2}{n_1}$$
$$\therefore \frac{\sin \theta_c}{\sin \theta_w} = \frac{n_w}{n_g}$$
$$\Rightarrow \sin \theta_c = \frac{n_w \sin \theta_w}{n_g}$$
$$= \frac{(1.33)\sin 90.0°}{1.55}$$
$$= 0.8581$$
$$\therefore \theta \cong 59.1°$$

5. B

$$\frac{1}{f} = \frac{1}{d_o} + \frac{1}{d_i}$$

$$\frac{1}{-5.00 \text{ cm}} = \frac{1}{15.0 \text{ cm}} + \frac{1}{d_i}$$

$$\frac{-3.00 - 1.00}{15.0} = \frac{1}{d_i}$$

$$d_i = \frac{15.0}{-4.00} = -3.75 \text{ cm}$$

$$M = \frac{-d_i}{d_o}$$

$$= \frac{-(-3.75 \text{ cm})}{15.0 \text{ cm}}$$

$$= 0.250$$

6. B

Light can pass through polarized glass, but it cannot pass through two polarized windows with perpendicular planes of polarization. Person Y can therefore see both person X and person Z, but person X and person Z cannot see each other.

7. B

Sources are in phase because the crests were produced simultaneously. We see that the distance RS_1 is 4λ and the distance RS_2 is 2.5λ. Therefore the path difference between RS_1 and RS_2 is 1.5λ.

8. WR

During Young's double-slit experiment, light passes through two slits to create an interference pattern on the screen opposite the slits. This pattern has alternating bright and dark fringes (antinodes and nodes of the interference pattern). This is evidence of a wave superposition. Each slit acts as an in-phase wavesource whose waves interact with one another to form an interference pattern.

If the light were composed of particles, two bright fringes would appear opposite the slits.

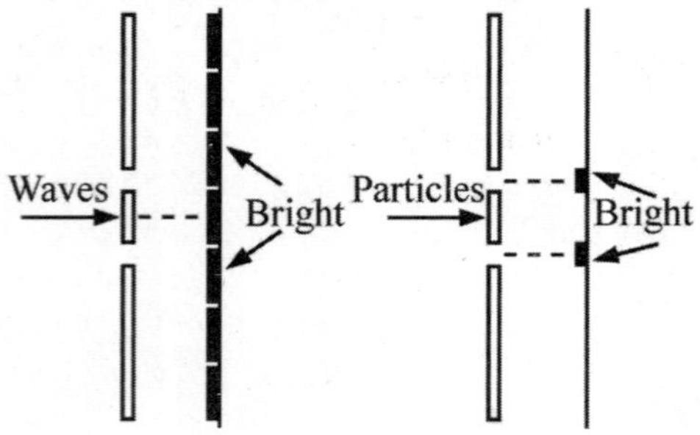

The diffraction interference pattern can be algebraically expressed by the following formula:
$n\lambda = d\sin\theta$

or $\sin\theta = \frac{n\lambda}{d}$

As the value of d becomes smaller, the angle formed between the light waves and the screen with the slits becomes greater. This causes the distance between the fringes to become farther apart. Therefore, varying the distance between the slits changes the size of the diffraction pattern on the screen.

9. B

$$\lambda = \frac{d\sin\theta}{n}$$

$$\sin\theta = \frac{n\lambda}{d}$$

where $d = \frac{1}{425\,000 \text{ lines/m}} = 2.35 \times 10^{-6}$ m/line

First line $n = 1$

$$\sin\theta = \frac{1\lambda}{d} = \frac{600 \times 10^{-9} \text{ m}}{2.35 \times 10^{-6} \text{ m}} = 0.255$$

$$\theta_1 = 14.77°$$

Second line $n = 2$

$$\sin\theta = \frac{2\lambda}{d} = \frac{2(600 \times 10^{-9} \text{ m})}{2.35 \times 10^{-6} \text{ m}} = 0.51$$

$$\theta_2 = 30.66°$$

$$\theta_2 - \theta_1 = 30.66° - 14.77° = 15.9°$$

10. 4987

$$n\lambda = \frac{dx}{l}$$

$$\lambda = \frac{dx}{nl}$$

$$= \frac{(4.24 \times 10^{-4} \text{ m})(2.35 \times 10^{-3} \text{ m})}{2(1.00 \text{ m})}$$

$$= 4.98 \times 10^{-7} \text{ m}$$

11. 2602

$$\frac{\lambda_a}{\lambda_m} = \frac{v_a}{v_m}$$

$$\Rightarrow \lambda_m = \frac{\lambda_a v_m}{v_a}$$

$$= \frac{(3.45 \times 10^{-2} \text{ m})(3.00 \times 10^8 \text{ m/s})(0.755)}{3.00 \times 10^8 \text{ m/s}}$$

$$= 2.60 \times 10^{-2} \text{ m}$$

12. B

$n\lambda = \frac{dx}{l}$ shows that $x \propto n\lambda$

The distance of the nth order bright fringe from the central maximum is directly proportional to the wavelength of the light being diffracted.
$\therefore$ x will be larger for red light than for blue light since red light has a longer wavelength. This means that red light will be positioned farther away from the central antinode than blue light.

13. C

First, equate the momentum of an electron to the momentum of a photon. Next, solve for the velocity of the electron required.

$$p_{\text{electron}} = p_{\text{photon}}$$
$$m_e v_e = \frac{h}{\lambda}$$
$$v_e = \frac{h}{m_e \lambda}$$
$$= \frac{6.63 \times 10^{-34}\ \text{J·s}}{(9.11 \times 10^{-31}\ \text{kg})(450 \times 10^{-9}\ \text{m})}$$
$$v_e = 1.62 \times 10^{3}\ \text{m/s}$$

14. B

Planck's constant can be found by taking the slope of the given graph.

$$h = \text{slope} = \frac{\text{rise}}{\text{run}} = \frac{\Delta E_{k_{\max}}}{\Delta f}$$
$$= \frac{(6.0 - 0.0) \times 10^{-19}\ \text{J}}{(16.0 - 4.0) \times 10^{-14}\ \text{Hz}}$$
$$h = 5.0 \times 10^{-34}\ \text{J·s}$$

15. 6014

$$W = hf_0$$
$$\therefore f_0 = \frac{W}{h} = \frac{2.5\ \text{eV}}{4.14 \times 10^{-15}\ \text{eV·s}}$$
$$= 6.0 \times 10^{14}\ \text{Hz}$$

16. B

Einstein proposed that light travelled as photons, or tiny "packets" of energy.

17. WR

The photoelectric effect occurs when light (or another type of EMR) shines on a surface and emits electrons from the surface. Waves and particles are two methods for transferring energy, so either form could be responsible for the photoelectric effect. However, the following experimental results supported the particle theory.

1. There is a threshold frequency below which no current flows, even if the light intensity is high. Any frequency of wave can have enough energy to remove an electron if its amplitude (intensity) is large enough, but this does not happen. Individual photons interacting one-to-one with electrons is consistent with this experimental result.
2. Above the threshold frequency, the current is proportional to intensity of light, but all photoelectrons have the same kinetic energy for a given frequency. A one-to-one collision between a photon and electron is consistent with this result.

The photoelectric current measures the number of electrons emitted by the photoelectric surface. Above the threshold frequency, this current is directly proportional to the intensity of the light because each indiviual photon of light has enough energy to remove an electron from the atoms in the surface. The more intense the light, the more electrons can be turned into a photoelectric current.

18. B

The Compton experiment showed that photons have the particle property of momentum.

19. WR

Several answers are possible. Here is a sample.

Experiments in favour of a particle model:

The photoelectric effect—experiments showed the existence of a threshold frequency below which no emissions would occur no matter how intense the light shining on the photoelectric surface was.
The classical wave theory predicted that the wave should become energetic enough to remove the electron if its amplitude were big enough.
The concept of the photon, quantized packets of light, explains why the electrons are not emitted despite the intensity of the light.

The Compton effect—experiments with incident X-rays on metal targets produced scattered X-rays and electrons. Measurements of the energies and the momenta of these X-rays and electrons verify the conservation laws for both energy and momentum (if the momentum of a photon is $\frac{h}{\lambda}$). Therefore, the X-rays behave as particles do in a collision.

Experiments in favour of a wave model:

Interference effects only occur with waves, which have the ability to pass through one another. Young's double-slit experiment shows a diffraction, interference pattern when light passes through two slits close together.

Refraction can occur with both waves and particles. However, particles refract toward the normal when they speed up, and waves refract away from the normal when they speed up. Observations show that light refracts toward the normal when passing from air into water, and measurements of the speed of light in water showed that this speed is less in water. This is consistent with a wave model for light.

Electromagnetic radiation has properties consistent with waves, but it also has properties consistent with particles. The wave-particle duality model is used to convey this idea that light shares properties with both phenomena.

20. WR

Find the momentum of the incident and scattered X-ray.

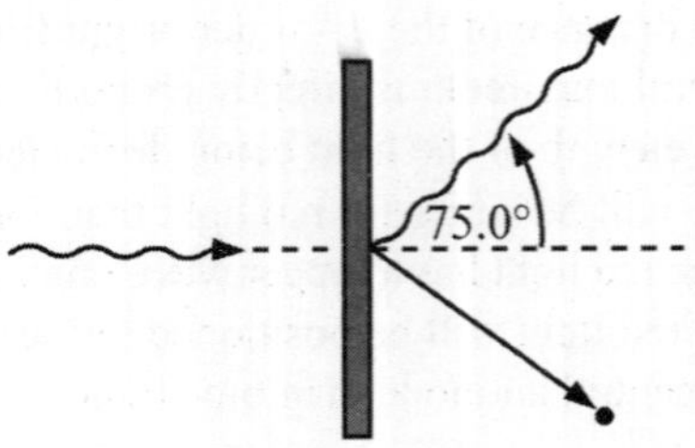

Momentum is conserved in this collision

$$p_\text{i} = \frac{h}{\lambda_\text{i}}$$

$$p_\text{i} = \frac{6.63 \times 10^{-34}\ \text{J·s}}{7.00 \times 10^{-11}\ \text{m}}$$
$$= 9.471 \times 10^{-24}\ \text{kg·m/s}$$

$$\Delta\lambda = \frac{h}{mc}(1 - \cos\theta)$$

$$= \frac{6.63 \times 10^{-34}\ \text{J·s}}{(9.11 \times 10^{-34}\ \text{kg})(3.00 \times 10^{8}\ \text{m/s})}$$
$$\times (1 - \cos 75.0°)$$
$$= 1.798 \times 10^{-12}\ \text{m}$$

$$\lambda_\text{s} = \lambda_\text{i} + \Delta\lambda$$
$$= 7.00 \times 10^{-11}\ \text{m} + 1.798 \times 10^{-12}\ \text{m}$$
$$= 7.18 \times 10^{-11}\ \text{m}$$

$$p_\text{s} = \frac{h}{\lambda_\text{s}}$$

$$p_\text{s} = \frac{6.63 \times 10^{-34}\ \text{J·s}}{7.18 \times 10^{-11}\ \text{m}}$$
$$= 9.234 \times 10^{-24}\ \text{kg·m/s}$$

You can solve for $p_{\bar{e}}$ using the component method or by using the cosine law.

To solve using a component method, the steps will be as follows:

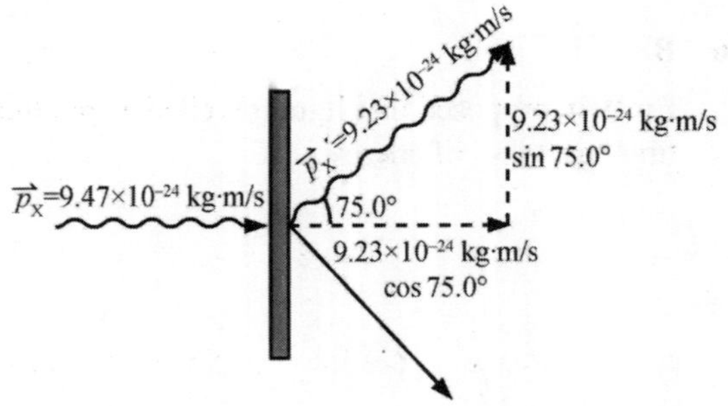

$$\sum p_\text{i} = \sum p_\text{f}$$

Vertical Momenta:

$$0 + 0 = (9.23 \times 10^{-24}\ \text{kg·m/s})\sin 75.0° + p_{e^-}$$

$$p_{e^-} = -8.92 \times 10^{-24}\ \text{kg·m/s}$$

Horizontal Momenta:

$$9.47 \times 10^{-24}\ \text{kg·m/s} + 0 = (9.23 \times 10^{-24}\ \text{kg·m/s})\cos 75.0° + p_{e^-}$$

$$\therefore p_{e^-} = (9.47 \times 10^{-24}\ \text{kg·m/s}) - (9.23 \times 10^{-24}\ \text{kg·m/s})\cos 75.0° = 7.08 \times 10^{-24}\text{kg·m/s}$$

Now construct a vector addition diagram to find the value of p_{e^-}.

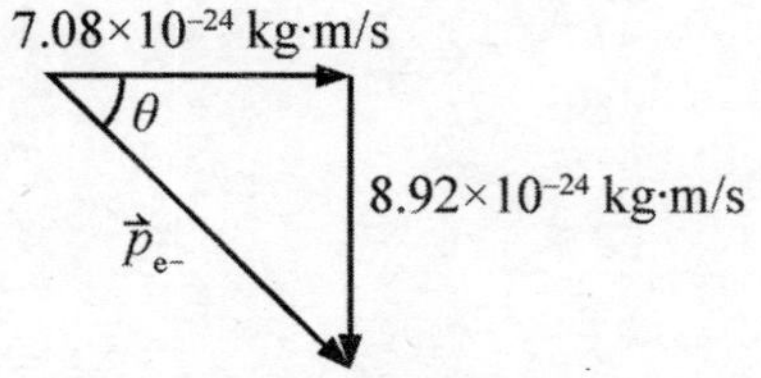

$$p_{e^-} = \sqrt{(7.08 \times 10^{-24}\ \text{kg·m/s})^2 + (8.92 \times 10^{-24}\ \text{kg·m/s})^2}$$
$$= 1.14 \times 10^{-23}\ \text{kg·m/s}$$

$$\theta = \tan^{-1}\left(\frac{8.92 \times 10^{-24}}{7.08 \times 10^{-24}}\right) = 51.6°$$

The electron's momentum is 1.14×10^{-23} kg·m/s at 51.6° down from the right of the diagram.

To solve using the cosine law method, the steps would be as follows:

Construct a vector addition diagram.

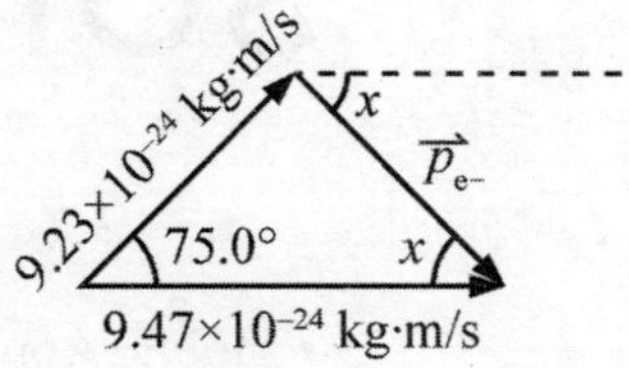

$$c^2 = a^2 + b^2 - 2ab\cos\gamma$$

$$\therefore p_{e^-}^2 = \begin{pmatrix} (9.23 \times 10^{-24}\ \text{kg·m/s})^2 \\ + (9.47 \times 10^{-24}\ \text{kg·m/s})^2 \\ - 2(9.23 \times 10^{-24}\ \text{kg·m/s}) \\ \times (9.47 \times 10^{-24}\ \text{kg·m/s})\cos 75.0° \end{pmatrix}$$

$$\Rightarrow p_{e^-} = 1.14 \times 10^{-23}\ \text{kg·m/s}$$

To find the angle of deflection for p_{e^-}, use the sine law to calculate the value of angle x in the diagram.

$$\frac{1.14 \times 10^{-23}}{\sin 75.0°} = \frac{9.23 \times 10^{-24}}{\sin x}$$
$$\therefore x = 51.4°$$

The momentum of the electron is 1.14×10^{-23} kg·m/s at an angle of 51.4° down from right in the diagram.

21. 321

The speed of electromagnetic radiation (EMR) is constant in a vacuum. Frequency and wavelength are inversely proportional. The frequency of EMR decreases from the gamma rays to the radio waves, whereas the wavelength increases from the gamma rays to the radio waves.

Description	Number
Remains the same regardless of location in the electromagnetic spectrum	3
Decreases from gamma rays to radio waves	2
Increases from gamma rays to radio waves	1

22. 3443

Violet light has a larger index of refraction than red light and is refracted through a larger angle than red is. Both colours must bend downward. Red has a larger wavelength than violet and appears in phase farther from the central antinode than does violet light. (Diffraction positions 1 and 3 could both be for blue light).

The values of *a*, *b*, *c*, and *d* are 3, 4, 4, and 3, respectively.

NOTES

Atomic Physics

ATOMIC PHYSICS

Table of Correlations

Outcome		Practice Questions	Unit Test Questions	Practice Test 1	Practice Test 2
D1	describe the electrical nature of the atom				
30-D1.1k	*describe matter as containing discrete positive and negative charges*	1		50	
30-D1.2k	*explain how the discovery of cathode rays contributed to the development of atomic models*	2	1, 2		52
30-D1.3k	*explain J.J. Thomson's experiment and the significance of the results for both science and technology*	3, 4, 5, 6, 7	3	51	
30-D1.4k	*explain, qualitatively, the significance of the results of Rutherford's scattering experiment, in terms of scientists' understanding of the relative size and mass of the nucleus and the atom*	8	4	52, 53	53
D2	describe the quantization of energy in atoms and nuclei				
30-D2.1k	*explain, qualitatively, how emission of EMR by an accelerating charged particle invalidates the classical model of the atom*	9			
30-D2.2k	*describe that each element has a unique line spectrum*	13	5		
30-D2.3k	*explain, qualitatively, the characteristics of, and the conditions necessary to produce, continuous line-emission and line-absorption spectra*	10, 11	6		54
30-D2.4k	*explain, qualitatively, the concept of stationary states and how they explain the observed spectra of atoms and molecules*	12		54	
30-D2.5k	*calculate the energy difference between states, using the law of conservation of energy and the observed characteristics of an emitted photon*	14a, 14b, 14c	7	55a, 55b	55, 56
30-D2.6k	*explain, qualitatively, how electron diffraction provides experimental support for the de Broglie hypothesis*	15	8		57
30-D2.7k	*describe, qualitatively, how the two-slit electron interference experiment shows that quantum systems, like photons and electrons, may be modelled as particles or waves, contrary to intuition*	16		56	58
D3	describe nuclear fission and fusion as powerful energy sources in nature				
30-D3.1k	*describe the nature and properties, including the biological effects, of alpha, beta and gamma radiation*	17, 18		57	
30-D3.2k	*write nuclear equations, using isotope notation, for alpha, beta-negative and beta-positive decays, including the appropriate neutrino and antineutrino*	19, 20, 21	9, 10		59a, 59b, 60
30-D3.3k	*perform simple, nonlogarithmic half-life calculations*	22, 23a, 23b	11	58	61
30-D3.4k	*use the law of conservation of charge and mass number to predict the particles emitted by a nucleus*	24	12, 13	59	62
30-D3.5k	*compare and contrast the characteristics of fission and fusion reactions*	25, 26a, 26b	18	60, 61	63
30-D3.6k	*relate, qualitatively and quantitatively, the mass defect of the nucleus to the energy released in nuclear reactions, using Einstein's concept of mass–energy equivalence*	27, 28, 29	14		64

D4	describe the ongoing development of models of the structure of matter.				
30-D4.1k	*explain how the analysis of particle tracks contributed to the discovery and identification of the characteristics of subatomic particles*	30		62	65
30-D4.2k	*explain, qualitatively, in terms of the strong nuclear force, why high-energy particle accelerators are required to study subatomic particles*	31	15		
30-D4.3k	*describe the modern model of the proton and neutron as being composed of quarks*	32	16		66
30-D4.4k	*compare and contrast the up quark, the down quark, the electron and the electron neutrino, and their antiparticles, in terms of charge and energy (mass-energy)*	33		63	
30-D4.5k	*describe beta-positive (β+) and beta-negative (β–) decay, using first-generation elementary fermions and the principle of charge conservation (Feynman diagrams are not required)*	34	17	64	67

30-D1.1k describe matter as containing discrete positive and negative charges

THOMSON'S MODEL OF THE ATOM

The concept of the atom in the first half of the 1800s was that atoms were featureless, indivisible spheres. Each atom was believed to have a neutral charge and no internal structure. The atoms of one element were clearly different from the atoms of another element, but the nature of this difference was unclear. This concept of the atom began to change as scientists learned more about electricity.

The evidence that supported the existence of atoms by the 1850s was primarily based on chemical investigations. By that time, chemists were learning about electrolysis and ions. The idea of a particle of electric charge began to emerge. In order to observe these charged particles, it was necessary to make an electric current pass through a vacuum. Tubes were made with a significant enough vacuum inside them that this was finally possible.

Experiments with these cathode ray tubes showed that something was flowing in straight lines across the tube from the cathode to the anode. These lines were originally called cathode rays. These rays were later understood to be beams of particles called electrons.

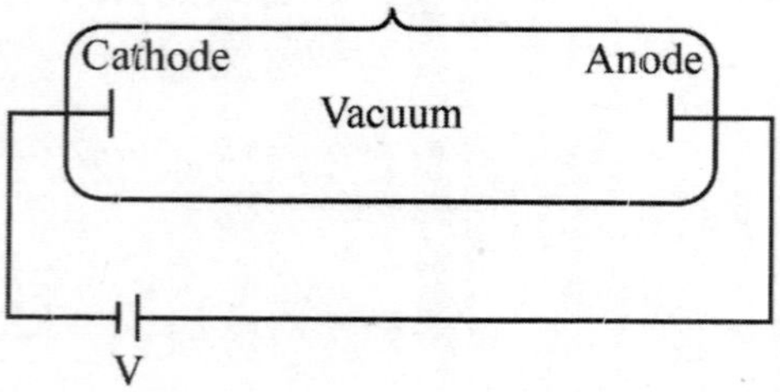

Based on these observations, J.J. Thomson reasoned that all atoms contain electrons. Since atoms are neutral, Thomson concluded that atoms must also contain sufficient positive charge to balance the negative charge of the electrons.

Use the following information to answer the next question.

The following observations were made about different evacuated glass tubes with various shapes and an electrode embedded at each end.

1. The rays in the L-shaped tube caused a green glow in the glass surface directly opposite the electrode attached to the negative pole of the high voltage source.
2. When a straight tube with a solid metal disk embedded in the middle of the tube was used, a shadow was cast on the side where the electrode was attached to the positive pole of the high voltage source.
3. When a straight tube was oriented with its negative electrode on the left, the ray in the tube was deflected downward when the north end of a bar magnet was brought near the tube along the horizontal plane.
4. When a tube was filled with hydrogen gas at a low pressure, it glowed a bright magenta color when a high voltage was applied across the electrodes.

1. Which of the given observations **best** support the hypothesis that cathode rays are composed of negative charge?

A. 2 and 4 **B.** 3 and 4

C. 1, 3 and 4 **D.** 1, 2, and 3

30-D1.2k explain how the discovery of cathode rays contributed to the development of atomic models

30-D1.3k explain J.J. Thomson's experiment and the significance of the results for both science and technology

THE DISCOVERY OF THE ELECTRON

J.J. Thomson demonstrated that cathode rays are beams of negatively charged particles called electrons. Thomson's experiment involved a cathode ray tube and perpendicular electric and magnetic fields that were also perpendicular to the motion of the cathode rays. The apparatus for Thomson's experiment appeared as shown

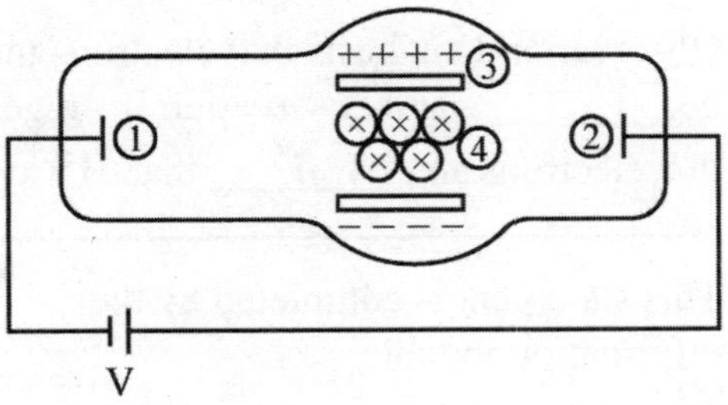

Cathode ray tube with perpendicular electric and magnetic fields

The apparatus setup included the following:

1. A cathode producing the cathode rays.
2. An anode attracting the cathode rays.
3. An electric field $\vec{E}$ directed downward and perpendicular to the cathode rays.
4. A magnetic field $\vec{B}$ directed into the page and perpendicular to both the electric field $\vec{E}$ and the cathode rays.

The electric field was formed by two charged parallel plates within the cathode ray tube, while the magnetic field was formed by external loops of wire that created a constant magnetic field through the apparatus. Both fields had to be mutually perpendicular to the motion of the cathode rays.

The directions of the fields were important for determining the nature of the charge on the cathode rays. A positive charge will experience a force in the same direction as the electric field, while a negative charge will experience a force in the opposite direction as the electric field. The nature of the charge of the cathode rays was established by removing the magnetic field around the apparatus. This resulted in the beam being deflected upward by the electric field.

Once the nature of the charge was determined using only the electric field, the magnetic field was set up to balance out the electrical force with a magnetic force using the left-hand rule for negative charges. In the given diagram, since the motion of the charges was toward the right and the magnetic force needed to direct the rays down (since the electric field deflected the ray up toward the positive plate), the magnetic field must be directed into the page.

The electric field $\vec{E}$ and the magnetic field $\vec{B}$ are adjustable. These two fields are the key to this experiment.

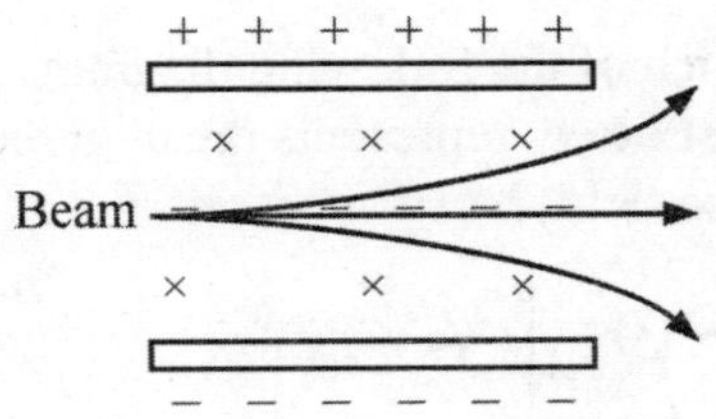

When the electric field attracts the beam upward in a parabolic trajectory, then $F_e = Eq$.
When the magnetic field deflects the beam downward in a circular trajectory, then $F_m = qvB_\perp$.

If the beam is undeflected, then $F_e = F_m$, since the forces due to each cancel out and the beam will pass undeflected through the region of perpendicular electric and magnetic fields.

Thomson was able to calculate the speed of the particles in the beam using the following formula:

$$F_e = F_m$$
$$Eq = qvB_\perp$$
$$v = \frac{E}{B_\perp}$$

After the speed of the particles was found, the electric field $\vec{E}$ was turned off, and Thomson measured the radius of the circular motion. Having found the values of v and r, Thomson was able to manipulate the magnetic force equation as follows:

$$F_{\text{m}} = qvB_{\perp} = ma_{\text{c}}$$
$$= qvB_{\perp} = \frac{mv^2}{r}$$
$$\Rightarrow \frac{q}{m} = \frac{v}{B_{\perp}r}$$

This allowed Thomson to calculate the charge-to-mass ratio of the particles as approximately 1.76×10^{11} C/kg. He then concluded that the cathode rays possessed both charge and mass, which was evidence that the rays were composed of particles.

Use the following information to answer the next question.

> A cathode ray passes undeflected through perpendicular electric and magnet fields.

2. Which of the following diagrams **most likely** represents the alignment of these fields?

A.
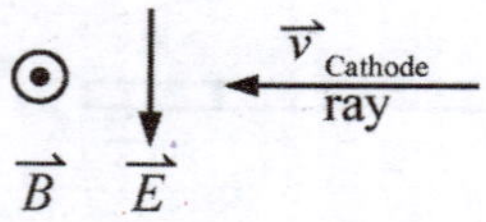

B.
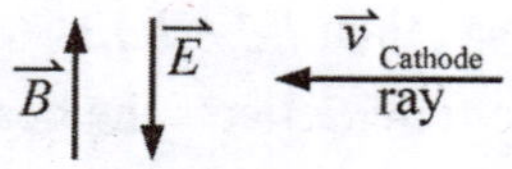

C.
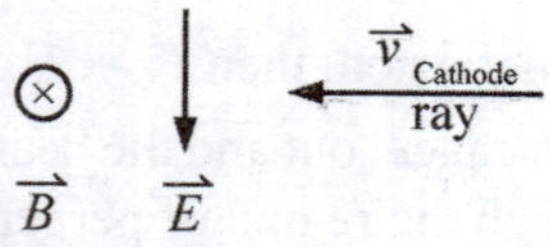

D.
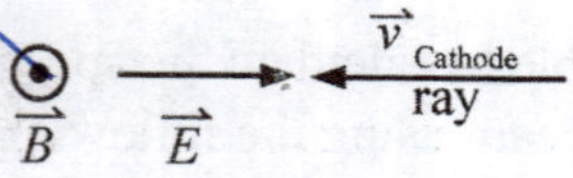

Use the following information to answer the next question.

> Two observations are made about J.J. Thomson's charge-to-mass-ratio experiment
>
> I. Thomson performed his experiment with several different materials for the cathode. The charge-to-mass ratio was the same for the cathode ray particles.
>
> II. The charge-to-mass ratio of these particles was about 2 000 times larger than the charge-to-mass ratio of hydrogen ions (thought to be the smallest particles in existence).
>
> Observation I suggests that electrons may be ___***i***___, and observation II suggests that electrons are ___***ii***___ than H^+ ions.

3. This statement is completed by the information in table

	i	***ii***
A.	part of all atoms	heavier
B.	part of all atoms	lighter
C.	a new form of matter	lighter
D.	a new form of matter	heavier

Use the following information to answer the next question.

Thomson proved that cathode rays were made of negatively charged particles. A student makes the following observations based upon a brief classroom demonstration on cathode rays.

I. Cathode rays are attracted to a positively charged plate.
II. The magnetic deflection of the cathode rays follows the left-hand rule.
III. Cathode rays move in straight lines.

4. Which of the given observations favour Thomson's prediction?

A. I only
B. III only
C. I and II only
D. II and III only

5. An electron, with a speed of 5.25×10^5 m/s and charge-to-mass ratio of 1.76×10^{11} C/kg, enters into a uniform magnetic field of 175 μT. If the electron travels perpendicular to the magnetic field direction, what will be the radius of curvature of the electron's path in the magnetic field?

A. 1.28 cm **B.** 1.70 cm
C. 2.55 cm **D.** 2.95 cm

Use the following information to answer the next question.

The speed of cathode ray particles that pass undeflected through a 0.0500 T magnetic field and a 1.20×10^5 N/C electric field, that are mutually perpendicular to the path of the cathode rays, is $a.bc \times 10^d$ m/s.

Numerical Response

6. What are the values of *a*, *b*, *c*, and *d*? __________ (Record your answer as a four-digit number.)

Use the following information to answer the next question.

An electron accelerated through a potential difference of 1.50 kV and was directed into the space between two parallel plates 2.50 cm apart with a potential difference of 100 V across them.

Numerical Response

7. Assume that the electron travelled perpendicularly to the uniform electric field between the plates. If the magnetic field was mutually perpendicular to both the electric field and the direction of the electron's motion, the magnitude of the magnetic field required to permit the electron to pass through the fields without deflection was $a.bc \times 10^{-d}$ T. The values of *a*, *b*, *c*, and *d* are __________, and __________. (Record your answer as a four digit number.)

30-D1.4k explain, qualitatively, the significance of the results of Rutherford's scattering experiment, in terms of scientists' understanding of the relative size and mass of the nucleus and the atom

Rutherford's Scattering Experiments

Thomson's model of the atom consisted of a positively charged solid sphere with electrons embedded throughout. Ernest Rutherford set out to test this idea by passing a beam of alpha particles through a thin gold foil to see how they scattered.

In Rutherford's gold foil scattering experiment, he found that alpha particles scattered much more than predicted by a uniformly dense model of the atom. He concluded that almost all of the mass and all of the positive charge of the atom must be located in a very tiny volume, which he called the nucleus.

The largest part of the atom's volume contained negative electrons orbiting the nucleus just as planets orbit the sun. The planetary model of the atom was mainly empty space. The atomic diameter is approximately 10^4 times larger than its nuclear diameter. If the nucleus were the size of a period on this page, the first orbit would be about 50 m away.

Use the following information to answer the next question.

These atomic structures represent two possible options for the structure of atomic nuclei. Ernest Rutherford's scattering experiment with gold foil was intended to shed some light on this structure.

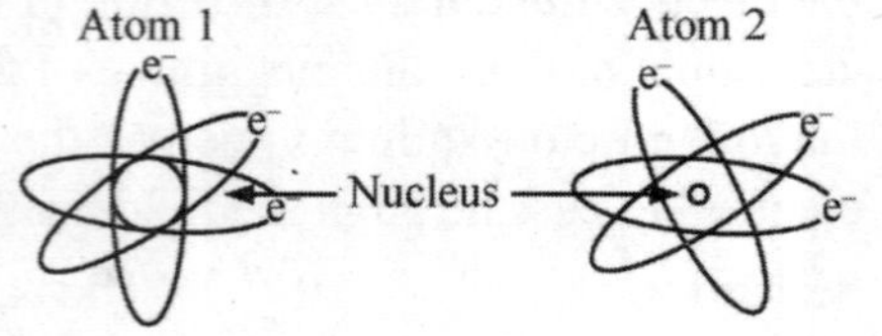

Two possible scattering results are graphed as shown.

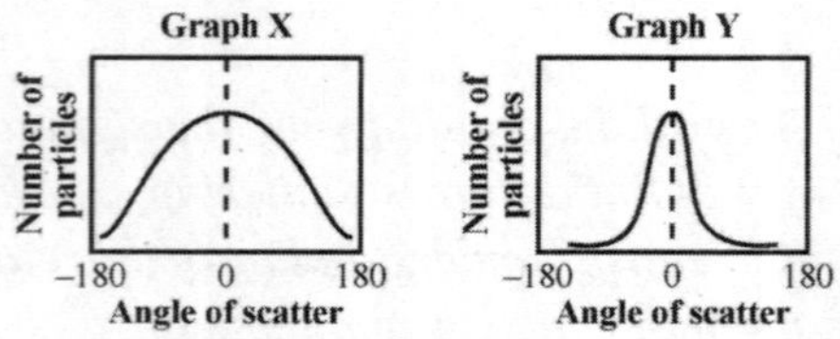

Numerical Response

8. The result illustrated in graph X supports the structure of atom _________, and the result illustrated in graph Y supports the structure of atom _________. (Record your answer as a two-digit number.)

30-D2.1k explain, qualitatively, how emission of EMR by an accelerating charged particle invalidates the classical model of the atom

A Problem with Rutherford's Atomic Model

James Maxwell's theory of electromagnetism states that an accelerating charge will produce an electromagnetic radiation (EMR) wave. A charged particle travelling in a circle, such as an electron in orbit around a nucleus, undergoes centripetal acceleration. Therefore, an orbiting electron should continually radiate energy in the form of EMR. The kinetic energy and electric potential energy of the electron should continually decrease, and the electron should spiral inward until it makes contact with the nucleus.

However, this collapse of the electron into the nucleus is not observed. The theory that negative electrons are separated from the small, positive nucleus by a large distance was necessary to explain Rutherford's observations, but orbiting electrons could not be stable, according to Maxwell. Thus, classical physics could not explain the atom and its makeup.

9. Which of the following statements explains a weakness in the planetary model of the atom?

A. The negative electron would be attracted by the positive nucleus with a Coulomb force sufficient to collapse the atom.

B. The centripetal force acting on the electron exceeds the electrostatic force of attraction between electron and nucleus.

C. The calculated orbital velocity could not be counterbalanced by the centripetal force due to the electrostatic attraction between the electron and nucleus.

D. The orbiting electron would be in a state of constant acceleration, so it should radiate energy continuously, reducing its kinetic energy until it spirals into the nucleus.

30-D2.3k explain, qualitatively, the characteristics of, and the conditions necessary to produce, continuous line-emission and line-absorption spectra

Types of Spectra

A continuous spectrum is observed when the light coming from an incandescent solid is divided into its component frequencies. Either a prism or a diffraction grating, incorporated in an instrument called a spectroscope, can be used to form a continuous spectrum. The spectrum is a smooth blending of colours from the longest wavelength of red light (then orange, yellow, green, blue, and indigo) to the shortest wavelength of violet light.

If a gas at low pressure is excited either electrically or thermally, light is emitted. If the emitted light is viewed through a spectroscope, only certain definite frequencies (colours) will be observed. This is called a bright-line or emission spectrum.
This spectrum is unique to the gas being excited, and it can be used to identify the gas.

If a beam of white light is directed through a low-pressure gas that is not energized electrically or thermally and the emergent beam is viewed through a spectroscope, the spectrum observed will consist of dark lines against a continuous spectrum. This is called a dark-line or absorption spectrum. The dark lines of the absorption spectrum correspond exactly to the bright lines of the emission spectrum for a given substance.

10.

A student sets up a diffraction spectroscope as shown in the diagram. The resulting spectrum viewed through the spectroscope will be a

A. dark-line emission spectrum

B. bright-line emission spectrum

C. dark-line absorption spectrum

D. bright-line continuous spectrum

11. A student has a glass tube filled with neon gas at low pressure. The tube has an electrode embedded at each end. First the student passes full-spectrum white light through the tube and views this light through a spectroscope. Then the student excites the gas with a high voltage and views the glowing tube through the same spectroscope. Which of the following statements **best** describes the student's observations from the experiment?

A. The student first observed a continuous spectrum and then an emission spectrum.

B. The student first observed an emission spectrum and then an absorption spectrum.

C. The two spectra were identical in line spacing, but the second spectrum was slightly less intense.

D. The dark lines of the first observed spectrum match the bright lines of the second observed spectrum.

30-D2.4k explain, qualitatively, the concept of stationary states and how they explain the observed spectra of atoms and molecules

Explaining Line Spectra Using the Atomic Model

Stationary States

In order to reconcile the planetary model of the atom with Maxwell's prediction that accelerating electrons emit EMR, Niels Bohr proposed the idea of **stationary states**, also called **energy levels.** According to this theory, electrons could have only certain permitted values of energy within the atom, and electrons with these specific energy values, or levels, were stable. If, however, an electron in a lower energy state gained the right amount of energy, it could jump to a higher energy state.
A specific frequency of light would then be absorbed.

Conversely, electrons moving from a higher stationary state to a lower one would emit only very specific amounts of energy. These specific energies, either absorbed or emitted, correspond exactly to the frequencies seen in the absorption and emission spectra for these atoms. Each element has a different line spectrum because each element has a different number and arrangement of electron energy levels.

Bohr was able to determine the stationary states of the hydrogen atom. His equation can be used to determine the energy of an electron in any of the states based on the energy of the electron in the **ground state** (the lowest energy level).

$E_n = E_1\left(\frac{1}{n^2}\right)$, where n must always be a whole number because electrons cannot exist between stationary states.

$E_1 = -13.6$ eV. This is the ground state for an electron in a hydrogen atom.

Electrons in higher energy levels than the ground state are said to be in excited states. For example, the energy of an electron in the first excited state ($n = 2$) can be calculated as follows:

$$E_2 = E_1\left(\frac{1}{2^2}\right)$$
$$= -13.6 \text{ eV}\left(\frac{1}{4}\right)$$
$$= -3.4 \text{ eV}$$

Bohr was only able to determine the energy levels of the hydrogen atom, but experimental evidence has since supported the idea that all atoms and molecules have stationary states. An example is illustrated in the given diagram. Note that the energies are given as negative numbers. The more excited an electron is, the closer its energy is to zero. Zero energy is defined as the energy needed for the electron to escape the atom completely. This event is called ionization.

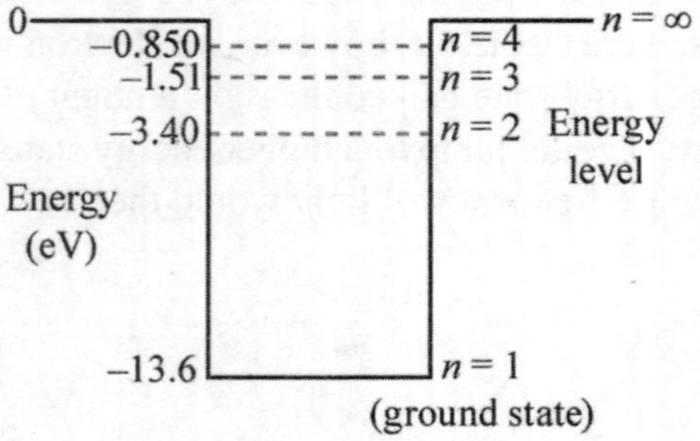

In the Bohr atom, energy is quantized. This model helped lay the groundwork for the quantum mechanical model of the atom.

12. Which of the following statements is **false**?

A. Electrons moving from higher energy levels to lower energy levels within an atom absorb energy.

B. An absorption spectrum occurs when electrons in stable stationary states within an atom gain energy.

C. An emission spectrum occurs when excited electrons within an atom radiate energy and move into stationary states of lower energy.

D. Each bright-line within a spectrum corresponds to a specific change of an electron from a higher energy level to a lower energy level within the atom.

30-D2.2k describe that each element has a unique line spectrum

Unique Line Spectra

A specific frequency of light is emitted or absorbed when an electron jumps from one energy state to another within the orbit of an atom. Each element has a different line spectrum because each element has a different number and arrangement of electron energy levels.

13. A bright-line emission spectrum would be seen if a spectroscope was used to view the

A. sun from Earth

B. glowing coals in a camp fire

C. incandescent filament of an ordinary light bulb

D. glow of a gas-filled tube excited by a high voltage

30-D2.5k calculate the energy difference between states, using the law of conservation of energy and the observed characteristics of an emitted photon

Energy States and Spectral Lines

Neils Bohr found values for the stationary states (now called energy levels) for hydrogen atoms. Franck and Hertz measured energy levels in mercury atoms. When spectral lines of hydrogen and mercury matched the predicted energy levels, the concept of energy levels was verified. This diagram demonstrates this idea.

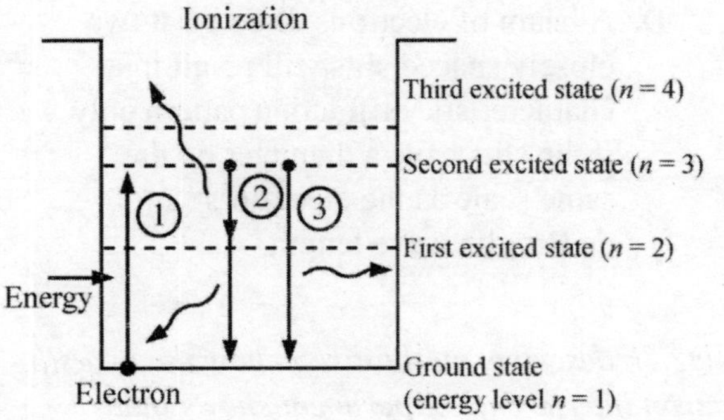

1. Electrons absorb only certain amounts of energy to move to higher levels.
2. Electrons emit only certain amounts of energy (as photons) when they return to their ground state.
3. Electrons can return to their ground state either directly or indirectly. For example, an electron in the second excited state may return directly to the ground state or may drop first to the first excited state and then to the ground state.

Use the following information to answer the next multipart question.

14. The diagram shows the predicted energy levels for an atom.

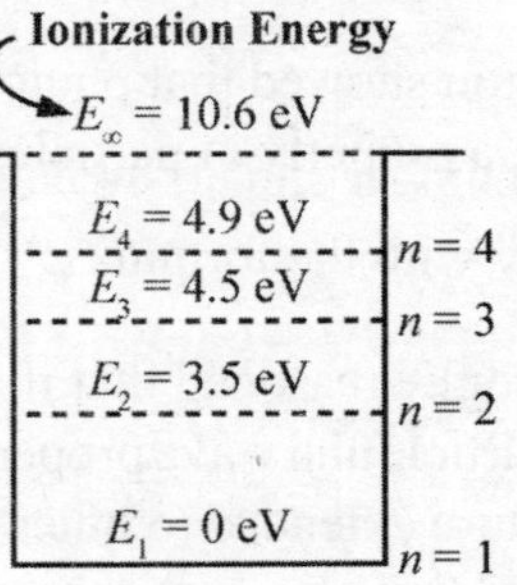

When this substance is bombarded with electrons of increasing energy, it is found that electrons with 3.5 eV lose their energy when colliding with the substance's atoms. Subsequently, the atoms emit photons with a frequency of $a.b \times 10^{cd}$ Hz.

Numerical Response

a) What are the values of *a*, *b*, *c*, and *d*? (Record your answer as a four-digit number.)

b) If an electron drops from $n = 4$ to $n = 3$, the wavelength of the emitted photon will be

A. 2.8×10^{-7} m

B. 3.5×10^{-7} m

C. 1.2×10^{-6} m

D. 3.1×10^{-6} m

c) If the electrons are excited to $n = 4$, the number of different spectral lines observed is

A. 3 **B.** 4

C. 5 **D.** 6

30-D2.6k explain, qualitatively, how electron diffraction provides experimental support for the de Broglie hypothesis

De Broglie's Hypothesis

A.H. Compton showed that photons had momentum, a property of particles. He represented this property with the formula $p = \frac{h}{\lambda} = \frac{hf}{c}$.

Louis de Broglie reasoned that if a photon could have both particle and wave properties, then perhaps this dual nature extended to other particles as well. He suggested that electrons, neutrons, and even baseballs have a wave nature. By combining the formulas for photon momentum and the momentum of matter, de Broglie derived a formula that suggested particles of matter have wave properties.

De Broglie's hypothesis was verified experimentally in 1927 by C. J. Davisson and L. H. Germer. A few years earlier, W.H. Bragg predicted and empirically verified that X-rays could be diffracted by thin crystals. He showed that the regular spacing of the atoms in the crystal behaved like a multi-slit diffraction grating. Davisson and Germer showed that a beam of electrons reflect off a thin crystal in a very similar manner, producing a diffraction pattern essentially the same as the pattern observed by Bragg.

This observation was convincing evidence for de Broglie's matter waves. It also supported the wave–particle duality theory, because it showed that a particle could have wave properties, just as a wave could have particle properties.

15. Which of the following statements does **not** describe the matter wave of an electron?

A. In any experiment, it is not possible to simultaneously observe both wave and particle properties.

B. The wavelength of an electron is inversely proportional to the velocity with which the electron travels.

C. The wavelength of an electron is directly proportional to the particle's constant rate of acceleration.

D. A beam of electrons directed at two closely spaced slits will result in a characteristic diffraction pattern only if the slits have a diameter on the same scale as the electron's de Broglie wave length.

30-D2.7k describe, qualitatively, how the two-slit electron interference experiment shows that quantum systems, like photons and electrons, may be modelled as particles or waves, contrary to intuition

Two Slit Electron Diffraction

Physicists now have the ability to conduct ever more sensitive and precise experiments involving light, which enables them to observe single photons as they pass through slits and strike a detector. The particle nature of the photon is apparent as they strike a photosensitive screen behind the slits. Over a longer period of time, individual photons, acting independently, strike the photosensitive screen to reveal a typical diffraction pattern of alternating bright and dark bands. This is an astonishing phenomenon!

This behaviour has also been observed for other particles, such as electrons. The current consensus is that the quantum mechanics theory best explains this phenomenon. The de Broglie wave seems to determine the probability that a particle will behave in a certain way. Certain trajectories through the slits have a higher probability and bright bands in the diffraction pattern are the result. The paths with low probability correspond to the dark bands.

Written Response

16. Explain how a beam of electrons directed at a crystalline substance would produce an interference pattern.

____

____

____

____

30-D3.1k describe the nature and properties, including the biological effects, of alpha, beta and gamma radiation

NUCLEAR RADIATION

Physicists have determined that a nucleus undergoing a transformation emits one of three types of radiation: alpha rays, beta rays, or gamma rays.

Alpha rays are beams of alpha particles (helium nuclei, consisting of two protons and two neutrons) and are represented by the symbol ${}_{2}^{4}\alpha$. Alpha particles can travel only very short distances in matter. For example, a 5 MeV alpha particle (a high-energy particle) can travel only 4 cm in air, and higher energy alpha particles can barely penetrate a sheet of paper. However, an alpha particle will collide with many atoms in the short distance it travels. Although they cannot penetrate skin, alpha particles are the most dangerous type of radiation because they will ionize many atoms in a small location if inhaled or ingested.

Beta rays are beams of beta particles (high-speed electrons emitted from the nucleus) and are represented by the symbol ${}_{-1}^{0}\beta$. The positron is the antiparticle of the beta particle and is represented by the symbol ${}_{+1}^{0}\beta$. Beta particles have a range typically one hundred times greater than that of alpha particles. Beta particles ionize fewer particles than alpha particles do, so although they can penetrate skin, they are not as damaging as alpha particles.

Gamma rays are beams of high-energy photons. They can travel great distances in air and can penetrate the human body completely. They interact with relatively few atoms, however, and are about as damaging as beta particles.

Alpha, beta, and gamma radiation are all ionizing forms of radiation. They turn atoms in the human body into ions, making normally non-reactive substances in the body reactive. Even atoms in DNA can become reactive, which can cause genetic mutations.

The symptoms caused by exposure to radiation are collectively called radiation sickness. In the short term, these symptoms may include loss of appetite, nausea, and vomiting. Long-term symptoms may include a weakening of the immune system (more severe with greater exposure), cataracts, and serious gastric disorders. Severe radiation sickness usually results in death within three weeks.

Use the following information to answer the next question.

Particle 1—can only penetrate a sheet of paper or thin metal foil
Particle 2—can penetrate up to 3 mm of aluminum
Particle 3—can penetrate several centimetres of lead

17. Which of the following lists shows the particles that make up alpha, beta, and gamma radiation, respectively?

A. Particles 1, 2, and 3

B. Particles 1, 3, and 2

C. Particles 2, 1, and 3

D. Particles 3, 1, and 2

Use the following information to answer the next question.

Three types of radiation pass through an electric field along the paths shown.

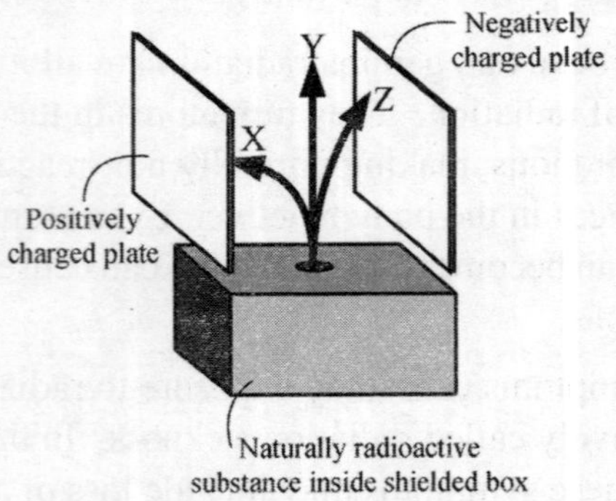

18. The types of radiation taking paths X, Y, and Z are, respectively,

A. beta, alpha, and gamma

B. beta, gamma, and alpha

C. gamma, alpha, and beta

D. alpha, gamma, and beta

30-D3.2k write nuclear equations, using isotope notation, for alpha, beta-negative and beta-positive decays, including the appropriate neutrino and antineutrino

NUCLEAR DECAY EQUATIONS

An isotope of element X is represented by ${}^{A}_{Z}X$, where Z is the element's atomic number (number of protons or charge number) and A is the element's mass number (number of nucleons: protons + neutrons).

The emission of an alpha particle from an isotope causes the atomic number and the atomic mass of the daughter nuclide to decrease by two and four, respectively.

$${}^{A}_{Z}X \rightarrow {}^{A-4}_{Z-2}Y + {}^{4}_{2}\alpha$$

Beta decay is the emission of high-energy electrons from the nucleus. It occurs when a neutron changes to a proton, releasing a high-energy electron and an antineutrino $\bar{\nu}$. Beta-negative decay causes the atomic number of the daughter nuclide to increase by one but does not change the mass number.

$${}^{A}_{Z}X \rightarrow {}^{A}_{Z+1}Y + {}^{0}_{-1}\beta + \bar{\nu}$$

The opposite reaction can also occur: a proton changes into a neutron, reducing the atomic number of the daughter nuclide by one. In the process, the atom emits a positron (the antielectron) and a neutrino. This is called beta-positive decay.

$${}^{A}_{Z}X \rightarrow {}^{A}_{Z-1}Y + {}^{0}_{+1}\beta + \nu$$

Gamma rays are very high-energy photons emitted when the nucleus of an atom jumps to a lower energy state. These photons often accompany alpha or beta decay.

$${}^{A}_{Z}X \rightarrow {}^{A}_{Z+1}Y + {}^{0}_{-1}\beta + \bar{\nu} + \gamma$$

Since photons have no rest mass, gamma emission does not change the atomic number or the atomic mass of the daughter nuclide.

An example of alpha decay, using isotope notation, is ${}^{227}_{90}\text{Th} \rightarrow {}^{223}_{88}\text{Ra} + {}^{4}_{2}\alpha$.

An example of beta-negative decay is ${}^{14}_{6}\text{C} \rightarrow {}^{14}_{7}\text{N} + {}^{0}_{-1}\beta + \bar{\nu}$.

19. The isotope ${}^{131}_{53}\text{I}$ emits a beta-negative particle. The products of this reaction include

A. ${}^{131}_{53}\text{Xe} + {}^{0}_{-1}\beta + \nu$

B. ${}^{131}_{53}\text{I} + {}^{0}_{-1}\beta + \nu$

C. ${}^{131}_{54}\text{Xe} + {}^{0}_{-1}\beta + \nu$

D. ${}^{131}_{52}\text{Xe} + {}^{0}_{-1}\beta + \nu$

20. The isotope ${}^{22}_{11}\text{Na}$ spontaneously decays to form ${}^{22}_{10}\text{Ne}$. What are the additional particles released in order to conserve mass, energy, and momentum?

A. ${}^{0}_{-1}\beta + \bar{\nu}$

B. ${}^{0}_{1}\beta + \nu$

C. ${}^{0}_{-1}\beta + \bar{\nu}$

D. ${}^{0}_{1}\beta + \bar{\nu}$

21. Uranium-238 is a known alpha emitter. The correct alpha-decay equation for this isotope is

A. ${}^{238}_{92}U + ? \rightarrow {}^{239}_{92}U$

B. ${}^{238}_{92}U \rightarrow ? + {}^{238}_{91}Pa + \bar{\nu}$

C. ${}^{238}_{92}U \rightarrow ? + {}^{234}_{90}Th$

D. ${}^{238}_{92}U + ? \rightarrow {}^{242}_{94}Pu$

30-D3.3k perform simple, nonlogarithmic half-life calculations

CALCULATING HALF-LIVES

The half-life of an element is the time it takes for a sample of an element to decay to one-half its original mass. In contrast, the activity of a sample is the number of decays that occur per second.

The activity decreases at the same rate as the mass of the sample because the two are proportional to one another.

The activity of a sample can be determined after a given amount of time using the formula

$N = N_0\left(\frac{1}{2}\right)^n$, where N is the activity after the given amount of time, N_0 is the activity of the original sample, and n is the number of half-lives.

The value of n can be found using the formula

$n = \frac{t}{t_{1/2}}$, where t is the elapsed time and $t_{\frac{1}{2}}$ is the element's half-life.

A sample's mass can be determined simply by substituting the mass after the given amount of time (m) for the activity of the sample after the given amount of time (N), and substituting the original mass (m_0) for the original activity (N_0).

$$m = m_0\left(\frac{1}{2}\right)^n$$

Half-life can be given in any unit of time, from seconds to years. However, the units for the elapsed time and the time for half-life must be in the same units.

Use the following information to answer the next question.

Mass spectrometers are used in archaeological studies to help date ancient artifacts. The relative amounts of carbon-12 and carbon-14 isotopes in a sample of organic material may be used to determine the age of the sample. Carbon-14 is a radioactive isotope that undergoes beta decay and has a half-life of 5 730 years.

22. An archaeological sample is dated using the carbon-14 dating process and is found to be 2 865 years old. What percentage of the original carbon-14 remains?

A. 25.0% **B.** 29.3%
C. 70.7% **D.** 75.0%

Use the following information to answer the next multipart question.

23. The graph shows the mass of a radioactive isotope as a function of time.

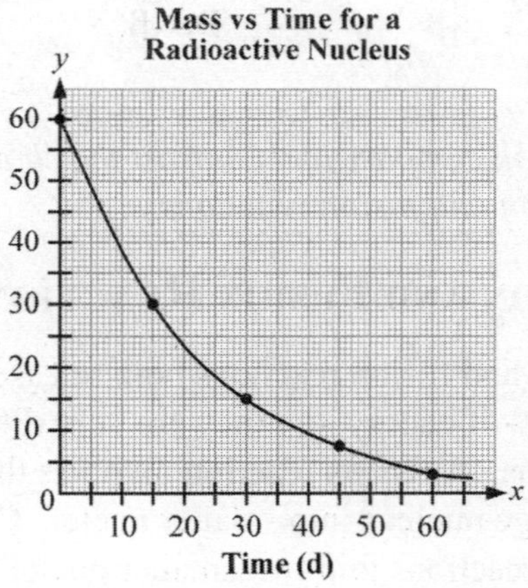

a) The half-life of this isotope is closest to

A. 30 days **B.** 15 days
C. 15 g **D.** 30 g

b) The mass of this isotope remaining after 2.5 half-lives is

A. 11 g **B.** 20 g
C. 25 g **D.** 56 g

30-D3.4k use the law of conservation of charge and mass number to predict the particles emitted by a nucleus

PREDICTING NUCLEAR EMISSIONS

When an element is bombarded by another particle or element, the result may yield many different elements, but all transmutations must conserve mass number (number of nucleons) as well as the charge of the system. For example, in the following reaction, there are 18 nucleons on both sides of the equation. Of these, nine are protons on both sides. Thus, both the mass and charge are conserved in this reaction.

$${}^{14}_{7}N + {}^{4}_{2}He \rightarrow {}^{17}_{8}O + {}^{1}_{1}H$$

Use the following information to answer the next question.

$${}^{14}_{7}N + {}^{4}_{+2}He \rightarrow {}^{17}_{8}O + x$$

24. What particle will complete the given nuclear equation?

A. ${}^{1}_{1}H$ **B.** ${}^{0}_{-1}\beta$

C. ${}^{0}_{+1}\beta$ **D.** ${}^{1}_{1}\beta$

30-D3.5k compare and contrast the characteristics of fission and fusion reactions

FISSION AND FUSION REACTIONS

Fission and fusion reactions both release large amounts of energy, but they are very different reactions. A fission reaction involves the splitting of a large nucleus into smaller nuclei. Contrastly, fusion reactions join two smaller nuclei together to make one larger nucleus.

The atom bombs used at the end of the Second World War generated their energy using the fission of uranium-235. The energy produced by the sun occurs when four hydrogen nuclei are fused into one helium nucleus. This fusion reaction produces much more energy than the splitting of the uranium atom.

Use the following information to answer the next question.

A particular nuclear fission reaction of uranium-235 is represented by

$${}^{235}_{92}U + {}^{1}_{0}n \rightarrow {}^{141}_{55}Cs + {}^{ab}_{cd}X + 3{}^{1}_{0}n$$

where element X is unknown.

Numerical Response

25. The fission product in this reaction is represented by ${}^{ab}_{cd}X$. The values of a, b, c, and d are ________, ________, ________, and ________. (Record your four-digit answer.)

Use the following information to answer the next multipart question.

26. Nuclear fission reaction:

$${}^{1}_{0}n + {}^{235}_{92}U \rightarrow {}^{141}_{56}Ba + {}^{ab}_{cd}Kr + 3{}^{1}_{0}n$$

Nuclear fusion reaction:

$${}^{3}_{1}H + {}^{3}_{1}H \rightarrow {}^{4}_{2}He + x{}^{1}_{0}n$$

Numerical Response

a) The values of a, b, c, and d in the fission reaction are ________, ________, ________, and ________. (Record your answer as a four-digit number)

b) In the fusion reaction, the number of neutrons produced (x) is

A. 0 **B.** 1

C. 2 **D.** 3

30-D3.6k relate, qualitatively and quantitatively, the mass defect of the nucleus to the energy released in nuclear reactions, using Einstein's concept of mass–energy equivalence

Einstein's Mass-Energy Equivalence

Einstein derived the equation $E = mc^2$.
This equation indicates that mass can be converted into energy. It also indicates that the conversion of very small amounts of matter will create vast amounts of energy.

In radioactive decay, nuclear fission, and nuclear fusion, the energy released is the result of the mass defect. The mass defect is the difference in the masses of the reactants and products. Since the mass defect in these subatomic reactions is always very small, the masses must be known to very precise figures (five or six decimal places) to determine the mass defect.

During any nuclear reaction, the difference in mass between the reactants and products is used to find the energy released (or absorbed). $E = \Delta mc^2$

Atomic Mass Units

When working with atomic masses and interactions on the atomic scale, it can be helpful to use a unit that is much smaller than the standard kilogram.

The atomic mass unit (u) is defined as exactly $\frac{1}{12}$ the mass of a carbon-12 atom:

$1\ \text{u} = 1.660\ 539 \times 10^{-27}\ \text{kg}$

The following equivalences for the atomic mass unit may also be useful:

$1\ \text{u} = 931.5\ \text{MeV}/c^2 = 1.492 \times 10^{-10}\ \text{J}/c^2$

These values are a direct result of mass-energy equivalence.

The given tables are helpful to use when calculating mass defects. The values for mass and charge are given to six decimal places to allow for more accurate calculations.

Particle	Electron
Charge (C)	$-1.602\ 177 \times 10^{-19}$
Mass (kg)	$9.109\ 383 \times 10^{-31}$
Mass (u)	$5.485\ 799 \times 10^{-4}$

Particle	Proton
Charge (C)	$+1.602\ 177 \times 10^{-19}$
Mass (kg)	$1.672\ 622 \times 10^{-27}$
Mass (u)	1.007 276

Particle	Neutron
Charge (C)	0
Mass (kg)	$1.674\ 927 \times 10^{-27}$
Mass (u)	1.008 665

Each atom also has a mass defect. The mass of a neutral atom is less than the mass of its individual particles (protons, neutrons, and electrons). This drop in mass occurs because a portion of the particles' masses is converted to energy that binds the nucleus together. This energy, called the binding energy of the atom, must be re-added to the atom to break it up into its particles.

Use the following information to answer the next question.

Binding Energy per Nucleon Versus the Atomic Mass Number

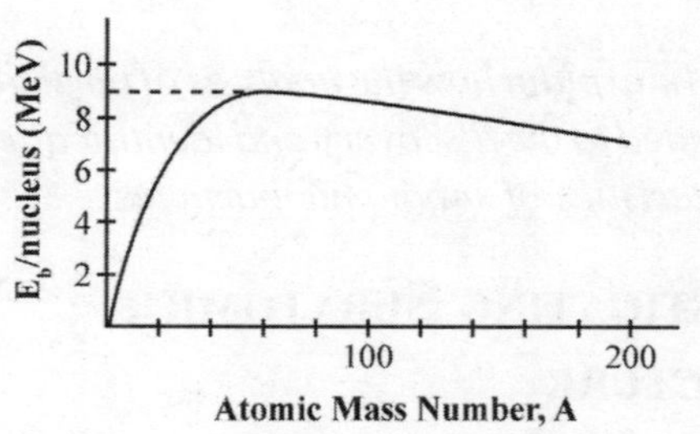

The given graph shows the average binding energy per nucleon versus the atomic mass number of the nucleus.

27. The most difficult atom's nucleus to break is

A. uranium **B.** neon

C. iron **D.** tin

Numerical Response

28. The reactants in a nuclear reaction have a mass 0.010 g larger than the mass of the products. The energy released by this nuclear reaction is $a.b \times 10^{cd}$ J. The value of *abcd* is ________. (Record your answer as a four-digit number.)

Use the following information to answer the next question.

The given chemical equation shows the fission reaction of uranium-235 in most modern nuclear reactors.

$^{235}_{92}U + ^{1}_{0}n \rightarrow ^{136}_{56}Ba + ^{97}_{36}Kr + 3^{1}_{0}n + \text{energy}$

The given table of data lists some species and their masses.

Species	Mass (kg)
Uranium-235	$3.903\,00 \times 10^{-25}$
Neutron	$1.674\,93 \times 10^{-27}$
Barium-136	2.2567×10^{-25}
Krypton-97	1.6099×10^{-25}

Numerical Response

29. The total amount of energy produced by the given nuclear reaction is $a.b \times 10^{-cd}$ J. What are the values of *a*, *b*, *c*, and *d*? ________ (Record your answer as a four-digit number.)

30-D4.1k explain how the analysis of particle tracks contributed to the discovery and identification of the characteristics of subatomic particles

Investigating Subatomic Structure

Particle physicists use instruments of ever-increasing complexity to probe the internal structure of matter. The simplest instrument they use is the cloud chamber. This is a device that permits the observation of the trail of condensed droplets left in the wake of a high-speed subatomic particle that travels through supersaturated vapour in the presence of a perpendicular magnetic field. It is possible to infer some of the properties (charge and mass for example) of these particles by measuring the radius of curvature of their trajectories when known uniform magnetic fields are applied and then using the laws of conservation of mass, energy, momentum, and charge.

The bubble chamber used the formation of bubbles caused when particles travelled through superheated liquids (although a super-heated neon and hydrogen mix occurs at only 30 K (above absolute zero). By the 1950s, over 100 different subatomic particles had been detected.

Use the following information to answer the next question.

This diagram shows two tracks formed in a cloud chamber. There is a constant magnetic field within the chamber that is directed into the page.

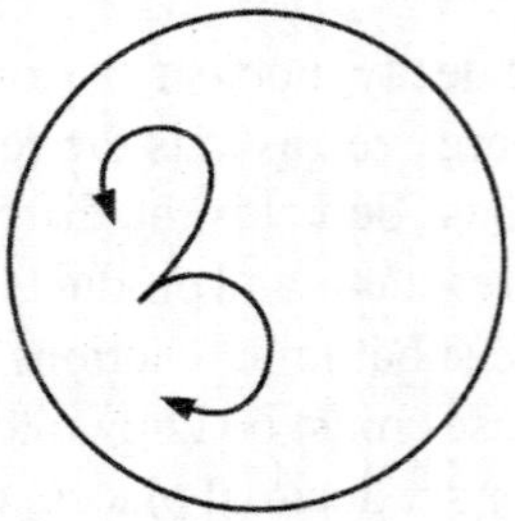

30. Which of the following statements is **true** about this cloud chamber?

A. Both particles are positively charged.

B. Both particles are negatively charged.

C. One particle is a proton, and the other is a neutron.

D. One particle is an electron, and the other is a positron.

30-D4.2k explain, qualitatively, in terms of the strong nuclear force, why high-energy particle accelerators are required to study subatomic particles

Particle Accelerators

In order to study the substructure of the atom, physicists have to add energy to the atom. They add this energy either thermally, electrically, or by collisions with high-speed subatomic particles. Collisions with visible light photons are often sufficient to remove the outer electrons from atoms, because they are relatively easy to remove (photoelectric effect). The inner core electrons can be ejected from atoms using *X*-ray photons.

Nucleons are very tightly bonded within the nucleus, so they are not easily removed.
For example, the binding energy of the helium nucleus (an alpha particle) is 28.3 MeV. This is a million times larger than the binding energy of the electrons in a helium atom. Therefore, studying the nucleus requires very large particle accelerators that can produce bombarding particles with kinetic energies large enough to overcome the strong nuclear force holding the nucleus together.

One of the largest energy particle accelerators in the world is a synchrotron that accelerates protons and antiprotons in a 6.3 km ring to achieve kinetic energies of up to 1 TeV(10^{12} eV). The results of experiments using these energies have revealed that even protons and neutrons have smaller components. These components are called quarks.

Use the following information to answer the next question.

> The following observations were made about the energies involved in studying the atom.
>
> 1. An energy of 13.6 eV will remove the electron from a hydrogen atom.
> 2. Rutherford's alpha particles required an energy of about 10 MeV in order to approach the nuclei in gold atoms closely enough to enable Rutherford to infer the nuclear size.
> 3. In order to cause a nucleus to break apart, subatomic particles with energies of 100 MeV or more are required.

31. Which of the following statements about the given observations is **true**?

A. Chemical reactions proceed faster than nuclear reactions.

B. Electromagnetic forces are stronger than strong nuclear forces.

C. Chemical reactions provide the energy needed to study the nucleus.

D. The bonds holding nucleons together are more than 10^6 times stronger than electromagnetic bonds.

30-D4.3k describe the modern model of the proton and neutron as being composed of quarks

Quarks

Since the discovery of electrons by J.J. Thomson in 1897 and the discovery of the nucleus by Ernst Rutherford in 1907, scientists have endeavoured to gain a clear understanding of what matter is made of and how it gets put together. As early success with quantum theory began to shed new light on the subatomic structure of the universe, a wide range of even smaller subatomic particles became necessary to explain certain behaviours in terms of mass and charge conservation. It seemed that the more that people looked into the structure of matter, the more they were able to find.

In order to make sense of all the subatomic particles, it was proposed that some of these particles (hadrons) are made of smaller particles called quarks. The quarks combine in various ways to make the many larger particles. For example, up and down quarks combine to form protons and neutrons. Different types of quarks, such as up and down quarks, are known as quark flavours.

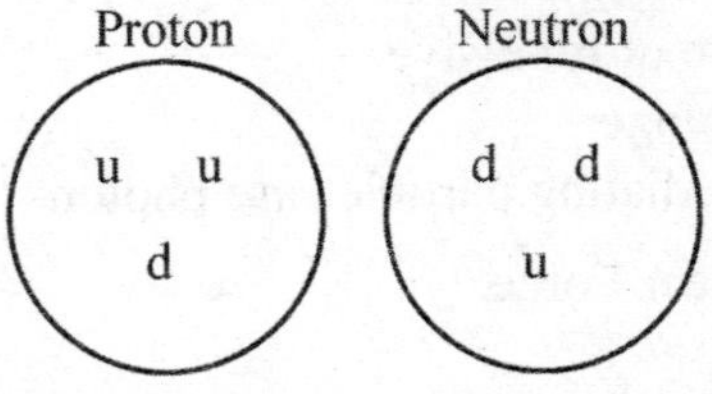

Quarks have charges that are fractions of the elementary charge. Up quarks have a $+\frac{2}{3}$e charge, and down quarks have a $-\frac{1}{3}$e charge.

Electrons do not seem to be made of smaller particles. Neither do neutrinos. These lighter particles are called leptons.

32. Which of the following particles consists of two up quarks and one down quark?

A. Proton **B.** Meson

C. Neutron **D.** Electron

30-D4.4k compare and contrast the up quark, the down quark, the electron and the electron neutrino, and their antiparticles, in terms of charge and energy (mass-energy)

Fundamental Forces

There appear to be four fundamental forces acting in the universe today. Some characteristics and properties of the four forces are given.

Gravitational Force

- Acts on masses
- Weakest force
- Always attractive
- Infinite range

Strong Nuclear Force

- Acts on hadrons
- Strongest of all forces
- Always attractive
- Very short range
- Force-mediating particles are gluons

Electromagnetic Force

- Acts on charges
- Second strongest force
- Attractive or repulsive
- Infinite range
- Force-mediating particles are photons

Weak Nuclear Force

- Acts on mass
- Second weakest force
- Always attractive
- Infinite range
- Force-mediating particles are gauge bosons

Only three of these forces are explained by the Standard Model, which is the new organization of particles and the forces that operate on them. Gravitation is left out due to the difficulty in determining what the force transfer particle is for gravity. With the creation of the Large Hadron Collider at CERN, many important questions about gravitation should soon be answered.

There are six quark flavours and three pairs of leptons in the current Standard Model. Of these six quark flavours and numerous leptons, only the first-generation species will be used with any frequency. The first-generation quarks are known as the up and down quarks, while the first-generation leptons are the electron and the electron neutrino. The important information regarding up and down quarks and first-generation leptons is given in the following table.

First Generation Quarks and Leptons	
Quarks	Leptons
up $q = +\frac{2}{3}e$	electron $q = -e$
down $q = -\frac{1}{3}e$	electron neutrino $q = 0$

33. What is the charge on an up quark, an electron antineutrino, and a down antiquark, respectively?

A. $+\frac{2}{3}e,\ 0,\ +\frac{1}{3}e$

B. $+\frac{2}{3}e,\ 0,\ -\frac{1}{3}e$

C. $-\frac{2}{3}e,\ -1e,\ +\frac{1}{3}e$

D. $-\frac{2}{3}e,\ +1e,\ +\frac{1}{3}e$

30-D4.5k describe beta-positive (β+) and beta-negative (β–) decay, using first-generation elementary fermions and the principle of charge conservation (Feynman diagrams are not required)

Radioactivity and the Standard Model

A large nucleus like uranium-238 is fairly stable. The total strong force from the protons and neutrons overcomes the total electromagnetic repulsion forces among the protons. However, at the edge of the nucleus, the repulsion forces occasionally overcome the attraction forces and an alpha particle is ejected from the nucleus. It is important to note that the conservation of charge must be maintained for all decay reactions.

BETA-NEGATIVE DECAY

The weak force acts upon the quarks inside a hadron. In β^- decay, a down quark in a neutron changes into an up quark to form a proton, releasing an electron and an antineutrino.

β^- decay: $n \rightarrow p^+ + e^- + \bar{\nu}_e$

Since the charge on a neutron is always zero, the products formed by the decay of a neutron must also have a null total charge. Antineutrinos have no associated charge. The charge on one electron and one proton cancel one another out exactly to achieve a total charge of zero for the products.

BETA-POSITIVE DECAY

In β^+ decay, the weak force and some additional energy changes an up quark in a proton to a down quark. This creates a neutron, releasing a positron and a neutrino.

β^+ decay: $\text{energy} + p^+ \rightarrow n + e^+ + \nu_e$

Since the charge on a proton is always 1.60×10^{-19} C, the total charge of the products formed by the decay of one proton must also equal 1.60×10^{-19} C. Since the charges of a neutron and a neutrino are always zero, and the charge on a positron is always 1.60×10^{-19} C, the conservation of charge in beta decay reactions is confirmed.

34. In the equation $udd \rightarrow uud + {}^{\;0}_{-1}\beta + \bar{\nu}$, the correct charges on each of the components is

A. $\left[\left(\frac{+2}{3}\right)+\left(\frac{-1}{3}\right)+\left(\frac{-1}{3}\right)\right]\rightarrow \left[\left(\frac{+2}{3}\right)+\left(\frac{+2}{3}\right)+\left(\frac{-1}{3}\right)\right]+(-1)+(+1)$

B. $\left[\left(\frac{+2}{3}\right)+\left(\frac{-1}{3}\right)+\left(\frac{-1}{3}\right)\right]\rightarrow \left[\left(\frac{+2}{3}\right)+\left(\frac{+2}{3}\right)+\left(\frac{-1}{3}\right)\right]+(-1)+(0)$

C. $\left[\left(\frac{+1}{3}\right)+\left(\frac{-2}{3}\right)+\left(\frac{-2}{3}\right)\right]\rightarrow \left[\left(\frac{-2}{3}\right)+\left(\frac{-2}{3}\right)+\left(\frac{+1}{3}\right)\right]+(+1)+(0)$

D. $\left[\left(\frac{+2}{3}\right)+\left(\frac{-1}{3}\right)+\left(\frac{-1}{3}\right)\right]\rightarrow \left[\left(\frac{+1}{3}\right)+\left(\frac{+1}{3}\right)+\left(\frac{+1}{3}\right)\right]+(-1)+(0)$

Answers and Solutions
Atomic Physics

1. D	9. D	15. C	23. a) B	29. 2611
2. A	10. C	16. WR	b) A	30. D
3. B	11. D	17. A	24. A	31. D
4. C	12. A	18. B	25. 9237	32. A
5. B	13. D	19. C	26. a) 9236	33. A
6. 2406	14. a) 8514	20. B	b) C	34. B
7. 1744	b) D	21. C	27. C	
8. 12	c) D	22. C	28. 9011	

1. D

The first observation would indicate that the cathode rays are repelled by the negative electrode, which would indicate a negative charge. This does support the hypothesis, and therefore alternatives A and B are incorrect. Observation 2 shows that a shadow is being cast towards the positive electrode. This also supports the hypothesis, so alternative C is incorrect. The downward deflection of cathode rays by the north end of a bar magnet when the negative electrode is on the left also supports the hypothesis, but the glowing effect of excited hydrogen gas does not, since there is no polarity information that can be drawn from the observation. Alternative D is the correct answer.

2. A

When a negative charge passes perpendicularly through an $\vec{E}$ field, it will be deflected in the opposite direction of the field. When a negative charge passes perpendicularly through a constant magnetic field, the deflection of the negative charge can be found using the left-hand rule. Therefore, the correct diagram must show the $\vec{E}$ field, the $\vec{B}$ field, and the cathode rays as being perpendicular to each other.

In diagram A, the electric field creates an electric force on the cathode ray upward along the page. The magnetic field points out of the page with the electrons moving from right to left. This will result in a magnetic force directed downward along the page. This can be found using the left-hand rule for negative particles, as the thumb will point to the left and the fingers will point out of the page. The palm then faces downward along the page. Therefore, diagram A shows the only possible setup for the cathode ray to pass through the fields undeflected.

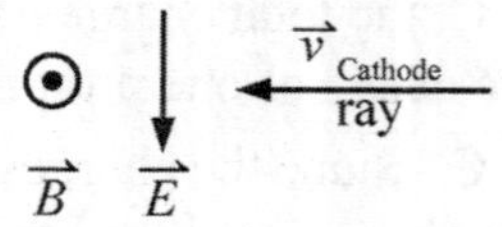

Diagram B is incorrect since the $\vec{E}$ and $\vec{B}$ fields are parallel, and diagram D is incorrect because the $\vec{E}$ field is parallel with the cathode rays. While the $\vec{E}$ and $\vec{B}$ fields are perpendicular in diagram C, the magnetic force on a negative particle will be in the same direction as the electric force on the negative particle, so the particle would be deflected.

3. B

If electrons are released from several different metals, this suggests that they may be part of all atoms. A large charge-to-mass ratio indicates a small mass.

4. C

Negatively charged particles will be attracted to a positive plate and will follow the left-hand rule within a magnetic field. Waves and particles both go in straight lines, but only observations I and II favour Thomson's finding that cathode rays are composed of negative particles.

5. B

$$F_m = F_c$$
$$qvB_\perp = \frac{mv^2}{r}$$
$$r = \frac{mv^2}{qvB_\perp}$$
$$= \left(\frac{m}{q}\right)\frac{v}{B_\perp}$$
$$= \left(\frac{1}{1.76 \times 10^{11}\ \text{C/kg}}\right)\left(\frac{5.25 \times 10^5\ \text{m/s}}{175 \times 10^{-6}\ \text{T}}\right)$$
$$= 1.70 \times 10^{-2}\ \text{m}$$
$$= 1.70\ \text{cm}$$

6. 2406

Since the particles pass undeflected, use the formula $F_m = F_e$, and solve for v.

$$F_m = F_e$$
$$qvB_\perp = Eq$$
$$v = \frac{E}{B_\perp} = \frac{1.20 \times 10^5\ \text{N/C}}{0.0500\ \text{T}}$$
$$= 2.40 \times 10^6\ \text{m/s}$$

The values of a, b, c, and d are 2, 4, 0, and 6, respectively.

7. 1744

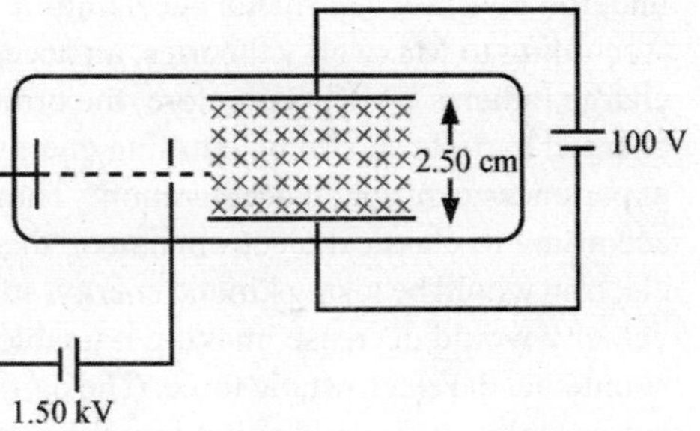

$$qV = \frac{1}{2}mv^2$$
$$v = \sqrt{\frac{2qV}{m}}$$
$$= \sqrt{\frac{2(1.60 \times 10^{-19}\ \text{C})(1.50 \times 10^3\ \text{J/C})}{9.11 \times 10^{-31}\ \text{kg}}}$$
$$= 2.295 \times 10^7\ \text{m/s}$$
$$F_e = F_m$$
$$qE = qvB_\perp$$
$$q\frac{V}{d} = qvB_\perp$$
$$B_\perp = \frac{V}{dv}$$
$$= \frac{100\ \text{J/C}}{(2.50 \times 10^{-2}\ \text{m})(2.295 \times 10^7\ \text{m/s})}$$
$$= 1.74 \times 10^{-4}\ \text{T}$$

$= 1.74 \times 10^{-4}$ T into the page.

8. 12

A large nucleus will scatter a higher percentage of particles at larger angles than a smaller nucleus will. Therefore, graph X supports the structure of atom 1, and graph Y supports the structure of atom 2.

9. D

If all the positive matter in the atom resides in a tiny cluster in the atom's centre separated from the negative particles (components of cathode rays), the negative particles can have orbital velocities large enough to counteract the force of attraction between the positive and negative charges.

However, the orbiting charged particles would undergo constant centripetal acceleration. According to Maxwell's theories, an accelerating charge radiates EMR. Therefore, the orbiting charged particle should be emitting energy as it experiences centripetal acceleration. Thus, according to classical electromagnetic theory, the electron would be losing kinetic energy, so its orbital velocity would decrease, making it unable to counteract the electrostatic force. The particle would not be stable and would spiral into the nucleus.

10. C

The transmission of light through a sample of gas would cause molecules of that gas to interfere with the light, much like holding a hand in front of a flashlight casts a shadow. The gas would absorb some of the spectrum of light, producing a dark-line absorption spectrum at the diffraction spectroscope. Bright-line emission spectra are created by exciting molecules of a substance, and then recording the luminescence using a spectrometer. The gas in this question is not emitting any light, and it is absorbing light produced elsewhere, so it produces a dark-line absorption spectrum.

11. D

Atoms absorb energy of the same specific values that they characteristically emit. In other words, the visible portions of a bright-line emission spectrum of a substance correlate directly with the darkened bars found in the dark-line absorption spectrum of that substance. The sum of the two spectra will produce a complete full-spectrum white light spectrum.

12. A

As an electron moves from a higher energy level to a lower one, it will emit energy. When an electron absorbs energy, it will increase its energy and move from a lower energy level to a higher one.

13. D

Electrically excited gases at low pressure emit light of only specific frequencies. This is viewed as a brigh-line emission spectrum when viewed with a spectroscope.

14. a) 8514

The atoms' electrons absorbed 3.5 eV of energy and moved to level 2.

Find the frequency.

$$\Delta E = hf$$
$$f = \frac{\Delta E}{h}$$
$$= \frac{3.5 \text{ eV}}{4.14 \times 10^{-15} \text{ eV} \cdot \text{s}}$$
$$= 8.5 \times 10^{14} \text{ Hz}$$

The values of *a*, *b*, *c*, and *d* are 8, 5, 1, and 4, respectively.

b) D

Use the formula for the change in energy of the valence electron to calculate the wavelength of the emitted photon.

$$\Delta E = \frac{hc}{\lambda}$$
$$\therefore \lambda = \frac{hc}{\Delta E}$$
$$= \frac{(4.14 \times 10^{-15} \text{ eV·s})(3.00 \times 10^{8} \text{ m/s})}{(4.9 - 4.5) \text{ eV}}$$
$$= 3.1 \times 10^{-6} \text{ m}$$

c) D

As the electron drops back down to the ground state from the third excitation level, it can make all the following jumps that will each result in a photon being released with a different wavelength:

$n = 4 \rightarrow n = 3$
$n = 4 \rightarrow n = 2$
$n = 4 \rightarrow n = 1$
$n = 3 \rightarrow n = 2$
$n = 3 \rightarrow n = 1$
$n = 2 \rightarrow n = 1$

Therefore, there are 6 possible different photons that could be released that correspond to 6 different spectral lines.

15. C

A de Broglie wave is often referred to as a matter wave. It is calculated from the particle's momentum.

$$\lambda = \frac{h}{mv}$$

From this formula, the de Broglie wavelength of an electron is inversely related to its velocity.

The wavelength does not depend on acceleration. It is impossible to observe both particle and wave traits of an electron simultaneously in an experiment, and a beam of electrons will produce a diffraction pattern if directed through slits that have the appropriate diameter.

16. WR

The atoms in the crystal will act much like a diffraction grating. This is because the atomic spacing within the crystal lattice matches the de Broglie wavelength of electrons quite well. This means that the electrons would be diffracted as they passed through the spaces between the atoms in the crystal. If there is diffraction, there will also be some form of interference pattern formed when the diffracted electrons interact.

17. A

Alpha, beta, and gamma particles are listed appropriately in order of increasing penetrating power. Alpha particles are basically helium nuclei that have more mass than the other two, but less momentum. It would be unlikely that an alpha particle could penetrate anything thicker than foil. Beta particles are high speed electrons or positrons that could penetrate a few millimetres of aluminum, but would be unable to penetrate lead. Gamma particles are high-energy photons that would be able to penetrate any of the three materials listed.

18. B

The radiation taking path X is attracted to the positive plate; it must be the beta ray.

The radiation taking path Y is unaffected by the plates; it must be the gamma ray, which is a form of electromagnetic radiation and is uncharged.

The radiation taking path Z is attracted to the negative plate; it must be the alpha ray, which has a charge of 2^+ on each particle in the ray.

19. C

The beta negative decay for ${}^{131}_{53}\text{I}$ is:

$${}^{131}_{53}\text{I} \rightarrow {}^{131}_{54}\text{Xe} + {}^{0}_{-1}\beta + \bar{\nu}$$

20. B

$${}^{22}_{11}\text{Na} \rightarrow {}^{22}_{10}\text{Ne} + {}^{0}_{1}\beta + \nu$$

This decay reaction required the production of a positron in order to conserve charge. The production of a positron is also accompanied by the production of a neutrino. This is a case of β^+ decay.

21. C

The alpha decay equation for uranium-238 is as follows:

$${}^{238}_{92}\text{U} \rightarrow {}^{4}_{2}\alpha + {}^{234}_{90}\text{Th}$$

Equation (B) is a beta decay, equation (D) is not a decay since the alpha particle has been captured by the uranium nucleus to form the larger mass Pu nucleus. Equation (A) shows a neutron capture which merely increases the mass number of the nucleus.

22. C

Number of half-live

$$\begin{aligned} n &= \frac{\text{elapsed time}}{\text{half-life}} \\ &= \frac{2\ 865 \text{ years}}{5\ 730 \text{ years}} \\ n &= 0.500 \\ \frac{N}{N_0} &= \left(\frac{1}{2}\right)^n \\ &= \left(\frac{1}{2}\right)^{0.500} \\ &= \left(\frac{1}{2}\right)^{\frac{1}{2}} \\ &= \sqrt{\frac{1}{2}} = \frac{1}{\sqrt{2}} \\ &= 0.707 \\ &= 70.7\% \end{aligned}$$

23. a) B

The graph shows that the original amount of the isotope was 60 g (plotted on the *y*-axis).

The half-life of the isotope is the time required to go from the original mass to half its mass. In this case, the mass of the isotope will be 30 g at its half-life. Find 30 on the *y*-axis, and follow the curve. The point is plotted at 15 on the *x*-axis.

The half-life of the isotope is closest to 15 days.

b) A

Expressed in terms of days, 2.5 half lives is equal to 37.5 days. On the graph, read up from the x-axis at the midpoint between 35 and 40 up to the curve. Read from the point on the curve and over to the y-axis to read the mass of 11 g.

Mass vs Time for a Radioactive Nucleus

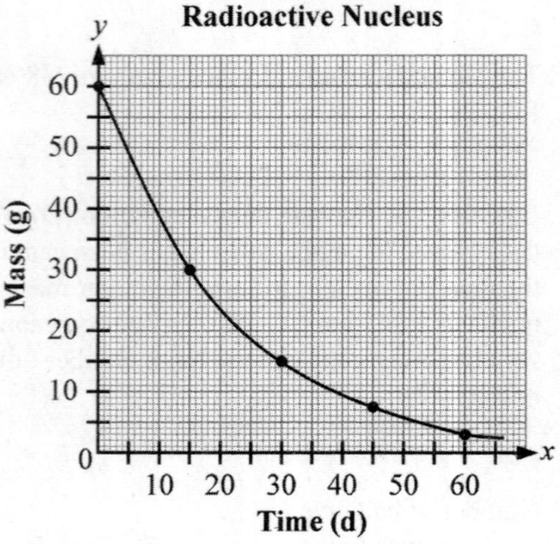

This can also be found using the half-life equation.

$$m = m_0\left(\frac{1}{2}\right)^n$$

$$m = (60\text{ g})\left(\frac{1}{2}\right)^{2.5}$$

$$m = 11\text{ g}$$

24. A

In order to find the missing particle, one only need look at the atomic mass and numbers of the components of the equation on the left side.
The nitrogen atom depicted has 7 protons and 7 neutrons for a combined atomic mass of 14.
The helium atom has 2 protons and 2 neutrons for a net atomic mass of 4. If they fuse to form an oxygen atom, the extra hadrons in the equation that are left over are $(7+2)-8=1$ protons. The remaining atom in the equation is a hydrogen atom, which is reflected in alternative A.

25. 9237

To determine the identity of this "daughter" nucleus, the subscripts (charge values) and the superscripts (mass numbers) must balance on both sides of the equation.

Superscripts:

$$235+1 = 141+ab+3(1)$$
$$236 = 144+ab$$
$$ab = 92$$

Subscripts:

$$92+0 = 55+cd+3(0)$$
$$92 = 55+cd$$
$$cd = 37$$

The fission product is ${}^{92}_{37}X = {}^{92}_{37}\text{Ru}$.

$\therefore abcd = 9\ 237$

26. a) 9236

Of the given reaction equations, the fission reaction appears first.

$${}^{1}_{0}\text{n} + {}^{235}_{92}\text{U} \rightarrow {}^{141}_{56}\text{Ba} + {}^{ab}_{cd}\text{Kr} + 3{}^{1}_{0}\text{n}$$

In order to balance this equation, a mass number of 92 is needed to conserve mass, and an atomic number of 36 is needed to conserve charge in the reaction.

b) C

Following the laws of conservation of mass, 2 neutrons are needed to conserve the mass numbers. The total mass number before the reaction is 6, so the total mass number after the reaction must be 6. Since the helium has 4 particles in its nucleus, there needs to be 2 neutrons to balance the equation.

27. C

The graph is highest near mass number 56. This is where the nuclei are bound together the strongest. Iron is the element with a mass number of 56.

28. 9011

$$0.010\text{ g} = 1.0 \times 10^{-5}\text{ kg}$$

$$E = mc^2$$
$$= (1.0 \times 10^{-5}\text{ kg})(3.00 \times 10^8\text{ m/s})^2$$
$$= 9.0 \times 10^{11}\text{ J}$$

29. 2611

Find the mass of the reactants.

$$\begin{array}{r} 3.903\ 00 \times 10^{-25}\ \text{kg} \\ +\underline{1.674\ 93 \times 10^{-27}\ \text{kg}} \\ 3.919\ 75 \times 10^{-25}\ \text{kg} \end{array}$$

Find the mass of the products.

$$\begin{array}{r} 2.2567 \times 10^{-25}\ \text{kg} \\ 1.6099 \times 10^{-25}\ \text{kg} \\ +3\underline{(1.674\ 93 \times 10^{-27}\ \text{kg})} \\ 3.916\ 85 \times 10^{-25}\ \text{kg} \end{array}$$

Find the energy produced.

$$\begin{aligned} E &= \Delta mc^2 \\ &= (2.90 \times 10^{-28}\ \text{kg})(3 \times 10^8\ \text{m/s})^2 \\ &= 2.6 \times 10^{-11}\ \text{J} \end{aligned}$$

The values of a, b, c, and d are 1, 8, 1, and 0, respectively.

30. D

Since the particles bend in different directions, they must have opposite charges. Since the size of the circular paths are equal, both particles must have approximately the same mass.

Therefore, one particle is an electron, and the other is a positron. The proton and neutron do not work since the neutron carries no charge and would be undeflected by the magnetic field.

31. D

There is no information in the three statements that compares the rate of chemical reactions with that of nuclear ones, so alternative A is incorrect.
The amount of energy required to remove an electron from hydrogen is miniscule compared to the energy required to break apart a nucleus, so alternative B is incorrect. There is no information to indicate that Rutherford used chemical reactions to energize his alpha particles, so alternative C is incorrect.
If nucleon bond strengths exceed 100 MeV, and the electron of a hydrogen atom can be removed with 13.6 eV, it can be shown that

$\dfrac{1.00 \times 10^8}{1.36 \times 10^1} \approx 7.35 \times 10^6$, which is greater than 10^6, so alternative D is correct.

32. A

Protons consist of two up quarks and one down quark; neutrons consist of two down quarks and one up quark. Quarks are a type of fermion. Electrons are a type of lepton and are not made up of quarks.

33. A

Antiparticles have opposite charges of the same magnitude.

A down quark has a charge of $-\frac{1}{3}e$, so a down antiquark has a charge of $+\frac{1}{3}e$.

Neutrinos are uncharged and an up quark has a charge of $+\frac{2}{3}e$.

34. B

The charge of an up quark is $+\frac{2}{3}$, the charge of a down quark is $-\frac{1}{3}$, the charge of a beta particle is negative one, and the charge of an antineutrino is zero. Therefore, the equation that expresses the correct charges on each component is as follows:

$$\left[\left(\frac{+2}{3}\right)+\left(\frac{-1}{3}\right)+\left(\frac{-1}{3}\right)\right] \to \left[\left(\frac{+2}{3}\right)+\left(\frac{+2}{3}\right)+\left(\frac{-1}{3}\right)\right]+(-1)+(0)$$

UNIT TEST — ATOMIC PHYSICS

1. Early experiments to determine if cathode rays were composed of waves or particles were inconclusive. Early evidence that cathode rays were composed of individual particles included the fact that they

A. are emitted from a cathode

B. do not move in straight lines

C. are deflected by an electric field

D. do not fall under the influence of gravity

Use the following information to answer the next question.

The given diagram shows a beam of electrons passing through perpendicular electric and magnetic fields.

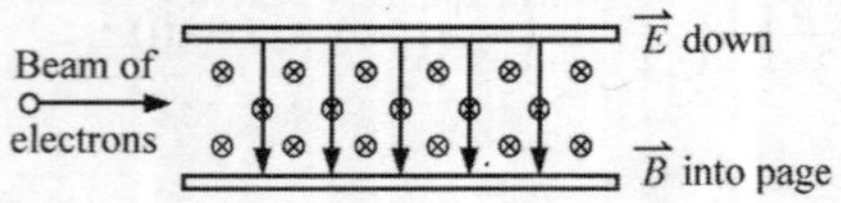

$E=$
$B=$

The beam passes straight through the two fields when the electric field strength is 1.80×10^3 N/C and the magnetic field strength is 3.00×10^{-4} T. When the $\vec{E}$ field is turned off, the beam deflects into a circular path with a radius of 11.0 cm.

Written Response

2. Use this data to determine the charge-to-mass ratio of electrons.

____

____

____

____

____

____

____

3. A beam of positive ions accelerated to a speed of 6.25×10^5 m/s and then entered into a magnetic field with a strength of 1.50×10^{-1} T, oriented perpendicular to the ion's velocity. The positive ions were deflected by the magnetic field into a circular path of radius 8.66 cm. What is the charge-to-mass ratio for the ions?

A. 4.81×10^7 C/kg

B. 7.22×10^7 C/kg

C. 9.58×10^{10} C/kg

D. 1.76×10^{11} C/kg

Use the following information to answer the next question.

The following inferences are made about a Rutherford type experiment using empirical data or calculations from data.

1. Particle *A* which collides elastically with particle *B*, can only rebound at an angle greater than 90° if particle *B* is much more massive than particle *A*.
2. The alpha particle and gold nucleus undergo very intense Coulomb repulsions when they collide head-on.
3. Large Coulomb repulsions in the alpha particle experiment imply an alpha particle was often far from the gold nucleus.
4. A piece of gold foil 1.0 μm thick would be about 2 800 atoms thick.

4. Which of the given statements support the observation that about 1 in 8 000 alpha particles would scatter at very large angles to their original direction?

A. 1 and 2 **B.** 2 and 4

C. 1, 2, and 3 **D.** 1, 2, and 4

Use the following information to answer the next question.

Four types of spectra are given.

1. Bright-line emission spectra
2. Dark-line absorption spectra
3. Continuous spectra
4. X-ray spectra

5. Which of the given types of spectra are **most commonly** used to identify specific elements?

A. 1 and 2 **B.** 1 and 3
C. 2 and 3 **D.** 3 and 4

6. Molten steel is poured into a mould, and its light is viewed through a diffraction grating. Which type of spectrum would be observed?

A. Continuous spectrum
B. Absorption spectrum
C. Bright-line spectrum
D. Dark-line spectrum

CHALLENGER QUESTION

Use the following information to answer the next question.

An experiment is carried out to test the predicted energy levels in an atom. Theoretical calculations predict the following energy levels.

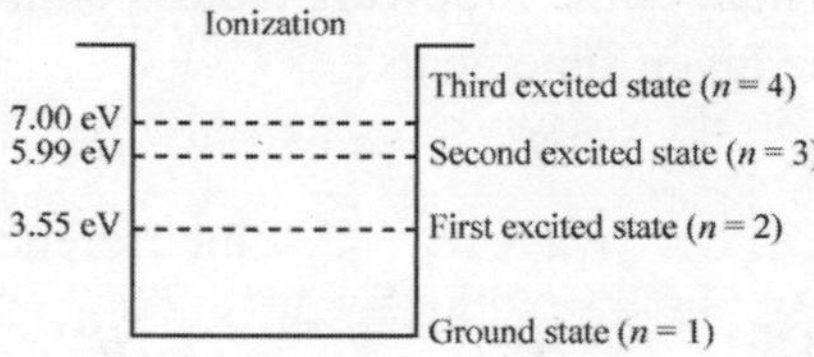

During the experiment, electrons are accelerated to a speed of 1.45×10^6 m/s. A velocity selector (as shown in the diagram) is used to ensure the consistency of this speed. A magnetic field $\vec{B}$ directed into the page is used together with an electric field $\vec{E}$ directed down to allow only the electrons at the chosen speed to pass through undeflected.

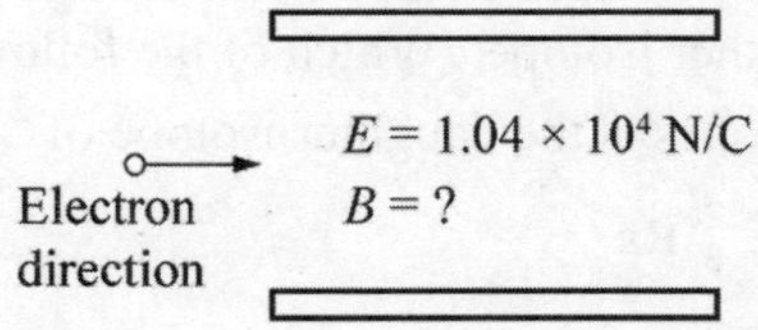

Written Response

7. Find the magnitude of the magnetic field, $\vec{B}$, used in the velocity selector and the wavelength of a visible light photon that might result from the bombardment of the atoms with the electrons.

Use the following information to answer the next question.

Louis de Broglie proposed that electrons can behave as ___*i*___. He predicted that they should produce ___*ii*___ effects in atomic crystals.

8. Which of the following tables completes the given statements?

A.

i	*ii*
waves	interference

B.

i	*ii*
waves	momentum

C.

i	*ii*
particles	interference

D.

i	*ii*
particles	momentum

9. The isotope ${}^{230}_{90}\text{Th}$ undergoes spontaneous decay to form an alpha particle and another isotope. Which of the following isotopes is the daughter isotope of ${}^{230}_{90}\text{Th}$?

A. ${}^{226}_{87}\text{Ra}$

B. ${}^{225}_{88}\text{Ra}$

C. ${}^{226}_{88}\text{Ra}$

D. ${}^{225}_{87}\text{Ra}$

10. Which of the following equations is an example of β^- decay?

A. ${}^{20}_{11}\text{Na} \rightarrow {}^{0}_{1}\text{e} + {}^{20}_{10}\text{Ne} + \nu$

B. ${}^{210}_{83}\text{Bi} \rightarrow {}^{0}_{0}\gamma + {}^{210}_{83}\text{Bi}$

C. ${}^{14}_{6}\text{C} \rightarrow {}^{0}_{-1}\text{e} + {}^{14}_{7}\text{N} + \bar{\nu}$

D. ${}^{235}_{92}\text{U} \rightarrow {}^{4}_{2}\text{He} + {}^{231}_{90}\text{Th}$

Numerical Response

11. The half-life of ${}^{90}_{38}\text{Sr}$ is 28.5 years. If a sample of soil contains 62.8 g of radioactive strontium, the amount of ${}^{90}_{38}\text{Sr}$ remaining after 84.6 years will be __________g. (Give your answer to three digits.)

Use the following information to answer the next question.

The given diagram shows two tracks in a cloud chamber.

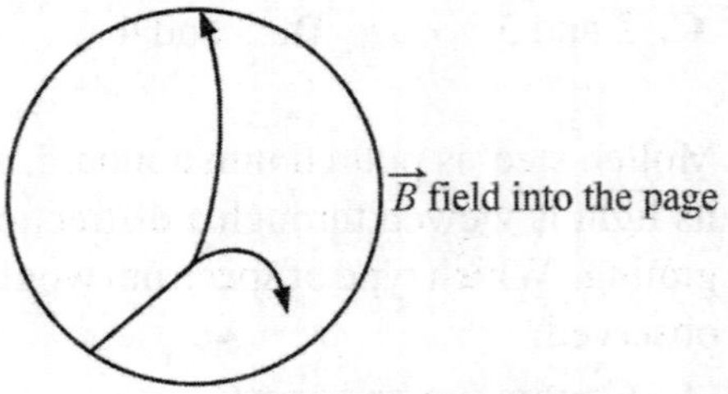

12. Given the diagram, which of the following statements is **true**?

A. A positive particle hits a negative particle.

B. Three neutral particles meet and annihilate.

C. A negative particle hits and sticks to a positive particle.

D. A neutral particle decays into a positive and a negative particle.

Use the following information to answer the next question.

Plutonium can be produced by bombarding neptunium atoms with neutrons, as shown.

${}^{239}_{93}\text{Np} + {}^{1}_{0}\text{n} \rightarrow {}^{240}_{94}\text{Pu} + X$

13. The unknown X represents

A. more neutrons **B.** an electron

C. a neutrino **D.** a photon

14. The reason that a nuclear reaction releases energy is that

A. some energy turned into mass during the reaction

B. some mass turned into energy during the reaction

C. new atoms were formed

D. charge was conserved

15. Which of the following statements is **not** a reason that high-energy particle accelerators are required to study many subatomic particles?

A. The strong force that holds the nucleus of atoms together is extremely strong and requires a relatively large amount of energy to break.

B. The energy required to generate temperatures that are comparable to the origins of the universe are extremely high and require a huge amount of energy to be reached.

C. Huge amounts of energy are required to create small amounts of mass, so high-energy accelerators are needed to generate extremely short half-life subatomic particles.

D. In order for charged particles to actually make contact in collisions, a large amount of energy is required to overcome the repulsion of like charges since all nuclei are positively charged.

16. A particle composed of two anti-up quarks and one anti-down quark would be

A. a proton

B. a positron

C. an antiproton

D. an antipositron

Use the following information to answer the next question.

During a beta decay, this interaction occurs.

$u \rightarrow d + x + y$

The decay could be releasing any of the following particles:

1. an electron
2. a positron (antielectron)
3. a photon
4. a neutrino
5. an antineutrino

Numerical Response

17. Match the two particles released with x and y.

Use the following information to answer the next question.

A nuclear reactor produces electricity from a fission reaction using uranium-235. The energy produced in this reaction is used to produce steam, which turns a turbine to generate electricity. Here is a list of isotopes and some information about them.

Particle	Mass (kg)	Decay mode
${}^{1}_{0}n$	$1.674\ 93 \times 10^{-27}$	β^-
${}^{235}_{92}U$	$3.903\ 00 \times 10^{-25}$	α, γ
${}^{92}_{38}Sr$	$1.526\ 22 \times 10^{-25}$	β^+
${}^{140}_{54}Xe$	$2.323\ 45 \times 10^{-25}$	β^+

Written Response

18. Using the concepts of radioactive decay, mass-energy equivalence, and energy conservation, analyze the energy output of this process by completing the following points:

- Write the fission equation if U-235 splits into Sr-92 and Xe-140 after a neutron bombards it.
- Calculate the energy produced for each U-235 atom split.
- Describe a safety procedure for entering and cleaning up a spill of radioactive isotopes in a small room.

Marks will be awarded for the physics you use to solve this problem and for effective communication of your response.

ANSWERS AND SOLUTIONS — UNIT TEST

1. C	6. A	11. 8.02	16. C
2. WR	7. WR	12. D	17. 24
3. B	8. A	13. B	18. WR
4. A	9. C	14. B	
5. A	10. C	15. B	

1. C

The ability to be deflected by electric fields is a property of charged particles, not waves. Therefore, the fact that cathode rays were deflected by electric fields was early evidence that the rays were composed of particles.

2. WR

Use the balanced forces to find the initial velocity of the electrons.

$$F_e = F_m$$
$$Eq = qvB_\perp$$
$$v = \frac{E}{B_\perp}$$
$$= \frac{1.80 \times 10^3 \text{ N/C}}{3.00 \times 10^{-4} \text{ T}}$$
$$= 6.00 \times 10^6 \text{ m/s}$$

With the electric field turned off, the magnetic field is then equal to the centripetal force. These force equations can be used to find the charge-to-mass ratio of the electrons.

$$F_m = F_c$$
$$qvB_\perp = \frac{mv^2}{r}$$
$$\frac{q}{m} = \frac{v}{B_\perp r}$$
$$= \frac{6.00 \times 10^6 \text{ m/s}}{(3.00 \times 10^{-4} \text{ T})(0.11 \text{ m})}$$
$$= 1.82 \times 10^{11} \text{ C/kg}$$

Therefore, the electrons have a charge-to-mass ratio of 1.82×10^{11} C/kg.

3. B

$$F_m = F_c$$
$$qvB_\perp = \frac{mv^2}{r}$$
$$\frac{q}{m} = \frac{v}{B_\perp r}$$
$$= \frac{6.25 \times 10^5 \text{ m/s}}{(1.50 \times 10^{-1} \text{ T})(8.66 \times 10^{-2} \text{ m})}$$
$$= 4.81 \times 10^7 \text{ C/kg}$$

4. A

If it is observed that alpha particles scatter at very large angles to their original direction, and considering that the nuclei of gold atoms are much more massive than alpha particles, inference 1 is valid and supports the observation. It is also valid to infer that both the alpha particle and the gold nucleus would undergo intense Coulomb repulsions upon a head on collision, which would support the observation of a comparatively large proportion of alpha particles that do not scatter at very large angles. Inference 2 is therefore valid. The distance of an alpha particle from a gold nucleus is not directly related to the angle at which the particle scattered following a collision, so the third inference is not valid for supporting the observation.
The thickness of gold foil is unrelated to the mechanics of collision and dispersion, so the fourth inference is not valid support for the observation. The alternative that lists the first two inferences as support for the observation is A.

5. A

Bright-line and dark-line spectra are used to identify the component atoms within gaseous samples, so 1 and 2 are correct.

Continuous spectra are emitted by all heated materials and only give information as to the temperature and not the composition. X-ray spectra are simply continuous spectra in the X-ray region of the electromagnetic radiation (EMR) spectrum.

6. A

Incandescent, or glowing, liquids emit light of all frequencies, so a continuous spectrum would form when viewed through a transmission diffraction grating.

7. WR

Use the principle of uniform motion—balanced forces. In the velocity selector, the magnetic and electric forces are equal and opposite.

$$F_m = F_e$$
$$qvB_{\perp} = Eq$$
$$B_{\perp} = \frac{E}{v}$$
$$= \frac{1.04 \times 10^4 \text{ N/C}}{1.45 \times 10^6 \text{ m/s}}$$
$$= 7.17 \times 10^{-3} \text{ T}$$

Use the conservation of energy to find the electron's energy transfer to the atom's electrons.

$$E_{\text{excitation}} = E_k$$
$$= \frac{1}{2}mv^2$$
$$= \frac{1}{2}(9.11 \times 10^{-31} \text{ kg})(1.45 \times 10^6 \text{ m/s})^2$$
$$= \frac{9.58 \times 10^{-19} \text{ J}}{1.60 \times 10^{-19} \text{ J/eV}}$$
$$= 5.99 \text{ eV}$$

The electrons in the atoms move to the second excited state ($n = 3$). The electrons produce three different photons when they return to their ground state: $n = 3$ to $n = 2$; $n = 2$ to $n = 1$; and $n = 3$ to $n = 1$. Each photon will have its own specific wavelength.

$$\Delta E = \frac{hc}{\lambda}$$
$$\lambda = \frac{hc}{\Delta E}$$
$$= \frac{(4.14 \times 10^{-15} \text{ eV·s})(3.0 \times 10^8 \text{ m/s})}{\Delta E}$$

For each of the state changes, the given equation will result in the following wavelengths:

$\Delta E = 2.44 \text{ eV} \Rightarrow \lambda = 509 \text{ nm}$ (visible light)
$= 3.55 \text{ eV} \Rightarrow \lambda = 350 \text{ nm}$ (UV)
$= 5.99 \text{ eV} \Rightarrow \lambda = 207 \text{ nm}$ (UV)

The photon with a wavelength in the range of visible light is 509 nm.

8. A

Louis de Broglie hypothesized that particles have wave properties and all waves should exhibit interference and diffraction effects.

9. C

An alpha particle has an atomic number of 2 and a mass number of 4. Both the mass number and the atomic numbers must be conserved on both sides of the chemical equation. So the complete equation of for the alpha-decay of thorium-230 is:

$${}^{230}_{90}\text{Th} \rightarrow {}^{226}_{88}\text{Ra} + {}^{4}_{2}\alpha$$

10. C

Equation C is an example of β^- decay. Equation A is an example of β^+ decay, equation B is an example of gamma decay, and equation D is an example of alpha decay.

11. 8.02

$$m = m_0\left(\frac{1}{2}\right)^{\frac{t}{t_{\frac{1}{2}}}}$$
$$= (62.8 \text{ g})\left(\frac{1}{2}\right)^{\frac{84.6}{28.5}}$$
$$= 8.02 \text{ g}$$

12. D

The initial track is straight (no magnetic deflection of a neutral particle) and branches into two curved tracks of opposite bend (which means they have opposite charges). Therefore, the diagram shows a neutral particle decaying into a positive and a negative particle.

13. B

A mass number of zero and a charge of −1 will balance the equation. Therefore, to complete the equation, X must be an electron (${}^{0}_{-1}\text{e}$).

$${}^{239}_{93}\text{Np} + {}^{1}_{0}\text{n} \rightarrow {}^{240}_{94}\text{Pu} + {}^{0}_{-1}\text{e}$$

14. B

Nuclear reactions release energy because a small portion of the mass involved in the reaction converts into energy. The mass defect is the portion of mass missing from the products that was initially present in the reactants. This mass gets converted into energy during the reaction.

15. B

The temperatures in the universe shortly after the big bang do not directly relate to the study and analysis of hard-to-find subatomic particles, so statement B is not a reason for using high-energy particle accelerators.

16. C

Because the particle would be composed of anti-quarks, it would thus be an antiparticle, so alternative A is incorrect. Positrons and electrons are leptons, and thus are not constructed from up and down quarks. Alternatives B and D are therefore incorrect. Protons are composed of two up quarks and one down quark, so an antiproton would be composed of two anti-up quarks, and one anti-down quark. The correct answer is C, an antiproton.

17. 2 4

The charges on the up and down quarks are as follows:

$u = +\frac{2}{3}$

$d = -\frac{1}{3}$

In order to decay from $+\frac{2}{3}$ to $-\frac{1}{3}$, a charge of -1 is lost. To balance this interaction, the equation needs a positron $({}^{0}_{1}e)$. The neutrino goes with this antiparticle.

Therefore, particle *x* should be a positron (2) and particle *y* should be a neutrino (4).

18. WR

Write the fission equation for U-235 splitting into Sr-92 and Xe-140.

$${}^{235}_{92}U + {}^{1}_{0}n \rightarrow {}^{92}_{38}Sr + {}^{140}_{54}Xe + 4\left({}^{1}_{0}n\right) + \text{energy}$$

Find the mass of the reactants.

$$\begin{array}{r} 3.903\,00 \times 10^{-25}\ \text{kg} \\ \underline{+1.674\,93 \times 10^{-27}\ \text{kg}} \\ 3.919\,75 \times 10^{-25}\ \text{kg} \end{array}$$

Find the mass of the products.

$$\begin{array}{r} 1.526\,22 \times 10^{-25}\ \text{kg} \\ 2.323\,45 \times 10^{-25}\ \text{kg} \\ \underline{+4\left(1.674\,93 \times 10^{-27}\ \text{kg}\right)} \\ 3.916\,67 \times 10^{-25}\ \text{kg} \end{array}$$

The mass lost in the reaction is 3.08×10^{-28} kg, which can be used to find the energy produced.

$$\begin{aligned} E &= \Delta mc^2 \\ &= \left(3.01 \times 10^{-28}\ \text{kg}\right)\left(3.00 \times 10^{8}\ \text{m/s}\right)^2 \\ &= 2.77 \times 10^{-11}\ \text{J} \end{aligned}$$

Therefore, splitting one atom of U-235 produces 2.77×10^{-11} J of energy.

A respirator will prevent only alpha radiation from penetrating a person's body, and a radiation suit will prevent beta radiation from penetrating. However, gamma radiation will always be able to penetrate the suit, so in the case of a radioactive spill involving gamma radiation, it would be best to use a mobile robotic device to handle the clean up. It would be best to place any type of radioactive spill inside a container that is impervious to the different types of radiation, such as a lead lined box.

NOTES

KEY Strategies for Success on Tests

KEY STRATEGIES FOR SUCCESS ON TESTS

AN OVERVIEW OF THE TEST

This section is all about the skills and strategies you need to be successful on the Alberta Physics 30 Grade 12 Diploma Exam. It is designed for you to use together with your classroom learning and assignments.

Finding Out About the Test

Here are some questions you may wish to discuss with your teacher to help you prepare for the Alberta Physics 30 Diploma Examination.

1.	What will this test assess, or cover?	The test assesses the expectations from four content strands: Momentum and Impulse, Forces and Fields, Electromagnetic Radiation and Atomic Physics. The questions will test your ability to understand and apply the scientific concepts you have learned throughout the year.
2.	What materials do I need to bring to write the test?	You need a pencil, an eraser, and a calculator.
3.	Can I use a calculator during the test?	Yes, you are allowed to use an approved calculator.
4.	Are there any materials provided for the test?	Data pages containing references such as the periodic table, a list of physical constants, a list of pertinent equations, etc. will be provided with the exam. .
5.	What kinds of questions are on the test?	Your teacher can answer this question..
6.	How much time do I have to write the test?	You will have two hours, plus 60 minutes of additional time to complete the examination.
7.	How important is this test to my final grade?	Your teacher can answer this question for you.
8.	How many questions will be on each content strand?	The Process of Science Strand is integrated into the questions for the other strands. The breakdown of questions will be approximately: 15% Momentum and Impulse, 30% Forces and Fields, 30% Electromagnetic Radiation and 25% Atomic Physics.

Having an understanding of effective test-taking skills can help your performance on the test. Being familiar with the question formats may help you to prepare for quizzes, unit tests, and year-end assessments.

TEST PREPARATION AND TEST-TAKING SKILLS

THINGS TO CONSIDER WHEN TAKING A TEST

- It is normal to feel anxious before you write a test. You can manage this anxiety by:
  - Thinking positive thoughts. Imagine yourself doing well on the test.
  - Making a conscious effort to relax by taking several slow, deep, controlled breaths. Concentrate on the air going in and out of your body.
- Before you begin the test, ask questions if you are unsure of anything.
- Jot down key words or phrases from any instructions your teacher gives you.
- Look over the entire test to find out the number and kinds of questions on the test.
- Read each question closely and reread if necessary.
- Pay close attention to key vocabulary words. Sometimes these are **bolded** or *italicized*, and they are usually important words in the question.
- If you are putting your answers on an answer sheet, mark your answers carefully. Always print clearly. If you wish to change an answer, erase the mark completely and then ensure your final answer is darker than the one you have erased.
- Use highlighting to note directions, key words, and vocabulary that you find confusing or that are important to answering the question.
- Double-check to make sure you have answered everything before handing in your test.

When taking tests, students often overlook the easy words. Failure to pay close attention to these words can result in an incorrect answer. One way to avoid this is to be aware of these words and to underline, circle, or highlight them while you are taking the test.

Even though some words are easy to understand, they can change the meaning of the entire question, so it is important that you pay attention to them. Here are some examples:

all	**always**	**most likely**	**probably**	**best**	**not**
difference	**usually**	**except**	**most**	**unlikely**	**likely**

1. Which of the following equations is **not** considered abiotic?

A. wind

B. bacteria

C. sunlight

D. precipitation

HELPFUL STRATEGIES FOR ANSWERING MULTIPLE-CHOICE QUESTIONS

A multiple-choice question gives you some information, and then asks you to select an answer from four choices. Each question has one correct answer. The other answers are distractors, which are incorrect. Below are some strategies to help you when answering multiple-choice questions.

- Quickly skim through the entire test. Find out how many questions there are and plan your time accordingly.
- Read and reread questions carefully. Underline key words and try to think of an answer before looking at the choices.
- If there is a graphic, look at the graphic, read the question, and go back to the graphic. Then, you may want to underline the important information from the question.
- Carefully read the choices. Read the question first and then each answer that goes with it.
- When choosing an answer, try to eliminate those choices that are clearly wrong or do not make sense.
- Some questions may ask you to select the best answer. These questions will always include words like *best*, *most appropriate*, or *most likely*. All of the answers will be correct to some degree, but one of the choices will be better than the others in some way. Carefully read all four choices before choosing the answer you think is the best.
- If you do not know the answer, or if the question does not make sense to you, it is better to guess than to leave it blank.
- Do not spend too much time on any one question. Make a mark (*) beside a difficult question and come back to it later. If you are leaving a question to come back to later, make sure you also leave the space on the answer sheet, if you are using one.
- Remember to go back to the difficult questions at the end of the test; sometimes clues are given throughout the test that will provide you with answers.
- Note any negative words like *no* or *not* and be sure your choice fits the question.
- Before changing an answer, be sure you have a very good reason to do so.
- Do not look for patterns on your answer sheet, if you are using one.

Helpful Strategies for Answering Open-Response Questions

A written response requires you to respond to a question or directive such as **explain**, **predict**, **list**, **describe**, **show your work**, **solve**, or **calculate.** In preparing for open-response tasks you may wish to:

- Read and reread the question carefully.
- Recognize and pay close attention to directing words such as *explain*, *show your work*, and *describe*.
- Underline key words and phrases that indicate what is required in your answer, such as *explain*, *estimate*, *answer*, *calculate*, or *show your work*.
- Write down rough, point-form notes regarding the information you want to include in your answer.
- Think about what you want to say and organize information and ideas in a coherent and concise manner within the time limit you have for the question.
- Be sure to answer every part of the question that is asked.
- Include as much information as you can when you are asked to explain your thinking.
- Include a picture or diagram if it will help to explain your thinking.
- Try to put your final answer to a problem in a complete sentence to be sure it is reasonable.
- Reread your response to ensure you have answered the question.
- Think: Does your answer make sense?
- Listen: Does it sound right?
- Use appropriate subject vocabulary and terms in your response.

ABOUT SCIENCE TESTS

What You Need to Know about Science Tests

To do well on a science test, you need to understand and apply your knowledge of scientific concepts. Reading skills can also make a difference in how well you perform. Reading skills can help you follow instructions and find key words, as well as read graphs, diagrams, and tables.

Science tests usually have two types of questions: knowledge questions and skill questions. Knowledge questions test for your understanding of science ideas. Skill questions test how you would use your science knowledge.

How You Can Prepare for Science Tests

Below are some strategies that are particular to preparing for and writing science tests.

- Note-taking is a good way to review and study important information from your class notes and textbook.
- Sketch a picture of the process or idea being described in a question. Drawing is helpful for learning and remembering concepts.
- Check your answer to practice questions the require formulas by working backward to the beginning. You can find the beginning by going step-by-step in reverse order.
- When answering questions with graphics (pictures, diagrams, tables, or graphs), read the test question carefully.
  - Read the title of the graphic and any key words.
  - Read the test question carefully to figure out what information you need to find in the graphic.
  - Go back to the graphic to find the information you need.
- Always pay close attention when pressing the keys on your calculator. Repeat the procedure a second time to be sure you pressed the correct keys.

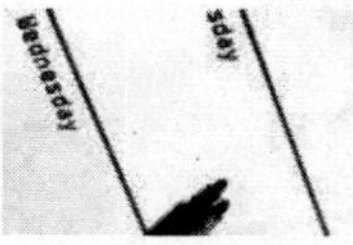

TEST PREPARATION COUNTDOWN

If you develop a plan for studying and test preparation, you will perform well on tests.

Here is a general plan to follow seven days before you write a test.

Countdown: 7 Days before the Test

1. Use "Finding Out About the Test" to help you make your own personal test preparation plan.

2. Review the following information:
- Areas to be included on the test
- Types of test items
- General and specific test tips

3. Start preparing for the test at least 7 days before the test. Develop your test preparation plan and set time aside to prepare and study.

Countdown: 6, 5, 4, 3, 2 Days before the Test

1. Review old homework assignments, quizzes, and tests.

2. Rework problems on quizzes and tests to make sure you still know how to solve them.

3. Correct any errors made on quizzes and tests.

4. Review key concepts, processes, formulas, and vocabulary.

5. Create practice test questions for yourself and then answer them. Work out many sample problems.

Countdown: The Night before the Test

1. The night before the test is for final preparation, which includes reviewing and gathering material needed for the test before going to bed.

2. Most important is getting a good night's rest and knowing you have done everything possible to do well on the test.

Test Day

1. Eat a healthy and nutritious breakfast.

2. Ensure you have all the necessary materials.

3. Think positive thoughts: "I can do this." "I am ready." "I know I can do well."

4. Arrive at your school early so you are not rushing, which can cause you anxiety and stress.

SUMMARY OF HOW TO BE SUCCESSFUL DURING A TEST

You may find some of the following strategies useful for writing a test.

- Take two or three deep breaths to help you relax.
- Read the directions carefully and underline, circle, or highlight any important words.
- Look over the entire test to understand what you will need to do.
- Budget your time.
- Begin with an easy question, or a question you know you can answer correctly, rather than following the numerical question order of the test.
- If you cannot remember how to answer a question, try repeating the deep breathing and physical relaxation activities first. Then, move on to visualization and positive self-talk to get yourself going.
- When answering a question with graphics (pictures, diagrams, tables, or graphs), look at the question carefully.
  - Read the title of the graphic and any key words.
  - Read the test question carefully to figure out what information you need to find in the graphic.
  - Go back to the graphic to find the information you need.
- Write down anything you remember about the subject on the reverse side of your test paper. This activity sometimes helps to remind you that you do know something and you are capable of writing the test.
- Look over your test when you have finished and double-check your answers to be sure you did not forget anything.

Practice Tests

Practice TEST

Practice Test 1

1. A plane had a velocity of 694 km/h due east. If the momentum of the plane was 5.49×10^5 kg·m/s in the same direction, the mass of the plane was
   A. 791 kg
   B. 2.85×10^3 kg
   C. 1.06×10^8 kg
   D. 3.81×10^8 kg

Use the following information to answer the next question.

A hockey puck with a mass of 250 g slides along a smooth ice surface at 17.4 m/s due west. It encounters some snow cover and 1.92 s later returns to smooth ice, continuing with a velocity of 11.0 m/s due west.

2. What is the change in the hockey puck's momentum?
   A. 1.60 kg·m/s due west
   B. 1.60 kg·m/s due east
   C. 1.60×10^3 kg·m/s due west
   D. 1.60×10^3 kg·m/s due east

Use the following information to answer the next question.

A 2.50 kg skateboard is rolling due east with negligible friction along a smooth surface. The skateboarder exerts a force of 7.50 N for 0.500 s in the same direction, causing the skateboard to accelerate to 5.25 m/s due east.

3. What impulse does the skateboarder impart to the skateboard?
   A. 3.75 N·s due west
   B. 13.1 N·s due west
   C. 3.75 kg·m/s due east
   D. 13.1 kg·m/s due east

Use the following information to answer the next question.

A ball is thrown at four different walls. The resulting bounces are shown in the diagram.

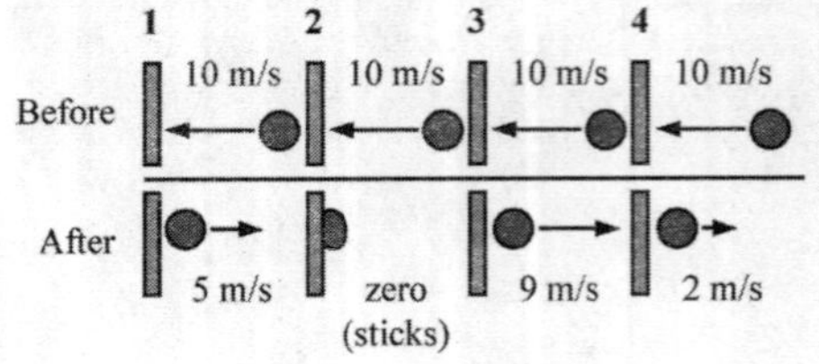

Numerical Response

4. The order of the scenarios when listed from the smallest to the largest impulses are scenarios, __________, __________, __________, and __________. (Record your answer as a four digit number.)

5. The following statements all relate to a collision between any two objects on a horizontal frictionless surface. Which of these statements is **always true**?
   A. The momentum of each object before and after the collision is the same.
   B. The kinetic energy of each object before and after the collision is the same.
   C. The total kinetic energy of the two objects before and after the collision is the same.
   D. The total momentum of the two objects before and after the collision is the same.

6. A railcar moving west at constant speed collides and couples with a similar railcar that was stationary. Which of the observations best supports the conservation of momentum?

A. The momentum of the initially moving railcar decreased after the collision.

B. The coupled railcars move west with a lower speed after the collision.

C. The momentum of the stationary railcar increased after the collision.

D. Sound and heat energy are emitted when the railcars collide.

Use the following information to answer the next question.

A student sits facing forward on a chair that has been fixed to a cart that moves on frictionless rails.

7. If the cart is moving at 3.00 m/s and the student throws a heavy sandbag off the side of the cart, the cart will

A. speed up

B. slow down

C. change direction

D. not change speed

8. A 115 g arrow travelling east at 20 m/s embeds itself in a 57 g tennis ball moving north at 42 m/s. The direction of the ball-and-arrow combination after impact is

A. 46° north of east

B. 46° east of north

C. 25° east of north

D. 25° north of east

9. In an inelastic collision, the energy that appears to be missing is converted into

A. sound and momentum

B. force and momentum

C. sound and heat

D. heat and force

Use the following information to answer the next question.

A positively charged rod is placed near, but not touching, a neutral metal ball.

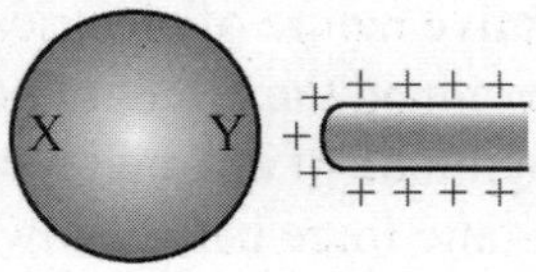

10. As a result of the rod's position, side X of the ball becomes relatively

A. negative and the ball is repelled from the rod

B. positive and the ball is repelled from the rod

C. negative and the ball is attracted to the rod

D. positive and the ball is attracted to the rod

Use the following information to answer the next question.

A group of students were asked to positively charge a neutral sphere by induction. Here is a set of possible steps.

1. Remove the ground from the sphere.
2. Touch the rod to the sphere.
3. Bring the positively charged rod near the sphere.
4. Ground the sphere by touching it.
5. Remove the charged rod.
6. Bring a negatively charged rod near the sphere.

Numerical Response

11. In order, the four steps the students should follow are __________, __________, __________, and __________. (Record your answer as a four-digit number.)

Use the following information to answer the next question.

Charles Augustin de Coulomb performed a series of investigations on the quantitative nature of electrical forces. He determined the effect of both distance and magnitude of charge on the electrostatic force between two charged metal spheres.

12. Which of the following graphs represents the relationship that Coulomb determined between force and the distance between two charged metal spheres?

A.

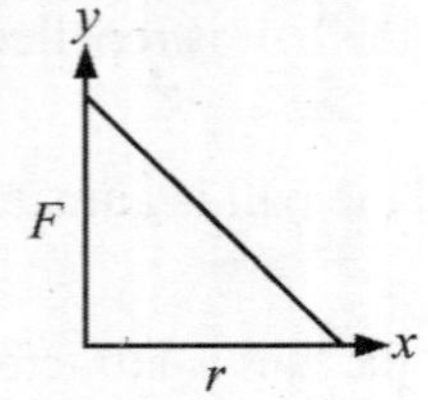

B.

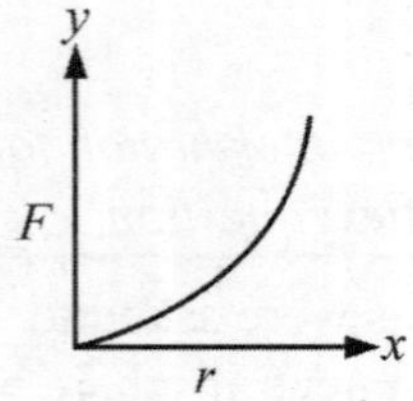

C.

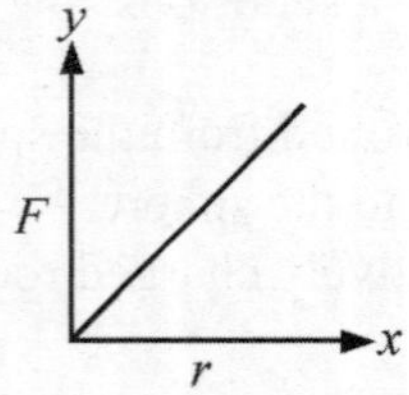

D.

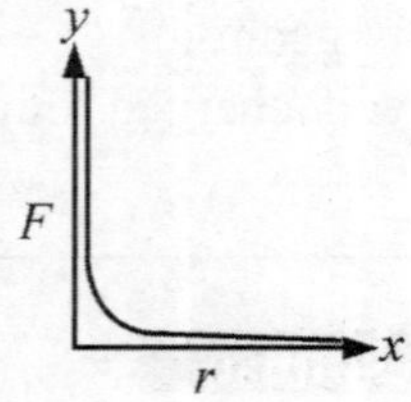

Use the following information to answer the next question.

Two conducting spheres have identical surface areas. Sphere A has a charge of 4.50 μC. Sphere B has a charge of −2.40 μC. Spheres A and B are brought into momentary contact and separated to a distance of 2.50 cm.

Numerical Response

13. The magnitude of the electric force exerted by sphere A on sphere B after contact and separation is ________ N. (Record your answer to three digits.)

Use the following information to answer the next question.

Charles Augustin de Coulomb performed a series of investigations on the quantitative nature of electrical forces. He was able to determine the effect of both distance and magnitude of charge on the electrostatic force between two charged metal spheres.

14. Coulomb again separated the identically charged spheres by a distance r. The force between the spheres was F. Coulomb touched one of the spheres with a third, identical neutral sphere. The third sphere was then moved far away from the other spheres. If he then measured the force between the original spheres, the new force between the spheres would have been

A. $\frac{1}{2}F$ **B.** $\frac{1}{4}F$

C. $2F$ **D.** $4F$

CHALLENGER QUESTION

Use the following information to answer the next question.

The three point charges *A*, *B*, and *C* are located at the vertices of a right triangle. The charge on each sphere is +40.0 μC, –50.0 muC, and +60.0 μC, respectively.

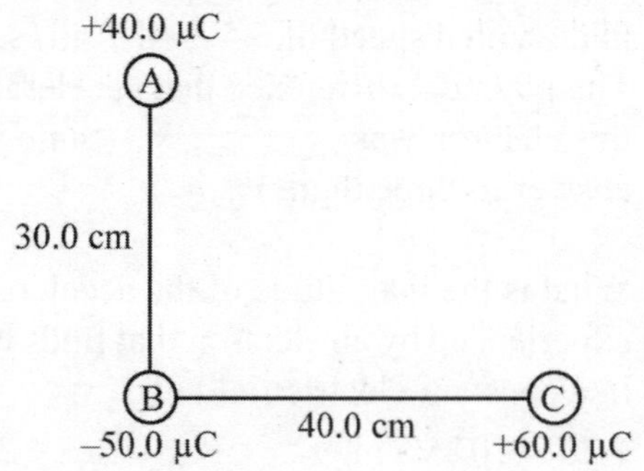

15. The electrical force acting on charge C because of the presence of charges A and B is

A. 255 N at 272° **B.** 112 N at 259°

C. 82.3 N at 272° **D.** 81.7 N at 189°

16. Which of the following statements **best** describes a scenario using charges that is similar to the increase in gravitational energy that occurs when a mass is raised at constant speed in a uniform gravitational field?

A. A small, negatively charged sphere is placed between two parallel, oppositely charged plates and moved at constant speed toward the negative plate.

B. A small, positively charged sphere is placed between two parallel, oppositely charged plates and moved at constant speed toward the negative plate.

C. A small, negatively charged sphere is placed near another small, negatively charged sphere and moved toward it at constant speed.

D. A small, positively charged sphere is placed near a small, negatively charged sphere and moved toward it at constant speed.

17. A mass falling from the top of a building is losing gravitational energy and gaining kinetic energy. Since the gravitational field can be considered uniform in this situation, this is **most** similar to a

A. negatively charged oil drop placed between charged, parallel plates, accelerating upward toward the positive plate

B. positively charged oil drop placed between charged, parallel plates, accelerating upward toward the positive plate

C. negatively charged oil drop accelerating toward a small, positively charge sphere

D. an electron when it is repelled by another electron

18. Two parallel charged plates are 15.0 cm apart. The top plate is connected to the positive pole of a battery and the bottom plate is attached to the negative pole of this battery. The battery is rated at 90.0 V. If a positive 100 μC charge is moved from a position 2.00 cm from the negative plate to a position 3.00 cm from the positive plate, the potential difference between these two points is

A. 12.0 V **B.** 30.0 V

C. 60.0 V **D.** 90.0 V

19. The intensity and direction of the electric field produced by an alpha particle at a distance of 5.0×10^{-11} m from the particle is

A. 5.8×10^{11} N/C, toward the alpha particle

B. 5.8×10^{11} N/C, away from the alpha particle

C. 1.2×10^{12} N/C, toward the alpha particle

D. 1.2×10^{12} N/C, away from the alpha particle

Use the following information to answer the next question.

> An ammeter reads 1.5 A when placed in a circuit. The number of electrons passing through the ammeter each second is $a.b \times 10^{cd}$.

Numerical Response

20. What are the values of *a*, *b*, *c*, and *d*? _________ (Record your answer as a four-digit number.)

Numerical Response

21. An electron entered into a space between two parallel plates, which were 10.0 cm apart, through a small hole in one of the plates. The electron was travelling with a speed of 2.50×10^5 m/s when it passed through the hole, and it reached the other plate with a speed of 6.50×10^6 m/s. The potential difference that accelerated this electron was ________V. (State your answer to three digits)

22. What is the magnitude of the acceleration experienced by an electron that finds itself in a constant electric field of 1.20×10^4 V/m?

A. 7.03×10^{13} m/s^2

B. 1.60×10^{15} m/s^2

C. 2.11×10^{15} m/s^2

D. 8.86×10^{13} m/s^2

Use the following information to answer the next question.

A student is given 11 identical cardboard boxes of negligible mass, each filled with a different number of identical marbles. The student determines the mass of each box and records them in the given table.

Box	Mass (g)
1	3.0
2	4.5
3	7.5
4	9.0
5	12
6	13.5
7	15
8	18
9	19.5
10	22.5
11	30

23. Using this data, the mass of a single marble is **most likely**

A. 1.0 g
B. 1.5 g
C. 2.5 g
D. 3.0 g

Use the following information to answer the next question.

A student holds a compass near the top of a filing cabinet and observes the direction that the needle points. When the student holds the compass near the bottom of the filing cabinet, the student observes that the compass needle is deflected 180° from its direction at the top of the cabinet.

24. A possible explanation for the deflection of the compass needle is that the

A. bottom of the filing cabinet is positively charged
B. bottom of the filing cabinet is negatively charged
C. induced magnetic polarity of the bottom of the filing cabinet is opposite to that at the top of the filing cabinet
D. bottom of the filing cabinet is closer to Earth, so it is more strongly magnetized than the top of the filing cabinet

Use the following information to answer the next question.

The given diagrams show three different fields: an electric field, a magnetic field, and a gravitational field. The direction that a beam of electrons are deflected as they travel from left to right through each field is indicated below each diagram.

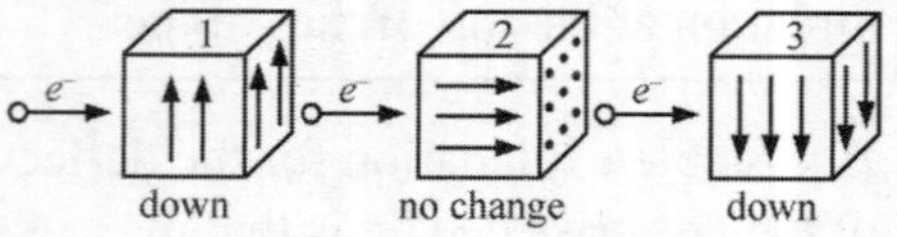

25. Which of the following tables shows the **most likely** field type represented by diagrams 1, 2, and 3?

A.

1	2	3
gravitational	magnetic	electric

B.

1	2	3
electric	magnetic	gravitational

C.

1	2	3
magnetic	gravitational	electric

D.

1	2	3
electric	gravitational	magnetic

Numerical Response

26. A 50.0 cm length of wire has a weight of 0.389 N and a current of 0.250 A running through it. The wire remains suspended against gravity when placed perpendicularly through a magnetic field. The strength of the magnetic field is __________ T. (Record your **three-digit** answer.)

Use the following information to answer the next question.

Cathode-ray tubes (CRTs) are used for television and computer screens. They are set up as shown in the diagram.

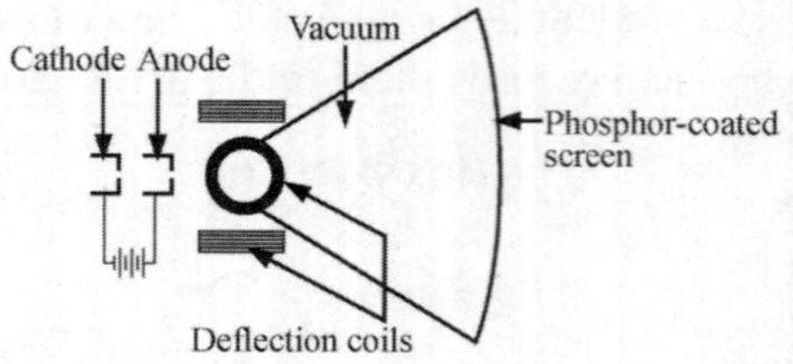

Electrons are "boiled off" the surface of the cathode and are accelerated toward the anode. The cathode is 4.5 cm from the anode. A potential difference of 2.5×10^3 V exists between the cathode and the anode. The electrons are deflected both side-to-side and up-and-down by pairs of magnetic deflection coils mounted on the neck of the tube.

An electron travels perpendicularly to the magnetic deflection coils, into the page, as shown in the following diagram.

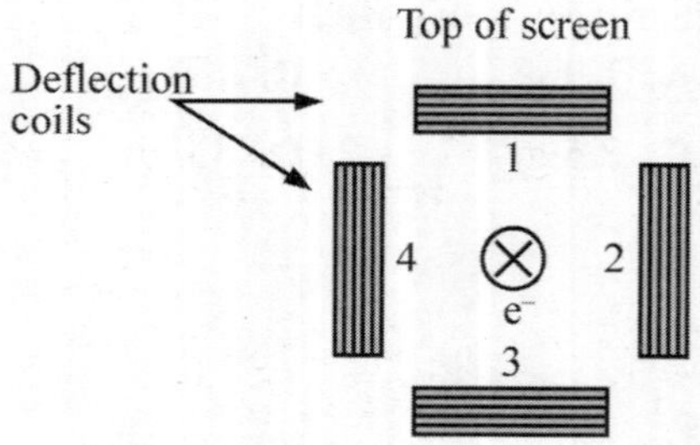

27. The coils that can produce a deflection toward the top of the screen are numbered

A. 1 and 3 **B.** 2 and 4

C. 1 and 2 **D.** 3 and 4

Use the following information to answer the next question.

An electron with a velocity of 4.0×10^6 m/s due west enters into a uniform magnetic field of 5.0 mT directed down.

28. What will be the radius and the orientation of the electron's circular path?

A. 4.6 mm on the horizontal plane

B. 4.6 mm on the vertical plane

C. 4.6 m on the horizontal plane

D. 4.6 m on the vertical plane

Use the following information to answer the next question.

Diagrams **1** and **2** below each show an electron as it enters a field. The fields are different but the electrons enter them with the same instantaneous velocity, $\vec{v}_{inst}$

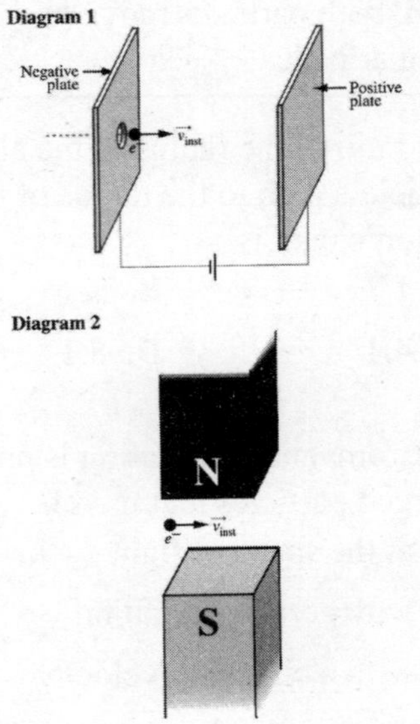

Statements about the Motion of the Charged Particles as They Travel Through the Fields

I. The speed of the particle remains constant.
II. The speed of the particle increases.
III. The direction of the particle's motion remains constant.
IV. The direction of the particle's motion changes.

29. The statements that describe the motion of the charged particle in diagram **1** are

A. I and III **B.** I and IV

C. II and III **D.** II and IV

30. A charged particle moves without deflection through electric and magnetic fields, where *v*, *E*, and *B* are mutually perpendicular. If the electric field is divided by the magnetic field, the units will be

A. $\frac{\text{N·kg}}{\text{A·s}}$ **B.** $\frac{\text{N·C}}{\text{T}}$

C. m/s^2 **D.** m/s

Use the following information to answer the next question.

A proton enters a magnetic field at a right angle to the field. An alpha particle enters the same field at the same angle but with twice the speed. Once in the magnetic field, both particles move in a circular path.

31. The ratio of the radius of the alpha particle's path to the radius of the proton's path is

A. 1:1 **B.** 2:1

C. 4:1 **D.** 8:1

32. Electromagnetic radiation is produced by charged particles that travel

A. at the speed of light

B. with zero acceleration

C. with a changing velocity

D. parallel to a fixed magnetic field

Use the following information to answer the next question.

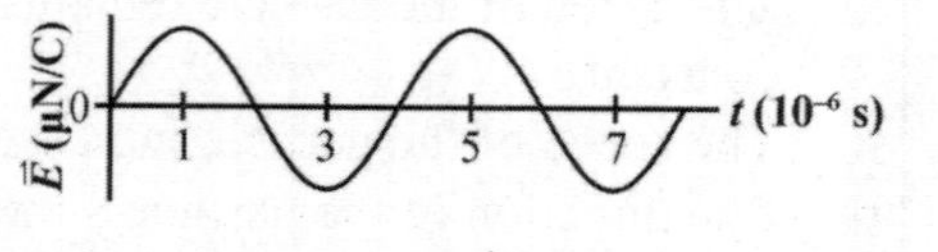

The Electric Field Component of an Electromagnetic Wave in a Vacuum

33. The wavelength of this electromagnetic wave is

A. 6.0×10^2 m

B. 1.2×10^3 m

C. 2.5×10^5 m

D. 7.5×10^{13} m

34.

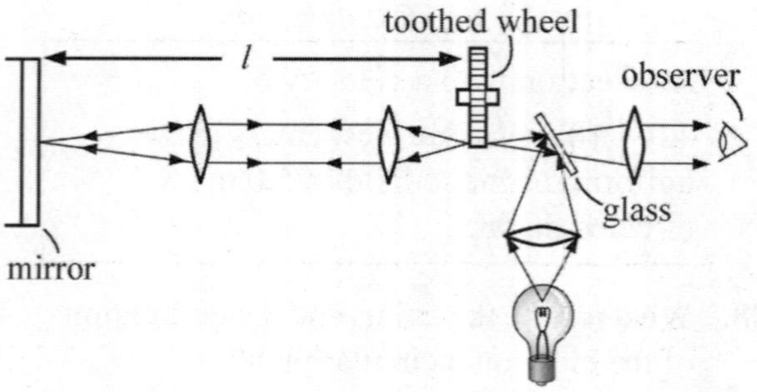

Light from a source, S, is collimated and reflected onto a spinning toothed wheel, which may interrupt the light beam as it travels to and from a distant fixed mirror, as shown in the diagram. If the distance to the fixed mirror is known, what other information is required in order to determine the speed of light?

A. The amount of time the light spends in the focusing lenses, where it has a lower speed

B. The frequency of rotation of the toothed wheel and the number of teeth in the wheel

C. The distance between the light source and the toothed wheel

D. The angular velocity of the toothed wheel

35. In an experiment designed similar to Michelson's, light reflects off an octagonal rotating mirror toward a fixed mirror 30.0 km away, and then back again in the time that the octagonal mirror rotates through an angle of 45.0°. If the octagonal mirror has a rotational frequency of 6.15×10^2 Hz, what is the value for the experimental error in this calculation of c?

A. 87.7% **B.** 9.83%

C. 1.67% **D.** 0%

Use the following information to answer the next question.

Monochromatic red light with a wavelength of 700 nm is mixed with monochromatic blue light with a wavelength of 434 nm. The mixture is directed as a single ray toward an equilateral prism made of crown glass, and it is travelling parallel to the base of the prism when it first strikes the prism. The index of refraction of crown glass is 1.510 for red light and 1.528 for blue light.

36. The difference in angles of refraction of the two components at the first surface is

A. 19.3° **B.** 19.1°

C. 0.237° **D.** 0°

Use the following information to answer the next question.

A girl is looking at her reflection in a full length mirror.

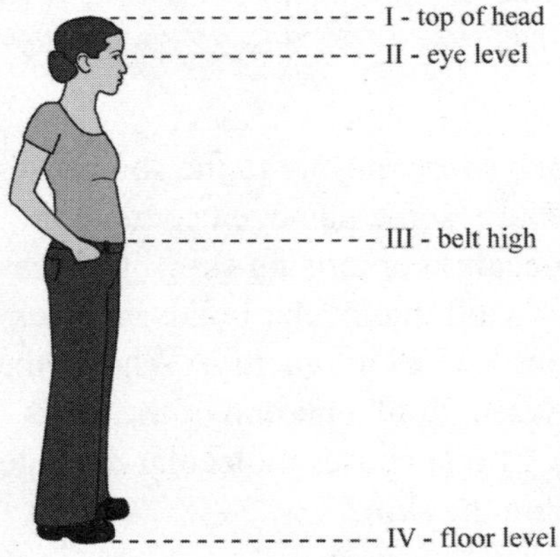

37. Using the given points of reference, the smallest mirror that can still show her complete reflection would extend from

A. I to IV

B. I to III

C. halfway between I and II to IV

D. halfway between I and II to halfway between II and IV

Use the following information to answer the next question.

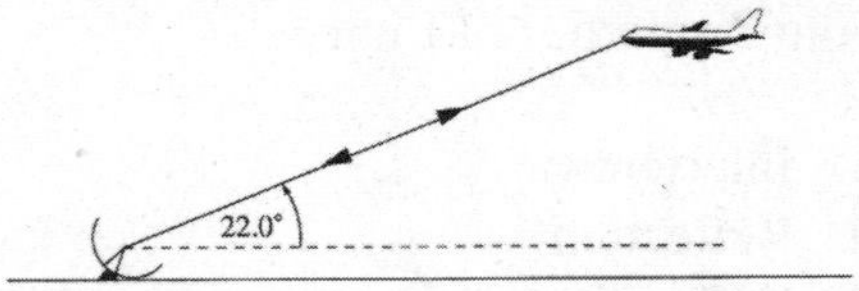

A radar pulse projected at an angle of elevation of 22.0° is reflected from an aircraft and returned.

(**Note:** The diagram is not drawn to scale. The height of the radar transmitter/receiver can be ignored.)

Numerical Response

38. If the pulse takes 1.28×10^{-4} s to make the round trip, then the vertical height of the aircraft is __________ km. (Record your answer to three digits.)

39. A typical single lens reflex (SLR) camera has a converging lens with a focal length of 50.0 mm. What is the position and size of the image of a 25.0 cm candle located 1.00 m in front of the camera?

A. 4.27 cm, 1.30 cm

B. 5.26 cm, 1.32 cm

C. 6.25 cm, 1.30 cm

D. 50.0 cm, 13.2 cm

Numerical Response

40. An object is located 30.0 cm from a converging mirror with a focal length of 5.00 cm. If the image distance is 1 / 5 as large as the object distance, and the object is 4.00 cm tall, the image height is __________ cm. (Express your answer to three significant digits.)

Use the following information to answer the next question.

Four Properties of Light
i. Interference
ii. Reflection
iii. Diffraction
iv. Dispersion

41. Which of the given properties of light are strong evidence that light has a wave nature?

A. iii and iv **B.** ii and iv

C. i and iii **D.** i and iv

Numerical Response

42. Monochromatic light illuminated two slits separated by 1.50×10^{-2} cm and formed a pattern of a screen 2.34 m away. The fifth maximum, not including the central maximum, was 6.22 cm from the centre of the screen. The wavelength of this light was $a.bc \times 10^{-d}$ m. The values of a, b, c, and d are _________, _________, _________, and _________. (Record your answer as a four-digit number.)

Use the following information to answer the next question.

> A diffraction grating with 550 lines per millimetre is used to examine a hydrogen spectrum. A red line is measured at 21.1° from the central antinode.

Numerical Response

43. The wavelength of this light is $a.bc \times 10^{-d}$ m. What are the values of a, b, c, and d? ________ (Record your answer as a four-digit number.)

Use the following information to answer the next question.

> A student is using a prism to produce a rainbow on a wall with blue on the top and red on the bottom.

44. Which of the following diagrams shows the correct placement of the prism?

A.

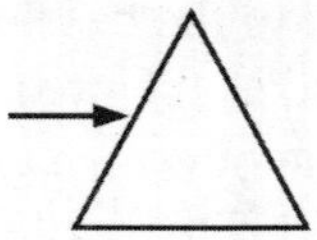

B.

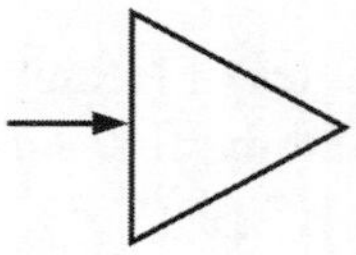

C.

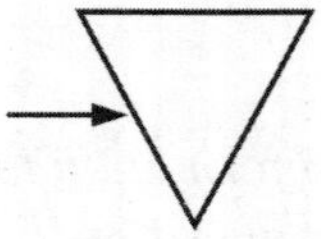

D.

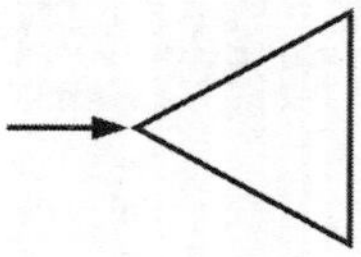

45. When overexposure to the sun causes sunburn, some damage occurs to the molecules comprising skin. To break the skin's intramolecular bonds requires about 3.65 eV of energy. What is the wavelength of a photon of the sun's energy that causes molecular damage within the skin?

A. 5.45×10^{-26} m

B. 3.41×10^{-25} m

C. 5.45×10^{-8} m

D. 3.41×10^{-7} m

46. Photons with an energy of 1.00×10^{-6} eV are found in the radiation of which of the following sections of the electromagnetic radiation (EMR) spectrum?

A. Ultraviolet **B.** Infrared

C. Visible **D.** Radio

47. Violet light striking the negative electrode in a phototube causes a current to flow in the tube. Under the same conditions, another form of light that will always cause a current to flow is

A. blue **B.** green

C. infrared **D.** ultraviolet

Numerical Response

48. When light with a wavelength of 350 nm shines on a photoelectric metal, the maximum kinetic energy of the emitted photoelectrons is 1.20 eV. To three significant digits, the work function of the metal is __________ eV.

Use the following information to answer the next question.

X-rays with a wavelength of 2.20×10^{-12} m and an energy of 56.0 keV are scattered from a carbon target.

49. If the radiation is scattered at 85.0° to the incident beam of X-rays, the change in wavelength of the scattered X-rays is

A. 9.23×10^{-15} m

B. 2.11×10^{-13} m

C. 2.21×10^{-12} m

D. 1.21×10^{-12} m

50. Assuming the mass of a single atom of hydrogen is identical to the sum of the masses of the positive and negative particles within the atom, the total charge and the total negative charge in 0.500 kg of hydrogen would be

A. 0 C and 4.79×10^{7} C

B. 0 C and 2.99×10^{26} C

C. 9.58×10^{7} C and 4.79×10^{7} C

D. 9.58×10^{7} C and 2.99×10^{26} C

51. J.J. Thomson's experiment that confirmed the existence of the electron showed that cathode rays are made of

A. a type of EM radiation

B. positively charged particles

C. negatively charged particles

D. atoms with electrons in them

Use the following information to answer the next question.

After Ernest Rutherford sent alpha particles to collide into gold atoms in a sheet of gold foil and measured how the alpha particles scattered, he concluded that atoms have a nucleus.

52. Which of the following graphs **best** shows the size of the nucleus?

A.

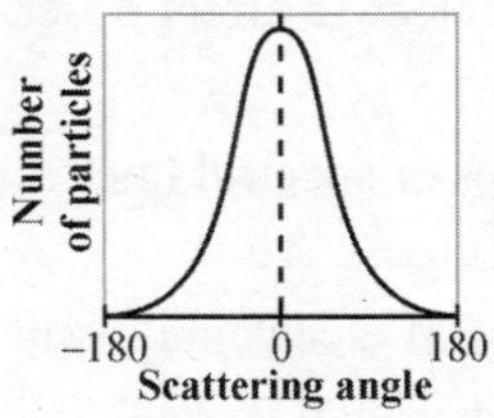

B.

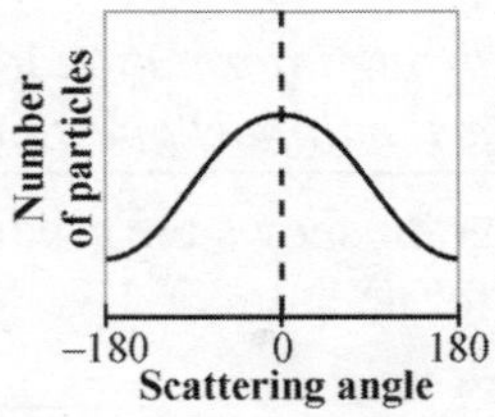

C.

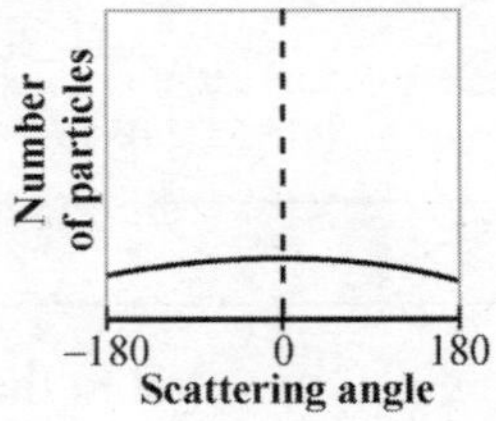

D.

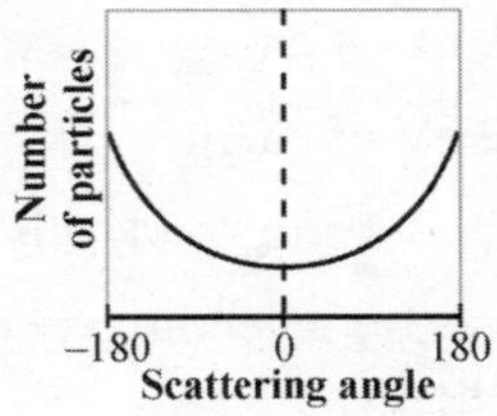

53. Rutherford proposed that electrons orbit a nucleus much like planets orbit the sun. This was discovered to be false because electrons moving in this manner would

- **A.** travel faster than light
- **B.** be pulled in toward the strongly charged nucleus
- **C.** produce antimatter during collisions, eventually disappearing
- **D.** be accelerating and would have to emit electromagnetic radiation

54. Which of the following phenomena provided striking evidence supporting Bohr's theory for the stationary electron orbits in the atom?

- **A.** The emission spectra studied by Balmer
- **B.** The photoelectric effect observed by Hertz
- **C.** The studies of spectral lines made by Kirchhoff
- **D.** The nature of electromagnetic radiation as stated by Maxwell

Use the following information to answer the next multipart question.

55. The given diagram shows the predicted energy levels for an atom.

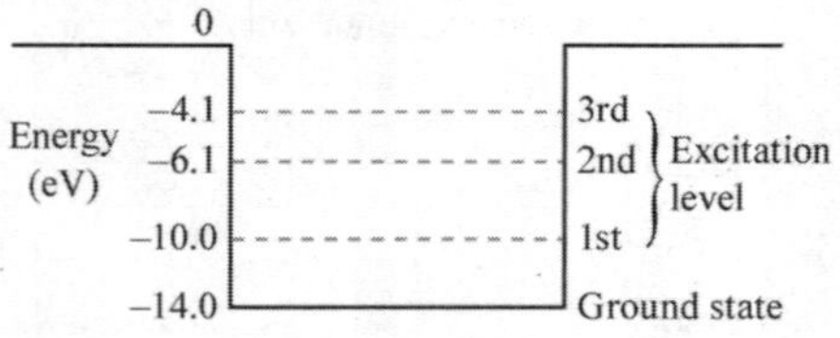

a) In order for an electron to get to the 3rd excitation level, it had to

- **A.** absorb 9.9 eV of energy
- **B.** absorb 5.2 eV of energy
- **C.** move to the 1st and 2nd levels first
- **D.** move to the 3rd level directly by emitting energy

Numerical Response

b) Visible light photon energies are from 1.8 eV for red to 3.1 eV for violet. The wavelength of visible light that an electron in the 3rd excitation level can emit is $a.bc \times 10^{-d}$ m. The values of a, b, c, and d are __________.

56. Imagine a beam of light with a sufficiently low intensity shines upon a single slit so that the photons pass through the slit one at a time. The photons then pass through one of two slits and then strike photographic film. Which of the following statements provides the correct description of the processed photographic image and the quantum mechanical explanation of this image?

- **A.** The photographic film will show two bright bands because the wave nature of the photon will direct the photons through either slit in random, unpredictable fashion.
- **B.** The photographic film will show an exposed central maximum with alternating bands of exposure on each side of center because every photon is directed to one of the two slits in an alternating pattern.
- **C.** The photographic film will be completely unexposed because the particle nature of the photons means that they will strike the point directly opposite the single slit; in other word, the photons will strike the midpoint between the double slits.
- **D.** The photographic film will show an exposed central maximum with alternating bands of exposure on each side of the centre because the wave nature of the photon will determine the probability the photon will strike the photographic film in a given location.

Use the following information to answer the next question.

> Compared with beta and gamma radiation, alpha radiation penetrates ___*i*___, moves ___*ii*___, and causes ___*iii*___ ionizing damage when inside a body.

57. This statement is completed by the information in table

A.

i	*ii*	*iii*
more	faster	less

B.

i	*ii*	*iii*
more	slower	more

C.

i	*ii*	*iii*
less	faster	less

D.

i	*ii*	*iii*
less	slower	more

58. Cobalt-60 is used as a radiation source in medicine. It has a half-life of 5.25 years. How long will it take for the sample of the radioisotope to decay to one-eighth of its original activity?

A. 0.656 years **B.** 10.5 years

C. 15.8 years **D.** 42.0 years

Use the following information to answer the next question.

> When uranium-238 is bombarded by neutrons, the following reaction occurs:
> $^{238}_{92}U + ^{1}_{0}n \rightarrow ^{0}_{-1}e + ^{abc}_{de}X$

Numerical Response

59. What are the values of *a*, *b*, *c*, *d*, and *e* in the given reaction? _______ (Record your answer as a five digit number.)

Use the following information to answer the next question.

> The fusion of hydrogen to helium releases ___*i*___ energy per reaction than the fission of uranium does, and this fusion process produces ___*ii*___ radioactive waste than the fission process does.

60. This statement is completed by the information in which of the following tables?

A.

i	*ii*
more	more

B.

i	*ii*
more	less

C.

i	*ii*
less	more

D.

i	*ii*
less	less

Use the following information to answer the next question.

> The binding energy per nucleon for U-238 is about 7.6 MeV, while the binding energy for a nucleus that is half this mass is about 8.6 MeV.

61. Which of the following statements about these nuclei is **true**?

A. The nucleus of U-238 is more stable than the smaller nucleus.

B. The stability of U-238 can only be inferred from the half-life of this nuclide.

C. The nucleus of U-238 can become more stable through nuclear fission because the binding energy per nucleon of the smaller product nuclei will decrease.

D. The nucleus of U-238 can become more stable through nuclear fission because the binding energy per nucleon of the smaller product nuclei will be greater than 7.6 MeV.

Use the following information to answer the next question.

A physicist drew the following diagram to represent the observed trajectories of subatomic particles in a bubble chamber. The uniform magnetic field within the bubble chamber is oriented out of the plane of the page.

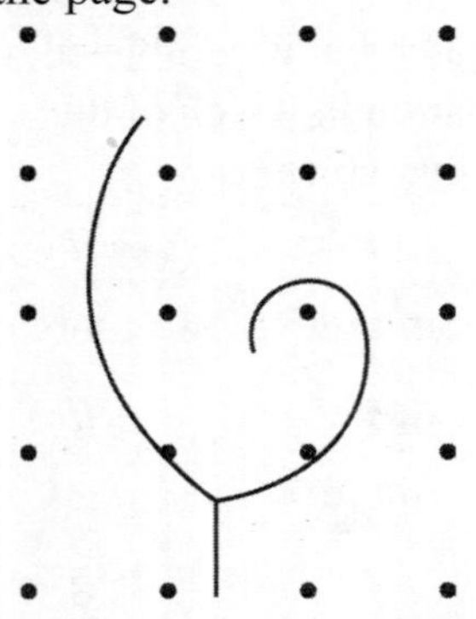

62. Which of the following inferences about the observed particles did the physicist **most likely** make?

A. A neutral particle travelled up along the plane of the page and converted into two particles, a proton and an electron.

B. A neutral particle travelled up along the plane of the page and converted into two particles, a positron and an electron.

C. A neutral particle travelled up along the plane of the page and converted into two particles, one of which was a positive particle that deflected counterclockwise.

D. A neutral particle travelled up along the plane of the page and converted into two particles, one of which was a negative particle that deflected clockwise.

63. Three particles have masses of 0.511 MeV/c^2, 938 MeV/c^2 and 7.00×10^{-6} MeV/c^2. The three particles, respectively, are **most likely** the

A. electron neutrino, neutron, and electron

B. electron, proton, and electron neutrino

C. positron, neutron, and antiproton

D. electon, proton, and antiproton

Use the following information to answer the next question.

Isotopes that are much lighter than average tend to be β^+ decay isotopes. During this decay, ___*i*___ changes into ___*ii*___ with the release of ___*iii*___.

64. Which of the following tables completes the given statement?

A.

i	*ii*	*iii*
an up quark	a down quark	a neutrino

B.

i	*ii*	*iii*
an up quark	a down quark	an antineu-trino

C.

i	*ii*	*iii*
a down quark	an up quark	a neutrino

D.

i	*ii*	*iii*
a down quark	an up quark	an antineu-trino

Practice TEST

PRACTICE TEST 2

1. A block of ice, with a mass of 8 350 g, slides across a smooth ice surface. If the block has a momentum of 56.4 kg·m/s west, the velocity of the block is
   A. 6.75 m/s east
   B. 6.75 m/s west
   C. 6.75×10^{-3} m/s east
   D. 6.75×10^{-3} m/s west

2. In an automobile collision, the severity of injury to the driver can be reduced by an airbag. In a car initially travelling at 100 km/h, the airbag stops a 62 kg driver in 90 ms. The magnitude of the average force exerted by the airbag on the driver is
   A. 6.9×10^4 N
   B. 1.9×10^4 N
   C. 9.6×10^3 N
   D. 6.1×10^2 N

Use the following information to answer the next question.

Cathode-ray tubes (CRTs) are used for television and computer screens. They are set up as shown below.

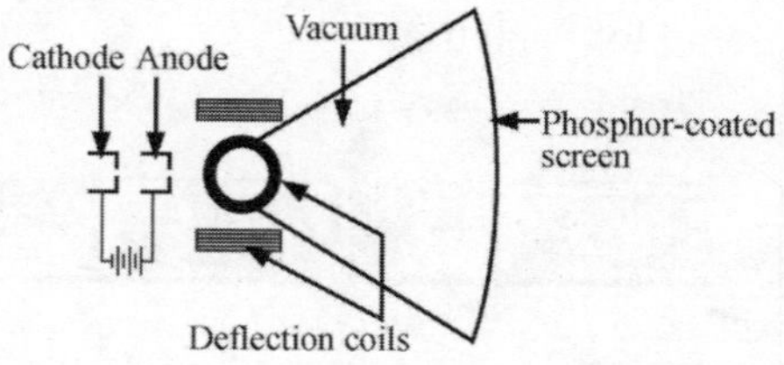

Electrons are "boiled off" the surface of the cathode and are accelerated toward the anode. The cathode is 4.5 cm from the anode. A potential difference of 2.5×10^3 V exists between the cathode and the anode. The electrons are deflected both side-to-side and up-and-down by pairs of magnetic deflection coils mounted on the neck of the tube.

3. What is the speed of an electron immediately before it hits the screen?
   A. 1.0×10^7 m/s
   B. 1.5×10^7 m/s
   C. 3.0×10^7 m/s
   D. 8.8×10^{14} m/s

Use the following information to answer the next question.

A student performs an experiment to investigate the time required to stop a toy van. In each of four trials, the student varies the speed and mass of the van. The toy van is brought to rest by a piston that applies a uniform force that is the same for each trial.

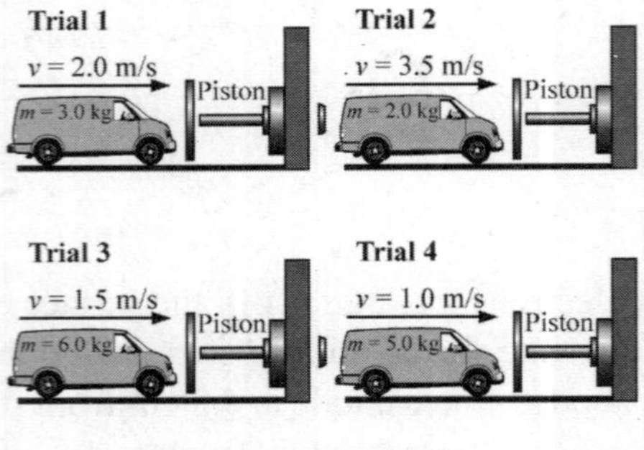

Numerical Response

4. When the trials above are listed in order from the trial that has the longest stopping time to the trial that has the shortest stopping time, the order is __________, __________, __________, __________.
(Record your answer as a four-digit number.)

5. A 65.0-kg girl running north at 3.00 m/s jumped onto a 15.0-kg sled that was already moving on a level, frictionless surface at 2.50 m/s north. What was the velocity of the girl and sled after she landed on the sled?
   A. 5.50 m/s north
   B. 3.58 m/s north
   C. 2.91 m/s north
   D. 2.75 m/s north

6. Which of the following statements **best** describes the conditions of an elastic collision?
   A. An elastic collision conserves both the kinetic and potential energies.
   B. An elastic collision is one in which both the kinetic energy and momentum are conserved.
   C. A collision that is completely elastic will have some kinetic energy converted to heat, light, or sound.
   D. The directions of all the colliding particles must be considered in order to determine if the collision is elastic.

Use the following information to answer the next question.

A car crashes into a cliff wall and comes to rest. The car is not ____*i*____ system, since its momentum changed. In order to show the conservation of momentum, ____*ii*____ must be included in the system.

7. The given statements are **best** completed by the information in which of the following tables?

A.

i	*ii*
an isolated	Earth's surface

B.

i	*ii*
a mechanical	Earth's surface

C.

i	*ii*
an isolated	the road

D.

i	*ii*
a mechanical	the road

Practice TEST

CHALLENGER QUESTION

8. A 0.500 kg steel ball rolling with a velocity of 2.00 m/s east collides with a second steel ball, which has a mass of 0.350 kg and is at rest. The collision deflects the first ball, and its velocity becomes 1.50 m/s E 30.0° N. What is the velocity of the second ball after the collision?
   A. 0.513 m/s E 76.9° S
   B. 0.754 m/s E 7.31° S
   C. 1.47 m/s E 47.0° S
   D. 3.50 m/s E 30.0° S

Use the following information to answer the next question.

At a coal mine, a train engine bumps an empty hopper car that has a mass of 1.00×10^4 kg such that it rolls at a constant speed of 2.00 m/s under a coal storage bin. When the hopper car triggers an electromagnetic switch on the track below the storage bin, the bin drops a load of 1.20×10^4 kg of coal into the hopper car.

Numerical Response

9. The speed of the hopper car immediately after receiving the load of coal, expressed in scientific notation, is $b \times 10^{-w}$ m/s. The value of b is ________.
(Record your answer to three digits.)

Use the following information to answer the next question.

A football player with a mass of 105 kg is running at 6.00 m/s west when another player, with a mass of 85.0 kg, tackles him. The tackler hangs on to the other player, and the two players continue to move at 4.00 m/s at 34.0° N of W.

Numerical Response

10. The tackler's speed before the collision was ________ m/s.

Use the following information to answer the next question.

Two cars collide at an unmarked intersection.

Just before collision

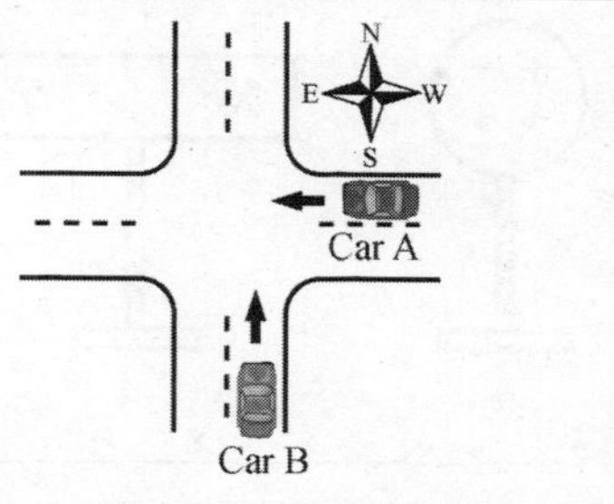

Just after collision

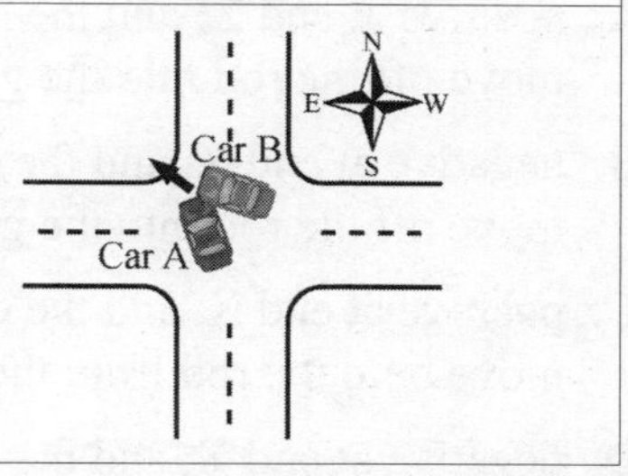

11. Which of the following statements **best** describes the inelastic collision in the given diagram?
   A. Both momentum and kinetic energy are conserved.
   B. Neither momentum nor kinetic energy are conserved.
   C. Momentum is not conserved but kinetic energy is conserved.
   D. Momentum is conserved but kinetic energy is not conserved.

Use the following information to answer the next question.

A student places a positively charged sphere near a metal rod. Both are on insulated stands and the rod is grounded.

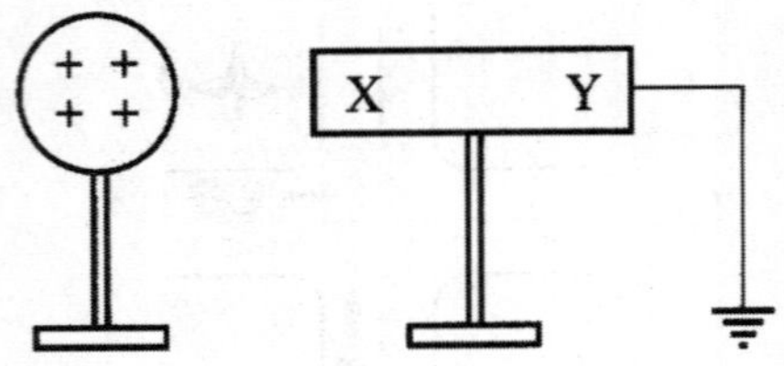

12. The distribution of charge on the rod is
A. positive at end X, and the electrons move off the rod into the ground
B. negative at end X, and the electrons move off the rod into the ground
C. positive at end X, and the electrons move onto the rod from the ground
D. negative at end X, and the electrons move onto the rod from the ground

13. A small sphere with a metallic coating is placed at the end of a bamboo skewer that electrically insulates the sphere from its surroundings. A negatively charged rod is brought into contact with the sphere, which is initially neutral. After the rod is removed, the sphere will **most likely** be
A. negatively charged with the charges uniformly distributed on the sphere's surface
B. negatively charged with the charges concentrated where the rod touched the sphere
C. positively charged with the charges uniformly distributed on the sphere's surface
D. neutral because no charge was transferred by induction

14. Which of the following statements about electrical conductors and insulators is **false**?
A. Electrons within an insulator are free to move from one place to another.
B. Electrons in a metal are loosely bound to the metallic nuclei and can easily move within the metal.
C. Electrons uniformly distribute themselves on a metallic sphere due to mutual electron repulsions.
D. Electrons can be deposited on one side of a rod composed of a substance that is an electrical insulator.

CHALLENGER QUESTION

Use the following information to answer the next question.

Four identical charged spheres, spheres A, B, C, and D, are placed at the corners of a square, as shown in the diagram. Each of the spheres has a charge with a magnitude of 5.0 μC. Two diagonally opposite charges, spheres A and C, are positive, and the other two charges are negative, as shown.

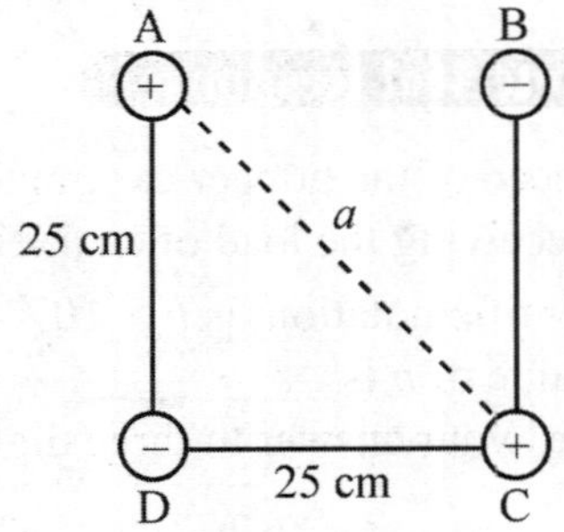

15. The magnitude of the net force acting on sphere A is
A. 1.8 N
B. 3.3 N
C. 3.6 N
D. 5.1 N

Numerical Response

16. Two positively charged pith balls are separated by a distance of 25.0 cm. If the charge on one ball is doubled, the charge on the second is increased by a factor of 3.5, and the force of repulsion is 4 times larger than the original force of repulsion, the pith balls must now be separated by a distance of________ cm. (Record your answer to three significant figures.)

Numerical Response

17. Two point charges were placed 6.75×10^{-2} m apart. Point charge A had a mass of 125 mg and a charge 200 μC, and point charge B had a mass of 450 mg and a charge of 350 μC. Charge A was fixed to a non-conducting rod while charge B was released and became free to move. The instantaneous acceleration of charge B as soon as it was released was $a.bc \times 10^{d}$ m/s². The values of a, b, c, and d are __________, __________, _________, and _________. (Record your answer as a four-digit number.)

18. If a mass is raised a small distance in a gravitational field that can be considered uniform over this small distance, the gravitational potential energy is given by $E_p = mgh$. The formula that is analogous to this is

A. $E = \frac{F}{q}$ **B.** $W = qEd$

C. $E = \frac{kq}{r^2}$ **D.** $E = Fd$

19. Which of the following statements **best** describes voltage?

A. Voltage and electrical potential energy are equivalent terms and have the units N/C.

B. Voltage is the measure of the change in electric potential energy per unit charge.

C. Voltage is the electric potential energy of a charge placed in a uniform electric field.

D. Voltage is the measure of the total work done to move a given charge within an external electric field.

Numerical Response

20. An 850 volt source is applied across two parallel, horizontal plates that are 12.0 cm apart. If point A is 1.50 cm above the lower plate and point B is 1.00 cm below the upper plate, the potential difference between the points A and B is ________ V. (State your answer to three digits.)

Numerical Response

21. The potential difference between two parallel plates is 7.00 kV. If a free electron is released from the midpoint between the plates, it will reach the positive plate with a speed of $a.bc \times 10^{d}$ m/s. The values of a, b, c, and d are _________, _________, _________, and _________. (Record your answer as a four-digit number.)

22. The magnitude of an electric field at a distance x from a point charge Q is 8.3×10^{-4} N/C. If the distance is increased to $3x$ and the charge is reduced to $\frac{Q}{4}$, then the magnitude of the electric field will be

A. 1.9×10^{-3} N/C

B. 3.7×10^{-4} N/C

C. 6.9×10^{-5} N/C

D. 2.3×10^{-5} N/C

Numerical Response

23. An electrical spark transfers 3.00 μC of charge in 4.50×10^{-5} s. This corresponds to a current of $a.bc \times 10^{-d}$ A. What are the values of *a*, *b*, *c*, and *d*? (Record your answer as a four-digit number.)

24. An electron is moving with a velocity of 1.03×10^{7} m/s when it enters the region between two parallel plates. The electric potential difference between these two plates is 500 V and the separation is 4.0 cm. If the plate that the electron came through was the positive plate, what is the closest approach that the electron will make to the other plate?

A. 1.2 cm **B.** 1.6 cm

C. 2.0 cm **D.** 2.4 cm

Use the following information to answer the next question.

> The Millikan oil-drop experiment demonstrated that charge is ___*i*___, and the smallest charge possible is ___*ii*___.

25. The information in which of the following tables completes the given statement?

A.

i	*ii*
quantized	1 eV

B.

i	*ii*
quantized	1.60×10^{-19} C

C.

i	*ii*
smoothly variable	1.60×10^{-19} C

D.

i	*ii*
smoothly variable	1 eV

26. If the source of Earth's magnetic field were a bar magnet, then the **best** diagram to show this field would be

A.

B.

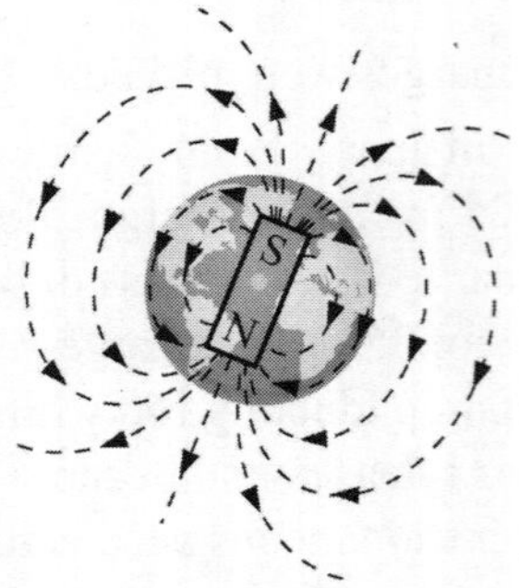

C.

D.

27. An electric field is oriented upward, a magnetic field is acting northward, and the gravitational field is acting downward. If an alpha particle travels eastward through these fields simultaneously, in which direction will the forces due to each field act upon the particle?

A. The electric force will act upward, the magnetic force will act downward, and the gravitational force will act downward.

B. The electric force will act upward, the magnetic force will act upward, and the gravitational force will act downward.

C. All three forces will act downward.

D. All three forces will act upward.

28. A straight, current-carrying conductor is placed between the poles of two bar magnets as shown. If the current shown in the diagram is conventional current, what is the direction of the magnetic force on the wire?

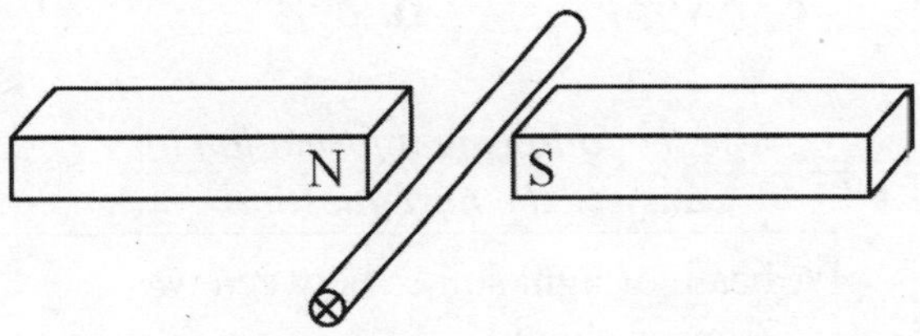

A. down **B.** right

C. left **D.** up

Numerical Response

29. A proton, travelling at 2.55×10^5 m/s east, entered into a uniform magnetic field produced by two large, horizontal solenoids. If the magnetic field strength was 7.35×10^{-2} T upward, the radius of curvature of the electron's trajectory was $a.bc \times 10^{-d}$ m. The values of a, b, c, and d are __________, __________, __________, and __________. (Record your answer as a four-digit number.)

Use the following information to answer the next question.

A proton with an energy of 894 eV travels perpendicularly into a magnetic field and then travels in a circular path with a radius of 3.60×10^{-4} m.

Numerical Response

30. The strength of the magnetic field, expressed in scientific notation, is $a.bc \times 10^d$ T. The values of a, b, c, and d are __________, __________, __________, and __________. (Record your answer as a four-digit number.)

Use the following information to answer the next question.

An electron travelling with a velocity of 2.50×10^6 m/s east entered into a uniform magnetic field of 9.58 mT downward. Two vertical, parallel plates, placed 15.0 cm apart, are located in the region of the uniform magnetic field.

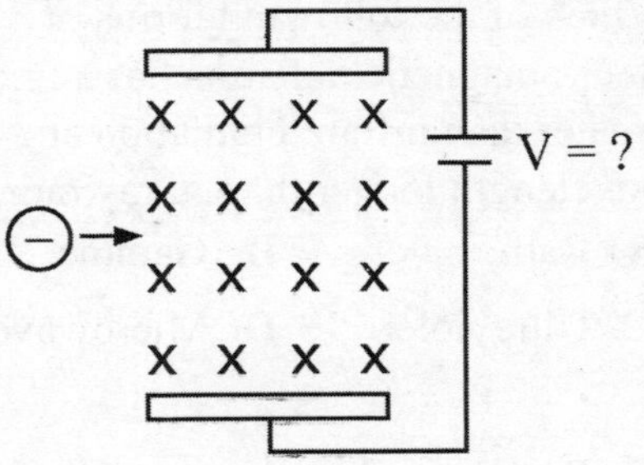

Numerical Response

31. The voltage across the plates necessary to permit the electron to travel without deflection through the crossed electric and magnetic fields is $a.bc \times 10^d$ V. The values of a, b, c, and d are __________. (State your answer as a four-digits number.)

32. A copper wire is connected to a battery so that it has a current in it. A segment of the wire is perpendicular to a horizontal 1.5 T magnetic field. The length of the wire in the magnetic field is 3.0 cm, and the mass of the wire affected by the magnetic field is 20 g. In order to suspend the segment of wire, the minimum current in the wire must be

A. 0.044 A **B.** 0.23 A

C. 4.4 A **D.** 44 A

Numerical Response

33. A wire that is 75.0 cm long carries a current of 6.00 A. The wire is at right angles to a uniform magnetic field and experiences a magnetic force of 0.350 N. The magnitude of the magnetic field, expressed in scientific notation, is $b \times 10^{-w}$ T. The value of b is ________. (Record your answer as a three-digit number.)

34. Which of the following forms of electromagnetic radiation has a frequency greater than infrared radiation and a wavelength longer than X-ray radiation?

A. Radio **B.** Gamma

C. Ultraviolet **D.** Microwave

35. Ole Rømer used the observed timings of Jupiter's moons to get a measurement for the speed of light. Which of the following statements about Rømer's method is **true**?

A. The occurence of eclipses of Jupiter's moons increases throughout the year.

B. The lateness of the eclipses of Jupiter's moons is due to the large distance between Earth and Jupiter.

C. The time taken for light from Jupiter to reach Earth can be used to time the eclipses of Jupiter's moons.

D. The maximum delay in an eclipse of Jupiter's moons is the duration of time for light to cross Earth's orbit.

Numerical Response

36. In an experiment to determine the speed of light, a hexagonal mirror, rotating with a frequency of 2.35 kHz, was used to reflect light to a distant, fixed mirror, which reflected the light back again in the time the hexagonal mirror rotated through a 60.0° turn. If the distance from the rotating mirror to the fixed mirror was 9.75 km, the experimentally determined speed of light was $a.bc \times 10^{d}$ m/s. The values of a, b, c, and d are ______. (State your answer to four digits.)

37. A layer of oleic acid ($n = 1.43$) sits undisturbed above a layer of carbon disulphide ($n = 1.46$) in a glass tank ($n = 1.50$) with a thick base. If all the layer interfaces are parallel and a ray of light travelling in the glass from below enters into the carbon disulphide at an angle of incidence of 35.0°, the angle of refraction of the emergent ray into the air is

A. 22.5° **B.** 35.1°

C. 56.9° **D.** 59.4°

Use the following information to answer the next question.

A beam of light shines between two mirrors as shown.

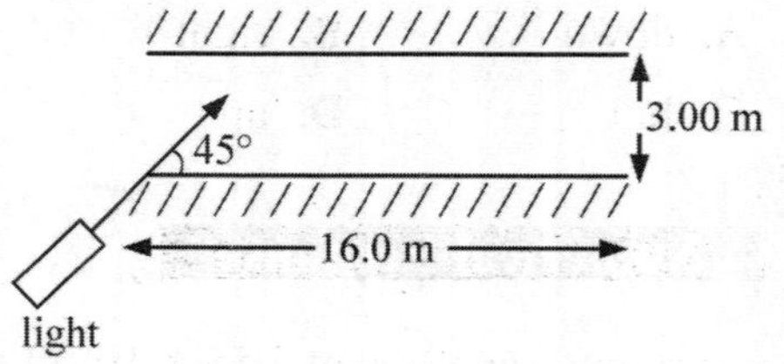

38. The number of reflections the beam will make between the mirrors is

A. 3 **B.** 4

C. 5 **D.** 6

39. A lens has a focal length of 20.0 cm and a magnification of 4.00. The distance between an object and its image is

A. 15.0 cm **B.** 45.0 cm

C. 60.0 cm **D.** 75.0 cm

Use the following information to answer the next question.

A person looks into a concave mirror with a focal length of 45 cm. When the person's face is 25 cm from the mirror, the image is ___***i***___ and is found ___***ii***___ the mirror.

40. The given statement is completed by the information found in which of the following tables?

A.

i	*ii*
real	56 cm behind

B.

i	*ii*
virtual	56 cm behind

C.

i	*ii*
real	56 cm in front of

D.

i	*ii*
virtual	56 cm in front of

Use the following information to answer the next question.

Light passes through two slits as shown.

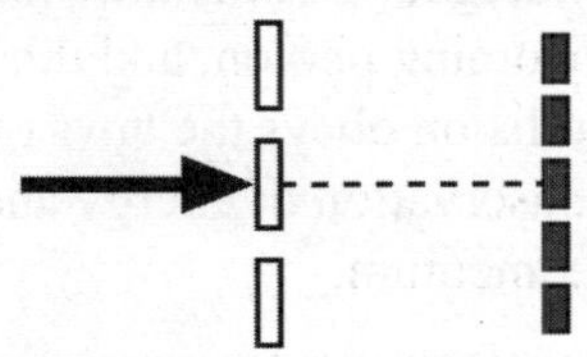

41. Bright fringes will appear on a screen when the path difference from each slit to the screen is

A. $1\frac{3}{4}\lambda$ **B.** 2λ

C. $2\frac{1}{4}\lambda$ **D.** $2\frac{1}{2}\lambda$

Numerical Response

42. Yellow light (λ = 588 mm) shines through two slits and projects onto a screen 3.50 m away. Bright fringes appear on the screen at distances 4.00 cm apart. The distance between the slits is $a.bc \times 10^{-d}$ m. What are the values of *a*,*b*,*c*, and *d*? __________ (Record your answer as a four-digit number.)

Numerical Response

43. A diffraction grating with $d = 2.50 \times 10^{-6}$ m is used to analyze an emission spectrum. A red line is measured at an angle of 15.2°. The wavelength of the red light is $a.bc \times 10^{-d}$ m. What are the values of *a*,*b*, *c*, and *d*? __________ (Record your answer as a four-digit number.)

Numerical Response

44. Green light, with a wavelength of 565 nm, enters into crown glass (n = 1.50) at an angle of incidence of 43.5°. The frequency of this green light as it passes through the crown glass is $a.bc \times 10^{de}$ Hz. The values of *a*, *b*, *c*, *d*, and *e* are __________, __________, __________, __________, and __________. (Record your answer as a five-digit number.)

45. In order to obtain a continuous spectrum in which the red wavelengths of light bend more than the blue wavelengths of light, which of the following methods for light dispersion should be used?

A. A triangular prism only

B. A diffraction grating only

C. Either a diffraction grating and a triangular prism

D. Red light cannot be bent more than blue light by any method of dispersion

Numerical Response

46. During the radioactive decay of a certain nucleus, a gamma ray was emitted with a photon energy of 1.35 MeV.
The frequency of this photon was $a.bc \times 10^{de}$ Hz. The values of *a*, *b*, *c*, *d*, and *e* are ________, ________, ________, ________, and ________. (Record your answer as a five-digit number.)

47. It takes about 5 to 10 eV of energy to break chemical bonds. Electromagnetic radiation with photons with this energy can be found in the

- **A.** radio region of the EMR spectrum
- **B.** visible region of the EMR spectrum
- **C.** infrared region of the EMR spectrum
- **D.** ultraviolet region of the EMR spectrum

48. Which of the following statements about the photoelectric effect is **false**?

- **A.** Different metals obey the same photoelectric equation.
- **B.** Different photoelectric metals have different threshold frequencies.
- **C.** The wave model of light predicted the instantaneous ejection of a photoelectron if the incident EMR had low intensity.
- **D.** The graph of the maximum kinetic energy of the photoelectrons versus the frequency of the incoming EMR always has the same slope.

Use the following information to answer the next question.

The photoelectrons emitted from a surface illuminated by light with a wavelength of 491 nm have a stopping potential of 0.710 V. When the incident EMR was replaced with EMR of a different wavelength, the stopping potential was then 1.43 V.

49. What was the work function for the surface and the wavelength of the new light?

- **A.** 2.92×10^{-19} J, 382 nm
- **B.** 4.05×10^{-19} J, 3.82×10^{-9} m
- **C.** 1.83 eV, 869 nm
- **D.** 2.92 eV, 8.69×10^{-7} m

50. Which of the following descriptions of the photoelectric effect **best** illustrates the particle nature of EMR?

- **A.** A charged photoelectric surface will lose its charge if high-energy EMR radiates the surface.
- **B.** An electron near a metallic surface will be oscillated out of the metal as the electric field of the incident EMR exerts an oscillating electrical force on this electron.
- **C.** An electron near a metallic surface undergoes a collision with an incoming photon, and this elastic collision obeys the laws of conservation of energy and momentum.
- **D.** An electron near a metallic surface will be affected by a magnetic force as the magnetic field of the incident EMR sweeps across this electron, as predicted by the left-hand rule.

Numerical Response

51. In a Compton scattering experiment, an incoming X-ray beam with a wavelength of 2.35×10^{-12} m was found to change after collisions with electrons in the target material. If the X-ray wavelength after the collision was 3.95×10^{-12} m, the ejected electrons gained an energy of $a.bc \times 10^{d}$ eV. The values of *a*, *b*, *c*, and *d* are ________, ________, ________, and ________. (Record your answer as a four-digit number.)

52. Whose model of the atom was developed as a result of the discovery of cathode rays?

A. Rutherford's model of the atom, which proposed a very small, very dense positive nucleus surrounded by negative particles called electrons

B. Bohr's model of the atom, which suggested that electrons could exist in stationary states without constantly radiating EMR

C. Thomson's model of the atom, which hypothesized a uniformly dense positive sphere in which negative bits of matter were uniformly distributed

D. Dalton's model of the atom, which proposed that atoms were tiny, neutral spheres that could chemically bond in various integer ratios

53. Rutherford's scattering experiment showed that atoms are

A. mostly filled with empty space with separate positive and negative charges

B. filled with positive and negative charges mixed together

C. made of positive and negative particles of equal mass

D. dense solid objects with a net zero charge

54. A student connected the electrodes at the ends of a glass discharge tube, filled with hydrogen gas, to a variable high-voltage source. When the student connected the electrodes to the voltage source, the tube began to glow with a magenta color. The student used a transmission diffraction grating to view the glowing tube and expected to see a

A. dark-line emission spectrum

B. bright-line emission spectrum

C. dark-line absorption spectrum

D. bright-line continuous spectrum

Numerical Response

55. The emission spectrum of an element contains a green line with a wavelength of 565 nm. If the electron that emitted this light ended up at an excited level 3.50 eV above ground state, then it was originally _______eV above ground state. (Round and record your answer to 3 significant digits.)

56. An element is observed to have many spectral lines in the infrared region of the EMR spectrum. From this observation, a reasonable conclusion about the energy levels in the atom is that the

A. atoms have many energy levels far apart

B. atoms have many energy levels close together

C. electrons are making many low-energy transitions between the energy levels

D. electrons are making many high-energy transitions between the energy levels

Use the following information to answer the next question.

Louis de Broglie proposed that particles, such as electrons, have a wave nature. Some of the properties now attributed to electrons are as follows:

I. Exhibit interference effects
II. Are able to collide with atoms
III. Diffract around objects

57. The electron properties that were developed from de Broglie's hypothesis are properties

A. I only **B.** II only
C. I and II **D.** I and III

Use the following information to answer the next question.

An experiment is carried out to test the form of radiation emitted by a radioactive rock. The rock is placed in a vacuum, and the radiation is directed through a magnetic field. Radiation detectors A, B, and C are set up in the magnetic field as shown.

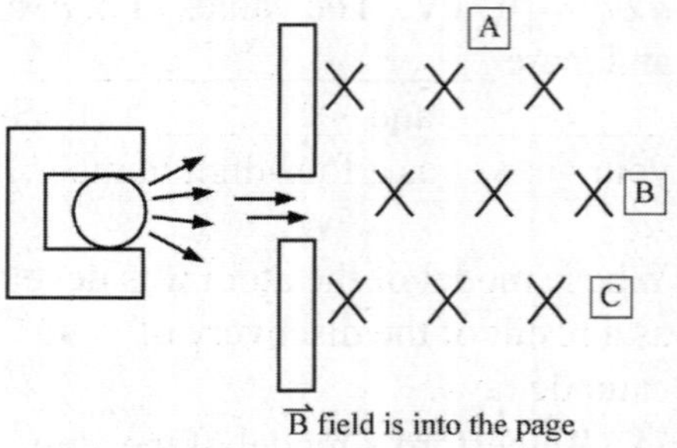

Detector A will detect ___*i*___ radiation and detector B will detect ___*ii*___ radiation.

58. The given statement is completed by the information in which of the following tables?

A.

i	*ii*
alpha	beta

B.

i	*ii*
beta	gamma

C.

i	*ii*
gamma	alpha

D.

i	*ii*
alpha	gamma

Use the following information to answer the next multipart question.

59. The given diagram shows the transformation of a nucleus during a number of decays.

Mass Number and Atomic Number of a Decaying Atom

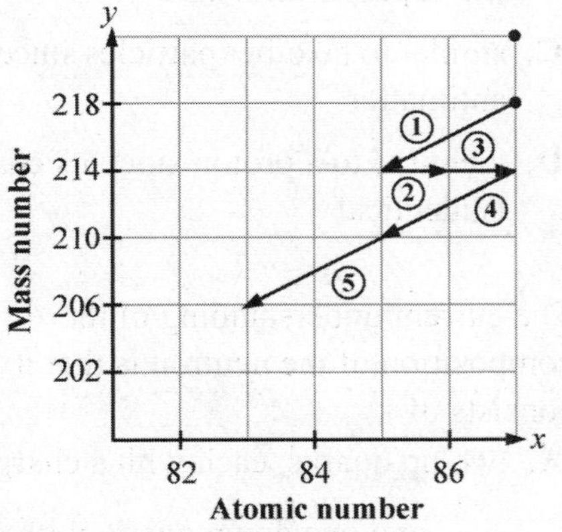

a) Of the decays represented by the given graph, the transitions that represent alpha decays are transitions

A. 1, 2 and 3 only

B. 1, 4, and 5 only

C. 2 and 3 only

D. 4 and 5 only

b) Which of the following arrows would represent a beta positive decay on the given diagram?

A.

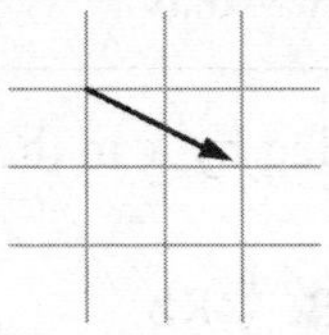

B.

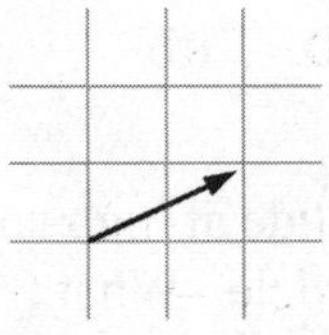

C.

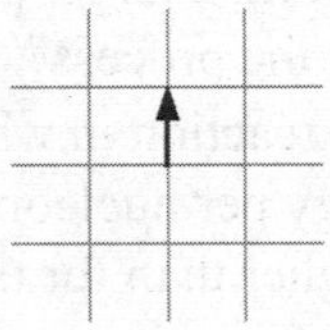

D.

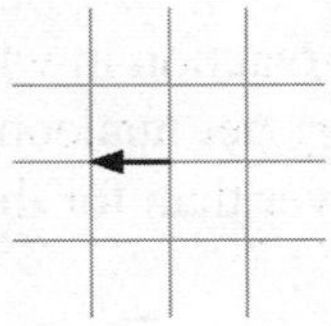

60. A $^{238}_{92}U$ ion undergoes four spontaneous radioactive decays in succession. If the ion first emits an alpha particle, followed by two beta-negative particles, and then a final alpha particle, the final daughter product will be

A. $^{234}_{90}Th$

B. $^{230}_{90}Th$

C. $^{234}_{91}Pa$

D. $^{234}_{92}U$

Numerical Response

61. If the radioactivity of a sample of $^{19}_{8}O$ decreased to $\frac{1}{16}$ of its initial value in 116 s, the half-life of this radioisotope is __________ s. (Give your answer to three digits.)

Use the following information to answer the next question.

$${}^{1}_{0}n + {}^{235}_{92}U \rightarrow {}^{141}_{55}Cs + X + 3{}^{1}_{0}n$$

62. The isotope represented by X in the given reaction is

A. ${}^{92}_{37}Rb$ **B.** ${}^{91}_{37}Rb$

C. ${}^{94}_{37}Rb$ **D.** ${}^{95}_{37}Rb$

63. Two small nuclei collide at high speeds and form a larger particle. What type of reaction occurred to form a larger particle and release energy in the process?

A. A nuclear fusion reaction in which the binding energy per nucleon for the product is higher than for the reactants.

B. A nuclear fusion reaction in which the binding energy per nucleon for the product is lower than for the reactants.

C. A pair production reaction in which the products have greater stability than the reactants.

D. A nuclear fission reaction in which energy is released.

Numerical Response

64. Given that the mass of a proton is 1.007 28 u, the mass of a neutron is 1.008 67 u, and the mass of the carbon-13 nucleus is 13.003 35 u, the binding energy of a carbon-13 nucleus is $a.bc \times 10^{-de}$ J. The values for a, b, c, d, and e are _______, _________, _________, _________, _________ (Record your answer as a five-digit number.)

65. The first antimatter particle discovered was the positron (the anti-electron). The appearance of the positron in a cloud chamber would be

A. much like an electron but with a larger radius of trajectory

B. much like an electron but turning in the opposite direction

C. similar to no other particles since it is antimatter

D. identical to a proton since its charge is identical

66. The current understanding of the composition of the neutron is that it consists of

A. two up quarks, each with a charge of $+\frac{2}{3}$, and one down quark, with a charge of $-\frac{1}{3}$

B. one up quark, with a charge of $+\frac{2}{3}$, and two down quarks, each with a charge of $-\frac{1}{3}$

C. one up quark, with a charge of $+\frac{1}{2}$, and one down quark, with a charge of $-\frac{1}{2}$

D. one up quark, with a charge of $+\frac{2}{3}$, and one down quark, with a charge of $-\frac{2}{3}$

Use the following information to answer the next question.

Beta decay comes in two kinds: β^+ and β^-. Both involve the ___*i*___ force which changes ___*ii*___ into different flavours (types).

67. The given statement is completed by the information in which of the following tables?

A.

i	*ii*
strong nuclear	quarks

B.

i	*ii*
strong nuclear	neutrinos

C.

i	*ii*
weak nuclear	quarks

D.

i	*ii*
weak nuclear	neutrinos

Answers and Solutions — Practice Test 1

1. B	14. A	27. B	40. 0.800	53. D
2. B	15. B	28. A	41. C	54. A
3. C	16. A	29. C	42. 7977	55. a) A
4. 3142	17. A	30. D	43. 6557	b) 6217
5. D	18. C	31. C	44. C	56. D
6. B	19. D	32. C	45. D	57. D
7. D	20. 9418	33. B	46. D	58. C
8. A	21. 120	34. B	47. D	59. 23993
9. C	22. C	35. C	48. 2.35	60. B
10. D	23. B	36. C	49. C	61. D
11. 6415	24. C	37. D	50. A	62. A
12. D	25. B	38. 7.19	51. C	63. B
13. 15.9	26. 3.11	39. B	52. A	64. A

1. B

$$m = \frac{\vec{p}}{\vec{v}}$$

$$= \frac{5.49 \times 10^5 \text{ kg·m/s due east}}{(694 \text{ km/h due east})\left(\frac{1\,000 \text{ m}}{1 \text{ km}}\right)\left(\frac{1 \text{ h}}{3\,600 \text{ s}}\right)}$$

$$= 2.85 \times 10^3 \text{ kg}$$

2. B

$$\begin{aligned}\Delta\vec{p} &= m\vec{v}_\text{f} - m\vec{v}_\text{i}\\ &= m(\vec{v}_\text{f} - \vec{v}_\text{i})\\ &= (250 \times 10^{-3} \text{ kg})\\ &\quad \times (11.0 \text{ m/s west} - 17.4 \text{ m/s west})\\ &= -1.60 \text{ kg·m/s west}\\ &= 1.60 \text{ kg·m/s east}\end{aligned}$$

3. C

The impulse is given by the following formula:

$$\begin{aligned}\text{Impulse} &= \vec{p}\\ &= \vec{F}t\\ &= (7.50 \text{ N east})(0.500 \text{ s})\\ &= 3.75 \text{ kg·m/s east}\end{aligned}$$

The skateboarder imparts an impulse of 3.75 kg·m/s east to the skateboard.

4. 3142

Use the formula for impulse to determine which ball experienced the largest impulse.

$$\text{Impulse} = F\Delta t = m\Delta v = m(v_\text{f} - v_\text{i})$$

When finding $v_\text{f} - v_\text{i}$, be sure to account for the direction change.

$$\begin{aligned}\text{Impulse}_1 &= m(-5 \text{ m/s} - 10 \text{ m/s})\\ &= m(-15 \text{ m/s})\end{aligned}$$

$$\begin{aligned}\text{Impulse}_2 &= m(0 \text{ m/s} - 10 \text{ m/s})\\ &= m(-10 \text{ m/s})\end{aligned}$$

$$\begin{aligned}\text{Impulse}_3 &= m(-9 \text{ m/s} - 10 \text{ m/s})\\ &= m(-19 \text{ m/s})\end{aligned}$$

$$\begin{aligned}\text{Impulse}_4 &= m(-2 \text{ m/s} - 10 \text{ m/s})\\ &= m(-12 \text{ m/s})\end{aligned}$$

Since the mass of the ball is constant, the impulse for each scenario is directly related to the change in velocity. Therefore, the scenarios should be in order of the increasing magnitudes of the change in velocity. The order is then scenario 3, scenario 1, scenario 4, and scenario 2.

5. D

The momentum of a system is always conserved if the objects in the system move under their mutual forces alone. In this case, the surface on which the objects move is frictionless, and the net external vertical forces on the objects must also be zero in order for them to remain on the surface.

The total kinetic energy remains constant only if the collision is elastic. If the individual kinetic energies are to be preserved, the two objects must approach each other with equal and opposite momenta before the collision.

The momentum of a colliding object cannot be the same before and after a collision.

6. B

Since momentum is conserved and the moving coupled mass is larger than the moving single car before the collision, the velocity of the coupled cars must be lower than the original speed of the single moving car.

7. D

Throwing the sandbag off the back will speed it up, and throwing it off the front will slow it down. Throwing it off the side will cause it to move to the opposite side, but the rails will prevent any motion in that direction. The speed of the cart will not change because there is no force exerted along the direction of its motion.

8. A

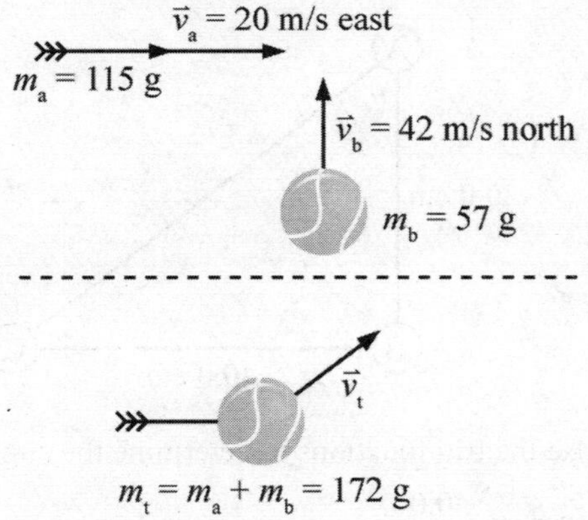

The conservation of momentum can be used to determine the relationship between the initial and final momenta.

$$\sum \vec{p}_i = \sum \vec{p}_f$$
$$\vec{p}_a + \vec{p}_b = \vec{p}_t$$
$$\therefore \vec{p}_t = m_a\vec{v}_a + m_b\vec{v}_b$$
$$= (115 \text{ g})(20 \text{ m/s east}) + (57 \text{ g})(42 \text{ m/s north})$$
$$= 2.30 \times 10^3 \text{ g·m/s east} + 2.40 \times 10^3 \text{ g·m/s north}$$

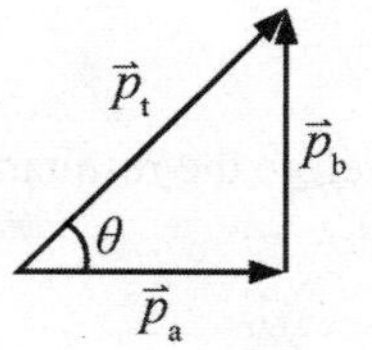

Since these two momenta are perpendicular, trigonometry may be used to calculate the direction of the final momentum.

$$\tan\theta = \frac{p_b}{p_a}$$
$$\therefore \theta = \tan^{-1}\left(\frac{p_b}{p_a}\right)$$
$$= \tan^{-1}\left(\frac{2.40}{2.30}\right)$$
$$= 46°$$

The arrow and ball combination end up traveling in the direction of 46° north of east.

9. C

In an inelastic collision, some of the original kinetic energy transforms to other types, such as heat and sound.

10. D

The diagram shows the process of electrostatic induction. Even though the ball is electrically neutral, electrons in the ball are attracted to the positive rod, making side X of the ball relatively positive. Because side Y of the ball is relatively negative, the ball is attracted to the rod.

11. 6415

To positively charge a neutral sphere by induction, the students should first bring a negatively charged rod near the sphere (6). Next, they should touch the sphere to ground it (4). Then, they should remove the ground from the sphere. (1). Lastly, they should remove the charged rod (5).

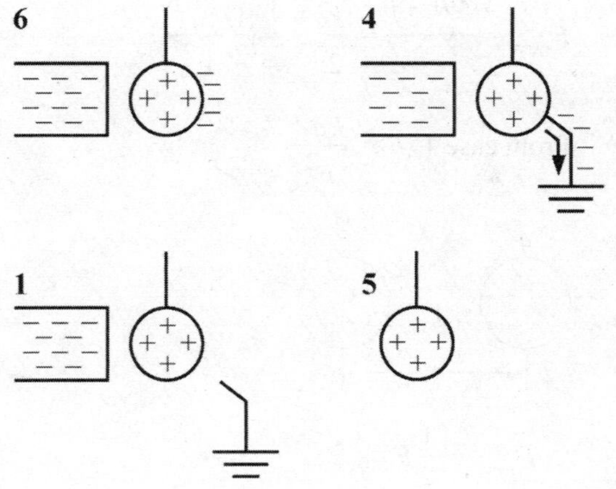

12. D

$F \propto \frac{1}{r^2}$, therefore the resultant graph must be hyperbolic.

13. 15.9

The charge on each sphere after touching is given by

$$\frac{q_1 + q_2}{2} = \frac{4.50\ \mu\text{C} + (-2.40\ \mu\text{C})}{2}$$
$$= 1.05\ \mu\text{C}$$

Use the value from above and Coulomb's Law of Electrostatic Forces

$$F_e = \frac{kq_1q_2}{r^2}$$
$$= \frac{(8.99 \times 10^9\ \text{N·m/C}^2)(1.05 \times 10^{-6}\text{C})(1.05 \times 10^{-6}\text{C})}{(2.50 \times 10^{-2}\ \text{m})^2}$$
$$F_e = 15.9\ \text{N}$$

Since the condition is one dimensional, the positive sign indicates that the force is repulsive.

14. A

Initially: Identical charges q separated by a distance r

$$\vec{F} = \frac{kqq}{r^2}$$
$$\vec{F} = \frac{kq^2}{r^2}$$

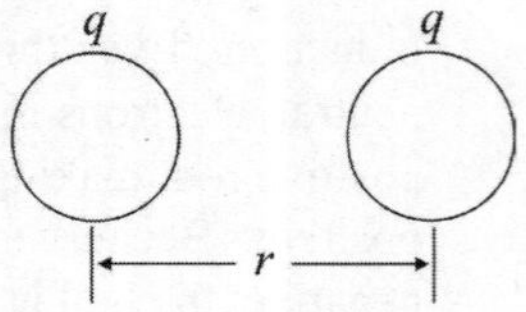

If a charge is touched to an identical neutral sphere, the charges will split evenly, thus leaving each sphere with a charge of $\frac{q}{2}$.

Finally: One sphere has charge $\frac{q}{2}$, the other sphere continues to have a charge of q.

$$F_{new} = \frac{kq\left(\frac{q}{2}\right)}{r^2} = \frac{kq^2}{2r^2} = \frac{1}{2}\frac{kq^2}{r^2}$$

From case 1, $F = \frac{kq^2}{r^2}$

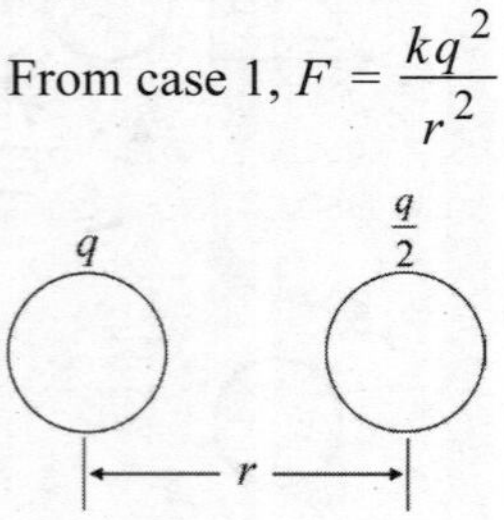

$$\therefore F_{new} = \frac{1}{2}F$$

15. B

$$F_{1,2} = \frac{kq_1q_2}{r_{1,2}^2}$$

Find the force between charges A and C.

$$F_{A,C} = \frac{(8.99 \times 10^9\ \text{N} \cdot \text{m}^2/\ \text{C}^2)(40.0 \times 10^{-6}\ \text{C})(60.0 \times 10^{-6}\ \text{C})}{(50.0 \times 10^{-2}\ \text{m})^2}$$
$$= 86.30\ \text{N}$$

Find the force between charges B and C.

$$F_{B,C} = \frac{(8.99 \times 10^9\ \text{N} \cdot \text{m}^2/\text{C}^2)(-50.0 \times 10^{-6}\ \text{C})(60.0 \times 10^{-6}\ \text{C})}{(40.0 \times 10^{-2}\ \text{m})^2}$$
$$= -168.6\ \text{N}$$
$$\therefore \vec{F}_{B,C} = 168.6\ \text{N left}$$

With the magnitudes of the forces known, determine the directions in which these forces act. For $F_{B,C}$, the force acts horizontally to the left on charge C since it is an attractive force between opposite charges. The direction of $F_{A,C}$ on charge C is more complex. It is possible to calculate the direction of $F_{A,C}$ from the original positions of the point charges.

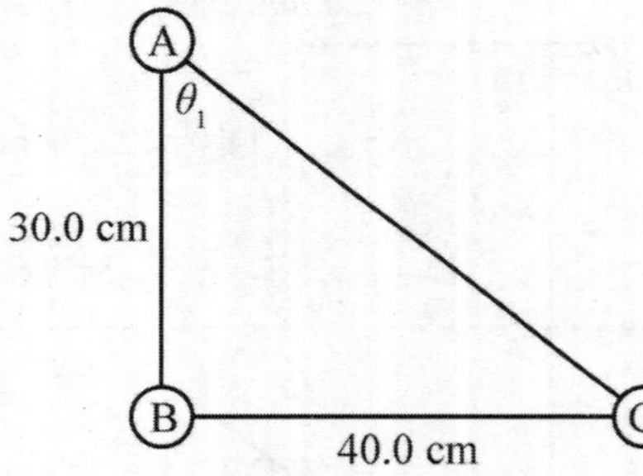

Use the trig functions to determine the angle θ_1.

$$\tan \theta_1 = \frac{40.0}{30.0}$$
$$\theta_1 = 53.1°$$

Using the cosine and sine law method

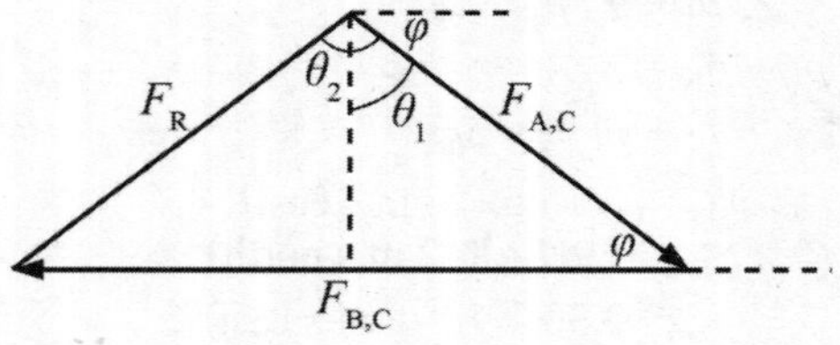

The directions of $F_{A,C}$ and $F_{B,C}$ can be used to find the direction, φ, of the resultant force, F_R.

$$\varphi = 90° - \theta_1$$
$$= 90° - 53.1°$$
$$= 36.9°$$

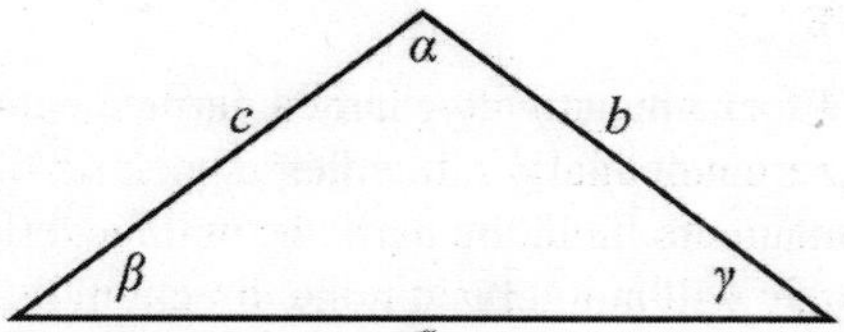

The cosine law can be used to calculate the magnitude of the resultant force.

$c^2 = a^2 + b^2 - 2ab\cos\gamma$

$F_R^2 = F_{B,C}^2 + F_{A,C}^2 - 2F_{B,C}F_{A,C}\cos\varphi$

$F_R^2 = (168.6\text{ N})^2 + (86.30\text{ N})^2 - 2(168.6\text{ N})(86.30\text{ N})\cos 36.9°$

$= 1.26 \times 10^4\text{ N}^2$

$F_R = 112\text{ N}$

Using the sine law, it is possible to calculate the angle θ_2.

The sine law: $\dfrac{c}{\sin\gamma} = \dfrac{b}{\sin\beta} = \dfrac{a}{\sin\alpha}$

$$\frac{F_{B,C}}{\sin\theta_2} = \frac{F_R}{\sin\varphi}$$

$$\frac{168.6\text{ N}}{\sin\theta_2} = \frac{112.3\text{ N}}{\sin 36.9°}$$

$$\sin\theta_2 = 0.901\ 43$$

$$\theta_2 = 64.3°$$

The total angle that the resultant force makes with the horizontal is $360° - \theta_2 - \varphi$, which is 259°.

Therefore, the resultant force has a magnitude of 112 N and acts at an angle of 259°.

16. A

Work must be done against the field in both scenarios. When a positive charge moves toward a negative charge or surface, no work is done against the field because the motion is in the same direction as the field. As well, the fields in both scenarios need to be uniform. The electric field around a point charge is not uniform. An electric field between two parallel plates is uniform. Thus the scenario that is similar to the increase in gravitational energy is the scenario in which a negatively charged sphere is lifted toward the negative plate.

17. A

The situation described is most similar to the negatively charged oil drop placed between charged, parallel plates, accelerating upward toward the positive plate. This is because in this case the electric field is uniform and the associated field is doing work on the oil drop. In the other cases, either the field is not uniform or the field does not do positive work.

18. C

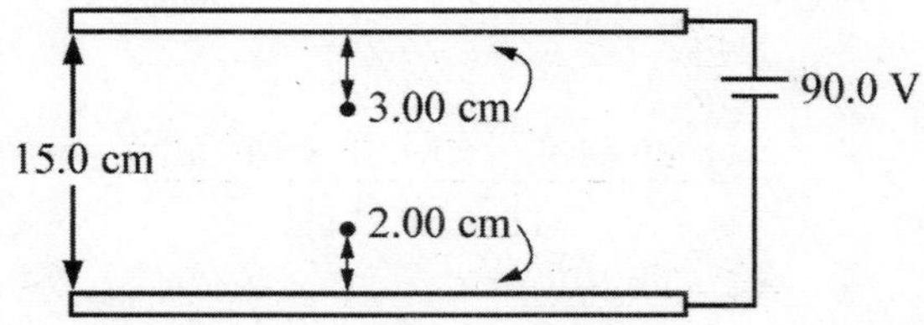

The electric potential (voltage) is equal to the work done on the charge in moving it at constant velocity through the uniform field the distance of 10.0 cm.

$V = Ed \Rightarrow V \propto d$

$$\frac{15.0\text{ cm}}{90.0\text{ V}} = \frac{10.0\text{ cm}}{x}$$

$$x = 60.0\text{ V}$$

19. D

The direction of an electric field at any location in space is the direction of the force on an imaginary positive "test charge" placed at this location.

Near an alpha particle, the direction of $\vec{E}$ will be away from the alpha particle.

The charge on the alpha particle is:

$(2)(+1.60 \times 10^{-19}\text{ C}) = (+3.20 \times 10^{-19}\text{ C})$

$$E = \frac{kq_1}{r^2}$$

$$= \frac{(8.99 \times 10^9\text{ N}\cdot\text{m/C}^2)(3.20 \times 10^{-19}\text{ C})}{(5.0 \times 10^{-11}\text{ m})^2}$$

$E = 1.2 \times 10^{12}\text{ N/C}$

$\therefore \vec{E} = 1.2 \times 10^{12}$ N/C away from the alpha particle

20. 9418

Find the number of electrons passing through the ammeter each second.

$$1.5\text{ A} = \frac{1.5\text{C/s}}{1.60 \times 10^{-19}\text{C/e}^-}$$

$$= 9.4 \times 10^{18}\text{e}^-/\text{s}$$

The values of *a*, *b*, *c*, and *d* are 9, 4, 1, and 8, respectively.

21. 120

$$\begin{aligned} qV &= \Delta E_{\text{k}} \\ &= \frac{1}{2}m\left(v_{\text{f}}^2 - v_{\text{i}}^2\right) \\ \Rightarrow V &= \frac{m\left(v_{\text{f}}^2 - v_{\text{i}}^2\right)}{2q} \\ &= \frac{\left(9.11 \times 10^{-31}\ \text{kg}\right)\left(\left(6.5 \times 10^6\ \text{m/s}\right)^2 - \left(2.5 \times 10^5\ \text{m/s}\right)^2\right)}{2\left(1.60 \times 10^{-19}\ \text{C}\right)} \\ &= 120\ \text{V} \end{aligned}$$

22. C

$$F_{\text{e}} = qE = ma$$

$$\begin{aligned} a &= \frac{qE}{m} \\ &= \frac{\left(1.60 \times 10^{-19}\ \text{C}\right)\left(1.20 \times 10^4\ \text{J/C}\right)}{9.11 \times 10^{-31}\ \text{kg}} \\ &= 2.11 \times 10^{15}\ \text{m/s}^2 \end{aligned}$$

23. B

Subtract successive masses to find the differences in the masses.

Box	Mass (g)	Difference (g)
1	3.0	1.5
2	4.5	3.0
3	7.5	1.5
4	9.0	3.0
5	12	1.5
6	13.5	1.5
7	15	3.0
8	18	1.5
9	19.5	3.0
10	22.5	7.5
11	30	

Since all the differences are multiples of 1.5 g, this is most likely the mass of one marble.

24. C

A compass acts as a "test magnet" and shows the direction of another magnetic field. Its north pole points in the direction of the field. There must be opposite poles at the top and bottom of the filing cabinet.

25. B

When a negatively charged particle enters perpendicularly into either an electric field or a magnetic field, the particles will be deflected, but they will not deflect in the direction of the field. However, a gravitational field always deflects massive objects in the direction of its field. Therefore, diagram 3 is most likely a gravitational field.

When negatively charged electrons are deflected in the opposite direction of a field, the field must be an electric field. Since diagram 1 depicts a field directed up and the electrons deflect down, then diagram 1 must represent an electric field.

Since diagram 1 is an electric field and diagram 3 is a gravitational field, then diagram 2 is most likely a magnetic field. When negatively charged particles travel parallel to a magnetic field, no magnetic force will act, so the direction of the particles should not change.

26. 3.11

The wire remains suspended against gravity, so $F_{\text{m}} = F_{\text{g}}$. Given this, you can use the weight, length, and current to determine the strength of the magnetic field.

$$\begin{aligned} IlB_{\perp} &= F_{\text{g}} \\ (0.250\ \text{A})(0.500\ \text{m})\left(B_{\perp}\right) &= 0.389\ \text{N} \\ B_{\perp} &= 3.11\ \text{T} \end{aligned}$$

27. B

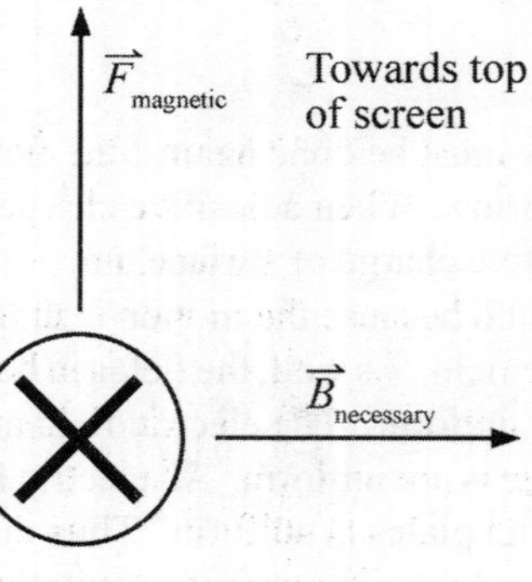

∴The deflecting coils that can produce a horizontal magnetic field to the right are coils 4 and 2 according to the left-hand rule. The magnetic field must be directed from left to right in order for the electrons to be deflected upwards.

28. A

The magnetic force caused the electron to move in a circular path, so it is a centripetal force.

$$F_m = F_c$$

$$qvB_\perp = \frac{mv^2}{r}$$

$$r = \frac{mv^2}{qvB_\perp} = \frac{mv}{B_\perp q} = \frac{(9.11 \times 10^{-31}\ \text{kg})(4.0 \times 10^6\ \text{m/s})}{(5.0 \times 10^{-3}\ \text{T})(1.60 \times 10^{-19}\ \text{C})} = 4.55 \times 10^{-3}\ \text{m} = 4.6\ \text{mm}$$

Use the left-hand rule for negative particles to find the direction of the electron's motion. With the thumb pointed along the electron's initial velocity westward, and the fingers pointed downward with the magnetic field, the palm points in the direction of the magnetic field to the north. Therefore, the electron's path will be in the horizontal plane.

29. C

The electron will be accelerated to the right by repulsion by the negative plate and attraction to the positive plate. The direction does not change because the motion is parallel to the electric field.

30. D

$$F_m = F_c$$

$$qvB_\perp = qE$$

$v = \dfrac{E}{B_\perp}$; thus the units for $\dfrac{E}{B}$ is m/s.

31. C

Since the magnetic force in this case acts as the centripetal force, determine the relation for the radius in terms of mass, velocity, charge, and magnetic field strength.

$$F = ma$$

$$F_m = ma_c$$

$$qvB_\perp = \frac{mv^2}{r}$$

$$\therefore r = \frac{mv}{qB_\perp}$$

Now, calculate the radius for each of the two particles.

Find the radius of the proton.

$$r_p = \frac{(1.67 \times 10^{-27}\ \text{kg})(v)}{(e)(B_\perp)}$$

Find the radius of the alpha particle.

$$r_a = \frac{(6.65 \times 10^{-27}\ \text{kg})(2v)}{(2e)(B_\perp)}$$

Calculate the ratio.

$$\frac{r_a}{r_p} = \frac{\dfrac{(6.65 \times 10^{-27}\ \text{kg})(2v)}{(2e)(B_\perp)}}{\dfrac{(1.67 \times 10^{-27}\ \text{kg})(v)}{(e)(B_\perp)}}$$

$$\frac{r_a}{r_p} = \frac{4}{1}$$

The radius of the alpha particle will be 4 times larger than that of the proton.

32. C

Maxwell proposed that electromagnetic radiation is produced by accelerating charged particles.

33. B

For an electromagnetic wave,

$v = c = f\lambda$ but $f = \dfrac{1}{T} = \dfrac{1}{\text{period}}$

According to the sketch, the period of one complete wave is 4.0×10^{-6} s.

$$f = \frac{1}{4.0 \times 10^{-6}\ \text{s}} = 2.5 \times 10^5\ \text{/s}$$

$$\lambda = \frac{c}{f} = \frac{3.00 \times 10^8\ \text{m/s}}{2.5 \times 10^5\ \text{/s}}$$

$$\lambda = 1.2 \times 10^3\ \text{m}$$

34. B

The frequency of rotation of the toothed wheel and the number of teeth in the wheel are also required in order to determine the speed of light. This is the basic set up of Fizeau's original experiment which led to later designs along the same line by Albert Michelson.

35. C

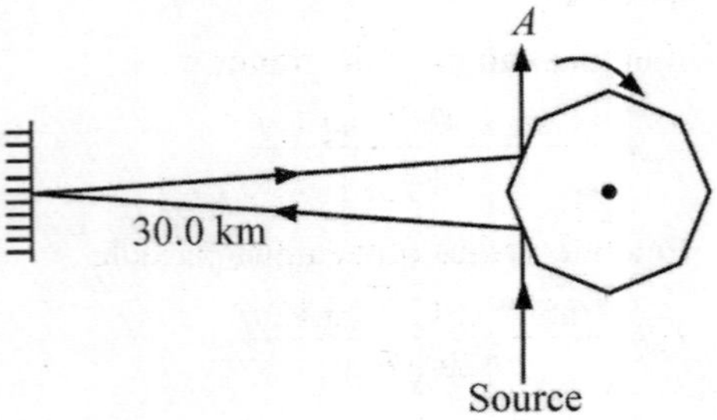

$f = 6.15 \times 10^2$ Hz

$$T = \frac{1}{f} = 1.627 \times 10^{-3} \text{ s}$$

$$\therefore \frac{1}{8}T = 2.034 \times 10^{-4} \text{ s}$$

We also know that $d = 60.0 \times 10^3$ m

$$v = \frac{d}{t}$$
$$= \frac{60.0 \times 10^3 \text{ m}}{2.034 \times 10^{-4} \text{ s}}$$
$$= 2.95 \times 10^8 \text{ m/s}$$

Now we need the % discrepancy

$$\% \text{ discrepancy} = \frac{\text{actual} - \text{calculated}}{\text{actual}} \times 100\%$$

$$\% \text{ discrepancy} = \frac{3.00 \times 10^8 \text{ m/s} - 2.95 \times 10^8 \text{ m/s}}{3.00 \times 10^8 \text{ m/s}} \times 100\%$$

$$\% \text{ discrepancy} = 1.67\%$$

36. C

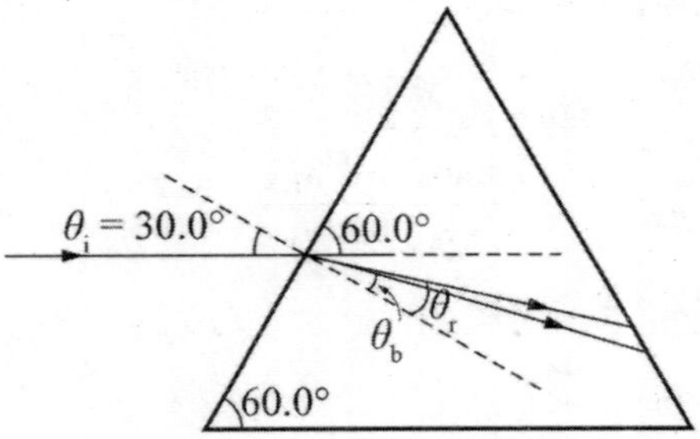

Find the angle of refraction for red.

$$\frac{n_g}{n_a} = 15.10 = \frac{\sin 30.0°}{\sin \theta_r}$$
$$= 1.510 = \frac{0.500}{\sin \theta_r}$$
$$\theta_r = \sin^{-1} \frac{0.500}{1.510} = 19.337°$$

Find the angle of refraction for blue.

$$\frac{n_g}{n_a} = 1.528 = \frac{\sin 30.0°}{\sin \theta_b}$$
$$\theta_b = \sin^{-1} \frac{0.500}{1.528} = 19.100°$$

Find the difference in the angles of refraction.

Dispersion $= 19.337° - 19.100°$
$= 0.237°$

The difference in angles of refraction of the two components at the first surface is 0.237°.

37. D

The angle of incidence and reflection are equal. When the girl looks at a spot halfway from eye level to the top of her head, it will show the top of her head in the mirror. The same holds for her lower half too, so the mirror would have to extend from the point halfway between her eyes and the top of her head down to the point halfway between her eyes and the floor.

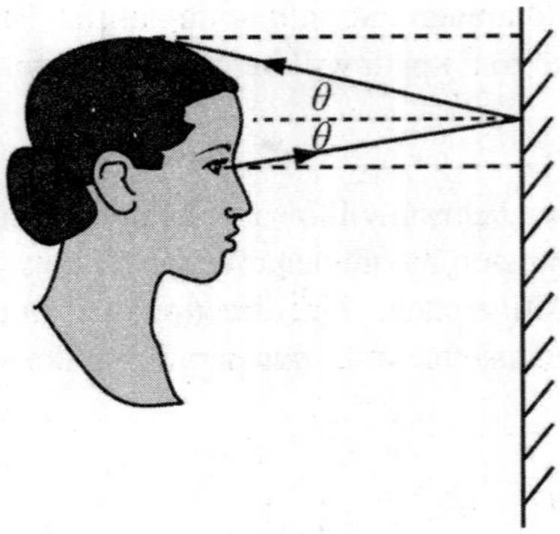

38. 7.19

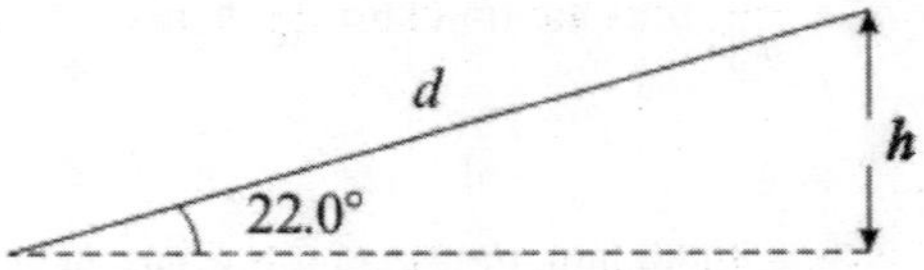

$$d_{\text{(from transmitter to aircraft)}} = ct$$
$$= (3.00 \times 10^8 \text{ m/s})\left(\frac{1.28 \times 10^{-4} \text{ s}}{2}\right)$$
$$d = 1.92 \times 10^4 \text{ m}$$

$$\sin 22.0° = \frac{h}{d}$$
$$h = d(\sin 22.0°)$$
$$= (1.92 \times 10^4 \text{ m})(\sin 22.0°)$$
$$h = 7.19 \times 10^3 \text{ m}$$
$$= 7.19 \text{ km}$$

Provincial TEST

39. B

$$\frac{1}{f}=\frac{1}{d_i}+\frac{1}{d_o}$$

$$\frac{1}{50.0\text{ mm}}=\frac{1}{d_i}+\frac{1}{1\,000\text{ mm}}$$

$$\frac{1}{d_i}=\frac{1}{50.0\text{ mm}}-\frac{1}{1\,000\text{ mm}}$$

$$=\frac{20-1}{1\,000\text{ mm}}$$

$$d_i=\frac{1\,000\text{ mm}}{19}$$

$$=52.6\text{ mm}$$

$$=5.26\text{ cm}$$

$$\frac{h_i}{h_o}=-\frac{d_i}{d_o}$$

$$h_i=\frac{-d_ih_o}{d_o}$$

$$=\frac{-5.26\text{ cm}\times 25.0\text{ cm}}{100\text{ cm}}$$

$$=-1.32\text{ cm}$$

∴ The image is 1.32 cm and inverted.

40. 0.800

$$M=\frac{-d_i}{d_o}$$

$$=-\frac{1}{5}=\frac{h_i}{h_o}$$

$$\therefore 5h_i=-h_o$$

$$=h_i$$

$$=-\frac{h_o}{5}$$

$$=-\frac{4.00\text{ cm}}{5}$$

$$=-0.800\text{ cm}$$

41. C

Interference and diffraction are typical wave phenomena, and are easily demonstrated in mechanical waves.

42. 7977

$$n\lambda=\frac{dx}{l}$$

$$\Rightarrow \lambda=\frac{dx}{nl}$$

$$=\frac{(1.50\times 10^{-4}\text{ m})(6.22\times 10^{-2}\text{ m})}{5(2.34\text{ m})}$$

$$=7.97\times 10^{-7}\text{ m}$$

43. 6557

Find the wavelength.

$$d=\frac{1}{550/\text{mm}}=1.82\times 10^{-6}\text{ m}$$

$$\lambda=\frac{d\sin\theta}{n}$$

$$=\frac{(1.82\times 10^{-6}\text{ m})\sin 21.1°}{1}$$

$$=6.55\times 10^{-7}\text{ m}$$

The values of *a*, *b*, *c*, and *d* are 6, 5, 5, and 7, respectively.

44. C

Blue light refracts through a prism more than red light does. All light will bend toward the horizontal base of the prism, creating the desired spectrum.

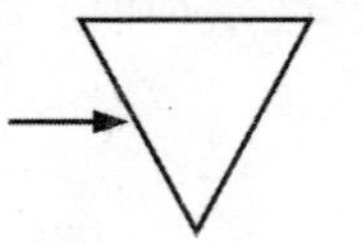

45. D

$$E=hf=\frac{hc}{\lambda}$$

$$\Rightarrow \lambda=\frac{hc}{E}$$

$$=\frac{(6.63\times 10^{-34}\text{ J·s})(3.00\times 10^{8}\text{ m/s})}{(3.65\text{ eV})(1.60\times 10^{-19}\text{ J/eV})}$$

$$=3.41\times 10^{-7}\text{ m}$$

46. D

Calculate the frequency of the given photons.

$$E=hf$$

$$\therefore f=\frac{E}{h}$$

$$=\frac{1.00\times 10^{-6}\text{ eV}}{4.14\times 10^{-15}\text{ eV·s}}$$

$$=2.42\times 10^{8}\text{ Hz}$$

Radio waves have frequencies that range from less than 1 Hz to approximately 3.50×10^{8} Hz.

Therefore, photons with the given energy would fall into the radio region of the electromagnetic spectrum.

47. D

In the photoelectric effect, the following equation describes how photon energy is distributed to the kinetic energy of the photoelectrons and the work function of the metal:

$$hf=E_{k_{max}}+W$$

Therefore, energy must be conserved. The photon (hf) gives its energy to the electron ($E_{k_{max}}$), which loses some energy to the metal (W). Each photon will release one electron. Only photons of higher energy will continue to release electrons. Ultraviolet is the only wavelength listed with a greater energy (frequency) than violet light.

48. 2.35

Use the formula for the maximum kinetic energy for photoelectrons to find the work function.

$$E_{k_{max}} = \frac{hc}{\lambda} - W$$

$$\Rightarrow W = \frac{hc}{\lambda} - E_{k_{max}}$$

$$= \frac{(6.63 \times 10^{-34}\ \text{J·s})(3.00 \times 10^{8}\ \text{m/s})}{(350 \times 10^{-9}\ \text{m})(1.60 \times 10^{-19}\ \text{J/eV})} - 1.20\ \text{eV}$$

$$= 3.55\ \text{eV} - 1.20\ \text{eV}$$

$$= 2.35\ \text{eV}$$

49. C

Find the change in the wavelength of the X-ray photons.

$$\Delta\lambda = \frac{h}{mc}(1 - \cos\theta)$$

$$= \frac{(6.63 \times 10^{-34}\ \text{J·s})(1 - \cos 85.0°)}{(9.11 \times 10^{-31}\ \text{kg})(3.00 \times 10^{8}\ \text{m/s})}$$

$$= 2.21 \times 10^{-12}\ \text{m}$$

50. A

$$m_H = m_p + m_e$$

$$= 1.67 \times 10^{-27}\ \text{kg} + 9.11 \times 10^{-31}\ \text{kg}$$

$$= 1.6709 \times 10^{-27}\ \text{kg}$$

$$\#\ \text{p + e pairs} = \frac{0.500\ \text{kg}}{1.6709 \times 10^{-27}\ \text{kg}} = 2.99 \times 10^{26}$$

$\therefore$ total charge = 0;
negative charge

$$= (2.99 \times 10^{26})(1.60 \times 10^{-19}\ \text{C}) = 4.79 \times 10^{7}\ \text{C}$$

51. C

In Thomson's experiment, the cathode rays are deflected by $\vec{E}$ and $\vec{B}$ fields in the same manner that individual negative particles are deflected by these fields in a velocity selector conformation. Thomson then measured the charge-to-mass ratio of these rays, proving that these rays consisted of moving negatively charged particles.

52. A

The smaller the nucleus is, the fewer alpha particles are scattered through large angles.

For an atom with a very small nucleus compared to the overall diameter of the atom, you would expect to find a graph with a narrow peak that drops off rapidly at large scattering angles.

53. D

Since uniform velocity includes a uniform direction, any particle travelling in a circular path must be accelerating because the particle's direction is changing. However, any accelerating charged particle emits electromagnetic radiation. If the electron emitted electromagnetic radiation due to its centripetal acceleration, the electron should eventually collapse into the nucleus since energy is being lost.

54. A

The photoelectric effect as discovered by Hertz was evidence of the particle nature of light and led to the eventual quantization of photons. Kirchhoff's observations of the emission spectra of different elements did not specifically relate to the Bohr model of the atom. Although we now know that the lines in the spectra of excited elements are a result of the electrons changing energy levels, at the time it was simply a case of studying the resulting spectra and so did not provide evidence for stationary electron orbits. Maxwell's explanation for electromagnetic radiation involved accelerating charges and did not involve stationary energy levels. Only Balmer's analysis of emission spectra gave direct evidence to defend Bohr's hypothesis by showing that all the lines of the Balmer series resulted from electrons falling from higher orbitals to the second stationary orbit.

55. a) A

The difference between ground state (where the electron started) and the third excitation level is 9.9 eV. This energy had to be absorbed for an electron to get to the 3rd excitation level.

Provincial TEST

b) 6217

You need a ΔE between 1.8 eV and 3.1 eV. The only two energy levels that are in this range are the 2nd and 3rd excitation levels.

$$\Delta E = \frac{hc}{\lambda}$$

$$\lambda = \frac{hc}{\Delta E} = \frac{(4.14 \times 10^{-15}\ \text{eV·s})(3.00 \times 10^{8}\ \text{m/s})}{(-4.1\ \text{eV}) - (-6.1\ \text{eV})}$$

$$= 6.21 \times 10^{-7}\ \text{m (Red)}$$

56. D

If either slit were covered in this experiment then the individual photons hitting the film would result in an ordinary diffraction pattern but with both slits left open the quantum mechanical nature of the photons takes over and the recognizable double slit interference pattern is restored. This result shows the dual nature of light. If light did not behave like a wave then no interference pattern could arise. But, if light were simply a wave then we would not expect individual photons to arive at the film.

57. D

Alpha particles are more massive than beta particles, so they move more slowly than beta particles at similar energies. Gamma rays are a form of electromagnetic radiation, so they have much higher energies than alpha and beta rays and move much faster. Alpha particles cannot penetrate matter deeply, but if they are ingested, this minor penetrating ability can cause a lot of damage to living tissues since the alpha particles will have to pass through living tissue.

58. C

$3t_{\frac{1}{2}}$ elapse since $\frac{1}{2} \times \frac{1}{2} \times \frac{1}{2} = \frac{1}{8}$

$$3t_{\frac{1}{2}} = 3 \times 5.25\ \text{years}$$

$$= 15.8\ \text{years}$$

59. 23993

Balance the nucleons on top (or mass number) and the charge on the bottom to get the following reaction:

$${}^{238}_{92}\text{U} + {}^{1}_{0}\text{n} \rightarrow {}^{0}_{-1}\text{e} + {}^{239}_{93}\text{Np}$$

The values of *a*, *b*, *c*, *d*, and *e* are 2, 3, 9, 9, and 3, respectively.

60. B

Fusion reactions involve larger mass defects than fission reactions, so they release more energy. The fusion of hydrogen to helium does not produce radioactive waste, whereas the fission of uranium does.

61. D

As the larger radioactive element undergoes fission, the daughter products have higher binding energy per nucleon. This means that they are more stable than the initial uranium parent.

62. A

The cloud-chamber diagram showed a particle initially travelling undeflected. The track then splits in two, with the two tracks bending in opposite directions. This means the two particles have opposite charges. Since the tracks also have different radii, the particles likely have different masses. Therefore, it is likely that the physicist inferred that the particle was initially neutral and converted into a negative particle and a positive particle that had different masses. It could then be inferred that the particle with the track on the left was a proton while the lighter particle with the track on the right was an electron. In the given magnetic field, a positive particle would be expected to be deflected in the clockwise direction while a negative particle would be expected to be deflected in the counterclockwise direction.

63. B

$$(0.511\ \text{MeV/c}^2)\left(1.78 \times 10^{-30} \frac{\text{kg}}{\text{MeV/c}^2}\right) = 9.10 \times 10^{-31}\ \text{kg}$$

Therefore the particle is either an electron or a positron.

$$(938\ \text{MeV/c}^2)\left(1.78 \times 10^{-30} \frac{\text{kg}}{\text{MeV/c}^2}\right) = 1.67 \times 10^{-27}\ \text{kg}$$

Therefore the particle is either a proton or a neutron.

$$(7.00 \times 10^{-6}\ \text{MeV/c}^2)\left(1.78 \times 10^{-30} \frac{\text{kg}}{\text{MeV/c}^2}\right) = 1.25 \times 10^{-35}\ \text{kg}$$

This mass is extremely small. Neutrinos are essentially without mass, so this particle is most likely some sort of neutrino.

The only option that includes the choice of a neutrino for the last particle is electron, proton, and electron neutrino. This means that the first particle is an electron and the second particle is a proton.

64. A

Light isotopes do not have enough neutrons to hold the nucleus together against the repulsion of the protons. A proton changes to a neutron (by the nuclear weak force). This means an up quark changes to a down quark. β^+ decay also produces a neutrino.

Provincial TEST

ANSWERS AND SOLUTIONS — PRACTICE TEST 2

1. B	**15. B**	**29. 3622**	**43. 6557**	**57. D**
2. B	**16. 33.1**	**30. 1201**	**44. 53114**	**58. D**
3. C	**17. 3078**	**31. 3593**	**45. B**	**59. a) B**
4. 3214	**18. B**	**32. C**	**46. 32620**	**b) D**
5. C	**19. B**	**33. 778**	**47. D**	**60. B**
6. B	**20. 673**	**34. C**	**48. C**	**61. 29.0**
7. A	**21. 3517**	**35. D**	**49. A**	**62. A**
8. C	**22. D**	**36. 2758**	**50. C**	**63. A**
9. 9.09	**23. 6672**	**37. D**	**51. 2145**	**64. 15111**
10. 5.00	**24. D**	**38. C**	**52. C**	**65. B**
11. D	**25. B**	**39. D**	**53. A**	**66. B**
12. D	**26. D**	**40. B**	**54. B**	**67. C**
13. A	**27. B**	**41. B**	**55. 5.70**	
14. A	**28. A**	**42. 5155**	**56. C**	

1. B

$$\vec{v} = \frac{\vec{p}}{m} = \frac{56.4\ \text{kg·m/s west}}{8.350\ \text{kg}} = 6.75\ \text{m/s west}$$

Remember that velocity requires both magnitude and direction as a vector quantity. The magnitude of velocity is just the speed.

2. B

$$\vec{v}_i = 100\ \text{km/h} = \frac{100 \times 1000\ \text{m}}{60 \times 60\ \text{s}} = 27.8\ \text{m/s forward}$$

$$\vec{F}_{net} = \frac{m\Delta\vec{v}}{\Delta t} = \frac{m(\vec{v}_f - \vec{v}_i)}{\Delta t} = \frac{62\ \text{kg}(0\ \text{m/s} - 27.8\ \text{m/s})}{9.0 \times 10^{-2}\ \text{s}}$$

$= -1.9 \times 10^4$ N forward or 1.9×10^4 N backward

$\therefore F_{net} = 1.9 \times 10^4$ N

3. C

$$E_p = E_k$$
$$Vq = \frac{1}{2}mv^2$$
$$\Rightarrow v^2 = \frac{2Vq}{m}$$
$$\therefore v = \sqrt{\frac{2Vq}{m}} = \sqrt{\frac{2(2.5 \times 10^3\ \text{V})(1.60 \times 10^{-19}\ \text{C})}{9.11 \times 10^{-31}\ \text{kg}}} = 3.0 \times 10^7\ \text{m/s}$$

4. 3214

The magnitudes of the changes in momentum in each case are:

Trial 1

$\Delta p = m\Delta v$
$= 3.0\ \text{kg}(0 - 2.0\text{m/s})$
$= -6.0$ kg·m/s

Trial 2

$\Delta p = m\Delta v$
$= 2.0\ \text{kg}(0 - 3.5\ \text{m/s})$
$= -7.0$ kg·m/s

Trial 3

$\Delta p = m\Delta v$
$= 6.0\ \text{kg}(0 - 1.5\ \text{m/s})$
$= -9.0$ kg·m/s

Trial 4

$\Delta p = m\Delta v$
$= 5.0\ \text{kg}(0 - 1.0\ \text{m/s})$
$= -5.0$ kg·m/s

Considering only magnitudes, since $\Delta p = F\Delta t$ and F is constant, the greater the magnitude of Δp, the greater the required time. Trial 3 will be longest, followed by trial 2, trial 1, and trial 4.

5. C

Consider the direction of motion of the girl and the sled (i.e., north) to be positive.

$$\sum \vec{p}_{\text{i}} = \sum \vec{p}_{\text{f}}$$

$$m_{\text{g}}\vec{v}_{\text{g}} + m_{\text{s}}\vec{v}_{\text{s}} = m_{\text{g+s}}\vec{v}_{\text{g+s}}$$

$$\vec{v}_{\text{g+s}} = \frac{m_{\text{g}}\vec{v}_{\text{g}} + m_{\text{s}}\vec{v}_{\text{s}}}{m_{\text{g+s}}}$$

$$= \frac{(65.0\text{ kg})(3.00\text{ m/s}) + (15.0\text{ kg})(2.50\text{ m/s})}{80.0\text{ kg}}$$

$$= \frac{195\text{ kg·m/s} + 37.5\text{ kg·m/s}}{80.0\text{ kg}}$$

$$= 2.91\text{ m/s north}$$

6. B

An elastic collision is one in which both the kinetic energy and momentum are conserved during the interaction.

7. A

The total momentum in an isolated system must be conserved. In this crash, the car transfers its momentum to Earth's surface through the cliff wall.

8. C

Before

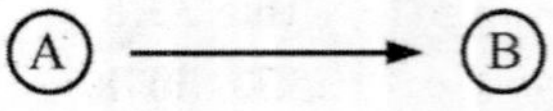

$m_{\text{A}} = 0.500$ kg $\quad m_{\text{B}} = 0.350$ kg

$\vec{v}_{\text{A}} = 2.00$ m/s E $\quad \vec{v}_{\text{B}} = 0$

$\vec{p}_{\text{A}} = 1.00$ kg·m/s E $\quad \vec{p}_{\text{B}} = 0$

After

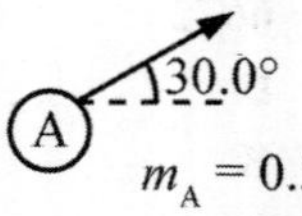

$m_{\text{A}} = 0.500$ kg

$\vec{v}_{\text{A}} = 1.50$ m/s E30.0°N

$\vec{p}_{\text{A}}' = 0.750$ kg·m/s E30.0°N

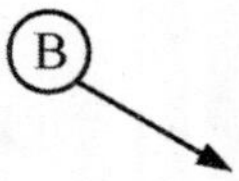

$m_{\text{B}} = 0.350$ kg

$\vec{v}_{\text{B}} = ?$

$\vec{p}_{\text{B}}' = ?$

First, determine the direction and magnitude of the momenta for the three instances where the velocity is known. You can use the conservation of momentum formula to help you see how the momentum vectors must add together.

$$\sum \vec{p}_{\text{i}} = \sum \vec{p}_{\text{f}}$$

$$\vec{p}_{\text{A}} + \vec{p}_{\text{B}} = \vec{p}_{\text{a}}' + \vec{p}_{\text{B}}'$$

$$m_{\text{A}}\vec{v}_{\text{A}} + m_{\text{B}}\vec{v}_{\text{B}} = m_{\text{A}}\vec{v}_{\text{A}}' + m_{\text{B}}\vec{v}_{\text{B}}'$$

$$(0.500\text{ kg})(2.00\text{ m/s E}) = (0.500\text{ kg}) \times (1.50\text{ m/s E }30.0°\text{ N}) + \vec{p}_{\text{B}}'$$

$$1.00\text{ kg·m/s E} = 0.750\text{ kg·m/s E }30.0°\text{ N} + \vec{p}_{\text{B}}'$$

In order for the conservation of momentum to be true, the vectors must add together.

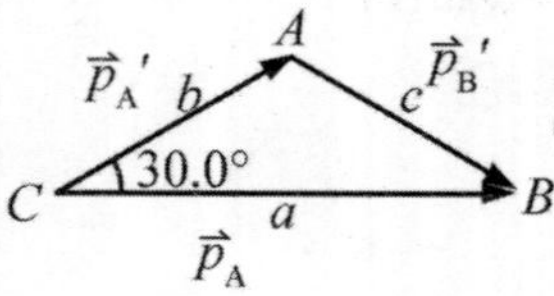

$$c^2 = a^2 + b^2 - 2ab(\cos C)$$

Use the cosine law to determine the magnitude of $\vec{p}_B'$.

$$c^2 = a^2 + b^2 - 2ab\cos C$$
$$(p_B')^2 = (p_A)^2 + (p_A')^2 - 2(p_A)(p_A')\cos 30.0°$$
$$= (1.00\ \text{kg·m/s})^2 + (0.750\ \text{kg·m/s})^2 - 2(1.00\ \text{kg·m/s})(0.750\ \text{kg·m/s})\cos 30.0°$$
$$= 0.2635\ \text{kg}^2\text{·m}^2/\text{s}^2$$
$$\therefore p_B' = 0.513\ \text{kg·m/s}$$

Next, use the sine law to calculate the direction of the momentum.

$$\frac{a}{\sin A} = \frac{b}{\sin B} = \frac{c}{\sin C}$$
$$\Rightarrow \frac{0.750\ \text{kg·m/s}}{\sin B} = \frac{0.513\ \text{kg·m/s}}{\sin 30.0°}$$
$$\therefore \sin B = \frac{(0.750\ \text{kg·m/s})\sin 30.0°}{0.513\ \text{kg·m/s}}$$
$$= 0.7310$$
$$\Rightarrow B = 47.0°$$

Now that you know the momentum of the second ball after the collision, calculate its velocity. The direction will be the same as that of the momentum.

$$\therefore \vec{p}_B' = 0.513\ \text{kg·m/s E } 47.0°\text{ S}$$

$$\vec{v}_B' = \frac{0.513\ \text{kg·m/s E } 47.0°\text{ S}}{0.350\ \text{kg}}$$
$$= 1.47\ \text{m/s E } 47.0°\text{ S}$$

9. 9.09

$$\sum p_i = \sum p_f$$
$$m_i v_i = m_f v_f$$
$$\therefore v_f = \frac{m_i v_i}{m_f}$$
$$= \frac{(1.00 \times 10^4\ \text{kg})(2.00\ \text{m/s})}{2.20 \times 10^4\ \text{kg}}$$
$$= 0.909\ \text{m/s}$$
$$= 9.09 \times 10^{-1}\ \text{m/s}$$

10. 5.00

Before the tackle:

$m_1 = 105$ kg

$\vec{v}_1 = 6.00$ m/s W

$m_2 = 85.0$ kg

$\vec{v}_2 = ?$

After the tackle:

$m_a = m_1 + m_2 = 190$ kg

$\vec{v}_a = 4.00$ m/s W 34.0° N

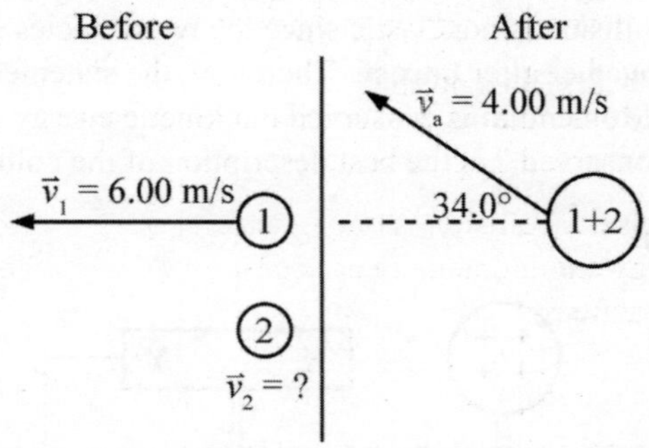

Apply the conservation of momentum to both the horizontal and vertical components of the momenta involved.

Horizontal momenta (west is positive):

$$\sum \vec{p}_{ix} = \sum \vec{p}_{fx}$$
$$\vec{p}_{1x} + \vec{p}_{2x} = \vec{p}_{ax}$$
$$m_1\vec{v}_{1x} + m_2\vec{v}_{2x} = m_a\vec{v}_{ax}$$
$$\therefore \vec{v}_{2x} = \frac{m_a\vec{v}_{ax}}{m_2} - \frac{m_1\vec{v}_{1x}}{m_2}$$
$$= \left(\frac{(190\ \text{kg})(4.00\ \text{m/s})\cos 34.0°}{85.0\ \text{kg}}\right) - \frac{(105\ \text{kg})(6.00\ \text{m/s})}{85.0\ \text{kg}}$$
$$= 0$$

Vertical momenta (north is positive):

$$\sum \vec{p}_{ix} = \sum \vec{p}_{fx}$$
$$\vec{p}_{1y} + \vec{p}_{2y} = \vec{p}_{ay}$$
$$m_1\vec{v}_{1y} + m_2\vec{v}_{2y} = m_a\vec{v}_{ay}$$
$$\therefore \vec{v}_{2y} = \frac{m_a\vec{v}_{ay} - m_1\vec{v}_{1y}}{m_2}$$
$$= \frac{(190\ \text{kg})(4.00\ \text{m/s})\sin 34.0° - 0}{85.0\ \text{kg}}$$
$$= \frac{425.0\ \text{kg·m/s}}{85.0\ \text{kg}}$$
$$= 5.00\ \text{m/s north}$$

Therefore,

$\vec{v}_{2x} = 0$

$\vec{v}_{2y} = 5.00 \text{ m/s}$

$\therefore \vec{v}_2 = 5.00 \text{ m/s N}$

The tackler's speed immediately before the impact was 5.00 m/s.

11. D

Momentum is conserved in all collisions, but kinetic energy is not conserved in an inelastic collision. This collision is not elastic since the two vehicles stick together after impact. Therefore, the statement "Momentum is conserved but kinetic energy is not conserved," is the best description of the collision.

12. D

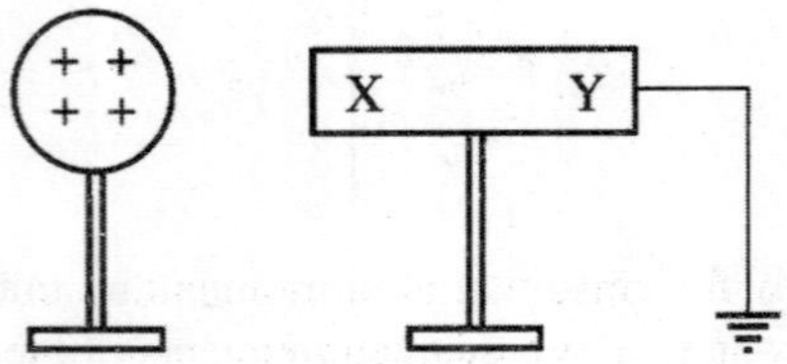

Since Earth is, practically speaking, an infinitely large conductor and source of electrons, the positive charge on the sphere will attract electrons from Earth to X, leaving end X with a negative charge.

13. A

The sphere becomes negatively charged by conduction. Since the sphere has a metallic coating, the excess electrons will repel one another and will rearrange themselves uniformly on the sphere's surface.

14. A

Insulators are substances that do not conduct electricity; they do not permit the free movement of electrons.

15. B

Begin by finding the diagonal distance and angle between sphere A and sphere C. The diagonal is the hypotenuse for a right triangle.

$d = \sqrt{25 \text{ cm}^2 + 25 \text{ cm}^2} = 35.4 \text{ cm}$

$\tan\theta = \dfrac{25 \text{ cm}}{25 \text{ cm}}$

$\theta = 45.0°$

Calculate the repulsion force acting on sphere A using the distance of the diagonal.

$$F_{\text{A,C}} = \frac{\left(8.99 \times 10^9 \frac{\text{N}\cdot\text{m}^2}{\text{C}^2}\right)(5.0 \times 10^{-6} \text{ C})^2}{(0.354 \text{ m})^2}$$

$= 1.79 \text{ N}$

$\therefore \vec{F}_{\text{A,C}} = 1.79 \text{ N at } 135°$

Calculate the magnitudes of the horizontal and vertical components of this force.

$F_{\text{A,C}\,x} = (1.79 \text{ N})(\cos 135°) = -1.27 \text{ N}$

$F_{\text{A,C}\,y} = (1.79 \text{ N})(\sin 135°) = 1.27 \text{ N}$

Calculate the total attractive forces acting on sphere A. These are the forces exerted by opposite charges.

$$F_e = \frac{kq_1q_2}{r^2}$$

$$F_{\text{A,B}} = \frac{\left(8.99 \times 10^9 \frac{\text{N}\cdot\text{m}^2}{\text{C}^2}\right)(5.0 \times 10^{-6} \text{ C})(-5.0 \times 10^{-6} \text{ C})}{(0.25 \text{ m})^2}$$

$= -3.60 \text{ N}$

$\therefore \vec{F}_{\text{A,B}} = 3.60 \text{ N at } 0°$

$$F_{\text{A,D}} = \frac{\left(8.99 \times 10^9 \frac{\text{N}\cdot\text{m}^2}{\text{C}^2}\right)(5.0 \times 10^{-6} \text{ C})(-5.0 \times 10^{-6} \text{ C})}{(0.25 \text{ m})^2}$$

$= -3.60 \text{ N}$

$\therefore \vec{F}_{\text{A,D}} = 3.60 \text{ N at } 270°$

The negative signs indicate that the force is attractive.

$$\begin{aligned}\Sigma\vec{F}_x &= \vec{F}_{\text{A,B}\,x} + \vec{F}_{\text{A,C}\,x} + \vec{F}_{\text{A,D}\,x} \\ &= 3.60 \text{ N} + (-1.27 \text{ N}) + 0 \\ &= +2.33 \text{ N}\end{aligned}$$

$$\begin{aligned}\Sigma\vec{F}_y &= \vec{F}_{\text{A,B}\,y} + \vec{F}_{\text{A,C}\,y} + \vec{F}_{\text{A,D}\,y} \\ &= 0 \text{ N} + (1.27 \text{ N}) + (-3.60 \text{ N}) \\ &= -2.33 \text{ N}\end{aligned}$$

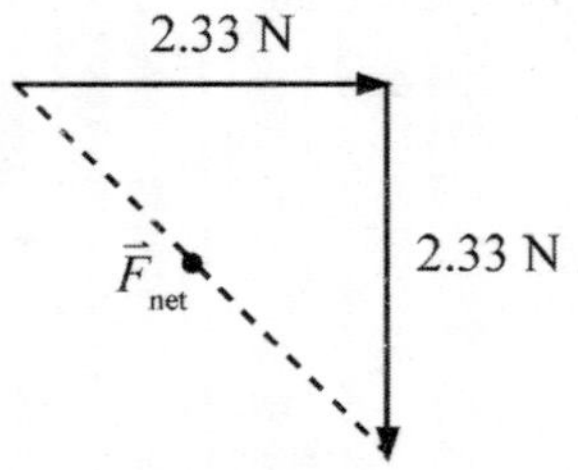

$F_{\text{net}} = \sqrt{(2.33 \text{ N})^2 + (2.33 \text{ N})^2}$

$= 3.3 \text{ N}$

Therefore, the magnitude of the net force on sphere A is 3.3 N.

16. 33.1

Let $r_1 = \sqrt{\frac{kq_1q_2}{F_e}}$

Then,

$$r_2 = \sqrt{\frac{k(2q_1)(3.5q_2)}{4F_e}}$$
$$= \sqrt{\frac{7}{4}\left(\frac{kq_1q_2}{F_e}\right)}$$
$$= \sqrt{\frac{7}{4}}\sqrt{\frac{kq_1q_2}{F_e}}$$
$$= \sqrt{\frac{7}{4}}r_1$$
$$= 1.323(25.0 \text{ cm})$$
$$= 33.1 \text{ cm}$$

17. 3078

$100\ \mu\text{C} = 1.00 \times 10^{-4}\ \text{C}$

$$F_e = \frac{kq_1q_2}{r^2}$$
$$= \frac{\left(8.99 \times 10^9\ \frac{\text{N}\cdot\text{m}^2}{\text{C}^2}\right)(2.00 \times 10^{-4}\ \text{C})(3.50 \times 10^{-4}\ \text{C})}{(6.75 \times 10^{-2}\ \text{m})^2}$$
$$= 1.381 \times 10^5\ \text{N}$$

$$a = \frac{F_{net}}{m}$$
$$= \frac{1.381 \times 10^5\ \text{N}}{450 \times 10^{-6}\ \text{kg}}$$
$$= 3.07 \times 10^8\ \text{m/s}^2$$

18. B

Work against the field = E_p gained

$= Fd$
$= (qE)d$
$\approx (mg)h$

So the given formula for gravitational potential energy is analogous to $E_p = qEd$ since both formulas involve the relative field strengths, the magnitude of the relevant quantities (i.e., mass and charge), and the position with the field (i.e., h and d).

19. B

Voltage is also the electric potential difference. This is the change in the electric potential energy per unit of positive charge.

20. 673

Since the electric field is constant between the two parallel plates it is possible to use the relation $E = \frac{V}{d}$ to determine the voltage across a given distance perpendicular to the plates.

$$\frac{850\ \text{V}}{12.0\ \text{cm}} = \frac{x}{9.50\ \text{cm}}$$
$$x = 673\ \text{V}$$

21. 3517

At the midpoint, the electrical potential (voltage) is 3.50 kV.

Work done on the electron = E_k gained

$$qV = \frac{1}{2}mv^2$$
$$v = \sqrt{\frac{2qV}{m}}$$
$$= \sqrt{\frac{2(1.60 \times 10^{-19}\ \text{C})(3.50 \times 10^3\ \text{J/C})}{9.11 \times 10^{-31}\ \text{kg}}}$$
$$= 3.51 \times 10^7\ \text{m/s}$$

22. D

$$E = \frac{kq_1}{r^2}$$

Case 1:

$$E = \frac{kQ}{x^2} = 8.3 \times 10^{-4}\ \text{N/C}$$

Case 2:

$$E_{new} = \frac{k\left(\frac{Q}{4}\right)}{(3x)^2} = \frac{kQ}{36x^2}$$
$$E_{new} = \frac{1}{36}\left(\frac{kQ}{x^2}\right) = \frac{1}{36}(8.3 \times 10^{-4}\ \text{N/C})$$
$$E_{new} = 2.3 \times 10^{-5}\ \text{N/C}$$

23. 6672

One ampere is equal to one coulomb of charge flow per second.

$$I = \frac{q}{t}$$
$$= \frac{3.00 \times 10^{-6}\ \text{C}}{4.50 \times 10^{-5}\ \text{s}}$$
$$= 6.67 \times 10^{-2}\ \text{A}$$

Therefore, the values of a, b, c, and d are 6, 6, 7, and 2, respectively.

24. D

$E_k(\text{lost}) = E_p(\text{gained})$

$\frac{1}{2}mv^2 = qEd$

$$E = \frac{V}{d}$$
$$= \frac{500 \text{ V}}{4.0 \times 10^{-2} \text{ m}} = 1.25 \times 10^4 \text{ V/m}$$

$$d = \frac{\frac{1}{2}mv^2}{qE}$$
$$= \frac{\frac{1}{2}(9.11 \times 10^{-31} \text{ kg})(1.03 \times 10^7 \text{ m/s})^2}{(1.60 \times 10^{-19} \text{ C})(1.25 \times 10^4 \text{ V/m})}$$
$$= 2.4 \times 10^{-2} \text{ m}$$

OR

$\vec{F}_e = q\vec{E} = m\vec{a}$

$$\therefore \vec{a} = \frac{q\vec{E}}{m}$$
$$= \frac{(-1.60 \times 10^{-19} \text{ C})(1.25 \times 10^4 \text{ V/m})}{9.11 \times 10^{-31} \text{ kg}}$$
$$= -2.195 \times 10^{15} \text{ m/s}^2$$

$v_f^2 = v_i^2 + 2ad$

$$d = \frac{v_f^2 - v_i^2}{2a}$$
$$= \frac{0 - (1.03 \times 10^7 \text{ m/s})^2}{2(-2.195 \times 10^{15} \text{ m/s}^2)}$$
$$= 2.4 \times 10^{-2} \text{ m} = 2.4 \text{ cm}$$

25. B

Millikan's oil-drop experiment showed that charge came in packets, or quanta. In other words, all charges were multiples of the elementary charge, which Millikan determined to be 1.60×10^{-19} C.

26. D

Earth's magnetic south pole is near its geographic North pole, so the magnetic field points toward Earth's surface. This is best represented by the S-pole of a bar magnet at this location and the magnetic field lines pointing toward Earth at the north geographic pole.

27. B

The direction of an electric field is defined as the direction that a positive test charge will move within that field. Since the alpha particle is positively charged, the electric force will act upward.
A positive charge moving through a perpendicular magnetic field will experience a force acting according to the right hand rule. That is the fingers of your right hand point northward and your thumb points eastward leaving your palm facing up in the direction of the magnetic force. Finally gravity will act downward on the alpha particle since it has mass.

28. A

Find the direction of the magnetic force on the current-carrying conductor by using the right-hand rule for positive charges moving in a perpendicular magnetic field. With the thumb of your right hand pointing in the direction of the current into the page and the fingers of your right hand pointing to the right, the magnetic force experienced by these charges will be in the direction that the palm of your right hand is facing. In this case the magnetic force will act downward.

29. 3622

$F_m = F_c$

$$qvB_\perp = \frac{mv^2}{r}$$
$$\therefore r = \frac{mv}{qB_\perp}$$
$$= \frac{(1.67 \times 10^{-27} \text{ kg})(2.55 \times 10^5 \text{ m/s})}{(1.60 \times 10^{-19} \text{ C})(7.35 \times 10^{-2} \text{ T})}$$
$$= 3.62 \times 10^{-2} \text{ m}$$

30. 1201

Use the kinetic energy of the proton to find the value of v

$$E_k = \frac{1}{2}mv^2$$
$$v = \sqrt{\frac{2E_k}{m}}$$
$$= \frac{\sqrt{2(894 \text{ eV})(1.60 \times 10^{-19} \text{ J/eV})}}{1.67 \times 10^{-27} \text{ kg}}$$
$$= 4.14 \times 10^5 \text{ m/s}$$

Since the proton travels in a circular path in the magnetic field, the magnetic force on the proton is the centripetal force.

$$F_c = F_m$$
$$\frac{mv^2}{r} = qvB_\perp$$
$$\therefore B_\perp = \frac{mv}{qr}$$
$$= \frac{(1.67 \times 10^{-27}\ \text{kg})(4.14 \times 10^5\ \text{m/s})}{(1.60 \times 10^{-19}\ \text{C})(3.60 \times 10^{-4}\ \text{m})}$$
$$B_\perp = 1.20 \times 10^1\ \text{T}$$

Therefore, the values of *a*, *b*, *c*, and *d* are 1, 2, 0, and 1.

31. 3593

This is a basic velocity selector used to allow only particles with a desired quantity of kinetic energy to pass. The forces due to the magnetic and electric fields cancel out when a charged particle travels at some specific velocity.

$$F_e = F_m$$
$$\frac{qV}{d} = qvB_\perp$$
$$\therefore V = dvB_\perp$$
$$= (15.0 \times 10^{-2}\ \text{m})(2.50 \times 10^6\ \text{m/s}) \times (9.58 \times 10^{-3}\ \text{T})$$
$$= 3.59 \times 10^3\ \text{V}$$

32. C

$$F_g = F_m$$
$$mg = B_\perp Il$$
$$\therefore I = \frac{mg}{B_\perp l}$$
$$= \frac{(2.0 \times 10^{-2}\ \text{kg})(9.81\ \text{m/s}^2)}{(3.0 \times 10^{-2}\ \text{m})(1.5\ \text{T})}$$
$$= 4.4\ \text{A}$$

33. 778

$$F_m = B_\perp Il$$
$$\therefore B_\perp = \frac{F_m}{Il}$$
$$= \frac{0.350\ \text{N}}{(6.00\ \text{A})(0.750\ \text{m})}$$
$$= 0.0778\ \text{T}$$
$$= 7.78 \times 10^{-2}\ \text{T}$$

34. C

Since both the frequency and wavelength are directly related to the photon energy of different types of electromagnetic radiation, it is easiest to approach the given question in terms of photon energies. The formula for the photon energy of different types of EMR is $E = hf = \frac{hc}{\lambda}$.

Therefore, the desired electromagnetic radiation must have an energy greater than infrared radiation, since a greater frequency results in a higher photon energy, and it will have less energy than X-rays, since a longer wavelength results in a lower photon energy.

This means that the form of EMR must fall in between infrared and X-ray radiation in the electromagnetic spectrum. Of the given forms of EMR, only ultraviolet radiation falls within this region.

35. D

The distance between Jupiter and Earth does not matter for calculating the speed of light; rather, it is the distance across Earth's orbit for which the light has to travel that is used to measure the speed of light using Rømer's method. The same effect can be used with the moons of any other planet in the solar system.

36. 2758

$$T = \frac{1}{f}$$
$$= \frac{1}{2.35 \times 10^3\ \text{Hz}}$$
$$= 4.26 \times 10^{-4}\ \text{s}$$
$$t = \frac{1}{6}T$$
$$= \frac{4.26 \times 10^{-4}\ \text{s}}{6}$$
$$= 7.09 \times 10^{-5}\ \text{s}$$
$$v = \frac{2d}{t}$$
$$= \frac{2(9.75 \times 10^3\ \text{m})}{7.09 \times 10^{-5}\ \text{s}}$$
$$= 2.75 \times 10^8\ \text{m/s}$$

37. D

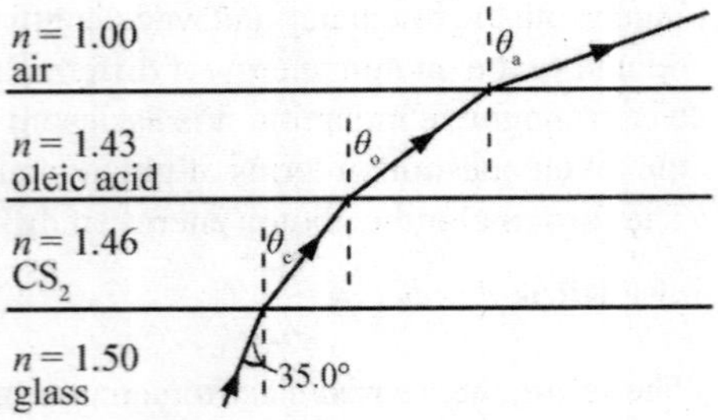

Since all the layers are parallel, you do not need to calculate the angles of refraction for each layer.

$$\frac{n_a}{n_g} = \frac{\sin\theta_g}{\sin\theta_a}$$

$$\sin\theta_a = \frac{\sin\theta_g}{\frac{n_a}{n_g}}$$

$$\theta_a = \sin^{-1}\left(\frac{\sin\theta_g}{\frac{n_a}{n_g}}\right)$$

$$\theta_a = \sin^{-1}\left(\frac{\sin 35.0°}{\frac{1.00}{1.50}}\right) = 59.4°$$

38. C

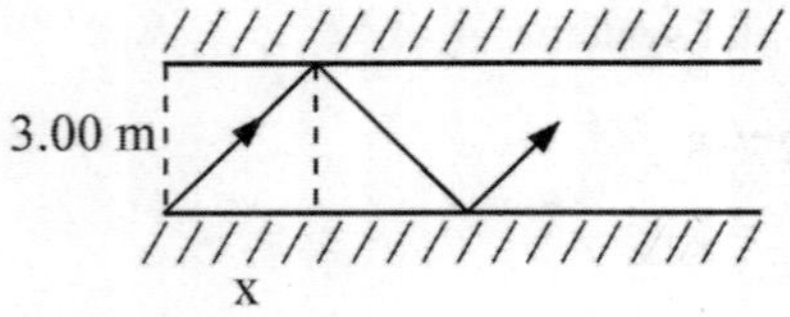

Since the angle between the light beam and the bottom mirror is 45 °, the light beam forms a right triangle with the two mirrors. Therefore, the beam will move the same vertical distance as it will horizontally as it passes to the top mirror. In other words, each reflection moves the beam 3 m to the right.

$$\frac{16 \text{ m}}{3 \text{ m per reflection}} = 5\frac{1}{3} \text{ reflections}$$

The beam makes 5 reflections off the mirrors.

39. D

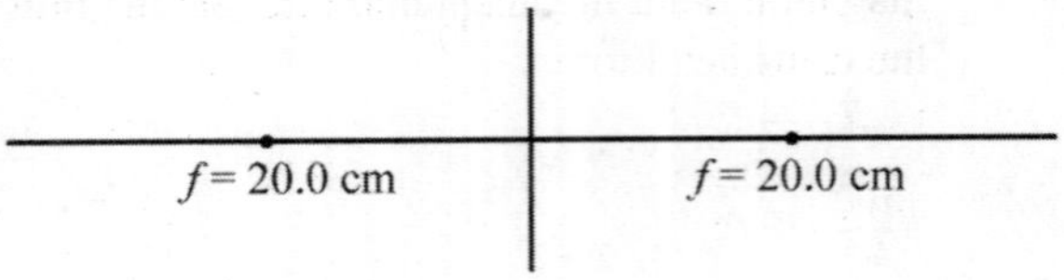

$$M = \frac{h_i}{h_o} = -\frac{d_i}{d_o} = 4.00 \Rightarrow d_i = -4.00d_0$$

$$\frac{1}{f} = \frac{1}{d_i} + \frac{1}{d_o}$$

$$\frac{1}{20.0 \text{ cm}} = \frac{1}{-4.00d_o} + \frac{1}{d_o}$$

$$\frac{1}{20.0 \text{ cm}} = \frac{1 + (-4.00)}{-4.00d_o} = \frac{-3.00}{-4.00d_o}$$

$$-4.00d_o = -(3.00)(20.0 \text{ cm})$$

$$\therefore d_o = 15.0$$

$$d_i = -4.00(15.0 \text{ cm})$$
$$= -60.0 \text{ cm}$$

Since the object and image appear on opposite sides of the lens, the distance between them can be calculated using the following.

$$\therefore |d_i| + |d_o| = 15.0 \text{ cm} + 60.0 \text{ cm} = 75.0 \text{ cm}$$

40. B

Use the formula for optics to find the distance of the image from the mirror.

$$\frac{1}{f} = \frac{1}{d_i} + \frac{1}{d_o}$$

$$\frac{1}{d_i} = \frac{1}{f} - \frac{1}{d_o}$$

$$\frac{1}{d_i} = \frac{1}{45 \text{ cm}} - \frac{1}{25 \text{ cm}}$$

$$\frac{1}{d_i} = -0.178 \text{ cm}^{-1}$$

$$\therefore d_i = -56 \text{ cm}$$

Since the image is a negative value, the image is a virtual image. Virtual images in concave mirrors are behind the mirror.

41. B

If the path difference is a whole number of wavelengths, constructive interference occurs to make a bright fringe (antinode).

Castle Rock Research, the creator of **The KEY** and the **SNAP Workbook**, has developed a new online study tool: **SOLARO**.

SOLARO - Student Oriented Learning, Assessment, and Reporting Online - is a grades 3-12 learning resource for math, science, and English language arts accessible both online and on mobile devices. **SOLARO** provides age-appropriate, curriculum-aligned lessons, activities, exercises, and quizzes with detailed solutions. Content, in the form of text, graphics, and multimedia is available 24 hours a day in a well-organized and highly engaging system.

SOLARO was designed by educators to respond to the needs of the three major stakeholders in education: students, parents, and teachers.

FOR TEACHERS

SOLARO's teacher interface makes it easy to manage a full suite of classes and students. The user-friendly system allows teachers to add classes and to populate them with students with just a click of the mouse.

Teachers can easily view all their course content, as well as the specific curriculum standards linked to each lesson. Educators can be confident that relevant content is covered in detail, as most curriculum standards have multiple lessons attached to them. Teachers can also use the playlist feature to add in their own customized content, including documents, media, and web links.

Properties of Air — Add an Assignment

Title	Standards	Lesson	Practice
Air Takes Up Space	SC6.1.5.1	View Lesson	View sample questions
Air Has Mass	SC6.1.5.1	View Lesson	View sample questions
Air Is A Fluid	SC6.1.5.2	View Lesson	View sample questions
Air Exerts Pressure	SC6.1.5.1	View Lesson	View sample questions
Air Can Be Compressed	SC6.1.5.2	View Lesson	View sample questions
Air Is Made Up of Many Gases	SC6.1.5.8	View Lesson	View sample questions

Forces of Flight — Add an Assignment

With the assignment generator feature in **SOLARO,** teachers can assemble customized assignments with problems selected from an extensive database of educator-reviewed questions automatically sorted by subject, topic, and lesson. Teachers manage student access to any given assignment, controlling the time available for completing each assignment. These assignments may be provided to students digitally or in print.

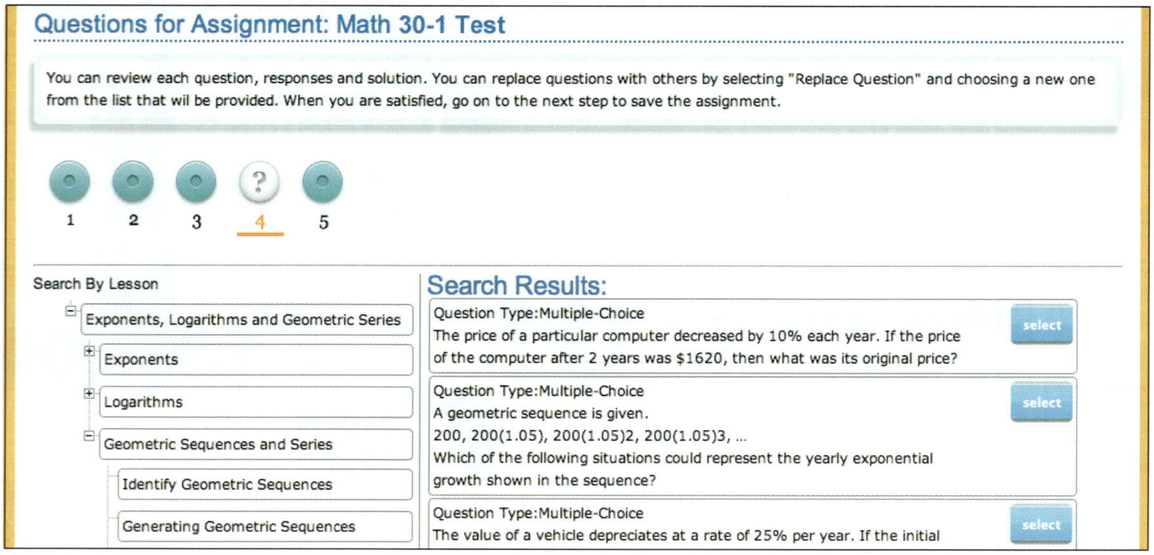

Immediate scoring and reporting enables teachers to track performance and helps them to determine if further instruction or remediation may be needed at the individual or class level. Class results can be anonymously displayed on a whiteboard for class-wide review.

FOR TEACHERS

Teachers can view progress reports for every student, detailing the student's achievements by date completed, lessons viewed, practice quizzes taken, and assessment results. The assessment results link individual questions to the related curriculum standards, showing the student's areas strength and weakness in great detail. The tools in **SOLARO** benefit teachers by reducing much of the time usually spent in planning, preparing, grading, and reporting.

FOR STUDENTS

SOLARO provides a secure and guided online environment for students as they study, work through exercises, and take assessments. The home screen encourages good study habits by providing a customizable, ordered to-do list and an overview of previously completed assessments and quizzes.

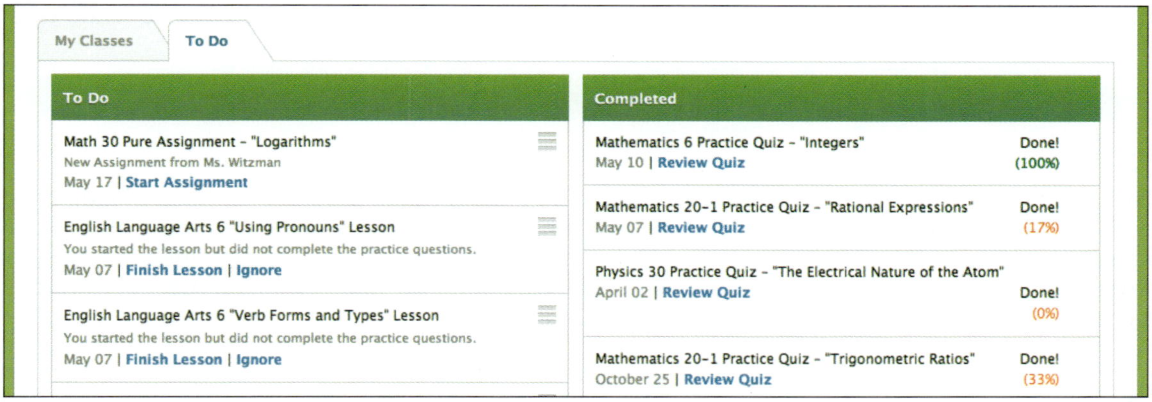

While viewing an individual lesson, students can easily create notes and flashcards for future studying. Notes and flashcards are linked to the original lesson and assembled under a separate tab, sorted by subject. Peer tutoring is also built into the lessons by a monitored discussion board shared by all **SOLARO** users.

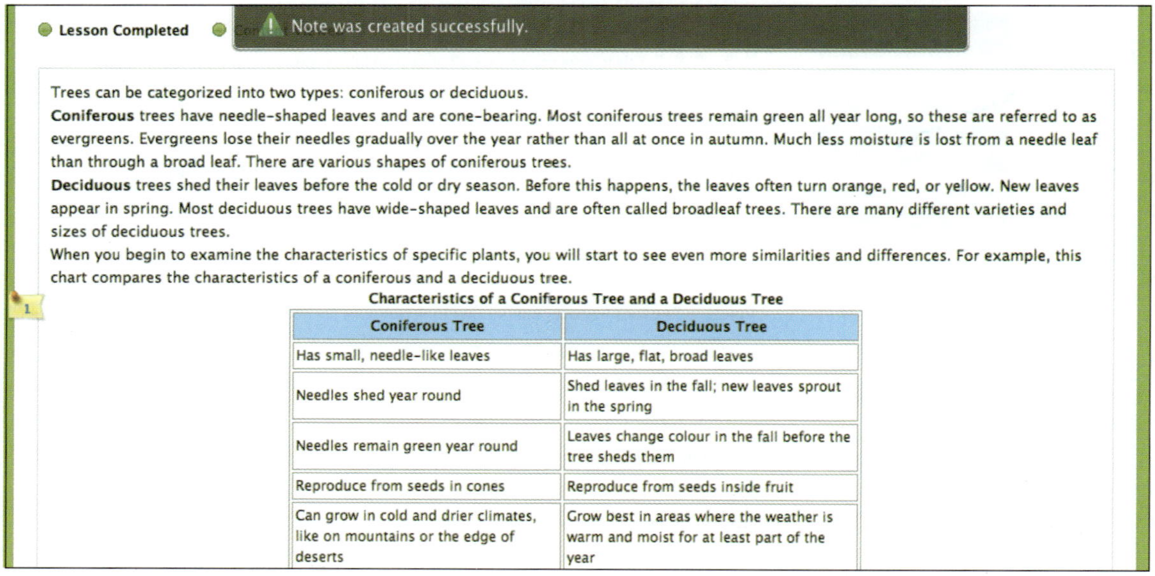

FOR STUDENTS

Students are awarded stars for each lesson they review or every assessment they complete. As students accumulate stars, they can use them to purchase rewards to build a personalized avatar. This provides incentive by providing a fun, interactive, motivational reward for participation and success.

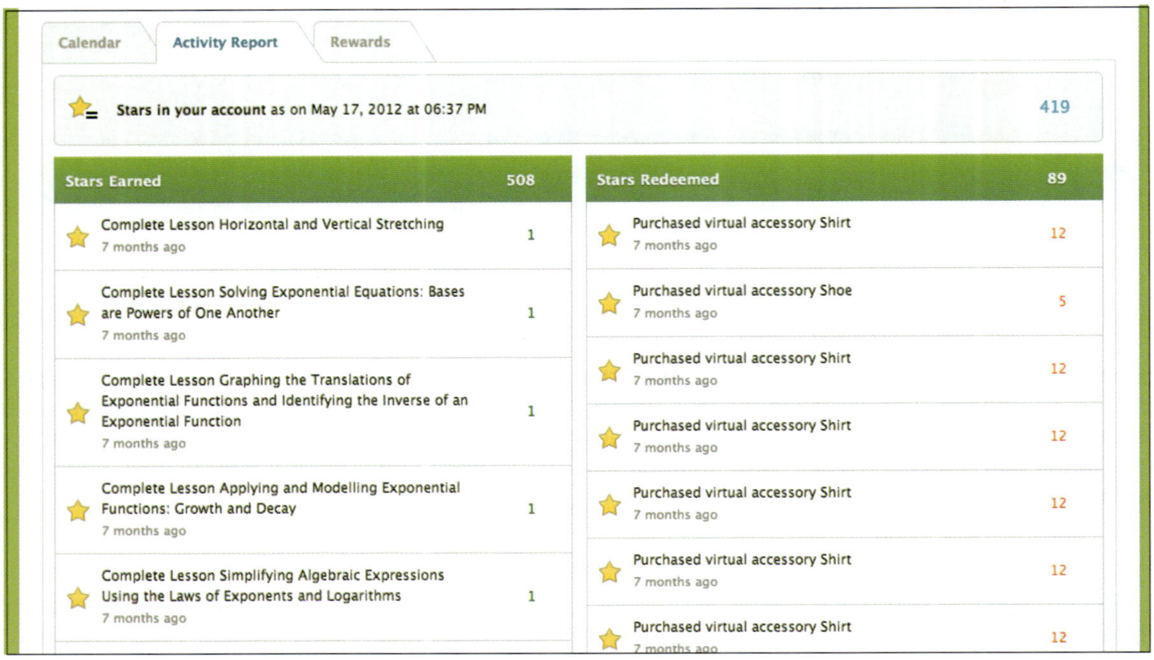

All progress is saved instantly so students can access pick up their mobile devices and continue where they left off on their home computers.

FOR PARENTS

The **SOLARO** parent interface allows parents to monitor the individual progress for each of their children, and it provides detailed reports for each child's account. These easy to read reports show how many activities have been completed, when they were reported, the progress of the student through their courses, the level of achievement on tests and assignments, and deficiencies that may need to be addressed. Parents can configure reports to automatically send to their mobile devices.

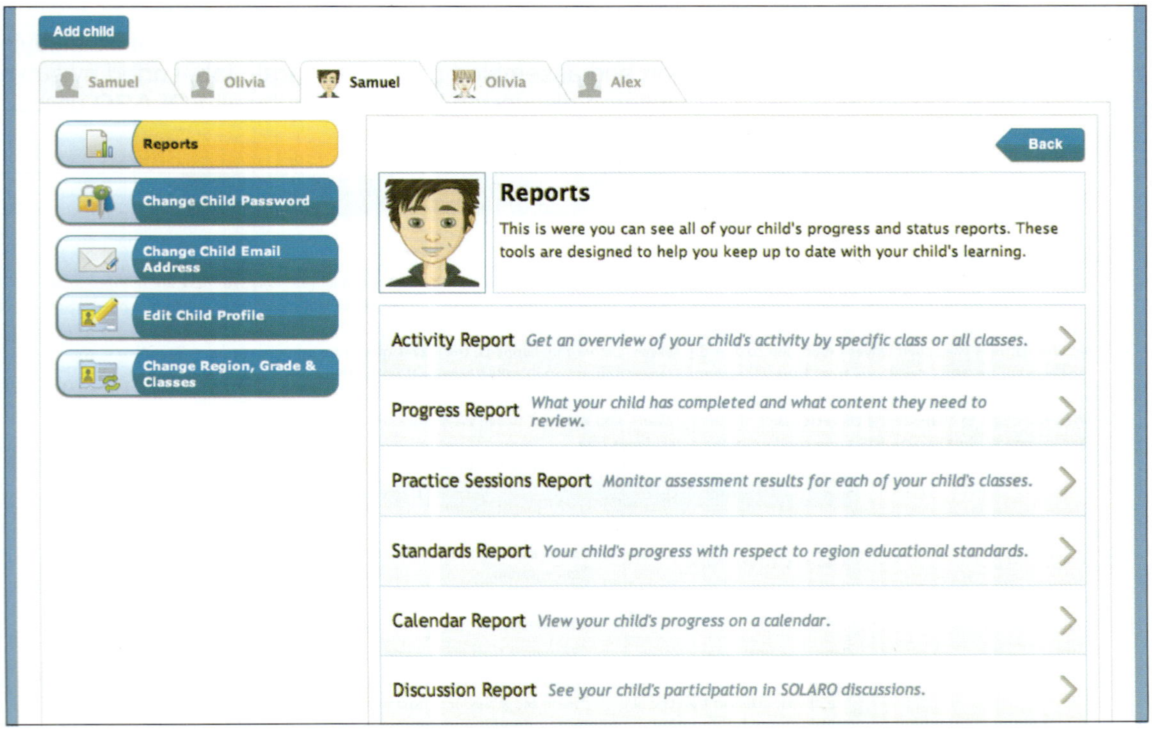

42. 5155

Use the formula for Young's double-slit experiment to find the distance between the slits.

$n\lambda = \frac{xd}{l}$ where $n = 1$

$d = \frac{\lambda l}{x}$

$d = \frac{(5.88 \times 10^{-7}\ \text{m})(3.50\ \text{m})}{4.00 \times 10^{-2}\ \text{m}}$

$d = 5.15 \times 10^{-5}\ \text{m}$

Therefore, the values of *a*, *b*, *c*, and *d* are 5, 1, 5, and 5, respectively.

43. 6557

Use the formula for the distance for multi-slit diffraction.

$n\lambda = d\sin\theta$ where $n = 1$

$= (2.50 \times 10^{-6}\ \text{m})(\sin 15.2°)$

$= 6.55 \times 10^{-7}\ \text{m}$

Therefore, the values of *a*, *b*, *c*, and *d* are 6, 5, 5, and 7, respectively.

44. 53114

From Snell's law it is known

$\frac{\sin\theta_1}{\sin\theta_2} = \frac{v_1}{v_2} = \frac{\lambda_1}{\lambda_2} = \frac{n_2}{n_1}$

$\therefore \frac{v_1}{v_2} = \frac{\lambda_1}{\lambda_2}$

or $\frac{v_1}{\lambda_1} = \frac{v_2}{\lambda_2} = f$

Therefore the frequency of the light does not change during refraction.

$v = f\lambda$

$f = \frac{v}{\lambda}$

$= \frac{3.00 \times 10^{8}\ \text{m/s}}{565 \times 10^{-9}\ \text{m}}$

$= 5.31 \times 10^{14}\ \text{Hz}$

Therefore, the values of *a*, *b*, *c*, *d*, and *e* are 5, 3, 1, 1, and 4, respectively.

45. B

Refraction will bend shorter wavelengths more than longer wavelengths while diffraction will bend longer wavelengths more than shorter wavelengths. Since red light has longer wavelengths than blue light, a diffraction grating will bend red light more than blue light.

46. 32620

$E = hf$

$\Rightarrow f = \frac{E}{h}$

$= \frac{(1.35 \times 10^{6}\ \text{eV})(1.60 \times 10^{-19}\ \text{J/eV})}{6.63 \times 10^{-34}\ \text{J·s}}$

$= 3.26 \times 10^{20}\ \text{Hz}$

47. D

Visible light energies run from 1.8 to 3.1 eV. Ultraviolet radiation energies run from approximately 3.1 eV to 124 eV. So ultraviolet radiation includes photons with enough energy to break chemical bonds of the given strength.

48. C

The wave model predicted that a substantial delay in the ejection of electrons would occur using low intensity incident light. Different metals do obey the same photoelectric equation with each metal having its own work function and threshold frequency. A graph of the maximum kinetic energy versus the frequency of incoming photons will result in a linear graph with a positive slope. The *x*-intercept of this graph is the threshold frequency of the given metal. The slope of this graph is always going to be Planck's constant *h* since the relation between the frequency of incoming light to maximum kinetic energy of photoelectrons is $E_{k_{max}} = h(f - f_0)$.

49. A

First, calculate the work function given the wavelength and stopping voltage of the initial experiment.

$qV_{stop} = E_{k_{max}} = \frac{hc}{\lambda} - W$

$qV_{stop} = \frac{hc}{\lambda} - W$

$qV_{stop} + W = \frac{hc}{\lambda}$

$W = \frac{hc}{\lambda} - qV_{stop}$

$= \frac{(6.63 \times 10^{-34}\ \text{J·s})(3.00 \times 10^{8}\ \text{m/s})}{491 \times 10^{-9}\ \text{m}}$

$- (1.60 \times 10^{-19}\ \text{C})(0.710\ \text{J/C})$

$= 2.915 \times 10^{-19}\ \text{J}$

$\cong 2.92 \times 10^{-19}\ \text{J}$

Next calculate the wavelength of the light in the second experiment using the calculated work function and the given stopping voltage.

$$qV_{stop} = \frac{hc}{\lambda} - W$$

$$qV_{stop} + W = \frac{hc}{\lambda}$$

$$\lambda = \frac{hc}{qV_{stop} + W}$$

$$= \frac{(6.63 \times 10^{-34} \text{ J·s})(3.00 \times 10^{8} \text{ m/s})}{(1.60 \times 10^{-19} \text{ C})(1.43 \text{ V}) + (2.915 \times 10^{-19} \text{ J})}$$

$$= \frac{1.989 \times 10^{-25} \text{ J·m}}{2.288 \times 10^{-19} \text{ J} + 2.915 \times 10^{-19} \text{ J}}$$

$$= 3.82 \times 10^{-7} \text{ m}$$
$$= 382 \text{ nm}$$

50. C

As the photon of light interacts with the electron near the surface of the metal, it imparts a certain amount of energy to the electron allowing it to be freed from the metal entirely. This transfer of energy acts in much the same manner as a particle hitting the electron with enough force to knock it out of the metal. The electron will have a kinetic energy directly related to the initial energy of the inbound photon.

51. 2145

$$E_e = E_i - E_f$$

$$= \frac{hc}{\lambda_i} - \frac{hc}{\lambda_f}$$

$$= \frac{(6.63 \times 10^{-34} \text{ J·s})(3.00 \times 10^{8} \text{ m/s})}{2.35 \times 10^{-12} \text{ m}} - \frac{(6.63 \times 10^{-34} \text{ J·s})(3.00 \times 10^{8} \text{ m/s})}{3.95 \times 10^{-12} \text{ m}}$$

$$= 8.464 \times 10^{-14} \text{ J} - 5.035^{-14} \text{ J}$$

$$= 3.43 \times 10^{-14} \text{ J}$$

$$\Rightarrow 3.43 \times 10^{-14} \text{ J}\left(\frac{1 \text{ eV}}{1.60 \times 10^{-19} \text{ J}}\right)$$

$$= 2.14 \times 10^{5} \text{ eV}$$

52. C

The explanation of cathode rays as a stream of negative particles was the first concrete evidence that atoms are composed of smaller structures. At the very least, atoms must consist of both positive matter and negative matter. Thompson's model was a direct result of these ideas.

53. A

Rutherford discovered that the atom consisted mostly of empty space with a dense, positively charged nucleus and an orbiting negative charge.

54. B

Gas at low pressure, when excited electrically or thermally, produces bright-line emission spectra.

55. 5.70

$$\Delta E = \frac{hc}{\lambda}$$

$$= \frac{(4.14 \times 10^{-15} \text{ eV·s})(3.00 \times 10^{8} \text{ m/s})}{5.65 \times 10^{-7} \text{ m}}$$

$$= 2.20 \text{ eV}$$

The electron ended up 3.50 eV above the ground state after the emission of this energy. The original energy level of this electron must have been $2.20 + 3.50 = 5.70$ eV above ground state.

56. C

Just because energy levels exist does not mean energy is absorbed or emitted. Electrons have to make transitions between the energy levels in order to absorb or emit energy in the form of EMR. Since infrared radiation has a lower energy than visible light, the transitions made by the electrons must be low-energy transitions.

57. D

The ability of a moving electron to diffract around objects and its tendency to exhibit interference effects are properties for all types of waves; collisions with atoms would be better associated with particles.

58. D

Alpha particles are positively charged, so the right-hand rule for moving positive charges shows that alpha particles will deflect toward detector A. Gamma rays have no charge and do not deflect. They will then be detected by detector B.
Beta particles are negatively charged, so the left-hand rule for moving negative charges shows that beta particles will deflect toward detector C.

59. a) B

Alpha decay emits an alpha particle from the original atom's nucleus. This creates a daughter nucleus two atomic numbers down and four mass numbers down from the parent nucleus. Therefore, each transition of a decrease of two atomic numbers and four mass numbers represents an alpha decay.

Therefore, the alpha decays are represented by transitions 1, 4, and 5.

b) D

During a beta plus (β^+) decay, the daughter nucleus will have the same mass number as the parent nucleus, but its atomic number will be lower by one because the beta plus decay involves the conversion of a single proton into a single neutron. Since the atomic number is a measure of the number of protons contained within the nucleus of an atom, the atomic number must decrease by one.

On the diagram, the change in the atomic number is indicated by a shift of one unit to the left (in the *x* direction).

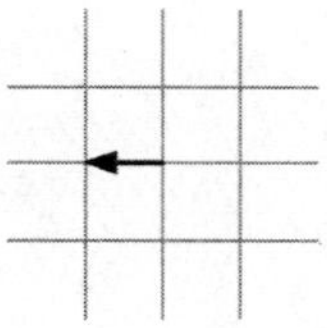

60. B

The described series of radioactive decays is shown below:

$${}^{238}_{92}\text{U} \rightarrow {}^{234}_{90}\text{Th} + {}^{4}_{2}\alpha$$

$${}^{234}_{90}\text{Th} \rightarrow {}^{234}_{91}\text{Pa} + {}^{0}_{-1}\beta + \bar{\nu}$$

$${}^{234}_{91}\text{Pa} \rightarrow {}^{234}_{92}\text{U} + {}^{0}_{-1}\beta + \bar{\nu}$$

$${}^{234}_{92}\text{U} \rightarrow {}^{230}_{90}\text{Th} + {}^{4}_{2}\alpha$$

Thus, the final daughter product will be ${}^{230}_{90}\text{Th}$.

61. 29.0

Start with the general formula for half life calculations and rearrange it to calculate how long it would take for the activity of a substance to drop to $\frac{1}{16}$ of its original activity.

$$\frac{N}{N_0} = \left(\frac{1}{2}\right)^{\frac{t}{t_{\frac{1}{2}}}}$$

$$\frac{1}{16} = \left(\frac{1}{2}\right)^{\frac{116\text{ s}}{t_{\frac{1}{2}}}}$$

$$\frac{1}{16} = \left(\frac{1}{2}\right)^{\frac{116\text{ s}}{t_{\frac{1}{2}}}}$$

$$\left(\frac{1}{2}\right)^4 = \left(\frac{1}{2}\right)^{\frac{116\text{ s}}{t_{\frac{1}{2}}}}$$

$$\therefore 4 = \frac{116\text{ s}}{t_{\frac{1}{2}}}$$

$$4t_{\frac{1}{2}} = 116$$

$$t_{\frac{1}{2}} = 29.0\text{ s}$$

62. A

To find the isotope represented by *X*, begin by balancing the nucleons (mass number).
$(1 + 235) - (141 + 3) = 92$

Balance the atomic number.
$92 - 55 = 37$

The isotope is ${}^{92}_{37}\text{Rb}$.

63. A

The release of energy means that mass disappears. In fusing these two elements, extra mass disappeared. The product has a higher binding energy per nucleon because it has a larger mass defect per nucleon.

Binding Energy per Nucleon Versus Atomic Mass Number

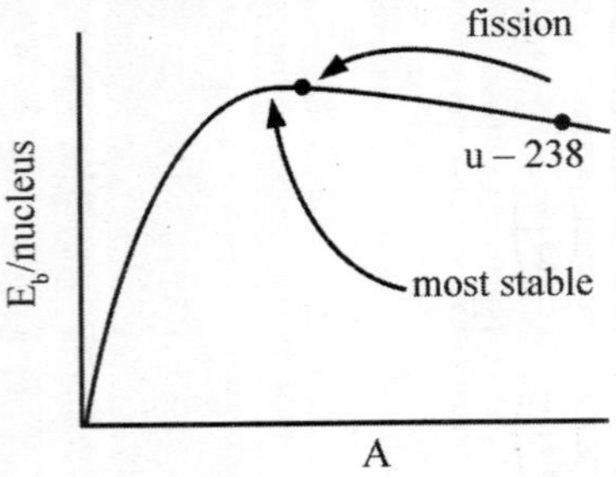

64. 15111

C-13 has:

6 Protons
$6(1.007\ 28\ \text{u}) = 6.043\ 68\ \text{u}$

7 neutrons
$7(1.008\ 67\ \text{u}) = 7.060\ 69\ \text{u}$

Total atomic mass of components of C-13:
$6.043\ 68\ \text{u} + 7.060\ 69\ \text{u} = 13.104\ 37\ \text{u}$

The mass defect is
$13.104\ 37\ \text{u} - 13.003\ 35\ \text{u}$
$= 0.101\ 02\ \text{u} \times 1.66 \times 10^{-27}\ \text{kg/u}$
$= 1.676\ 932 \times 10^{-28}\ \text{kg}$

$$\begin{aligned} E &= \Delta mc^2 \\ &= (1.676\ 932 \times 10^{-28}\ \text{kg})(3.00 \times 10^8\ \text{m/s})^2 \\ &= 1.51 \times 10^{-11}\ \text{J} \end{aligned}$$

Therefore, the values of *a*, *b*, *c*, *d*, and *e* are 1, 5, 1, 1, and 1, respectively.

65. B

The electron and the positron have the same mass and same magnitude of charge, but the nature of charge is opposite charges. Therefore, the motion of the positron in the cloud chamber will resemble the movement of the electron, but it will turn in the opposite direction.

66. B

Up quarks carry a charge of $+\frac{2}{3}$; down quarks carry a charge of $-\frac{1}{3}$.

Since neutrons are neutrally charged, it must consist of quarks that combine to have a total of zero charge. So $\left(+\frac{2}{3}\right)+2\left(-\frac{1}{3}\right) = 0$ appears to be appropriate for neutrons.
Proton (uud)
Antiproton $(\bar{u}\bar{u}\bar{d})$

67. C

The weak force only acts on quarks changing from one flavour (or type) into another. Both types of beta decay involves the conversion of one flavour of quark into another.

Appendices

PHYSICS DATA SHEET

Constants

Acceleration Due to Gravity Near Earth	$\lvert\vec{a}_g\rvert = 9.81$ m/s^2
Gravitational Constant	$G = 6.67 \times 10^{-11}$ N·m^2/kg^2
Radius of Earth	$r_e = 6.37 \times 10^6$ m
Mass of Earth	$M_e = 5.97 \times 10^{24}$ kg
Elementary Charge	$e = 1.60 \times 10^{-19}$ C
Coulomb's Law Constant	$k = 8.99 \times 10^9$ N·m^2/C^2
Electron Volt	1 eV = 1.60×10^{-19} J
Index of Refraction of Air	$n = 1.00$
Speed of Light in Vacuum	$c = 3.00 \times 10^8$ m/s
Planck's Constant	$h = 6.63 \times 10^{-34}$ J·s $h = 4.14 \times 10^{-15}$ eV·s
Atomic Mass Unit	$u = 1.66 \times 10^{-27}$ kg

Physics Principles

0 Uniform motion ($\vec{F}_{net} = 0$)
1 Accelerated motion ($\vec{F}_{net} \neq 0$)
2 Uniform circular motion ($\vec{F}_{net}$ is radially inward)
3 Work-energy theorem
4 Conservation of momentum
5 Conservation of energy
6 Conservation of mass-energy
7 Conservation of charge
8 Conservation of nucleons
9 Wave-particle duality

Prefixes Used with SI Units

Prefix	Symbol	Exponential Value
atto	a	10^{-18}
femto	f	10^{-15}
pico	p	10^{-12}
nano	n	10^{-9}
micro	μ	10^{-6}
milli	m	10^{-3}
centi	c	10^{-2}
deci	d	10^{-1}
deka	da	10^{1}
hecto	h	10^{2}
kilo	k	10^{3}
mega	M	10^{6}
giga	G	10^{9}
tera	T	10^{12}

Particles

	Charge	Mass
Alpha Particle	$+2e$	6.65×10^{-27} kg
Electron	$-1e$	9.11×10^{-31} kg
Proton	$+1e$	1.67×10^{-27} kg
Neutron	0	1.67×10^{-27} kg

First-Generation Fermions

	Charge	Mass
Electron	$-1e$	0.511 MeV/c^2
Positron	$+1e$	0.511 MeV/c^2
Electron neutrino, ν	0	< 50 eV/c^2
Electron antineutrino, $\bar{\nu}$	0	< 50 eV/c^2
Up quark, u	$+\frac{2}{3}e$	~5 MeV/c^2*
Anti-up antiquark, $\bar{u}$	$-\frac{2}{3}e$	~5 MeV/c^2*
Down quark, d	$-\frac{1}{3}e$	~10 MeV/c^2*
Anti-down antiquark, $\bar{d}$	$+\frac{1}{3}e$	~10 MeV/c^2*

*Current models seem to suggest a significantly lower mass of these quarks than those in this table.

EQUATIONS

Kinematics

$\vec{v}_{ave} = \frac{\Delta\vec{d}}{\Delta t}$ $\vec{d} = \vec{v}_f t - \frac{1}{2}\vec{a}t^2$

$\vec{a}_{ave} = \frac{\Delta\vec{v}}{\Delta t}$ $\vec{d} = \left(\frac{\vec{v}_f + \vec{v}_i}{2}\right)t$

$\vec{d} = \vec{v}_i t + \frac{1}{2}\vec{a}t^2$ ${v_f}^2 = {v_i}^2 + 2ad$

$|\vec{v}_c| = \frac{2\pi r}{T}$ $|\vec{a}_c| = \frac{v^2}{r} = \frac{4\pi^2 r}{T^2}$

Dynamics

$\vec{a} = \frac{\vec{F}_{net}}{m}$ $|\vec{F}_g| = \frac{Gm_1m_2}{r^2}$

$|\vec{F}_f| = \mu|\vec{F}_N|$ $|\vec{g}| = \frac{Gm}{r^2}$

$\vec{F}_s = -k\vec{x}$ $\vec{g} = \frac{\vec{F}_g}{m}$

Momentum and Energy

$\vec{p} = m\vec{v}$ $E_k = \frac{1}{2}mv^2$

$\vec{F}\Delta t = m\Delta\vec{v}$ $E_p = mgh$

$W = |\vec{F}||\vec{d}|\cos\theta$ $E_p = \frac{1}{2}kx^2$

$W = \Delta E$

$P = \frac{W}{t}$

Waves

$T = 2\pi\sqrt{\frac{m}{k}}$ $m = \frac{h_i}{h_o} = \frac{-d_i}{d_o}$

$T = 2\pi\sqrt{\frac{l}{g}}$ $\frac{1}{f} = \frac{1}{d_o} + \frac{1}{d_i}$

$T = \frac{1}{f}$ $\frac{\sin\theta_1}{\sin\theta_2} = \frac{n_2}{n_1} = \frac{v_1}{v_2} = \frac{\lambda_1}{\lambda_2}$

$v = f\lambda$ $\lambda = \frac{d\sin\theta}{n}$

$f = \left(\frac{v}{v \pm v_s}\right)f_s$ $\lambda = \frac{xd}{nl}$

Electricity and Magnetism

$|\vec{F}_e| = \frac{kq_1q_2}{r^2}$ $\Delta V = \frac{\Delta E}{q}$

$|\vec{E}| = \frac{kq}{r^2}$ $I = \frac{q}{t}$

$\vec{E} = \frac{\vec{F}_e}{q}$ $|\vec{F}_m| = Il_\perp|\vec{B}|$

$|\vec{E}| = \frac{\Delta V}{\Delta d}$ $|\vec{F}_m| = qv_\perp|\vec{B}|$

Atomic Physics

$W = hf_0$ $E = hf = \frac{hc}{\lambda}$

$E_{k_{max}} = q_e V_{stop}$ $N = N_0\left(\frac{1}{2}\right)^n$

Quantum Mechanics and Nuclear Physics

$\Delta E = \Delta mc^2$ $E = pc$

$p = \frac{h}{\lambda}$ $\Delta\lambda = \frac{h}{mc}(1 - \cos\theta)$

Trigonometry and Geometry

$\sin\theta = \frac{\text{opposite}}{\text{hypotenuse}}$

$\cos\theta = \frac{\text{adjacent}}{\text{hypotenuse}}$

$\tan\theta = \frac{\text{opposite}}{\text{adjacent}}$

$c^2 = a^2 + b^2$

$\frac{a}{\sin A} = \frac{b}{\sin B} = \frac{c}{\sin C}$

$c^2 = a^2 + b^2 - 2ab\cos C$

Line

$m = \frac{\Delta y}{\Delta x}$

$y = mx + b$

Area

Rectangle $= lw$

Triangle $= \frac{1}{2}ab$

Circle $= \pi r^2$

Circumference

Circle $= 2\pi r$

Graphing Calculator Window Format

x: $[x_{min}, x_{max}, x_{scl}]$

y: $[y_{min}, y_{max}, y_{scl}]$

Periodic Table of the Elements

Key

Atomic number →	3
Symbol →	Li
Atomic molar mass (g/mol) →	6.94
Name →	lithium

Based on $^{12}_{6}C$
( ) Indicates mass of the most stable isotope

1 H 1.01 hydrogen																	2 He 4.00 helium
3 Li 6.94 lithium	4 Be 9.01 beryllium											5 B 10.81 boron	6 C 12.01 carbon	7 N 14.01 nitrogen	8 O 16.00 oxygen	9 F 19.00 fluorine	10 Ne 20.18 neon
11 Na 22.99 sodium	12 Mg 24.31 magnesium											13 Al 26.98 aluminium	14 Si 28.09 silicon	15 P 30.97 phosphorus	16 S 32.07 sulfur	17 Cl 35.45 chlorine	18 Ar 39.95 argon
19 K 39.10 potassium	20 Ca 40.08 calcium	21 Sc 44.96 scandium	22 Ti 47.87 titanium	23 V 50.94 vanadium	24 Cr 52.00 chromium	25 Mn 54.94 manganese	26 Fe 55.85 iron	27 Co 58.93 cobalt	28 Ni 58.69 nickel	29 Cu 63.55 copper	30 Zn 65.39 zinc	31 Ga 69.72 gallium	32 Ge 72.64 germanium	33 As 74.92 arsenic	34 Se 78.96 selenium	35 Br 79.90 bromine	36 Kr 83.80 krypton
37 Rb 85.47 rubidium	38 Sr 87.62 strontium	39 Y 88.91 yttrium	40 Zr 91.22 zirconium	41 Nb 92.91 niobium	42 Mo 95.94 molybdenum	43 Tc (98) technetium	44 Ru 101.07 ruthenium	45 Rh 102.91 rhodium	46 Pd 106.42 palladium	47 Ag 107.87 silver	48 Cd 112.41 cadmium	49 In 114.82 indium	50 Sn 118.71 tin	51 Sb 121.75 antimony	52 Te 127.60 tellurium	53 I 126.90 iodine	54 Xe 131.29 xenon
55 Cs 132.91 cesium	56 Ba 137.33 barium	57-71	72 Hf 178.49 hafnium	73 Ta 180.95 tantalum	74 W 183.84 tungsten	75 Re 186.21 rhenium	76 Os 190.23 osmium	77 Ir 192.22 iridium	78 Pt 195.08 platinum	79 Au 196.97 gold	80 Hg 200.59 mercury	81 Tl 204.38 thallium	82 Pb 207.21 lead	83 Bi 208.98 bismuth	84 Po (209) polonium	85 At (210) astatine	86 Rn (222) radon
87 Fr (223) francium	88 Ra (226) radium	89-103	104 Rf (261) rutherfordium	105 Db (262) dubnium	106 Sg (266) seaborgium	107 Bh (264) bohrium	108 Hs (277) hassium	109 Mt (268) meitnerium	110 Ds (271) darmstadtium	111 Rg (272) roentgenium	112 Uub (285) ununbium	113 Uut (284) ununtrium	114 Uuq (289) ununquadium	115 Uup (288) ununpentium	116 Uuh (292) ununhexium	117 Uus (?) ununseptium	118 Uuo (294) ununoctium

57 La 138.91 lanthanum	58 Ce 140.12 cerium	59 Pr 140.91 praseodymium	60 Nd 144.24 neodymium	61 Pm (145) promethium	62 Sm 150.36 samarium	63 Eu 151.96 europium	64 Gd 157.25 gadolinium	65 Tb 158.93 terbium	66 Dy 162.50 dysprosium	67 Ho 164.93 holmium	68 Er 167.26 erbium	69 Tm 168.93 thulium	70 Yb 173.04 ytterbium	71 Lu 174.97 lutetium
89 Ac (227) actinium	90 Th 232.04 thorium	91 Pa 231.04 protactinium	92 U 238.03 uranium	93 Np (237) neptunium	94 Pu (244) plutonium	95 Am (243) americium	96 Cm (247) curium	97 Bk (247) berkelium	98 Cf (251) californium	99 Es (252) einsteinium	100 Fm (257) fermium	101 Md (258) mendelevium	102 No (259) nobelium	103 Lr (262) lawrencium

CREDITS

Every effort has been made to provide proper acknowledgement of the original source and to comply with copyright law. However, some attempts to establish original copyright ownership may have been unsuccessful. If copyright ownership can be identified, please notify Castle Rock Research Corp so that appropriate corrective action can be taken.

The data tables have been reproduced from http://education.alberta.ca/admin/testing/diplomaexams.aspx

NOTES

NOTES

NOTES

NOTES

NOTES

ORDERING INFORMATION

SCHOOL ORDERS

Please contact the Learning Resource Centre (LRC) for school discount and order information.

***THE KEY* Study Guides** are specifically designed to assist students in preparing for unit tests, final exams, and provincial examinations.

***THE KEY* Study Guides**—$29.95 each plus G.S.T.

Senior High		Junior High	Elementary
Biology 30	Biology 20	English Language Arts 9	English Language Arts 6
Chemistry 30	Chemistry 20	Mathematics 9	Mathematics 6
English 30-1	English 20-1	Science 9	Science 6
English 30-2	Mathematics 20-1	Social Studies 9	Social Studies 6
Mathematics 30-1	Physics 20	Mathematics 8	Mathematics 4
Mathematics 30-2	Social Studies 20-1	Mathematics 7	English Language Arts 3
Physics 30	English 10-1		Mathematics 3
Social Studies 30-1	Mathematics 10 Combined		
Social Studies 30-2	Science 10		
	Social Studies 10-1		

Student Notes and Problems (SNAP) Workbooks contain complete explanations of curriculum concepts, examples, and exercise questions.

SNAP Workbooks—$29.95 each plus G.S.T.

Senior High		Junior High	Elementary
Biology 30	Biology 20	Mathematics 9	Mathematics 6
Chemistry 30	Chemistry 20	Science 9	Mathematics 5
Mathematics 30-1	Mathematics 20-1	Mathematics 8	Mathematics 4
Mathematics 30-2	Physics 20	Science 8	Mathematics 3
Mathematics 31	Mathematics 10 Combined	Mathematics 7	
Physics 30	Science 10	Science 7	

Class Notes and Problem Solved—$19.95 each plus G.S.T.

Senior High		Junior High
Biology 30	Biology 20	Mathematics 9
Chemistry 30	Chemistry 20	Science 9
Mathematics 30-1	Mathematics 20-1	Mathematics 8
Mathematics 30-2	Physics 20	Science 8
Mathematics 31	Mathematics 10 Combined	Mathematics 7
Physics 30	Science 10	Science 7

Visit our website for a tour of resource content and features or order resources online at
www.castlerockresearch.com/store/

#2340, 10180 – 101 Street NW
Edmonton, AB Canada T5J 3S4
e-mail: learn@castlerockresearch.com

Phone: 780.448.9619
Toll-free: 1.800.840.6224
Fax: 780.426.3917

CASTLE ROCK
RESEARCH CORP

ORDER FORM

THE KEY	QUANTITY
Biology 30	
Chemistry 30	
English 30-1	
English 30-2	
Mathematics 30-1	
Mathematics 30-2	
Physics 30	
Social Studies 30-1	
Social Studies 30-2	
Biology 20	
Chemistry 20	
English 20-1	
Mathematics 20-1	
Physics 20	
Social Studies 20-1	
English 10-1	
Math 10 Combined	
Science 10	
Social Studies 10-1	
Social Studies 9	
English Language Arts 9	
Mathematics 9	
Science 9	
Mathematics 8	
Mathematics 7	
English Language Arts 6	
Mathematics 6	
Science 6	
Social Studies 6	
Mathematics 4	
Mathematics 3	
English Language Arts 3	

Student Notes and Problems Workbooks	QUANTITY	
	SNAP Workbooks	Solution Manuals
Mathematics 31		
Biology 30		
Chemistry 30		
Mathematics 30-1		
Mathematics 30-2		
Physics 30		
Biology 20		
Chemistry 20		
Mathematics 20-1		
Physics 20		
Mathematics 10 Combined		
Science 10		
Mathematics 9		
Science 9		
Mathematics 8		
Science 8		
Mathematics 7		
Science 7		
Mathematics 6		
Mathematics 5		
Mathematics 4		
Mathematics 3		

Problem Solved and Class Notes	QUANTITY	
	Class Notes	Problem Solved
Mathematics 31		
Biology 30		
Chemistry 30		
Mathematics 30-1		
Mathematics 30-2		
Physics 30		
Biology 20		
Chemistry 20		
Mathematics 20-1		
Physics 20		
Mathematics 10 Combined		
Science 10		
Mathematics 9		
Science 9		
Mathematics 8		
Science 8		
Mathematics 7		
Science 7		

Total Cost	
Subtotal 1	
Subtotal 2	
Subtotal 3	
Cost Subtotal	
Shipping and Handling*	
G.S.T	
Order Total	

Learning Resources Centre

Castle Rock Research is pleased to participate in an exclusive distribution arrangement with the Learning Resources Centre (LRC). Under this agreement, schools can place all their orders with LRC for order fulfillment. As well, these resources are eligible for applying the Learning Resource Credit Allocation (LRCA), which gives schools a 25% discount off LRC's selling price. Call LRC for details.

Orders may be placed with LRC by
Telephone: 780.427.2767
Fax: 780.422.9750
Internet: www.lrc.education.gov.ab.ca
Or mail: 12360 – 142 Street NW
Edmonton, AB T5L 4X9

PAYMENT AND SHIPPING INFORMATION

Name: ______________________
School
Telephone: ______________________
SHIP TO
School: ______________________
Address: ______________________
City: ____________ Postal Code: ______
PAYMENT
□ By credit card VISA/MC
Number: ______________________
Expiry Date: ______________________
Name on card: ______________________
□ Enclosed cheque
□ Invoice school P.O. number: ______

*(Please call for current rates)

CASTLE ROCK
RESEARCH CORP
#2340, 10180 – 101 Street NW, Edmonton, AB T5J 3S4 **Phone:** 780.448.9619 **Fax:** 780.426.3917
Email: learn@castlerockresearch.com **Toll-free:** 1.800.840.6224
www.castlerockresearch.com